THE ARCHAEOLOGY OF MODERN WORLDS IN THE INDIAN OCEAN

UNIVERSITY PRESS OF FLORIDA

Florida A&M University, Tallahassee
Florida Atlantic University, Boca Raton
Florida Gulf Coast University, Ft. Myers
Florida International University, Miami
Florida State University, Tallahassee
New College of Florida, Sarasota
University of Central Florida, Orlando
University of Florida, Gainesville
University of North Florida, Jacksonville
University of South Florida, Tampa
University of West Florida, Pensacola

The Archaeology of Modern Worlds in the Indian Ocean

Edited by Mark William Hauser
and Julia Jong Haines

UNIVERSITY PRESS OF FLORIDA

Gainesville/Tallahassee/Tampa/Boca Raton
Pensacola/Orlando/Miami/Jacksonville/Ft. Myers/Sarasota

Reproduction of color images was made possible by a grant from Northwestern University.

Copyright 2023 by Mark William Hauser and Julia Jong Haines
All rights reserved
Published in the United States of America

28 27 26 25 24 23   6 5 4 3 2 1

Library of Congress Cataloging-in-Publication Data
Names: Hauser, Mark W., editor. | Jong Haines, Julia, editor.
Title: The archaeology of modern worlds in the Indian Ocean / edited by
  Mark William Hauser and Julia Jong Haines.
Description: 1. | Gainesville : University Press of Florida, [2023] |
  Includes bibliographical references and index.
Identifiers: LCCN 2023012240 (print) | LCCN 2023012241 (ebook) | ISBN
  9780813069845 (hardback) | ISBN 9780813070612 (pdf)
Subjects: LCSH: Underwater archaeology—Indian Ocean. | Shipwrecks—Indian
  Ocean. | Indian Ocean—History. | BISAC: SOCIAL SCIENCE / Archaeology |
  HISTORY / Asia / South / General
Classification: LCC DS338 .A698 2023 (print) | LCC DS338 (ebook) | DDC
  909.0965—dc23/eng/20230419
LC record available at https://lccn.loc.gov/2023012240
LC ebook record available at https://lccn.loc.gov/2023012241

The University Press of Florida is the scholarly publishing agency for the State University System of Florida, comprising Florida A&M University, Florida Atlantic University, Florida Gulf Coast University, Florida International University, Florida State University, New College of Florida, University of Central Florida, University of Florida, University of North Florida, University of South Florida, and University of West Florida.

University Press of Florida
2046 NE Waldo Road
Suite 2100
Gainesville, FL 32609
http://upress.ufl.edu

Contents

List of Figures   vii
List of Tables   ix

1. The Archaeology of Modern Worlds in the Indian Ocean: An
   Introduction   1
   Mark William Hauser and Julia Jong Haines

2. The *Maqāmāt* Ship: Image as Source in Historical Archaeology of the
   Indian Ocean   24
   Mick de Ruyter

3. A Thousand Years of Connections between the Indian Ocean Region
   and Southeast Asia   48
   Ellen Hsieh and Takashi Sakai

4. Connectivity and Small Island Historical Archaeology in the Indian
   Ocean   71
   Krish Seetah, Stefania Manfio, and Akshay Sarathi

5. Healthcare Inequality and Reticence in the Mascarenes: The
   Contribution of Historical Archaeology   100
   Saša Čaval and Alessandra Cianciosi

6. The Archaeology of Portuguese Agricultural Outposts in the
   Seventeenth-Century Zanzibar Countryside   128
   Adria LaViolette and Neil Norman

7. Sources for Analyzing the Social and Economic Contexts of the
   Diaspora on the Coromandel Coast   152
   V. Selvakumar and Mark William Hauser

8. Diaspora in the Domestic: A Comparative Approach to Tamil Nadu and
   Mauritius   178
   Julia Jong Haines and Mark William Hauser

9. Approaching Past, Present, and Future Urbanisms in Goa, India   207
   Brian C. Wilson

10. Commentary: The Swahili World and Its Global Connections   228
   Chapurukha M. Kusimba

11. Commentary: A Perspective from South Asia   243
   Supriya Varma

   List of Contributors   249
   Index   253

Figures

1.1. Map of locations described in text   2

2.1. Ship illustration from the Schefer *Maqāmāt*   26

2.2. Illustration from the St. Petersburg *Maqāmāt*   27

2.3. Illustration similar to the St. Petersburg image   34

2.4. Elements of the *Maqāmāt* ships modeled on shadow puppets   36

3.1. Indian Ocean–Southeast Asia connections   49

3.2. Buddhist monuments with different shapes   51

3.3. Islamic tombs in Aceh and their origins in India   55

3.4. Islamic tiles of Southeast Asia and Central Asia   57

3.5. Persian wares   59

3.6. Anping jars   61

3.7. Art Nouveau tiles in different contexts   63

3.8. Double-happiness wares   65

4.1. Belle Mare Sugar Estate   85

5.1. Arrivals and departures of Indian immigrants to Mauritius   105

5.2. Le Morne Old Cemetery and Bois Marchand cemetery   107

5.3. General Plan of Lazaret no. 1 and Lazaret no. 2   112

5.4. Return of seven ships with immigrants from quarantine   114

5.5. Map of Flat Island with quarantine structures   115

5.6. "Latrines for females" and "Latrines in Coolies Camp"   118

6.1. Map of Unguja Island with project area   129

6.2. Drone images, Fukuchani and Mvuleni, and cave and pool, Mvuleni   137

6.3. Plans of redoubts at Fukuchani and Mvuleni   138

viii · Figures

6.4. Views of stone walling on escarpment above Mvuleni 142

7.1. Areas of the Tamil Diaspora 154

7.2. Weaving centers, European factories, and port towns 157

7.3. Weaver's pit loom, Thilyaidi, 2019 160

7.4. Nangur, Tamil Nadu 161

8.1. South Asian indentured immigration to various colonies 179

8.2. Location of Sathangudi and water infrastructure 189

8.3. Water tank and dried pond at Brothers' Garden 191

8.4. Tamil vernacular housing 192

8.5. Map of Bras d'Eau water infrastructure 198

9.1. Modern street overlay of Old Goa 213

9.2. Map of Velha Goa and accompanying market scene 215

9.3. Plan view of elite structure and detail of eighteenth-century map of Goa 220

9.4. Preserved terrace walls in Velha Goa 221

9.5. Non-elite structure, grinding stone, and house shrine 222

Tables

5.1. Return of immigrants landed in quarantine, Flat and Gabriel Islands   117

7.1. Select inscriptions and palm-leaf documents referencing enslavement   163

8.1. Indentured immigrants at Bras d'Eau arrived from different ports   185

8.2. Bras d'Eau log showing the "Return of Indian laborers," March 1845   186

10.1. Commodities of trade   231

10.2. Modes of exchange on the Swahili Coast   233

10.3. Renaissance in Asia (ca. 500–1450 CE)   237

1

The Archaeology of Modern Worlds in the Indian Ocean

An Introduction

MARK WILLIAM HAUSER AND JULIA JONG HAINES

In recent years an international community of scholars has focused attention on the study of the Indian Ocean's archaeological record over the relatively recent past. They search archives, survey the land, and excavate religious, production, institutional, and home spaces in South India, Africa, Southeast Asia, and the many islands that dot its seas, including Mauritius, Réunion, Zanzibar, Pemba, Madagascar, and Java. Their investigations have resulted in new stories that challenge dominant narratives of European hegemony in which capitalist logics impose order on a chaotic medieval ocean of commerce. This volume connects the modern worlds that emerge out of local stories, producing a transnational archaeology that acknowledges how modern nation states have shaped archaeological knowledge and transgresses such borders methodologically.

As scholars have previously noted, the Indian Ocean is in many ways defined by the far-reaching networks facilitated by the monsoon seasons. Early archaeological studies of the Indian Ocean emphasized how material residues enabled them to trace people and things that circulated among disparate parts of the Indian Ocean. Historians and archaeologists have been careful to chart these connected histories, aware that epochal fallacies can all too often dismiss the complexity and nuance of medieval and early modern relations in the Indian Ocean. Despite the "ongoingness" of European colonization, scholars across the ocean have continually argued for expansive definitions of modernity that move beyond narrow perspectives grounded in Western thought. As such, more recently, the Indian Ocean World has been described as its

2 · Mark William Hauser and Julia Jong Haines

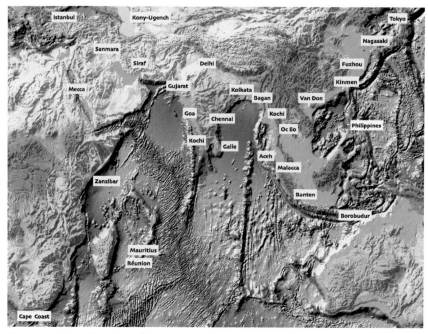

Figure 1.1. Map of locations described in text. Base map courtesy of Michael Schmeling.

own problem space (in sensu Scott 2004), rather than as a setting in which to see a set of processes play out (Hoogervorst and Hodos 2016; Mathew 2016; Seetah and Allen 2018). Questions about the social and political impacts of long-standing ecological, commercial, and political circulations guide many of these approaches to the archaeological record of the Indian Ocean, with increased attention on the years preceding and through the rise of European economic and political hegemony. Contributors in this volume place these impulses in conversation, along with their modes of inquiry, in investigations of the Indian Ocean and the settlements that dot its shores (Fig. 1.1).

Working in a region that has been largely overshadowed in historical archaeology by another ocean is a balancing act of learning from methodologies, frameworks, ideologies, and ethics that were developed by increasingly diverse and global North American and Atlantic-focused historical archaeologists over the last few decades, and simultaneously advocating for an Indian Ocean archaeology that gestures to these archaeologies but that is framed within its own oceanic temporalities and connections. The authors in this volume strike this balance by considering the archaeological record of modern worlds in the Indian Ocean through explicitly micro-historical, material, and situated approaches that emphasize relationality within the region. These chapters are locally situated studies that, when read collectively, connectively, and comparatively, describe the Indian Ocean through the relations that weave across its waters, islands, and coastlines, and extend beyond its currents.

Why Modern Worlds

This book contributes to archaeologies of the modern world by focusing on the experience of ordinary people in the Indian Ocean. By modern world, we reference not only a time period—from about 1500 to the 1800s—but also a body of scholarship popularized in the 1990s that focused on "planetary flows" (Trouillot 2003: 28). This body of scholarship gave rise to themes that remain in circulation today, including transnational and postcolonial archaeologies. In this way we rely on one definition of historical archaeology, without considering the totality of its praxis in the Indian Ocean. This period is not as extensively documented in the archaeological record as other times in the Indian Ocean World, which opens the opportunity to shape Indian Ocean archaeology and scholarship from the outset as a region and a field that centers on how ordinary people confronted the material conditions of their lives and by integrating multiple different sources, drawing intraregional comparisons to enrich their interpretations, and challenging the ways in which current politics influence research agendas and local memories and the memorialization of archaeological sites and heritage. It is worth noting that while our authors have provided chapter contributions from East Africa to Southeast Asia, we do not have any case studies from Australia, a rich body of historical archaeology in its own right. Archaeologists have used the Indian Ocean's archaeological record as a counterpoint to dominant narratives about the modern period which overemphasize Europe's influence in shaping the world (Lane 2016; Schmidt 2016; Wilson and Hauser 2016; Acabado 2017). Another counterpoint concerns the use of the Indian Ocean's present as a starting point to study history backward (Stahl 2001), arguing that the archaeological record is also one in which we can consider relationships to futures (Reilly 2019; Franklin et al. 2020).

This volume is guided by a vision that not only sees the archaeological record of the Indian Ocean within its own historical continuities, where the modern might carry ideological baggage with it (Chakrabarty 2009), but also sees the Indian Ocean and the modern integrated into one unit of analysis that the field of historical archaeology has yet to approach (Subrahmanyam 1997). The authors herein approach the field of historical archaeology from a variety of perspectives that might seem familiar to readers not familiar with the area. In some cases authors stress the value of archaeological thinking in confronting dominant narratives about the past that overlook the struggles of everyday life (Voss 2018). In other cases the authors rely on the empirical richness of textural and archaeological materials to generate and evaluate questions with major theoretical implications (Mrozowski 2010). Finally, others focus on the ability to examine the ideological and material legacies of capitalism as it manifests in landscape and artifactual assemblages (Leone 1995). While none of these perspectives is a perfect fit, they do provide a jumping-off point through which to interrogate the past 800 years in the Indian Ocean.

Our aim here is not to resuscitate a two-and-a-half-decade-old framing to talk about archaeology, yet authors in this volume demonstrate that the Indian Ocean is a scholarly and political zone in which such accounts are required. Scholars (Orser 1996; Hall 2000) have been largely concerned with mapping the relationship between the global, the local, and the spaces in between through a putative systematic or "variable-oriented" comparative approach in which cases were argued based on the presence or absence of certain features. There is value to such an approach, and many examples continue to operate today, as demonstrated by quantitively driven projects such as the Digital Archaeological Archive of Comparative Slavery (DAACS), which has facilitated a bourgeoning body of material culture-oriented scholarship on comparative enslavement in North America and the Caribbean (Galle et al. 2019) that has implications for opening up archaeology's accessibility and use in the classroom (Agbe-Davies et al. 2014). Such comparative databases are only as good as the variables considered, and if there are blind spots in these variables, they get reproduced in the analysis (Flewellen 2019). Rather, authors in this volume are concerned with shifting the very dimensions upon which comparison and connections are framed. As several authors point out (Wilson; LaViolette and Norman, this volume), the very grounds upon which archaeological research and heritage are framed must, by definition, encounter the epistemologies upon which the past is constructed.

We see this volume as putting forward transnationalism as a methodology and as a framing for historical archaeology. Historical archaeologists have used transnationalism as a way to describe the experiences and identities of people in diaspora who maintain a tie to their homeland, particularly as members of a collective diaspora's shared region, socioeconomic status, and as a result, cultural values. Today scholars are more interested in mapping the social, political, and economic sinews of everyday life that extend in between and beyond the "shadow-lines" of empire, through an "intensive" comparative approach wherein a small number of cases are analyzed in greater depth to produce highly nuanced accounts (Horning 2013; Voss et al. 2018) to trace "the different sources and roots" that brought about "many different forms of meaning it attends" (Subrahmanyam 1997: 735). Transnational approaches to archaeology follow this line of thought especially in consideration of diaspora (Lilley 2006), heritage (Samuels 2016), and environmental justice (Douglass and Cooper 2020). Additionally, a transnational approach does not assume the presence of nation states in the past but, rather, stresses that ideologies presuming the nation state have shaped the production of archaeological knowledge about the past (see Brighton 2009; Ross 2012; Davies et al. 2020).

Many chapters in this volume explore the lived experiences of resource and labor exploitation within the context of Euro colonization and capitalism that shaped modern worlds; however, western paradigms are not and should not be the only lens through which we define Indian Ocean landscapes, materials, debates, and predicaments. We hope these case studies can be read as a praxis of Enseng Ho's (2004) diasporic metaphor "the view from the other boat," which reverses the imperial point of view—Bernard Cohn's definition of imperialism as the "view from the boat" (1990)—by identifying and putting into discursive tension smaller boats "plying the same seas." The concentration on gender (Čaval and Cianciosi), the experience of marginalized communities (Haines and Hauser; Selvakumar and Hauser), highlight that transregional communities form a "view from the other boat," where they are simultaneously locals yet remain cosmopolitans with vital connections across the ocean. Other contributions (Wilson) have turned to transnational heritage to consider the ways in which boundaries are at work both in producing global inequalities and in rendering such forces less visible.

The mode of comparison involved in transnational approaches has been multisited (Voss 2008; Brighton 2009; Cobb and DePratter 2012; Hauser 2011; Voss et al. 2018). A multisited approach lends itself readily to Indian Ocean archaeologies of the past 500 years (Wilson and Hauser 2016). Archaeological perspectives on landscapes of eighteenth- and nineteenth-century colonial settlements provide a context for commercial connections between different regions, intensification of land use, and complex social orders in the long term (Lane 2016). These relations shaped Atlantic and Indian Ocean trade circuits and landscapes employed by Europeans beginning in the sixteenth century (Hauser 2018). Even on an island like Mauritius, where human habitation began in the 1600s, the precolonial historical depth of these connections is critical to archaeology since the majority of people who populated the island came from other parts of the Indian Ocean; they or their ancestors were an integral part of those circulations, and the persistence of such networks would continue to influence the landscapes they built, the plants they grew and consumed, the ways they adorned their bodies, and their relationships to the land, the sea, and other beings in it. We cannot understand heritage in this postcolonial nation without thinking transregionally about the island's history. Therefore, while three chapters in this volume are explicitly multisited projects of comparison (Haines and Hauser; Hsieh and Sakai; Seetah et al.), the volume might be read for the many implicit intraregional comparisons of smaller-scale themes within subsets of chapters—comparisons of Portuguese (LaViolette and Norman; Wilson) and British (Čaval and Cianciosi; Haines and Hauser; Selvakumar and Hauser) colonial contexts; approaches to visual and artistic data sources (DeRuyter; Hsieh and Sakai); tensions between the direct and indirect impacts of colonialism on local people (LaViolette and Norman; Selvakumar and Hauser; Wilson); the reshaping of Indian Ocean cultural practices within unequal labor systems (Čaval and Cianciosi; Haines and Hauser; Seetah et al.; Selvakumar and Hauser).

Approaches to Indian Ocean Historical Archaeology

How archaeologists engage with their sources and the material record has shifted significantly in the intervening decades. Authors in this volume approach the assemblage of the Indian Ocean in a variety of ways. Some (Čaval and Cianciosi; De Ruyter; Wilson) begin with observations of the material record and use a variety of sources to build out contexts creating new maps of the Indian Ocean. Others (Haines and Hauser; LaViolette and Norman; Seetah et al.) place heavy emphasis on the archaeological record and what it can contribute to narratives structured by documentary sources. Still others examine textural sources as part of the archaeological record, highlighting a long tradition of historical archaeology in South Asia which extends time frames back to the early centuries of the first millennium CE. All rely on the dialectic between artifact and text, plying the interpretive potential of their limitations as a source of the past as well as their strengths.

Departing from approaches that typically view landscape as a description of nature from the perspective of humans, scholars working in many times and places have demonstrated the import of approaching the landscape as an assemblage of actants that shape the social history of the people who negotiate it. Take, for example, Bauer and Bhan's (2018, 4) definition of climate as "constituted by the interrelationships and dependencies among a multitude of different materials, things, and organisms." Several contributions (Haines and Hauser; Seetah et al.; Wilson) highlight the recursive and political nature of discussing humans and their relations to the environment. Compared with the Atlantic, when the past 500 years is usually framed in reference, at least tacitly, to the Columbian exchange, these authors look at long-term circulations in which the assemblage that constitutes climate is constantly in flux. For laborers being brought to Mauritius, climate change was twofold—first, there was the change in climate for those who were brought from one part of the world to another. Second, there was the change in climate brought about by agricultural intensification. That being said, the nature of that change has taken on dramatic proportions in the last few decades.

We can look at institutions, such as the plantation, as part of that change. On the one hand—the "planetary" hand—new engagements with the land are being introduced through biota such as sugar cane and draught animals, features such as steam mills, or items of mass consumption (Seetah et al., this volume). We can look to experiences as part of the global and consider how those assemblages changed for human beings who were forcibly moved as labor to different latitudes, elevations, and proximities to ground water (Hauser 2021). Considering climate as assemblage allows us to rework traditional units of analysis. For example, some (Waters et al. 2018; Edgeworth et al. 2019) argue for tracking the archaeosphere as part of the planetary. The archaeosphere is that geologic layer accompanying the Anthropocene comprising human detritus. These scholars, along with Stephen Mrozowski (2018), have pointed out that the archaeosphere does not begin with late-stage capitalism but can be tracked to the eighteenth century. In conducting such research there are scalar challenges (see Robb and Pauketat 2013) wherein we must confront how long-term processes are reflected at an arm's distance in individual lives. Thinking through the connective sinews and comparative cases of the Indian Ocean World is one place to begin.

This introduction now turns to the relevance of each chapter to some of the major themes in the historical archaeology of the Indian Ocean, identifies critical absences, and suggests new lines of investigation.

Connecting Sources and the Material Record of the Indian Ocean World

Historical archaeology in the Indian Ocean must account for millennia of circulations and their material consequences. Archaeologists have typically relied on material remains and a wide host of sources such as historical accounts, literary works, commercial records, pictorial sources, oral traditions, environmental sources, and landscape features (Selvakumar 2011; Lane 2012;

Seland 2014; Douglass and Cooper 2020). There is a long-term history of first-handwritten accounts in Parsi, Arabic, Tamil, Brahmi, Aramaic, and Greek (to name a few) that document inter-regional trade, contact, conquest, and migration and extend the possibilities of a historical archaeology well beyond the date of European arrival by sea. A range of both historical and archaeological data attests to complex maritime networks, involving extensive connections stretching from China to eastern Africa and into the Mediterranean. There is inscription-based and other archaeological evidence for millennia-old networks between the Arabian Gulf and the Indian Ocean, with specific data for sea routes between the Indus region (northwest India and Pakistan) and ancient Melhua (Oman) (Edens 1993; Possehl 1996; Cleuziou and Tosi 1997). For example, ancient Tamil writing has been found on ostraca in Red Sea ports (Sidebotham 1992). In addition, ancient Tamil literature in South India describes the "Yavanna," generally regarded as a term derived from an old Persian ethnonym for Greeks, as people arriving with trade goods and returning with locally produced wares (Ray 2005).

Traditionally, trade has been rendered as a down-the-line system in which merchandise, including textiles, spices, and metals, is traded from a source or an area of original manufacture and then trafficked from group to group in different ports across the Indian Ocean World (Margariti 2008). Persian and Arabic sources (Moovsi 2009) suggest that there was more direct trade extending between the Persian Gulf and Southeast Asia as early as the ninth century CE (Risso 2018). Three shipwrecks documented in Southeast Asia confirm direct trade links between the western Indian Ocean and beyond. These include the Belitung shipwreck from the second quarter of the ninth century CE in Indonesia (Flecker 2001) and the Phanom Surin wreck from the eighth century CE in Thailand (Guy 2019). The presence of green-glazed West Asian jars containing bitumen (Connan et al. 2020) with Pahlavi inscriptions (Guy 2017) in the hold of these vessels further supports the argument for early direct exchanges. More important, the construction techniques of these vessels relied on a sewn-plank technique (Staples and Blue 2019). When Europeans entered the Indian Ocean World, they viewed these techniques to be inferior to and less durable than their rigid hull construction, however sewn watercrafts were used into the twentieth century.

The first two case studies in this volume make use of such diverse sources as they examine the ways in which these wide reaching historic transoceanic circulations resulted in multiple permutations of influence across the region. Mick DeRuyter maps the Indian Ocean through the iconic thirteenth-century ship illustration found in the Schefer *Maqāmāt* manuscript in Paris. This

Maqāmāt ship illustration is prized within a visual corpus devoid of other significant archaeological, iconographic, or documentary sources describing ships in entirety, even though its inherent rarity complicates the criticism required of historical visual sources. Comparing this famous image with other lesser known *Maqāmāt* ships, such as watercraft in contemporary Islamic manuscripts from Iran and Mesopotamia and other potential referents like shadow puppets, redefines its usefulness as an artifactual source on material culture. In this way, the technological particularism of nautical construction methods, features, and form provides a better social understanding of a visual artifact embedded in the circulation of people and things in the historical Indian Ocean.

Reliance on the material record poses challenges and opportunities for archaeologists. It has long been recognized that material culture and the way it is used cannot serve as proxies for social identity, world view, or ideology. Yet these very factors shape the meanings and values that objects take on. Take, for example, the mass-produced goods that inhabit the globalized worlds of the eighteenth and nineteenth centuries. The work of anthropologists Patricia Spyer (2000) and Nick Thomas (1991) in Southeast Asia reveals that long-term residents, subject to durian colonialism and its attendant discourses, used objects to their own ends, rejecting, embracing, or working with colonizing projects. This suggests not only that the indexes, measures, and frames of reference so popular in historical archaeology may miss the mark but also that such insights can be used more generally. They extend to the cultural attitudes that people held on those distant shores from which strangers came.

Hsieh and Sakai (this volume) discuss the connection between South Asia and Southeast Asia; a topic of interest to epigraphists, historians, anthropologists, and archaeologists. In contrast to text-based research that mostly focuses on the influences of Indian culture during the classical period, archaeological evidence reveals a long-term connection between the two maritime regions. These authors argue that the Indian Ocean had a far greater role in Indianizing South Asia than has been recognized and that it continued to play a significant role in shaping everyday life in the late medieval and early colonial periods in Southeast Asia. Evidence found in numerous sites in Southeast Asia, including artifacts (such as trade ceramics), monuments (such as tombstones), and architecture (such as mosques), not only attests to the development of dynamic networks that can be further integrated into our understanding of global systems but also reveals the characteristics of each period and place once contextualized with Hsieh and Sakai's interregional perspective.

Comparison of the Indian Ocean

To be fair, and to avoid painting too much of a straw man, the field of historical archaeology, especially as practiced in the Americas and West Africa, has for some time rejected traditional chronologies that frame the past along with concomitant categories, born through European encounters (e.g., prehistory vs. history; Amerindian vs. African; colonizer vs. colonized; and medieval vs. modern) (see Lightfoot 2005; Silliman 2005; Oland et al. 2012; Schmidt and Mrozowski 2013; Kusimba, this volume). They have done so through careful archaeological and ethnohistorical analyses of everyday life. Archaeologists working in the Caribbean and West Africa show that functions assigned to objects by manufacturers cannot be reliably used to predict how the objects were used and by whom. Instead, items were used in ways that graft onto traditional ways of doing things, meet the needs of the immediate and day-to-day, and serve as a material foundation for improvisation. It therefore stands to reason that comparing cases can be another way of thinking through the creation and connections of the archaeosphere.

Recasting the emergence of the modern world in a way that centers the Indian Ocean is not new to historians, anthropologists, and literary scholars who have spent decades documenting the varied ecologies, economies, and modes of difference that challenge the centrality of Europe in its account. Given the relative paucity of archaeological accounts of the Indian Ocean in discussions of the modern world, the focus of historical archaeology on multi-vocal, multi-methods, and multiscalar approaches to the past is invaluable to the formulation of questions and answers about how denizens of the Indian Ocean contributed to the modern world as well as how they shaped the character of the past 500 years. This collection of essays is aimed at demonstrating that a historical archaeological approach provides a critical bridge between the long-term, the large-scale, and the immediate concerns of everyday life for those who lived in the landmasses bordering this ocean and who circulated between its shores.

Since the 1980s historians, among others, have turned to global histories to explain the centrality of the Indian Ocean in the development of the modern world. These comparative transnational and global historical perspectives challenge approaches that took the nation or the Atlantic as the assumed unit of analysis in conceiving or explaining mercantilism, modes of difference (such as gender or race), colonialism, global circulations, imperial formation, consumption, production, and the material worlds of everyday life. Archaeologists have also been attuned to recasting the modern in a way that not only incorporates the Indian Ocean but also attempts to describe it in its own terms. This volume continues this approach but does so with an emphasis on a comparative, connective, and empirical nature of Historical Archaeology in the Indian Ocean.

Lately, historical archaeologists have paid little explicit attention to comparative approaches to the archaeology record. As has been discussed elsewhere, historical archaeology, as a field, has painted itself into a bit of an epistemic corner by employing a scale of analysis largely defined by the Atlantic Ocean (Orser 2018). While there are a few contemporary examples (Horning 2013; Galle et al. 2019), the heyday of such approaches took place in the 1990s with Chuck Orser's comparative study of globalization in Palmares, Brazil, and Gorttoose, Ireland, and Martin Hall's comparative study of structural inequality in Chesapeake, Virginia, and Cape Town, South Africa. Orser compares two disconnected cases to advance an argument about the conjuncture of capitalism and colonialism in the Atlantic World. More a proposed study than an analysis, Orser utilizes landscapes of displacement and objects of everyday life, such as tobacco pipes and locally made ceramics called colon ware by archaeologists, to map the relationship between the local and the global for its inhabitants. To dig locally and think globally, for Orser, is to contextualize such objects in a series of haunts including "colonialism, capitalism, Eurocentrism, racialization, and other entwined processes that were practiced after about 1500 CE" (Orser 1996).

Compare this approach with the one offered by Martin Hall (2000). He argues that the modern world is incomplete without an understanding of the material registers of lives and livelihoods under colonial regimes. To illustrate this argument he compares colonial South Africa and colonial Chesapeake because they "shared an underlying set of economic imperatives" (Hall 2000, 18). He tacks back and forth comparing transcripts (in sensu Scott 1985), both hidden and public, writ in the architecture, planning, and landscape of the two. In doing so, he maps the disjuncture between the local and the global, with implications for "statements" about gender, race, and slavery that framed so much of colonial interaction in both places.

In all cases, past and present, there is an issue of scale. When considered at all, the Indian Ocean is treated largely as epiphenomenal. To be fair, at the time, the number of studies through which modern and early modern materials could be contextualized was far smaller. But there was an unintended consequence. By making Atlantic World accounts the norm against which all other cases are compared, historical archaeology has obscured global flows from other regions that are, in fact, critical to understanding the modern world, particularly the workings of and resistance to colonialism and capitalism over the last 500 years (Lane 2016; Schmidt 2016). Not all transcripts of power can be directly ascribed to colonial prescriptions—though colonizing practices took advantage of them. Take, for example, *kala-pani* or the fear of losing caste status that coincided with crossing the "Black Water" of the ocean, which was prevalent among many Hindus until recently.

Haines and Hauser (this volume), in their multisited examination of domestic space in Mauritius and the Coromandel coast, tackle the materiality of this public transcript in labor migration. Linking households in two places subverts cultural or political boundaries of Indian Ocean geographies and shows that such boundaries reassert themselves in material and spatial ways. They argue that diaspora through the lens of the household recognizes that the haunts of race, colonialism, Eurocentrism, and modernity are "situated" (Haraway 1988) and enhances possibilities for understanding the ways in which individuals face complex issues in a global context.

There is a value to thinking comparatively—that is, making explicit the similarities and differences between Indian, Pacific and Atlantic oceans, acknowledging that drawing boundaries is fuzzy, particularly when we consider how people experience the world. European colonization, beginning in the sixteenth century but reaching its apogee in the eighteenth, nineteenth, and twentieth centuries, is associated with long-term consequential impositions at the individual, community, societal, and global level. As Lilley (2006) and Voss et al. (2018) point out, the shared experience of displacement may provide a methodological foundation for integrating archaeological research on indigenous, enslaved, settler, and immigrant populations in colonial and postcolonial contexts. The Indian Ocean complicates such a stance. Thinking comparatively *with* the Indian Ocean highlights some of the methodological assumptions we historical archaeologists use in our interpretations of landscapes and the artifacts within them, but thinking comparatively *across* the ocean highlights connections in the sociocultural ways Indian Ocean people confronted their own colonial and postcolonial predicaments.

Considering the region's many islands and archipelagos, Krish Seetah, Stefania Manfio, and Akshay Sarathi compare connectivity through the materiality of slavery from the ports and plantations on Zanzibar and Mauritius. The body of literature on artifacts, mortuary practices, and diet highlight the nuances and complexity of enslaved lifeways. They draw on several decades of research on the dynamics of forced and free labor on both islands and in the wider region, serving to enrich our understanding of slavery on a global scale. Framed through the concepts of connectivity and islands, they illustrate the nuances of enslavement and indenture as understood from this region: what do we know about arrival processes, working conditions, and daily existence? The chapter suggests insightful similarities to Atlantic counterparts as well the unique features that help contextualize the experience of slavery in this part of East Africa and the southwestern Indian Ocean.

At the level of the immediate and concrete, individuals and communities must contend with displacement, cultural appropriation, civilizing discourses of imperialism, and novel taxonomies through which structural inequality is ordered and must negotiate the norms of dominant ideologies in order to survive. There are profound and durable effects, such as alienation, displacement, colorist, and identity conflicts which reproduce colonizing forces in the intimate and the everyday. Documenting the ways in which individuals and communities have internalized the beliefs of colonizers and how, in response, they have adopted coping strategies such as silence, accommodation, evasiveness, ingratiation, or manipulation, seems necessary and important. Čaval and Cianciosi consider the everyday implications of disease and health management for South Asian workers in Mauritius and Réunion under novel labor regimes. With a range of sites and landscapes related to island epidemic, including the quarantining of ships carrying incoming migrant workers (Flat Island) and sick residents (Lazaret in Réunion), and final resting places (Bois Marchand Cemetery and Le Morne) of these populations, they connect different nodes within the colonial administration of Mauritius and beyond to French-controlled Réunion. The evidence suggests that novel labor regimes were detrimental to people migrating to this previously unsettled island in the Indian Ocean. They explore the significance of gender within this world by focusing on women's encounters with health management. Using a comparative analysis, they explore the seeds of different health policies for indentured communities in the Indian Ocean's colonies.

These latter studies point to a present but underrealized potential of studying the archaeological record of modern worlds in the Indian Ocean. In a series of essays (2009, 2016), and most recently a book (2021), Dipesh Chakrabarty argues that the globe, an account centering human experience and engagement, and the planet, an account that decenters human experience, represent two narratives of globalization and the Anthropocene. For Chakrabarty, these accounts become ineluctably tied through the lens of modern capitalism. Until recently, "'natural disasters' have occurred independent of human activities but have been central to the flourishing of human and other forms of life" (Chakrabarty 2021: 4). Today the twinned forces of socioeconomic institutions and human technologies shape those very planetary processes. To consider climate through the planetary and the global is an essential part of modern world Archaeology—which is to critique modernity as a condition and a concept.

Transnational Archaeologies of the Modern World

What difference does an Indian Ocean approach to modern world archaeology make? Quite simply, it allows us to understand the lives of people who were part of the modern world, though they might not have viewed themselves as such, in ways that are truer to their experience. Older approaches formulate historical archaeology in terms of European empires, companies, or agents and traced transatlantic materialities between Africa and Europe and the colonies or outposts in the Americas. In these narratives, each colony or outpost is an island of investigation that engaged only with its parent country. The ocean itself was both a setting of conflict and rivalry for distant overseas empires and also distinct from the histories and economies that made the ocean such a territorial prize.

If, by contrast, we approach the several hundred years following da Gama's landing in Calicut in 1498 through the lens of the Indian Ocean, we see that links and exchanges were as often between people of many different origins as they were within strictly political lines. As the long reach of South Asian textiles spread further, the ocean's capacity to consume silver from the west grew. One could go as far as to say that no mercantile venture, colonial enclave, or settlement, including slaveholding plantations of the Atlantic, could have survived if its people had not relied on the long-standing circulations, commerce, and ways of doing things in the Indian Ocean. African, Indian, and Southeast Asian leaders judged new opportunities and risks for themselves and chose to participate in internecine rivalries between vulnerable European enterprises. At the same time, ordinary people lost neither their precarity nor their agency as they negotiated the maelstrom of circumstances of novel colonial regimes.

The transregional approach allows us to remap what constitutes Indian Ocean heritage and where this heritage is located. This challenges geographies of heritage when national boundaries are no longer taken for granted; and we posit that we cannot allow the nation-state to define the flows of things and ideas in the present, but especially in the past. Colonial appropriations and acquisitions on the part of European powers during the modern time reveal interconnected object histories among communities in disparate parts of South Asia and European and North American museums (Nordin 2016). We can also consider the heritage of the Indian Ocean in material remains associated with histories of the less powerful. For example, Hauser (2021) and Flewellen (2017) describe the presence of bales of "Madras" fabric as a critical component of material worlds constructed by enslaved laborers in the Caribbean.

Attention to the cultural, economic, and social connections between inhabitants of the far-flung lands and islands of the Indian Ocean leads to another important theme that defines and drives Indian Ocean World historical archaeology. Archaeologists frequently use material residues of everyday life to make plain that travel, migration, and cultural interaction are not recent by-products of globalization, but endeavors that societies have always undertaken for economic, religious, ideological, strategic, or personal reasons (Knutsen 2021). Rather than elaborate the substantive and material transformations of economic arrangements between the late eighteenth and twentieth centuries, archaeologists explore a history where diverse communities subject to polities exercising power on regional scales were commercially interconnected to distant shores (Gurukkal 2016; Rajan 2019) and were cosmopolitan (LaViolette 2008; Fleisher and LaViolette 2013; Selvakumar 2017). As this volume's contributors show, the archaeological record broadens our knowledge of cultural interconnection at various moments in history, such as Roman trade diaspora in Muziris from the first century onward, interactions between South Indians and Southeast Asians during the twelfth century and thereafter, and the eighteenth- and nineteenth-century labor systems that populated islands such as Réunion and Mauritius.

Like Ferdinand Braudel's (1995) observation about material worlds of the Mediterranean, tracing the archaeological record including landscapes, features, and the artifacts that populate the record reminds us that there are many Indian oceans, none of which could be understood through what is exterior to it. The long perspective of the Indian Ocean positions Europe and the Atlantic as peripheral to a space driven by its own seasonal monsoons, tempo of life, power structures, empires, and modern politics. The eventual pull of European colonization in the Americas not only increased commercial activities between the Indian Ocean and the Pacific and Atlantic Worlds, but also intensified rural industry and commercial agriculture in Indian Ocean hinterlands. For example, Atlantic World demands for South Asian cloth, dyes, and other goods did not so much increase craft specialization or urbanization as transform the structure and organization of labor recruitment, the value of labor, and in some cases, demand for existing commodity circuits such as rice. For their part, Neil Norman and Adria LaViolette examine two fortified farmsteads operating together in the north Unguja countryside, Zanzibar archipelago. These sites of Portuguese colonial agricultural and commercial efforts lasted for a period beginning in the seventeenth century and ending no later than the Portuguese defeat in Mombasa in 1698 and expulsion from Stonetown in 1699. Although the Portuguese colonial project ultimately failed, Fukuchani and Mvuleni show us a rural, commercial effort away from the two regional centers of Portuguese power—Fort Jesus in Mombasa and the church and factory in the Zanzibar Stonetown—and explore a tense but practical equilibrium struck with local Swahili residents.

Transnational archaeologies also situate the many diasporas that circulated in the Indian Ocean. Some of these communities (Armenian, Jewish, Siddi, to name a few) were trade diasporas or "commercial specialists [who] would remove themselves physically from the home community and go to live as aliens in another town, usually not a fringe town, but a town important in the life of the host community" (Curtin 1984). To the preceding list, we might add Latin- and Greek-speaking merchants who may have occupied enclaves in Indian Ocean port cities of Muziris and Arikamedu (Fitzpatrick 2011; Tomber 2016; Selvakumar 2017). There is also diaspora related more directly to the conscription and valuation of labor. Selvakumar and Hauser argue that while there has been considerable effort by historians to describe the conditions and responses of indentured labor by South Asians in the Caribbean, Mauritius, and Fiji, less effort has been given to the social, economic, and political contexts from which laborers were emigrating. Such a focus highlights the diversity of experiences. In the case of South Asia, research is oriented toward North India (reflecting overwhelming numbers). Yet ports on the Coromandel Coast, such as Karaikal, Pondicherry, and Tharangambadi, played a vital role as transshipment ports in the transportation of indentured labor from Tamil country to Mauritius, Réunion, Fiji, and, to a lesser extent, the French Antilles. Such a focus also highlights the long-term histories of precarity that set the stage for labor recruitment in the nineteenth century.

A transregional approach similarly challenges temporalities about heritage. Archival sources provide meta-narratives of the "rise and fall" of colonial outposts, and our understanding of the material lives of their residents remains limited to these written sources. Brian Wilson revisits these histories, and the heritage management practices in Velha, Goa, the former capital of the Portuguese eastern empire. Archaeological survey provides traces suggestive of a range of socialites and endurances, revealing differing temporalities and material experiences of the city. Unfortunately, these alternative voices are silenced today. Heritage management practices in Goa erase non-elite socio-spatial production. Wilson argues that the site's UNESCO Heritage designation further perpetuates narratives so prevalent in the archive. Providing value to only one set of urban experiences re-creates colonial stereotypes that justified the exploitation of the socio-spatial landscape for colonial ends. An analysis of current heritage practices in conjunction with archaeological data widens our understanding of the recent material past in South Asia, helping us redefine both past and present colonial urban landscapes in the region. To reiterate, studies resulting from the emergence of transnational approaches push us toward a multisited approach that centers the Indian Ocean and connects distant places.

As a Starting Place

Archaeologists have yet to critically engage the study of agroecological transformations from a transnational perspective. A long tradition of scholarship on enclosures, which take many forms, including physical barriers or crops, during agrarian transition forecloses the possibility of other uses and increases the precarity of resources attached to the land (see Fanon 1963; Thompson 1964; Williams 1975; Johnson 1996; Hall et al. 2011). Scholars stress that enclosure was not a settled account for indigenous peoples, agricultural conscripts, or smallholders who relied on substantive understandings of the land and community to develop resolutions to the predicaments of enclosure (Li 2014). Heritage studies scholars have argued that economic development and social empowerment projects often implicate archaeological remains in new transnational heritages (see Meskell 2011; Jorgensen 2014; Selvakumar 2017). By calling attention to sites of potential significance, they introduce the scrutiny of state and non-state actors, who have the ability to regulate access and control narratives of interpretation that privilege some actors' roles over others, and thereby become sites of enclosure (Jorgensen 2014). Despite foreclosing other possibilities through physical and discursive measures, these forces of exclusion are not settled accounts (Flewellen 2017). A transregional approach would enable us to answer questions surrounding how people in the past resolved predicaments created when export agriculture made access to land and its resources (e.g., water) more precarious; how investigations of colonial archaeological heritage limit access to land and heritage for local communities; and how solutions developed in the past may be employed in the present for stakeholders facing predicaments of enclosure.

Overall, this collection of essays demonstrates the compelling nature of the archaeological record of modern worlds in the Indian Ocean. It is not exhaustive. Nor is it sufficient. It is a starting place. Interdisciplinary approaches are the very essence of Indian Ocean archaeology, especially in order to understand global entanglements through human migrations, economic circuits, biotic circulations, and the exercise of power. This volume suggests that there is something important in documenting these currents over the past five hundred years—in their own right. In some cases, scholars take a longitudinal approach, reaching back to the medieval and ancient to document the present. Others take a horizontal approach, highlighting the tenor of entangled lives in multiple places.

Bibliography

Acabado, Stephen. 2017. "The Archaeology of Pericolonialism: Responses of the 'Unconquered' to Spanish Conquest and Colonialism in Ifugao, Philippines." *International Journal of Historical Archaeology* 21: 1–26.

Agbe-Davies, Anna S., Jillian E. Galle, Mark W. Hauser, and Frasier D. Neiman. 2014. "Teaching with Digital Archaeological Data: A Research Archive in the University Classroom." *Journal of Archaeological Method and Theory* 21(4): 837–61.

Armstrong, Douglas. 1990. *The Old Village and the Great House: An Archaeological and Historical Examination of Drax Hall Plantation, St. Ann's Bay, Jamaica*. Urbana: University of Illinois Press.

Bauer, Andrew M., and Mona Bhan. 2018. *Climate without Nature: A Critical Anthropology of the Anthropocene*. Cambridge: Cambridge University Press.

Braudel, Ferdinand. 1995. *The Mediterranean and the Mediterranean World in the Age of Philip II. Vol. 2*. Berkeley: University of California Press.

Brighton, Stephen. A. 2009. *Historical Archaeology of the Irish Diaspora: A Transnational Approach*. Knoxville: University of Tennessee Press.

Chakrabarty, Dipesh. 2009. "The Climate of History: Four Theses." *Critical Inquiry* 35 (2): 197–222.

———. 2016. "Whose Anthropocene? A Response." Response to R. Emmett and T. Lekan, (eds.), "Whose Anthropocene? Revisiting Dipesh Chakrabarty's 'Four Theses,'" *Transformations in Environment and Society* 2, 103–13.

Chakrabarty, D. 2021. *The Climate of History in a Planetary Age*. Chicago: University of Chicago Press.

Cleuziou, Serge, and Maurizio Tosi. 1997. "Evidence for the Use of Aromatics in the Early Bronze Age of Oman." In *Profumi d'Arabia*, A. Avanzini, editor, 57–74. "L'Erma" di Bretschneider: Pisa, Italy.

Cobb, C. R., and C. B. DePratter. 2012. "Multisited Research on Colonowares and the Paradox of Globalization." *American Anthropologist* 114(3): 446–61.

Cohn, Bernard S. 1990. *An Anthropologist Among Historians and Other Essays*. New York: Oxford University Press.

Connan, Jacques, S. Priestman, T. Vosmer, A. Komoot, H. Tofighian, B. Ghorbani, . . . and T. Van De Velde. 2020. "Geochemical Analysis of Bitumen from West Asian Torpedo Jars from the c. 8th Century Phanom-Surin Shipwreck in Thailand." *Journal of Archaeological Science* 117: 105111.

Connaughton, Sean P., and J. Herbert. 2017. "Engagement Within: An Anthropological Exploration of First Nations Engagement and Consulting Archaeology within a Transnational Corporation." *Archaeologies* 13(2): 306–43.

Crossland, Christopher, J. Kremer, H. Hartwig, H. J. Lindeboom, J. I. Marshall Crossland, and M.D.A. Le Tissier (eds.). 2005. *Coastal Fluxes in the Anthropocene: The Land-Ocean Interactions in the Coastal Zone Project of the International Geosphere-Biosphere Programme.* IGBP Series. Berlin: Springer Verlag.

Curtin, Philip. 1984. *Cross Cultural Trade in World History.* Cambridge, U.K.: Cambridge University Press.

Davies, Peter, S. Lawrence, and A. Middleton. 2020. "Citizen of Empire: A Transnational Archaeology of James William Robertson." *International Journal of Historical Archaeology* 24(3): 483–501.

Douglass, Kristina, and J. Cooper. 2020. "Archaeology, Environmental Justice, and Climate Change on Islands of the Caribbean and Southwestern Indian Ocean." *Proceedings of the National Academy of Sciences* 117(15): 8254–62.

Edens, Christopher. 1993. "Indus-Arabian Interaction during the Bronze Age." In *Harappan Civilization: A Recent Perspective,* 2nd rev. edition, edited by Gregory L. Possehl, 335–63. New Delhi: American Institute of Indian Studies and Oxford & IBH Publishing Co.

Edgeworth, Matthew, D. deB. Richter, C. Waters, P. Haff, C. Neal, and S. J. Price. 2015. "Diachronous Beginnings of the Anthropocene: The Lower Bounding Surface of Anthropogenic Deposits." *Anthropocene Review* 2(1): 33–58.

Fanon, Frantz. 1963. *The Wretched of the Earth.* New York: Grove Press.

Fitzpatrick, Matthew P. 2011. "Provincializing Rome: The Indian Ocean Trade Network and Roman Imperialism." *Journal of World History* 22(1): 27–54.

Flecker, Michael. 2001. "A Ninth-Century AD Arab or Indian Shipwreck in Indonesia: First Evidence for Direct Trade with China." *World Archaeology* 32(3): 335–54.

Fleisher, Jeff, and A. LaViolette. 2013. "The Early Swahili Trade Village of Tumbe, Pemba Island, Tanzania, AD 600–950." *Antiquity* 87(338): 1151–68.

Flewellen, Ayana O. 2017. "Locating Marginalized Historical Narratives at Kingsley Plantation." *Historical Archaeology* 51(1): 71–87.

———. 2019. "African Diasporic Choices." *Nordisk Tidsskrift for Informationsvidenskab Og Kulturformidling* 8(2): 54–74.

Franklin, Maria, J. P. Dunnavant, A. O. Flewellen, and A. Odewale. 2020. "The Future Is Now: Archaeology and the Eradication of Anti-Blackness." *International Journal of Historical Archaeology* 24(4): 753–66.

Galle, Jillian E., E. Bollwerk, and F. D. Neiman. 2019. "A Case Study in Open Data and Collaboration in the Field of Archaeology." In *New Life for Archaeological Collections,* edited by Rebecca Allen and Ben Ford, 45–90. Lincoln: University of Nebraska Press.

Gurukkal, Rajan. 2016. *Rethinking Classical Indo-Roman Trade: Political Economy of Eastern Mediterranean Exchange Relations.* Oxford: Oxford University Press.

Guy, John. 2017. "The Phanom Surin Shipwreck, a Pahlavi Inscription, and Their Significance for the Early History of Lower Central Thailand." *Journal of the Siam Society* 105: 179–96.

———. 2019. "Long Distance Arab Shipping in the Ninth Century Indian Ocean: Recent Shipwreck Evidence from Southeast Asia." *Current Science* 117(10): 1647–53.

Hall, Derek, P. Hirch, and T. Li. 2011. "Introduction to Powers of Exclusion: Land Dilemmas in Southeast Asia." In *Powers of Exclusion: Land Dilemmas in Southeast Asia,* edited by D. Hall, P. Hirsch, and T. Li, 1–27. Singapore: National University of Singapore Press and University of Hawaii Press.

Hall, Martin. 2000. *Archaeology and the Modern World: Colonial Transcripts in South Africa and the Chesapeake.* London: Routledge.

Haraway, Donna. 1988. "Situated Knowledges: The Science Question in Feminism and the Privilege of Partial Perspective." *Feminist Studies* 14(3): 575–99.

Hauser, Mark W. 2011. "Routes and Roots of Empire: Pots, Power, and Slavery in the 18th-Century British Caribbean." *American Anthropologist* 113(3): 431–47.

———. 2018. "Huge Oceans, Small Comparisons: Danish Forts and Their Enclaves in the Indian and Atlantic Oceans." In *Power, Political Economy, and Historical Landscapes of the Modern World: Interdisciplinary Perspectives,* edited by C. R. DeCorse, 349–74. Binghamton, N.Y.: Binghamton University Press.

———. 2021. *Mapping Water on Dominica: Archaeologies of Water and Enslavement under Colonialism.* Seattle: University of Washington Press.

Ho, E. 2004. "Empire through Diasporic Eyes: A View from the Other Boat." *Comparative Studies in Society and History* 46(2): 210–46.

Hoogervorst, Tom, and T. Hodos. 2016. "Tracing Maritime Connections between Island Southeast Asia and the Indian Ocean World." In *The Routledge Handbook of Archaeology and Globalization.* London: Routledge.

Horning, Audrey. 2013. *Ireland in the Virginian Sea: Colonialism in the British Atlantic.* Chapel Hill: University of North Carolina Press.

Howson, J. E. 1990. "Social Relations and Material Culture: A Critique of the Archaeology of Plantation Slavery." *Historical Archaeology* 24(4): 78–91.

Johnson, Matthew. 1996. *An Archaeology of Capitalism.* Blackwell: London.

Jorgensen, Helle. 2014. *Tranquebar: Whose History? Transnational Cultural Heritage in a Former Danish Trading Colony in South India.* New Delhi: Orient Black Swan.

Knutson, S. A. 2021. "Archaeology and the Silk Road Model." *World Archaeology* 52(4): 619–38.

Lane, Paul J. 2016. "New Directions for Historical Archaeology in Eastern Africa?" *Journal of African History* 57(2): 173–81.

LaViolette, Adria. 2008. "Swahili Cosmopolitanism in Africa and the Indian Ocean World, A.D. 600–1500." *Archaeologies: Journal of the World Archaeological Congress* 4(1): 24–49.

Leone, Mark P. 1995. "A Historical Archaeology of Capitalism." *American Anthropologist* 97(2): 251–68.

Li, Tania Murray. 2014. *Land's End: Capitalist Relations on an Indigenous Frontier.* Durham: Duke University Press.

Lightfoot, Kent G. 2005. *Indians, Missionaries, and Merchants: the Legacy of Colonial Encounters on the California Frontiers.* Berkeley: University of California Press.

Lilley, Ian. 2006. "Archaeology, Diaspora and Decolonization." *Journal of Social Archaeology* 6(1): 28–47.

Margariti, Roxani E. 2008. "Mercantile Networks, Port Cities, and 'Pirate' States: Conflict and Competition in the Indian Ocean World of Trade before the Sixteenth Century." *Journal of the Economic and Social History of the Orient* 51(4): 543–77.

Mathew, K. S. (ed.). 2016. *Imperial Rome, Indian Ocean Regions and Muziris: New Perspectives on Maritime Trade.* London: Routledge.

Meskell, Lynn. 2021. "Toilets First, Temples Second: Adopting Heritage in Neoliberal India." *International Journal of Heritage Studies* 27(2): 151–169.

Moosvi, Shireen. 2009. "India's Sea Trade with Iran in Medieval Times." *Proceedings of the Indian History Congress* 70: 240–50.

Mrozowski, Stephen A. 2010. New and Forgotten Paradigms: The Environment and Economics in Historical Archaeology. *Historical Archaeology*44: 117–27.

———. 2018. "The Archaeology of Climate Change: Is Unbridled Commodity Production Sustainable?" In *Historical Archaeology and Environment,* edited by M.A.T. de Souza and D. M. Costa, 41–61. Cham, Switzerland: Springer.

Napolitano, Matthew F., J. H. Stone, and R. J. DiNapoli. 2021. *The Archaeology of Island Colonization: Global Approaches to Initial Human Settlement.* Gainesville: University Press of Florida.

Nordin, Jonas M. 2016. "The World in a Nutshell: A Historical Archaeology of Early Modern Entanglement of Scandinavia and India Studied through the Life Course of the Danish Nobleman Ove Gjedde, 1594–1660." *Journal of Post Medieval Archaeology* 50(2): 244–63.

Oland, Maxine, S. M. Hart, and L. Frink (eds.). 2012. *Decolonizing Indigenous Histories: Exploring Prehistoric/Colonial Transitions in Archaeology.* Tucson: University of Arizona Press.

Orser, Charles E. 1996. *A Historical Archaeology of the Modern World.* New York: Plenum Press.

———. 2018. *An Archaeology of the English Atlantic World, 1600–1700.* Cambridge: Cambridge University Press.

Possehl, Gregory L. 1996. Melhua. In *The Indian Ocean in Antiquity,* edited by Julian E. Reade, 133–208. London: Kegan Paul International.

Rajan, K. 2019 *Churning the Ocean: Maritime Trade of Early Historic India.* Thanjavur, India: Manoo Pathippakam.

Ray, Himanshu Prabha, and Jean-François Salles. 1996. Chinese Ceramics of Tamil Nadu and Kerala Coasts. In *Tradition and Archaeology: Early Maritime Contacts in the Indian Ocean,* edited by Himanshu Prabha Ray and Jean-François Salles, 109–14. Manohar, New Delhi, India.

Reilly, Matthew. 2019. "Futurity, Time, and Archaeology." *Journal of Contemporary Archaeology* 6(1): 1–15.

Risso, Patricia A. 2018. *Merchants and Faith: Muslim Commerce and Culture in the Indian Ocean.* London: Routledge.

Robb, John, and T. R. Pauketat. 2013. "From Moments to Millennia: Theorizing Scale and Change in Human History." In *Big Histories, Human Lives: Tackling Problems of Scale in Archaeology,* edited by J. Robb and T. R. Pauketat, 3–33. Santa Fe, NM: School for Advanced Research.

Ross, Douglas E. 2012. "Transnational Artifacts: Grappling with Fluid Material Origins and Identities in Archaeological Interpretations of Culture Change." *Journal of Anthropological Archaeology* 31(1): 38–48.

Samuels, Kathryn. 2016. "Transnational Turns for Archaeological Heritage: From Conservation to Development, Governments to Governance." *Journal of Field Archaeology* 41(3): 355–67.

———. 2012. "Roman Archaeology and the Making of Heritage Citizens in Tunisia." In *Making Roman Places: Past and Present,* edited by D. Totten and K. L. Samuels, 159–70. JRA Supplementary Series no. 89. Portsmouth, RI: Journal of Roman Archaeology.

Schmidt, Peter R. 2016. "Historical Archaeology in East Africa: Past Practice and Future Directions." *The Journal of African History* 57(2): 183–94.

Schmidt, P. R., and S. A. Mrozowski. 2013. "The Death of Prehistory: Reforming the Past, Looking to the Future." In *The Death of Prehistory,* edited by P. R Schmidt and S. A. Mrozowski, 1–30. Oxford: Oxford University Press.

Scott, David. 2004. *Conscripts of Modernity: The Tragedy of Colonial Enlightenment.* Durham: Duke University Press.

Scott, James C. 1985. *Weapons of the Weak: Everyday Forms of Peasant Resistance.* New Haven, Conn.: Yale University Press.

Seetah, Krish, and R. Allen. 2018. "Interdisciplinary Ripples across the Indian Ocean." In *Connecting Continents,* edited by K. Seetah, 1–29. Athens: Ohio University Press.

Seland, E. H. 2014. "Archaeology of Trade in the Western Indian Ocean, 300 BC–AD 700." *Journal of Archaeological Research* 22(4): 367–402.

Selvakumar, V. 2011. "Archaeology, Literary and Ethnographic Evidence for Traditional Boatbuilding in Kerala, South India." In *Proceedings of the Asia-Pacific Regional Conference on Underwater Cultural Heritage,* edited by M. Staniforth, J. Craig, S. C. Jago-on, B. Orillaneda, and L. Lacsina, 201–20. November 8–12, 2011. Manila, Philippines.

———. 2016. "Ancient Ports of Kerala: An Overview." In *Imperial Rome, Indian Ocean Regions and Muziris: New Perspectives on Maritime Trade,* edited by K. S. Mathew, 269–96. London: Routledge.

Sidebotham, Steven. 1992. "Ports of the Red Sea and the Arabia-India Trade." In *Rome and India: The Ancient Sea Trade,* edited by V. Begley and R. D. Puma, 12–38. Oxford: Oxford University Press.

Silliman, Stephen W. 2005 "Culture Contact or Colonialism? Challenges in the Archaeology of Native North America." *American Antiquity* 70(1): 55–74.

Spyer, Patricia. 2000. *The Memory of Trade: Modernity's Entanglements on an Eastern Indonesian Island.* Durham: Duke University Press.

Stahl, Ann B. 2001. *Making History in Banda: Anthropological Visions of Africa's Past.* Cambridge: Cambridge University Press.

Staples, Eric, and L. Blue. 2019. "Archaeological, Historical, and Ethnographic Approaches to the Study of Sewn Boats: Past, Present, and Future." *International Journal of Nautical Archaeology* 48(2): 269–85.

Subrahmanyam, Sanjay. 1997. "Connected Histories: Notes towards a Reconfiguration of Early Modern Eurasia." *Modern Asian Studies* 31(3): 735–62.

Thomas, Nicholas. 1991. *Entangled Objects: Exchange, Material Culture, and Colonialism in the Pacific.* Cambridge, Mass.: Harvard University Press.

Thompson, E. P. 1971. The Moral Economy of the English Crowd in the Eighteenth Century. *Past & Present* 50(1): 76–136.

Tomber, Roberta. 2008. *Indo-Roman Trade: From Pots to Pepper*. London: Bristol Classical Press.

Trouillot, Michel-Rolph. 2003. *Global Transformations: Anthropology and the Modern World*. New York: Palgrave Macmillan.

Voss, Barbara L. 2008. *The Archaeology of Ethnogenesis: Race and Sexuality in Colonial San Francisco*. Berkeley: University of California Press.

Voss, Barbara L., J. R. Kennedy, J. S. Tan, and L. W. Ng. 2018. "The Archaeology of Home: Qiaoxiang and Nonstate Actors in the Archaeology of the Chinese Diaspora." *American Antiquity* 83(3): 407–26.

Waters, Colin N., J. Zalasiewicz, C. Summerhayes, I. J. Fairchild, N. L. Rose, N. J. Loader, W. Shotyk, A. Cearreta, M. J. Head, J. P. M. Syvitski, M. Williams, M. Wagreich, A. D. Barnosky, A. Zhisheng, R. Leinfelder, C. Jeandel, A. Galuszka, J. A. Ivar do Sul, F. Gradstein, W. Steffen, J. R. McNeill, S. Wing, C. Poirier, and M. Edgeworth. 2018. "Global Boundary Stratotype Section and Point (GSSP) for the Anthropocene Series: Where and How to Look for Potential Candidates." *Earth-Science Reviews* 178: 379–429.

Williams, Raymond. 1975. *The Country and the City*. Oxford: Oxford University Press.

Wilson, Brian, and Mark W. Hauser. 2016. "Toward a South Asian Historical Archaeology." *Historical Archaeology* 50(4): 7–21.

Wurst, LouAnn, and S. A. Mrozowski. 2014. "Toward an Archaeology of the Future." *International Journal of Historical Archaeology* 18(2): 210–23.

2

The *Maqāmāt* Ship

Image as Source in Historical Archaeology of the Indian Ocean

MICK DE RUYTER

An iconic illustration of a ship in a thirteenth-century Islamic manuscript now in the Bibliothèque Nationale de France in Paris is one of the most significant individual images used in studies of Indian Ocean seafaring, and in nautical archaeology in particular. This painting, in the Arab manuscript known as the Schefer *Maqāmāt,* was the primary visual source for interpretations of the ninth-century shipwrecks from Belitung in Indonesia and Phanom Surin in Thailand and for the design and construction of two full-sized reconstructions (Severin 1985: 279; Vosmer 2010: 121, 134; Guy 2019: 125–28; Staples 2019: 316). This *Maqāmāt* ship illustration is prized because of the relative paucity of other archaeological, iconographic, or documentary sources, although this conversely makes validation difficult. The context of the image, and of several others in other illustrated versions of the manuscript, is troublesome for researchers of material culture, as the *Maqāmāt* text was a collection of witty short stories or fables written in the eleventh century, in which illustrations were designed to enhance the witticisms by clever compositions rather than to depict contemporary material culture faithfully, much as in the popular shadow theaters of the time. Using these ship pictures as historical evidence requires particular caution, as knowledge of the models or referents used by the artists—which may have included shadow puppets, the limitations imposed by the page size and shape, the skill of the artists, and the intended mode of reception—is integral to sound interpretations.

Thus, while some nautical researchers are content to consider these images at face value, many continue to be vexed by the *Maqāmāt* paintings and, in particular, the example in the Paris Schefer manuscript. Reflecting on the original audience and consumption of these manuscript paintings and their literary and entertainment contexts allows the Paris *Maqāmāt* painting to be reinterpreted as a caricature loaded with iconographic and metaphorical significance rather than as an attempted realistic impression of a ship. While the artist of the Paris manuscript produced the most celebrated and accomplished paintings (Grabar 1984: 10–11), this image of a ship was not the most reliable of the several *Maqāmāt* ships and was certainly not an original composition. These paintings retain evidentiary value when chronologically sequenced, when used together in comparison, and, most important, with appropriate recognition of their unique artistic and literary contexts. This chapter compares the famous image in the Paris manuscript with other lesser known *Maqāmāt* ships, and with other depictions of watercraft in contemporary manuscripts and shadow theater, and offers a critique specifically focused on the value of *Maqāmāt* ships as sources in historical nautical archaeology.

Ships in Thirteenth-Century Manuscripts

An important element of historical archaeology is criticism of the historical sources, including iconographic or visual sources, that provide context for our archaeological inquiries. This is especially important when there are few cross-references or opportunities to validate the data in, or interpretations of, individual sources. Arab manuscript painting is a good example of such an instance, with its brief flowering from the eleventh to the fourteenth centuries. Indeed, there are only around fifty extant full or partial Islamic manuscripts from the period before the fourteenth century (Hillenbrand 2007: 119). Within this restricted period, there are relatively few Indian Ocean watercraft depicted and few other contemporaneous visual or archaeological sources with which to compare them. The ships depicted in the thirteenth-century manuscripts of al-Hariri's *Maqāmāt* have therefore become quite familiar sources for interpretation in nautical archaeology of the Indian Ocean and warrant closer examination.

The most familiar image of a medieval Indian Ocean ship (Fig. 2.1) came to prominence in Hourani's interpretation of it as an Arab sewn-plank ship with the publication of *Arab Seafaring* in 1951, when there were few other pictorial or material sources available. This single image (Bibliothèque National de France MS Arabe 5847) has since come to represent Indian Ocean seafaring in general and is perhaps the most recognizable image of a ship from that ocean, the "most well-known depiction of a pre-modern western Indian Ocean vessel" (Staples 2019: 328). The Paris Schefer manuscript itself is widely recognized as a masterpiece and is celebrated in Arab and Islamic

26 · Mick de Ruyter

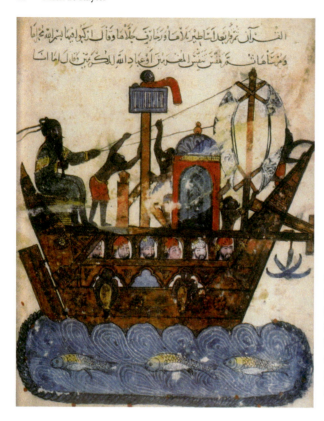

Figure 2.1. The ship illustration from the Schefer *Maqāmāt* in Paris, from 1237 CE, Bibliothèque National de France MS Arabe 5847 fol.119b (Album/Alamy stock photo).

art circles. The folio painted with a ship, on a page only some 37 cm high in the original, has been used on book covers and exhibition posters for decades, and the prominence, detail, state of preservation, and free availability of the image nearly 800 years after it was painted have ensured the popularity and ubiquity of this piece.

The *Maqāmāt* is a collection of stories or fables written in the eleventh century CE by Abou Mohammad al-Hariri al-Basri, better known simply as al-Hariri. There are more than 200 known versions of al-Hariri's *Maqāmāt*, 13 of which are illustrated, and of these, four can be ascribed to the Baghdad school, where there might have been Indian Ocean watercraft available to act as models for illustrators (Grabar 1984: 7–19). The thirty-ninth *maqāmah*, the story with the seagoing ship, is illustrated in three of the four Baghdad-style manuscripts, the earliest now in St. Petersburg in Russia (Fig. 2.2), the Schefer manuscript in Paris, and a later version now in Istanbul. The St. Petersburg manuscript image was originally far more difficult to access and has not been anywhere near as widely published and has been defaced by scratches on the

The *Maqāmāt* Ship: Image as Source in Historical Archaeology of the Indian Ocean · 27

Figure 2.2. Illustration from the St. Petersburg *Maqāmāt*, Russian Academy of Sciences Ms. S23 p. 260, dated 1225–1235 CE (akg-images/Roland and Sabrina Michaud).

faces of figures (Grabar 1984: 11). The third Istanbul version from a decade after the Paris manuscript is also quite damaged by iconoclastic defacing (MS Esad Efendi 2916 f.153, dated 1242–1258 CE; see James 2013: pl. 5.9). Grabar concluded that the stylistic and detail similarities between these images, particularly of the figures shown in them, means that they "clearly belong to one iconographic type" (1984: 88). These two other illustrations provide context in which to examine the more familiar Paris version, although there are other noteworthy versions.

The British Library manuscript AD 1200 from 1256 CE is very similar to the Baghdad-style manuscripts but may have been executed elsewhere, perhaps farther inland in Iraq. This manuscript is "so interconnected visually and technically" with the others that a clear link is presumed (James 2013: 5). The ship in the thirty-ninth *maqāmah* in this British Library manuscript is "almost exactly the same" as that in the Schefer manuscript and, although simplified, has obviously been directly copied from this or a similar source (James 2013: 63). A manuscript version in the John Rylands University Library in Man-

28 · Mick de Ruyter

chester (MS Arab 680) is very similar to the thirteenth-century Baghdad-style manuscripts, particularly the St. Petersburg version, but is from Ottoman-era Iraq in the sixteenth or seventeenth century CE (James 2013: 26–27). The Rylands manuscript is particularly obscure, and as the ship in the thirty-ninth *maqāmah* in this version is clearly not a seagoing vessel (James 2013: 63), it is not discussed further here. The last version worth mentioning is a forgery executed in the early twentieth century and originally passed off as a detached folio of a thirteenth-century manuscript (Hoare 2017: no. 207). The ship in the forgery is similar in outline to the Schefer manuscript ship, but the figures and colors are stylistically different. The anchor is also secured by a metal chain, a feature virtually unknown in Indian Ocean ships until much later. While painted on thirteenth-century paper, the pigments used have been confirmed as much later, probably twentieth-century (Damian Hoare, pers. comm., November 24, 2018). This leaves the St. Petersburg, Paris, and Istanbul manuscripts as the only reliably dated versions of the Baghdad school that include an image of a seagoing ship in the thirty-ninth *maqāmah*.

The *Maqāmāt* Ships in Archaeological Contexts

The preservation, detail, and easy availability of the Paris *Maqāmāt* ship has given it prominence among the several similar illustrations in interpretations of archaeological remains of Indian Ocean ships. The first major example of a supposedly medieval Indian Ocean ship in an archaeological context is the Belitung, or Tang, shipwreck from the ninth century, which showed features similar to those of the Paris *Maqāmāt* ship, particularly the sewn-plank construction (Flecker 2000: 213–14; see Haw 2019 for an alternative view). Significantly, the stern and rudder arrangements of this ship were not described by the salvors of this wreck, so reconstructions of the Belitung wreck have relied heavily on other sources of evidence, particularly these visual sources. The *Maqāmāt* ships have also enlightened interpretations of other archaeological sites around the Indian Ocean, such as the sewn planks from tombs at Qusier al-Qadim on the Red Sea (Blue 2006: 277), those from Al Baleed in Oman (Ghidoni 2021: 226), and the nautical petroglyphs from al-Jassasiya in Qatar (Facey 1987: 201).

The sewn-plank ship excavated at Phanom Surin in Thailand is also from around the ninth century, similar to the Belitung wreck, and has also been interpreted in light of the *Maqāmāt* ships (Guy 2019: 125–28). The method of lacing used to join the planks, the use of coir wadding in the seams, the stern rudder, and the presence of two masts have reinforced interpretations of this wreck that compare it with the "faithfully depicted" ship in the Paris

Maqāmāt and declare it to be an "Arab dhow" (Guy 2019: 126–27). Further excavation and analysis of timber species is expected to improve this interpretation, but the likeness to a painting of a ship from several hundred years after the shipwreck is a dubious basis for identification, and other evidence is clearly required. This case also highlights the potentially circular nature of evidence used for cultural identification of ships from the Indian Ocean and shows how the prominence of this painting effectively demands comparison. Those particular architectural features were widely used in the Indian Ocean and in parts of Southeast Asia, and are therefore insufficient evidence that the ship is "Arab" or even a "dhow." The ship in the Paris *Maqāmāt* painting is potentially Persian, Indian, or African (Agius 2013: 50–51). Identifications of the ships in the *Maqāmāt* paintings with cultural specificity are frequently misleading and often based on unproven assumptions.

Of the three illustrated Baghdad-style manuscripts that include a ship, in only one instance is the identity of the artist known (Grabar 1984: 10). In this case—Yaḥyā ibn Maḥmūd al-Wāsiṭī of the Paris *Maqāmāt*—the artist's origin can be traced to Wāsiṭ, a city in Iraq on the Tigris River above Basra (James 2013: 16). While it is clear that the three illustrated Baghdad manuscripts all accord with the same style, this does not necessarily imply that the ships shown in the images are Iraqi. Even if they were drawn from life, Basra attracted shipping from all over the Indian Ocean and Asia, so many of the vessels in port at any particular instant may have been foreign. This identification of the ships as Iraqi assumes that Iraqi artists would depict Iraqi watercraft, but nowhere in the text is the origin of the ship specified, and in the context of the story the ship may well be Omani, as it undertakes a passage to Oman. Nevertheless, some sources accept the ship as Iraqi on the basis of origin of the artist or artwork alone (Facey and Martin 1979: 108–9), and the port in Oman may well be a waystation on its voyage elsewhere. The manuscript's text is ambiguous on this matter and is as open to interpretation as the images themselves. Interpretations based on the structural features of the ship itself are rarely conclusive, and the characters illustrated in the image demonstrate a variety of clothing, skin colors, and hair styles, probably representing different cultural origins or status. As Agius concludes of this instance, "in the absence of written evidence and with hardly any archaeological finds it is wrong to claim that this *Maqāmāt* ship is Arabian on the basis that it is found in an Arabic work" (2013: 51).

Furthermore, the *Maqāmāt* ships are technically not dhows. While there is no evidence that the term dhow or its variants were used any earlier than the fifteenth century, the use of the word in a generic sense for any western Indian Ocean watercraft is a modern construct common only from the early nineteenth century (Al-Hijji 2001: 11; Staples 2018: 201–2). Prior to this, the name referred to a specific type of watercraft with a prominent projecting stern, a name now spelled as *dāw* or *daww* by way of differentiation (Al Salimi and Staples 2019: 67–68; Agius 2019: 61–62; De Ruyter 2020). None of the *Maqāmāt* ships appears to represent this specific type of dhow, and they have more commonly been associated with the *būm*, a double-ended craft of relatively modern origins (Al-Hijji 2001: 4, 21; Al Salimi and Staples 2019: 51–52). The *Maqāmāt* ships therefore cannot be properly referred to as dhows in either the generic or the specific sense. Naming such ships so is equivalent to naming all European wooden sailing vessels "galleons," regardless of their origin, size, or rig. This practice may have been correct for one type of ship during a particular period of history, but it is now misplaced, potentially confusing, and imprecise.

If the ship cannot be identified with confidence as a particular type, nor associated with a cultural origin with meaningful precision, then how does it provide useful evidence of Indian Ocean seafaring? This scenario relies then on context, just as does any analysis of a historical archaeological artifact. The tendency to classify artifacts or technology with cultural specificity may not even be a particularly useful approach in a region as diverse yet interconnected as the Indian Ocean and may obscure more than it reveals. In the case of the *Maqāmāt* ship, the illustration is most rewardingly considered in its context, with the story it was meant to illustrate and with the mediums through which it was meant to be consumed.

Words and Pictures in the *Maqāmāt*

The short stories, or *maqāmah,* that make up the *Maqāmāt,* were written by al-Hariri in the eleventh century and proved popular for several centuries later. The appeal of the work lay mainly in the clever use of language, in its wit and "in jokes," rather than in any particular literary merit or narrative value (Grabar 2005: 188–89). Even hundreds of years after it was written, it was still a "best seller of its age, with more than seven hundred copies of the text authorized by al-Hariri during his lifetime" (O'Kane 2012: 52). This sort of illustrated manuscript was enjoyed by being recited in a social setting in an era with low levels of textual literacy. The illustrations therefore served to entertain the audience, but they also allowed the copyist and artist(s) to demonstrate their skill at interpretation by including multiple layers of meaning in single images as visual accompaniments to the clever text. Each image is therefore not necessarily a single moment in time, but a passage of narrative with interwoven metaphors and jokes (James 2013: 39–42).

Within the *Maqāmāt*, two stories relate to watercraft: the twenty-second *maqāmah*, "Of the Euphrates," about a river crossing, and the thirty-ninth, "Of Oman," about a sea passage from Basra in Iraq to Oman. The twenty-second *maqāmah* takes place on a riverine craft (Chenery 1867: 229) and is illustrated with open boats. "Of Oman," the thirty-ninth *maqāmah*, describes a voyage in the Persian Gulf to Oman during which the ship is forced to shelter at an exotic island (Steingass 1898: 93–94), a story illustrated with seagoing vessels. Most of the images of watercraft in the *Maqāmāt* depict small riverine boats that would have been familiar to anyone in lower Mesopotamia, with artists using increasingly complex internal arrangements to show seagoing craft. The larger ships shown in the thirty-ninth *maqāmah* in the St. Petersburg, Paris Schefer, and Istanbul manuscripts are distinct and represent "an original innovation" (Grabar 1984: 120). In the thirty-ninth *maqāmah* from the St. Petersburg manuscript (Fig. 2.2), the protagonist of the story, Abū Zaid, is shown begging passage to Oman in exchange for a charm to ward off catastrophe at sea, a "shield against anxiety, when the wave of the deep rages" (Steingass 1898: 96). The Paris manuscript shows the ship at sea on a passage to Oman, and the Istanbul version shows a scene in Basra very similar to the earlier St. Petersburg manuscript (James 2013: 63, pls. 2.27 and 5.9). The scenes of the ship in the St. Petersburg and Istanbul versions therefore depict a different and earlier moment in the narrative than does al-Wāsiṭī's scene in the Paris manuscript. This is the first major issue of divergence between the St. Petersburg/Istanbul and Paris images, and potentially the most significant for the interpretation of historical archaeology.

"A Pictorial Evocation of a Conversation"

The fifty stories in the *Maqāmāt* can be separated by literary and narrative complexity into several groups. The thirty-ninth is one of five that James calls an "extended plot" *maqāmah,* the most complex type, that "cannot simply be divided into two or three areas of dialogue capable of pictorial representation" (James 2013: 39). The action in these more complex examples mixes characters and scenes, and sometimes even returns the reader to prior events. The extended plot stories offer the artist "more than usually elaborate adventures [and] extremely cunning tricks," allowing more scope for illustration than the simpler narrative or continuous dialogue versions elsewhere in the work (James 2013: 40). The illustrations in a complex *maqāmah* are therefore less reliant on the text, although still closely representative of it. The single illustration in the thirty-ninth *maqāmah* in the St. Petersburg manuscript depicts a "dialogue in progress" or "a pictorial evocation of a conversation," while the

32 · Mick de Ruyter

four illustrations in the Paris manuscript appear more linked to "episodes and occurrences" (James 2013: 41). These divergent themes are used in illustrations throughout the manuscripts, although the narrative style illustrations are used less frequently in the Paris *Maqāmāt* and "almost exclusively in the extended plot *maqāmahs*" (James 2013: 42). It is important to understand this point: that the two main images drawn from the St. Petersburg and Paris manuscripts illustrate different moments in the text by using different illustrative themes.

The artist of the St. Petersburg manuscript has used the only illustration in that *maqāmah* to show the conversation between the protagonist Abū Zaid and the master of the vessel in Basra (Fig. 2.2). At this moment, Abū Zaid is negotiating for a passage to Oman, before the ship sets out and before the storm interrupts its passage. Yet the ship already appears to be in distress, as the single mast is clearly broken, the oars are shipped, and the crew is bailing. This apparent chronological disconnect has been a major issue of contention in interpretations of this scene (James 2013: 63; Burningham 2019: 157) and has important implications for the use of these images as historical evidence. After Abū Zaid is accepted on board and reunited with the hero, the travelers continue the voyage until the ship takes shelter from a storm at an unnamed magical island, after suffering some damage. While at the enchanted island, Abū Zaid earns the local lord's eternal gratitude by helping to deliver his wife's child safely. The story ends there, and the ship goes no farther. While this ship is the only illustration in that *maqāmah* in the St. Petersburg manuscript, the Paris manuscript uses four images to depict the events in the narrative.

The images of the thirty-ninth *maqāmah* in the slightly later Paris manuscript are used to illustrate different moments in the story. In the earlier St. Petersburg image, the mast is broken, the oars are shipped, and the crew is bailing. In the later Paris version, these artistic elements are copied in the first of four illustrations showing the ship at sea before arriving at the magical island (Fig. 2.1). The first image has the ship already at sea with the characters embarked. The damaged ship is then shown hidden behind the island in the third illustration (James 2013: 203, pl. 3.19) and is not shown at all in the second or fourth. In this way al-Wāsiṭī has avoided showing the vessel in any more distress than it appears in the first image, where the figures bailing with ceramic pots are retained, as is the outline of the broken mast. The sails are shown hoisted on another mast to give the vessel the appearance of motion, and the oars of the St. Petersburg manuscript are not shown at all. The position of the illustrations within this story is particularly relevant as some have argued that they show the damage after the storm and hence the reason for resorting to the magical island. The sequence of four illustrations—the ship on passage, sheltering at the magical island, and the characters ashore on the island and in the palace—has convinced some that the *maqāmah* of the Paris manuscript is truer to the text of the story and that the mast shown in the St. Petersburg manuscript is not broken (Burningham 2019: 157). This common interpretation has enhanced the reputation for technical accuracy of al-Wāsiṭī's depiction of the ship.

Nevertheless, such an interpretation ignores the intent of the charm offered for passage as a "shield against anxiety" (Steingass 1898: 96). To illustrate the concept, the artist of the St. Petersburg manuscript has shown the ship in obvious distress, and the single image therefore appears to diverge from the narrative sequence of the text. The illustration from the Paris *Maqāmāt* is the most widely cited and has been used so often that it has developed into a caricature of Indian Ocean seafaring. Open access to good quality reproductions of this particular image through the French national library has facilitated the ease with which it is disseminated. The Paris *Maqāmāt* is also the only illustrated Baghdad manuscript where the name of the artist is known, and al-Wāsiṭī's other paintings throughout the manuscript have been lauded as remarkable renditions of Arabian material and social culture and are far more accomplished in general than others of the genre. Despite hailing from a river port north of Basra, al-Wāsiṭī appears not to have been as familiar with seagoing craft as some of his contemporary illustrators. His widely used depiction of the ship is neither the best nor the most technically accurate version and has clearly been copied from another source or sources.

Referents for the *Maqāmāt* Ships

There are two images of the ship in the Schefer *Maqāmāt* (BnF MS Arabe 5847), the principal image on folio 119b, and another of the bow only, with the rest of the vessel hidden by the island on folio 121b. This second image of the ship's bow does not exactly replicate the first image and has been reduced in proportion to the page. It still shows the sewn planks, stem finial, and grapnel anchor. Together, the four *Maqāmāt* ship images—two in the Paris manuscript and one each in the St. Petersburg and Istanbul manuscripts—display similarities in form and detail and are all represented in a distinct, if somewhat awkward, style (Grabar 1984: 88). While each has stylistic peculiarities, the illustrations of the three main manuscripts are set in two-dimensional space with depth provided by parallel outlines, as if each were on separate planes, an ancient convention. Representations of other material elements like buildings and campsites within this corpus appear similarly awkward when compared with illustrations less restricted by form and space, or that employ perspective

Figure 2.3. A ship illustration similar to the earlier St. Petersburg manuscript image (1225–1235 CE) on the left may have provided a model for the later Paris manuscript image (1237 CE) on the right, with the transfer achieved by pouncing.

and realism. Many of these architectural features, including the ships, comprise frames to which the figures are attached (Grabar 1984: 142).

Al-Wāsiṭī appears to have copied his ship from an earlier referent, perhaps one similar to the St. Petersburg manuscript or another long-lost model. This may even be evidenced by the process of pouncing, where versions are copied by pricking vellum and then reversed to trace onto paper (Roxburgh 2002: 61–63). The artistic elements of the St. Petersburg ship are retained—the broken mast, oars, and bailers—while new ones are added, such as the mast and crow's nest and banner sail on the foremast. When the outlines of the ships are traced in this way, it is easy to see the similarities (Fig. 2.3). The similar positions of the anchors, masts, and domed superstructures, as well as the angles of the ends, become apparent.

Indeed, some of these similarities are apparent in the other images as well. These similarities appear to support the contention that such images represent actual ships, in that they all seem to show the same arrangement of features. The referents could of course have been actual ships, several of which would have been available in riverine ports in Iraq where these works were illustrated, the common assumption in interpretations of these images (Burningham 2019: 147–50, 157). Grabar concluded that the paintings in the thirty-ninth *maqāmah* were "sufficiently different from the rest of their miniatures in human types, in the representation of boats, and in landscape to suggest some external origin," although his suggestions were limited to other contemporary illustrated texts (Grabar 1984: 143). It is safe to conclude that each of the *Maqāmāt* ships was based on similar referents, although these were not necessarily actual ships. Copying from earlier models was a common practice in Islamic art, and it was considered commendable to be able to recreate the work of an earlier master while adding minor embellishments (Rice 1975: 7; Roxburgh 2002: 57–61). The original models for these illustrations are probably long lost, and there are certainly many other versions that have not been preserved over the intervening centuries.

A probable candidate for the models of ships used in these illustrations is shadow play, a popular form of entertainment at the time, and very similar in its performative aspects to the way these manuscripts were intended to be delivered "orally during literary gatherings" (George 2011: 1; Guo 2020: 3–12). Indeed, George has concluded that "manuscript illustrators faced with the challenge of creating narrative imagery for the *Maqāmāt* drew much of their inspiration from the shadow play," and that this notion "represents a key element in our understanding of the *Maqāmāt*" (2011: 1). Examples of leather ship puppets from a collection acquired in Egypt in the early twentieth century show how the thirteenth-century manuscript artists may have envisaged watercraft. These puppets, purchased at a small Egyptian village of Menzaleh in 1909 (Kahle 1940: 22), are the earliest known examples of shadow puppets from the region, but similar puppets would have been used for shadow plays in medieval Iraq where the *Maqāmāt* manuscripts were illustrated (George 2011: 4). While the individual puppets may be of different ages, they have been dated to the seventeenth century with confidence (Milwright 2011). Puppets were more difficult to keep together, and perhaps less collectible than manuscripts, so none are known to have survived from the thirteenth century when these manuscripts were illustrated, but the *Maqāmāt* artists probably had similar ship puppets at hand as models or referents. The Menzaleh collection is now dispersed, and the whereabouts of many of the puppets, including most of the ships, are unknown (Milwright 2011: 43–44).

The Menzaleh puppets were made from individual sheets of prepared leather—"stretched and beaten to make them thin, hard and semi-transparent"—that were pinned or stitched together (Milwright 2011: 44). Some elements of thinner, colored leather were used to create colored panels when backlit (George 2011: 4). Many of the assembled puppets could be moved at the joints to create 'action' scenes. George (2011) has shown convincingly that

Figure 2.4. Some elements of the *Maqāmāt* ships appear to have been modeled on shadow puppets, like the examples here on the right from Egypt.

many of the *Maqāmāt* illustrations were actually based on shadow puppets, as indicated by figures shown in profile and structures shown in silhouette. Islamic art historians contend that the puppets came first, or at the very least served as models for many illustrations, because of the awkward articulated poses in some of the figures (Grabar 1984: 142–43; Roxburgh 2013: 205–6). This is possibly also indicated by the retention of arabesques or other features in the illustration that were intended to allow light or color through puppets but that served no purpose other than decoration on paper (Figure 2.4). The "flat outline" of ships, the "disproportionally large human figures" and devices for framing used in other structural puppets indicate the "imperatives of visibility in the shadow theatre" (George 2011: 10–11). The popularity of shadow plays and the exploding thirteenth-century demand for illustrated books combined with al-Hariri's bestselling text to create the extant versions of the *Maqāmāt* (George 2011: 5–6). The ships painted in these surviving manuscripts may therefore have more to do with the technical limitations of assembling shadow puppets from elements of leather than with actual wooden watercraft illustrated from life.

"A touch of their own humour"

The inclusion of unusual features in the ship illustrations, particularly in the Paris manuscript, has long vexed those who interpret the images out of their

The *Maqāmāt* Ship: Image as Source in Historical Archaeology of the Indian Ocean · 37

cultural context. Metaphorical imagery and symbolism were widely used in Islamic poetry and shadow play from this period (Hodgson 1964: 222–23; Guo 2020: 3–12), and the inclusion of visual metaphors in some of the *Maqāmāt* images may have enhanced the artist's prestige, much as the quips and tricks of the text did for the author. "Banner" sails similar to those in the ships from the Paris (Fig. 2.1) and Istanbul manuscripts, possibly depicting a Qur'anic metaphor (Beeston 1973: 94), are relatively common in Mesopotamian and Persian manuscript paintings from the thirteenth to the fifteenth century CE. The sail design is nonsensical, apparently operating in opposing directions, but if the intent was to emphasize the similarity with banners as they might appear on the horizon in the desert (Beeston 1973: 94–96), then such technical considerations might be laid aside. It is also worth noting that this device appears in the Paris and Istanbul images, although not in the earlier and apparently more competent St. Petersburg image. However, the artist of the Paris manuscript image, al-Wāsiṭī, may have been less concerned with technical accuracy than with illustrative magic, as a further example of visual metaphor shows.

The figure depicted in the crow's nest at the top of the main mast in the Paris manuscript ship serves a metaphorical purpose. This figure is painted with a long sleeve, a common visual symbol for a Sufi, or mystic. The Arabic word for Sufi, *tasawwuf*, means 'wearing wool,' making a Sufi mystic 'one who wears wool' (Anjum 2006: 225). The coarse wool cloaks worn by Sufis symbolized penitence, similarly to Christian monks (Anjum 2006: 226), while the later Persian word *darwish*, meaning pauper, became dervish in common English usage (Meier 1976: 117). The woolen sleeves stretched over time, especially from 'whirling' or dancing, and this feature therefore became a common visual metaphor for Sufism in Islamic art (e.g., Meier 1976: 128–36). The St. Petersburg *Maqāmāt* even shows Sufis dancing with stretched sleeves a decade before the Paris manuscript (St. Petersburg MS C23 f.76, shown in James 2013: 178, figure 2.9). Classical Sufism was established in Mesopotamia, where these manuscripts were illustrated, by the ninth century CE (Meier 1976: 118). The state of ecstasy sought by the Sufis, an elevation "in which they believed they experienced direct contact with God," was a form of religious experience that isolated some from society (Meier 1976: 117–18). The isolated hermitage of a Sufi was called a *ribāt*, a word that also means a "look-out post" (Anjum 2006: 243). Hence, the Sufi, identified by his stretched woolen sleeve, is depicted in the crow's nest or 'look-out post,' secluded and 'close to God.' The links in this visual metaphor would have been obvious to the intended educated audience, "before whom the text would be delivered orally during literary gatherings" (George 2011: 1), and such a detailed painting would have accompanied the witty text perfectly. The images were intended to bring "a visual dimension—a touch of their own humor—to these essentially aural events" (George 2011: 1).

Indeed, it may never have been the artist's intention to create a realistic representation of a contemporary watercraft; rather, the intent may have been a metaphorical caricature to run parallel with the tricks and jokes of the text. One may wonder at what other jokes remain hidden from the modern viewer. Drawing conclusions about structural arrangements—the number and configuration of masts, for instance—from single illustrations created in such a way is fraught. Roxburgh expresses concern, in fact, at the "incomplete, often misleading, presentation of the 1237 [Paris] *Maqāmāt* manuscript through scholarly publications" (Roxburgh 2013: 178), where art historians have tended to concentrate on the images rather than the manuscript as a whole. Interpretation of watercraft in iconographic depictions, and in Islamic art in particular, benefits from contextual information when available and, when not, from comparison with other spatially, temporally, or culturally related depictions (Wachsmann 2019: 9).

Reconstructing Ships from the *Maqāmāt*

Two major experimental archaeological projects have relied to varying degrees on the iconographic evidence of the *Maqāmāt*: Tim Severin's *Sohar* and the later *Jewel of Muscat*. Severin's sewn-plank ship *Sohar* was built in Oman in 1980 for the Sinbad Voyage, from a design based on "early illustrations" to resemble a modern *būm* (Severin 1985: 279). This "limited iconographic evidence" included the Paris *Maqāmāt* ship, but Severin's choices about the design of the craft were "constrained by the lack of meaningful archaeological evidence" (Staples 2019: 316). The salvage of the Belitung wreck was still two decades away, so the features Severin seems to have drawn from the *Maqāmāt* ship were its general shape and configuration, its sewn-plank construction, and perhaps the possibility of multiple masts. The resulting reconstruction has been termed "very hypothetical" (Staples 2019: 316), but the voyage and narrative were popular at the time. *Sohar* is now on display in a prominent traffic roundabout in Muscat, Oman.

The *Jewel of Muscat* project drew on far more evidence than was available to Severin but still relied to a degree on the illustrations from the *Maqāmāt*. *Jewel of Muscat* is a sewn-plank reconstruction built in Oman from 2008 to 2009 that is now on display in Singapore after its recreation voyage. The design of the vessel was based in large part on reports of the Belitung wreck, and the archaeologist who surveyed a portion of the wreck was included in the design team for *Jewel of Muscat* (Staples 2019: 317–18). Tom Vosmer, one of the principals of this project, called the sources for the design "a potpourri of information, direct and indirect, with elements of naval architecture and common sense stirred in," including the *Maqāmāt* ships and other visual sources (Vosmer 2010: 121, 134). An interpretation of the Paris *Maqāmāt* image, along with the absence of archaeological evidence from the stern of the Belitung shipwreck, greatly influenced the decision to employ the unusual configuration of both median and quarter rudders in the reconstruction (Vosmer et al. 2011: 420–21).

The *al-Hariri Boat* is a further reconstruction, albeit a scaled representative reconstruction of the vessel depicted in the Paris *Maqāmāt,* constructed in 2013. In this instance the designers used the Paris *Maqāmāt* ship painted by al-Wāsiṭī as the primary source, guided to degrees by archaeological evidence and previous experience with *Jewel of Muscat*. Despite being named for the eleventh-century author of the *Maqāmāt,* for the most part the design followed that painted by al-Wāsiṭī, the artist of the thirteenth-century Paris manuscript image, even down to the plank sewing method indicated by vertical lines, and the shapes and carvings of the ports. The 13-meter-long vessel is now displayed at the Museum of History of Islamic Science in Muscat, Oman (Staples 2019: 328–29). The influence of the *Maqāmāt* ships and the prominence of the Paris Schefer manuscript are amply demonstrated by these increasingly faithful reconstructions. Rather than diverging from the designs shown in the manuscript paintings as further evidence is brought to light, the tendency has been to represent them more closely.

Interpretations for Nautical Research

The ways in which nautical researchers interpret the *Maqāmāt* paintings inform not only decisions about reconstructions but also arguments for technological development and the exchange of influences and ideas in the Indian Ocean world. The most contentious issues in these debates and interpretations relate to the configuration of masts and steering gear. In both cases, it appears that further contextually aware source criticism can add significantly to historical archaeological outcomes. The debates are interlinked, as the element that appears as a broken mast in the earlier St. Petersburg manuscript (Fig. 2.2) is reused in the later Paris manuscript (Fig. 2.1), albeit far less convincingly. The interpretation that the mast is broken in the earlier image is by no means universally accepted, but only because the image is taken at its face value—isolated and decontextualized—rather than as an integral component of the original story.

The main issue with the apparently broken mast in the St. Petersburg image is its placement within the thirty-ninth *maqāmah*. The image represents the moment when Abū Zaid is negotiating his passage in Basra and before the ship is damaged at sea. In Grabar's view, the crew are shown here erecting the mast (1984: 88). Burningham concludes that the mast is lowered rather than broken, and that the otherwise broken stump represents a type of short strongpost used to support a mast. He posits that al-Wāsiṭī "was no mariner" and that he had misinterpreted the arrangement to show that the mast was scarfed or joined to the top of the strongpost, thereby explaining the jagged ends (Burningham 2019: 157). This argument is based solely on the contention that the damage related in the story should be represented after the ship left Basra. However, Abū Zaid is shown begging passage to Oman in exchange for a "shield against anxiety, when the wave of the deep rages" (Steingass 1898: 96). The original Arabic-speaking audience of this manuscript would have read the image from right to left, as they did with text, so the appearance of a ship in distress *from a previous voyage* would illustrate the inherent danger of a sea passage and therefore the potential value of Abū Zaid's charm. The "jagged ends"—apparently even eight centuries ago a recognized symbol for broken wood (Bolshakov 1997: 65)—consequently need no elaborate explanation, and the broken mast appears intertextually confirmed by other elements of the image. In an era when most ocean passages would have resulted in at least some damage to the ship, vessels might often limp into port under oars, with a broken mast, with the crew set to bailing and the passengers appearing decidedly queasy. Indeed, the artist required this distress to be obvious to an audience reading right to left to create the sense of dread of ocean passages that Abū Zaid's charm was intended to alleviate, and the ship appears to have "recently weathered a storm" (Bolshakov 1997: 65). Although al-Wāsiṭī chose not to illustrate this moment, he may have been working from different models taken out of context, such as shadow puppets, and simply repurposed elements like the broken mast in his painting.

Another contention influenced by interpretation of the broken mast is that the apparently woven mat at the base of the mast in the St. Petersburg manuscript image is evidence of "a woven palm sail" (Burningham 2019: 157; Staples 2018: 211). While there is no doubt as to the historiographic basis of this contention, which has been mentioned and observed in many cases (Agius 2008: 209–10), the context of the woven mat does not in this instance appear to indicate a sail. The mat is slightly raised from the lowest visible extent of the unbroken stump of the mast, while the broken upper part of the mast seems to have a cloth sail furled or wrapped in the arms of the figure. The white cloth sail and the white clothing of the figure blend to a certain extent, but the rope or rigging around what is here contended to be the furled sail separates it from the garment. These rigging lines are connected to the furled cloth and mast rather than the woven fabric. Woven mats were, however, used to cover cargo, both as a spray cover and to enable the crew to work the vessel better. If the broken mast does indeed support a furled sail, then this mat is more probably a cargo cover rather than a sail. It is nevertheless possible, although unlikely, that both woven and cloth sails are represented in this image (Burningham 2019: 157), although the lack of rigging connected to the woven sail requires explanation in that case.

The median rudder—one fitted to the centerline of the vessel—with a reverse tiller is a common device in western Indian Ocean watercraft that has been observed for centuries and has modern ethnographic parallels (Agius 2008: 206–7). The St. Petersburg ship shows a device like this in operation (Fig. 2.2), while the median rudder in the Paris manuscript has no obvious method of operation, being merely a board swinging freely from the stern post (Fig. 2.1). The inclusion of a side or quarter rudder along with a median rudder in the reconstruction *Jewel of Muscat* was influenced by an interpretation that the disarticulated angled device toward the stern of the Paris *Maqāmāt* ship represented a side rudder rather than a broken mast (Vosmer et al. 2011: 420–21). A twelfth-century Arab text seems to show the coexistence of a median rudder and side rudders (see Agius 2008: 205–6), thereby lending credence to this interpretation, although the side rudders in this case could also be oars placed to accord with the stars in the constellation that this common image depicts. It is more likely that the apparent single side rudder of the Paris *Maqāmāt* was copied from an earlier model, such as the St. Petersburg manuscript, in which the mast is broken to show the necessity for Abū Zaid's charm against catastrophe. In that case, the blade of the apparent stern rudder is actually the crow's nest of the broken mast. The presence of the median rudder with reverse tiller in the St. Petersburg *Maqāmāt* ship has even been used to date the petroglyphs at al-Jassasiya in Qatar, with the claim that they could not therefore be earlier than the second millennium CE (Facey 1987: 201). In these cases, images from the same decade were used to show simultaneously that a ninth-century CE ship could have a median rudder and that petroglyphs with median rudders had to be from the eleventh century CE or later because they had median rudders. While clearly a matter of interpretation, corroborating ethnographic or archaeological evidence for either of these contentions is sorely lacking.

The last element of interpretation for discussion here was also one of the first identified in Hourani's seminal interpretation in *Arab Seafaring* in 1951 (1995: 92). The Paris and the St. Petersburg *Maqāmāt* ship images both show an apparent stitching or sewing pattern on the side of the vessel, although in Hourani's interpretation he only used the Paris manuscript (1995: 92, pl. 7). The Paris vessel used by Hourani has parallel pairs of vertical stitches along the seams of several hull planks and on the rudder (Fig. 2.1), which means that they are unlikely to represent the stitching that may have been used in shadow puppets. This type of externally visible pattern is widely attributed throughout the western Indian Ocean and is still visible in "humble forms" of craft in the region today (Hourani 1995: 92–93). The St. Petersburg vessel shows a cross pattern of stitching on one seam rising toward the bow and stern and again on the rudder (Fig. 2.2). These two different patterns of plank stitching, and others not shown in the *Maqāmāt* ships, have been verified by considerable archaeological and ethnographic evidence (Staples 2019; Vosmer 2019). However, the point here is not to question these interpretations, but to note that the patterns are quite different in two vessels painted in very nearly the same place within a decade or so of each other. Were this detail not so small, it might be more prominent in arguments about the origins of the vessel, or even the technical competence of the artists. Instead, the presence of what appears to be external stitching in both paintings, *along with considerable archaeological and ethnographic evidence,* tends to confirm the interpretation that these ships were at least partially sewn. Such a conclusion would be troublesome if based primarily on iconographic evidence, obliging a more thorough inquiry "into the source of the artist/artisan's actual knowledge of the ship that is portrayed" (Wachsmann 2019: 6). This chapter has shown how different angles of inquiry can enlighten interpretations of even commonly accepted historical visual sources for nautical archaeology.

Conclusion

The ship illustrated in the thirteenth-century Paris *Maqāmāt* has become one of the most iconic and widely used individual images in studies of Indian Ocean seafaring. It is used as the primary iconographic source for interpretations of shipwrecks, for the design and construction of two full-sized replica ships, and more widely as visual evidence of "Arab" seafaring in general. Yet the notion that the ship in the painting can be identified as a particular type or associated with a specific cultural tradition is fraught. The circulation of ideas, designs, materials, and techniques throughout the Indian Ocean world effectively precludes such specificity on the basis of a single visual artifact alone. The story of the thirty-ninth *maqāmah* tells of a ship leaving Basra and bound for Oman, but that does not mean the illustrator intended to represent an Iraqi or Omani or even an Arab ship at all. It seems that the context of the story, and the literary witticisms contained within it, were more important to the illustrator and his intended audience than were the details of what type of ship was represented or from which building tradition it came.

From a modern archaeological perspective concerned with the detailed representation of nautical technology, the famous Paris manuscript illustration is not even the best or most technically competent of the several *Maqāmāt* ship illustrations known. While it is still a beautiful illustration by a very accomplished and acclaimed artist, it is not as good an illustration of a ship as that achieved by the artist of the more obscure rendition from the St. Petersburg manuscript. The artists of the *Maqāmāt* ships probably never aimed for technological accuracy, motivated or constrained as they were by the limits of their medium and the context of their audience, aiming instead for popularly understood caricatures, local renown, and further commissions. Conformance with broadly recognizable shadow puppets may have been a greater concern to the artists than technical accuracy, with the ship and its people turned into vessels for visual metaphors to parallel the witticisms of the popular text. If the various versions of the *Maqāmāt* ship painting are compared on this basis, on their conformance to and exposition of the texts into which they were painted, then the Paris illustration by al-Wāsiṭī, the only manuscript with a known artist, is exceptional. Simply by luck of circumstance, the manuscript by al-Wāsiṭī that ended up in Paris became more widely known and celebrated than the St. Petersburg manuscript, which contained paintings less accessible to Western scholars and less easily reproduced, so that ubiquity and artistic excellence established a veneer of nautical accuracy that has held ever since.

While the *Maqāmāt* ship illustrations as a group are so esteemed precisely because of the relative paucity of other archaeological, iconographic, or documentary sources, they should nevertheless be used with caution when applied to historical archaeological problems. As with any archaeological problem, context is especially important—physical, social, cultural, literary, and technological contexts, even the way the paintings themselves have been curated, restored, and reproduced. This source criticism parallels the practice of historical archaeologists examining artifacts excavated from terrestrial or underwater environments, where extensive records of context in three dimensions, of relative and absolute position, are required as a matter of course. Nevertheless, the present chapter is in no way an interpretation of the entire text of al-Hariri's *Maqāmāt,* or any illustrated retelling of it, and the present author

44 · Mick de Ruyter

is no literary expert; instead, this chapter highlights the importance of context in using visual sources for historical archaeology. Careful consideration of the intended audience and consumption of these visual artifacts from the *Maqāmāt*, of the models used to create them, and of their cultural and literary contexts—social context rather technological particularism—means that they can retain much of their ability to tell us about the circulation of people, ideas, and things in the historical Indian Ocean.

Acknowledgments

I am most indebted to Professor Dionisius Agius, who read and commented on an early version of this chapter. I have also benefited from the generous feedback from the editors and reviewers of this volume.

Bibliography

Agius, D. A. 2005. *Seafaring in the Arabian Gulf and Oman: People of the Dhow*. London: Routledge.
———. 2008. *Classic Ships of Islam: From Mesopotamia to the Indian Ocean*. Leiden: Brill.
———. 2010. *In the Wake of the Dhow: The Arabian Gulf and Oman*. Reading, U.K.: Ithaca Press.
———. 2013. "Oman Seafaring Identity Before the Early 1600s: Ethnic and Linguistic Diversity." In *Oman and Overseas*, edited by M. Hoffman-Ruf and A. Al Salimi, 39–56. Hildesheim, Germany: George Olms Verlag.
———. 2019. *The Life of the Red Sea Dhow: A Cultural History of Seaborne Exploration in the Islamic World*. London: I. B. Taurus.
Al-Hijji, Y. Y. 2001. *The Art of Dhow-building in Kuwait*. London: London Centre for Arab Studies.
Al Salimi, A., and E. Staples (eds.). 2019. *A Maritime Lexicon: Arabic Nautical Terminology in the Indian Ocean*. Hildesheim, Germany: Georg Olms Verlag.
Anjum, T. 2006. "Sufism in History and Its Relationship with Power." *Islamic Studies* 45(2): 221–68.
Beeston, A.F.L. 1973. "Ships in a Quranic Simile." *Journal of Arabian Literature* 4: 94–96.
Blue, L. 2006. "Sewn Boat Timbers from the Medieval Islamic Port of Quseir al-Qadim on the Red Sea Coast of Egypt." In *Connected by the Sea: Proceedings of the Tenth International Symposium on Boat and Ship Archaeology*, Denmark 2003, edited by L. K. Blue, F. Hocker, and A. Englert, 277–83. Oxford: Oxbow.
Bolshakov, O. G. 1997. "The St. Petersburg Manuscript of the Maqamat by al-Hariri and Its Place in the History of Arab Painting." *Manuscripta Orientalia* 3(4): 59–66.
Burningham, N. 2019. "Shipping of the Indian Ocean World." In *Early Global Interconnectivity across the Indian Ocean World, Vol. 2*, edited by A. Schottenhammer, 141–201. Palgrave Series in Indian Ocean World Studies. Cham, Switzerland: Palgrave Macmillan.

Chenery, T. (ed.). 1867. *The Assemblies of Al Hariri, Translated from the Arabic with an Introduction and Notes Historical and Grammatical.* Vol. I. London: Williams and Norgate.

De Ruyter, M. 2020. "*Kalbā* and *Dāw* in Khaliji Art: Tracing Extinct Dhows in Arab and Persian Iconography." *Proceedings of the Seminar for Arabian Studies* 50: 127–39.

Ettinghausen, R. 1977. *Arab Painting.* New York: Rizzoli International Publications.

Facey, W. 1987. "The Boat Carvings at Jabal Al-Jassasiyah, Northeast Qatar." *Proceedings of the Seminar for Arabian Studies* 17: 199–222.

Facey, W.H.D., and E. B. Martin. 1979. *Oman: A Seafaring Nation.* Muscat: Ministry of Information and Culture of the Sultanate of Oman.

Flecker, M. 2000. "A 9th-Century Arab or Indian Shipwreck in Indonesian Waters." *International Journal of Nautical Archaeology* 29(2): 199–217.

Furman, M. 2015. *Jewel of Muscat: On the High Seas in a 9th-Century Sailing Ship.* Muscat: Sultanate of Oman.

George, A. F. 2011. "The Illustrations of the Maqamat and the Shadow Play." *Muqarnas* 28: 1–42.

———. 2012. "Orality, Writing and the Image in the Maqamat: Arabic Illustrated Books in Context." *Art History* 35(1): 10–37.

Ghidoni, A. 2021. "Sewn-Plank Construction Techniques in the Western Indian Ocean: Evidence from the Timbers of Al Baleed, Oman." In *Archaeonautica* 21, edited by G. Boetto, P. Pomey, and P. Pveda, 225–32. Paris: CNRS Éditions.

Grabar, O. 1984. *The Illustrations of the Maqamat.* Chicago: University of Chicago Press.

———. 2005. "Pictures or Commentaries: The Illustrations of the Maqamat of al-Hariri." In *Islamic Visual Culture, 1100–1800, Vol. 2: Constructing the Study of Islamic Art*, 187–205. London: Routledge.

———. 2007 "What Does 'Arab Painting' Mean?" In *Arab Painting: Text and Image in Illustrated Arabic Manuscripts*, edited by A. Contadini, 17–22. Leiden: Brill.

Guo, L. 2020. *Arabic Shadow Theatre 1300–1900: A Handbook.* Leiden: Brill.

Guy, J. 2019. "Shipwrecks in the Late First Millennium Southeast Asia: Southern China's Maritime Trade and the Emerging Role of Arab Merchants in Indian Ocean Exchange." In *Early Global Interconnectivity across the Indian Ocean World, Vol. 1*, edited by A. Schottenhammer, 121–63. Palgrave Series in Indian Ocean World Studies. Cham, Switzerland: Palgrave Macmillan.

Haw, S. 2019. "The Genus Afzelia and the Belitung Ship." *Journal of the Royal Asiatic Society* 29(3): 505–18.

Hillenbrand, R. 2007. "The Schefer Ḥarīrī: A Study in Islamic Frontispiece Design." In *Arab Painting: Text and Image in Illustrated Arabic Manuscripts*, edited by A. Contadini, 117–34. Leiden: Brill.

Hoare, O. 2017. *Every Object Tells a Story.* Exhibition catalogue of Oliver Hoare Ltd., London. Accessed April 22, 2020, at https://issuu.com/pallasathene0/docs/every_object_tells_a_story_issuu

Hodgson, G. S. 1964. "Islâm and Image." *History of Religions* 3(2): 220–60.

Hourani, G. F. 1995 [1951]. *Arab Seafaring in the Indian Ocean in Ancient and Early Medieval Times.* Princeton: Princeton University Press.

Howarth, D. 1977. *Dhows*. London: Quartet Books.

James, D. 2013. *A Masterpiece of Arab Painting: The 'Schefer' Maqāmāt Manuscript in Context*. London: East & West Publishing.

Kahle, P. 1911. "Islamische Schattenspielfiguren aus Egypten. Teil II." *Der Islam* 2: 143–95.

———. 1940. "The Arabic Shadow Play in Egypt." *Journal of the Royal Asiatic Society of Great Britain and Ireland* 1: 21–34.

Loren, D. D., and U. Baram. 2007. "Between Art and Artifact: Approaches to Visual Representations in Historical Archaeology." *Historical Archaeology* 41(1): 1–5.

Meier, F. 1976. "The Mystic Path: The Sufi Tradition." In *The World of Islam*, edited by B. Lewis, 117–40. London: Thames & Hudson.

Milwright, M. 2011. "On the date of Paul Kahle's Egyptian Shadow Puppets." *Muqarnas* 28: 43–68.

Mott, L. V. 1997. *The Development of the Rudder: A Technological Tale*. College Station: Texas A&M University Press.

Nicolle, D. 1989. "Shipping in Islamic Art: Seventh through Sixteenth Century AD." *American Neptune* 49(3): 168–97.

O'Kane, B. 2012. "Text and Painting in the al-Wasiti *Maqāmāt*." *Ars Orientalis* 42: 41–55.

Rice, D. T. 1975. *Islamic Art*. New York: Praeger Publishers.

Roxburgh, D. J. 2002. "Persian Drawing, ca. 1400–1450: Materials and Creative Procedures." *Muqarnas* 19: 44–77.

———. 2013. "In Pursuit of Shadows: Al-Hariri's Maqamat." *Muqarnas* 30: 171–212.

Severin, T. 1985. "Constructing the Omani Boom Sohar." In *Sewn Plank Boats: Archaeological and Ethnographic Papers Based on Those Presented to a Conference at Greenwich in November, 1984*, edited by S. McGrail and E. Kentley, 279–87. BAR International Series. Greenwich: National Maritime Museum.

Staples, E. 2018. "Ships of the Gulf: Shifting Names and Networks." In *The Gulf in World History: Arabian, Persian and Global Connections*, edited by A. J. Fromherz, 201–18. Edinburgh: Edinburgh University Press.

———. 2019. "Sewn-Plank Reconstructions of Oman: Construction and Documentation." *International Journal of Nautical Archaeology* 48(2): 314–34.

Staples, E., and L. Blue. 2019. "Archaeological, Historical, and Ethnographic Approaches to the Study of Sewn Boats: Past, Present, and Future." *International Journal of Nautical Archaeology* 48(2): 269–85.

Steingass, F. (ed.). 1898. *The Assemblies of Al Hariri, translated from the Arabic with Notes, Historical and Grammatical. Volume II*. London: Royal Asiatic Society.

Toprak, F. A. 2012. "The Influence of Oral Narrating Traditions on a Frequently Illustrated Thirteenth-Century Manuscript." In *Islamic Art, Architecture and Material Culture: New Perspectives*, edited by Margaret S. Graves, 133–42. BAR International Series 2436. Oxford: Archaeopress.

Vosmer, T. 2010. "The Jewel of Muscat: Restructuring a Ninth-Century Sewn-Plank Boat." In *Shipwrecked: Tang Treasures and Monsoon Winds*, edited by R. Krahl, J. Guy, J. K. Wilson, and J. Raby, 120–35. Washington D.C.: Smithsonian Institution.

———. 2019. "Sewn Boats in Oman and the Indian Ocean." *International Journal of Nautical Archaeology* 48(2): 302–13.

Vosmer, T., and L. Belfioretti. 2010. "Al-Balid Ship Timbers: Preliminary Overview and Comparisons." *Proceedings of the Seminar for Arabian Studies* 40: 111–18.

Vosmer, T., L. Belfioretti, E. Staples, and A. Ghidoni. 2011. "The Jewel of Muscat Project: Reconstructing an Early Ninth-Century CE Shipwreck." *Proceedings of the Seminar for Arabian Studies* 41: 411–24.

Wachsmann, S. 2019. "On the Interpretation of Watercraft in Ancient Art." *Arts* 8(4): 165.

Weismann, N. 2002. "A Type of Ship on the Indian Ocean in the Fifteenth and Sixteenth Centuries." *Mariner's Mirror* 88(2): 132–43.

3

A Thousand Years of Connections between the Indian Ocean Region and Southeast Asia

ELLEN HSIEH AND TAKASHI SAKAI

This chapter addresses the long-term interaction between the Indian Ocean region and Southeast Asia from an archaeology perspective. When it comes to the connection between the two sides of the Bay of Bengal, the first thing that comes to mind is usually the "Indianization" effect beginning from the first century CE, which initiated the classical period of Southeast Asia (Cœdès 1968; Wolters 1999; Manguin 2010; Miksic and Goh 2017). Discussions focus primarily on those ancient Indianized kingdoms that left traces in stelae and monuments and the influence from the west side of the Indian Ocean to the east. However, the interaction between the Indian Ocean region and Southeast Asia did not start from, or finish in, the classical period. If archaeological studies of glass and stone beads, metal, and pottery have shown that exchange between the two regions can be traced back to the late centuries BCE (Bellina and Glover 2004), they also substantiate how later, during the period of Islamization and European colonization, the interactions between the two regions continued. Archaeological evidence, including various types of ceramics and religious monuments exemplified in this chapter, suggests a much more complex network extended geographically and chronologically beyond what we usually consider.

Within Southeast Asia, materials with Indian influence have been found in areas that are generally not considered Indianized. For example, the golden Tara statuette found in Agusan del Sur, Mindanao Island, suggests a more profound transmission of Indian religions to Southeast Asia (Capistrano-Baker 2015). Additionally, interactions within the Indian Ocean–Southeast Asia network linked these regions to civilizations in the Mediterranean Basin and East Asia (Fig. 3.1). Famous examples of this reach make clear that these networks continuously mediated the transport of goods over many centuries. The gold medallions from Roman emperors Antoninus Pius (86–161 CE)

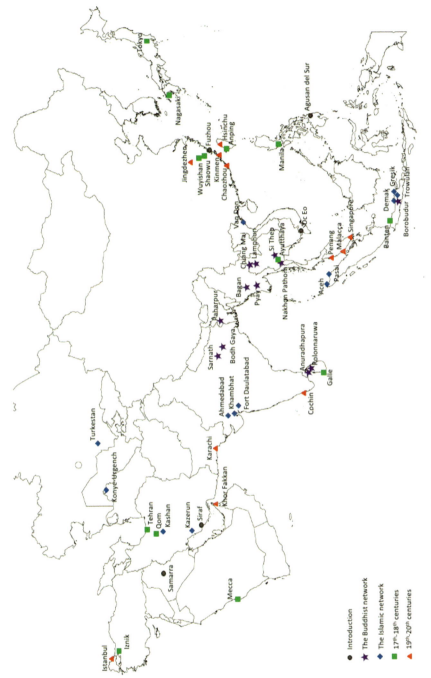

Figure 3.1. Sites involved in the Indian Ocean–Southeast Asia connections mentioned in this chapter.

and Marcus Aurelius (121–180 CE) in Oc Eo, the port city of Funan (present southern Vietnam), one of the earliest Indianized political entities in Southeast Asia, had not arrived in the region directly from Europe. Instead, the significant finding of Roman coins in South Asia, especially South India, suggests that from the first century CE, South Asia served as a critical node that received goods from farther west and redistributed them to coastal Southeast Asia and farther east. Moreover, the early ceramic trade during the ninth and tenth centuries offers an example of the two-directions cultural exchange among Asian waters. Carried by Arabian- and Persian-made dhow ships, the primary type of vessel sailing across the Asian waters at the time (see de Ruyter, this volume), a considerable number of turquoise blue glazed jars manufactured in the Persian Gulf region landed in cities in Southeast Asia. The same kind of object was also discovered in a tomb of a local queen in Fuzhou, southern China, dated 930 CE. Conversely, early Chinese trade ceramics were carried to Samarra, the capital of Abbasid, via port cities along the Persian Gulf, such as Siraf.

Instead of searching for the initial contact between the two regions, the authors believe that expanding the study timeframe to the modern period is critical to connecting the past and present of the Asian waters. We thus start from the ninth century, a point at which the early links between the two sides of the Bay of Bengal were present, and depict successive waves of networks against the backdrop of the transmission of Islam and European colonization until this connection declined due to the geopolitical policymaking after the Second World War (Amrith 2013). Archaeology, in particular, has the potential to illuminate new facets underlying this extensive network of interactions. Ceramics manufactured within or beyond these maritime regions, including architectural materials and containers, constitute critical evidence for tracing the development of the connections between the two regions. Considering these ceramics within their social milieu and the characteristics of some religious monuments, such as stupas and cenotaphs, provides valuable data revealing the long-term dynamics of networks and various faces of people who maintained and changed them.

Stupa, a Material Aspect of Indianization: Ninth to Fifteenth Centuries

The Hybrid Stupa of Borobudur

The early introduction of Buddhism in Southeast Asia can be traced back to the period between the fourth and sixth centuries. Among various types of

Figure 3.2. Buddhist monuments with different shapes: (*a*) Borobudur, Java, Indonesia; (*b*) Thuparamaya Stupa, Anuradhapura, Sri Lanka; (*c*) Dhamekh stupa, Sarnath, India; (*d*) Bawbawgyi Paya Stupa, Pyay, Myanmar; (*e*) Wat Chama Thevi, Lamphun, Thailand; (*f*) Satmahal Prasada, Polonnaruwa, Sri Lanka. Credit: Takashi Sakai.

monuments, architectural elements, and objects associated with this religion, the stupa is a perfect example of addressing the power of Indianization in transmitting Buddhism and its localization. The stupa is a type of monument that is geographically widespread in the Buddhist world. Regardless of its pre-Buddhist origin, it became the symbol of the mound under which Gautama Buddha's relics were buried. The designs of stupas have varied in different periods and locations and are good indicators for investigating cultural exchanges. The cases of Java, Myanmar, and Thailand show that northern India and Sri Lanka had multi-directional connections with insular and mainland Southeast Asia.

Built between the eighth and ninth centuries, Borobudur in Java, Indonesia, is not only the world's largest Buddhist temple but also a giant stupa

(Fig. 3.2a). Although it is generally accepted that the shape of the monument could be traced back to the Javanese mountain worship tradition blended with the idea of Mt. Sumeru in Mahayana Buddhism, some elements also reveal influences from particular places in South Asia (Miksic 1990). Borobudur is crowned with one big stupa surrounded by seventy-two smaller stupas, followed by 432 stupa-shaped niches for Buddha statues on the middle balustrades. Although the relief panels of Borobudur depict multiple forms of stupas from South Asia, the monument's stupas are all bell-shaped and are strikingly similar to the Thuparamaya Stupa in Anuradhapura, Sri Lanka (Fig. 3.2b). A similar style was also used for other temple ruins in central Java, such as Kalasan and Sewu, showing that Sri Lanka was an important religious and artistic source for Buddhism in central Java.

While the bell-shaped stupas unfold a connection between Sri Lanka and Java, other elements reveal connections with different regions in India. The carving of Buddha images can be traced back to the art style from Sarnath in northern India. Additionally, the cruciform plan of Borobudur is closely related to the early Vajrayana thinking from the Pala Dynasty (eighth to twelfth centuries) in present northeastern India and Bangladesh (Sakai 2014). The similar plans of a few stupas in mainland Southeast Asia have been linked to models in the old empire. For example, in Thailand, stupas with multiple layers of foundation and square upper structures could be found at Chedi Chula Prathon in Nakhon Pathom and Khao Khlang Nok in Si Thep. Both monuments were built by the Mons during the Dvaravati period and could be traced back to the structure of Sompur Mahavihara at Paharpur dated to the late eighth century. Revire (2015) argued that the archaeological artifacts associated with Chedi Chula Prathon reveal the commonalities between central Java and Thailand. However, more archaeological research is needed to address the religious ties between mainland Southeast Asia and Java in this period and how they related to the design of Borobudur.

The Diverse Stupas in Bagan

Contemporary to the apparent connections between a wide range of locations and the design of Borobudur, stupa styles in mainland Southeast Asia were influenced by the tall cylindrical stupas in northeast India. This similarity could be found between the Dhamekh Stupa in Sarnath (Fig. 3.2c) and those around Pyu cities, such as the Bawbawgyi Paya Stupa in Pyay (Fig. 3.2d). After the establishment of the Bagan Kingdom in central Myanmar between the eleventh and thirteenth centuries, a combination of the Pyu style with the Mon style generated a new form of the stupa, and the majority of Mahayana

Buddhist temples and stupas in Bagan city were constructed in the new Bagan style. Although this is the standard narrative for this vast Buddhist complex, some particular stupas reveal the religious connections between Bagan and Sri Lanka, from where the people of Bagan received Theravada Buddhism. As the earliest Sri Lankan–style stupa in mainland Southeast Asia, Sapada Paya (dated 1199 CE or early thirteenth century) is important evidence of such religious connection between Bagan and Sri Lanka after Buddhism declined in the subcontinent. It was believed to have been built by a monk who returned from Sri Lanka, and its shape could be traced back to the basic stupa style in Polonnaruwa.

Another stupa-related monument in Bagan city sheds light on the reverse direction of cultural influence across the Bay of Bengal. The Mahabodhi Temple of Bagan, constructed in 1215 CE, is known for its tall pyramid-shaped tower with many niches for Buddha statues over a cubic foundation. The design of the temple, which is very different from other architectures in Bagan, is thought to have been borrowed from the Mahabodhi Temple of Bodh Gaya, constructed around the seventh century in India.[1] In turn, the Mahabodhi Temple of Bagan was used as a model when Wat Chet Yot built Chiang Mai in 1455 in Thailand. However, this kind of tall, pyramid-shaped monument with niches for Buddha statues can be connected to the stupas in the Mon's contemporary Hariphunchai Kingdom (eighth century–1292 CE) in northern Thailand. Examples can be found at the Wat Chama Thevi (also known as Wat Ku Kut, Fig. 3.2e) and the Suwanna Chedi in the Wat Phra That Hariphunchai in Lamphun, the capital of the kingdom, dated around the twelfth to thirteenth centuries. Both stupas have five layers, decorated with three niches with standing Buddha statues on each side. As with the Mahabodhi Temple of Bagan, scholars traced the origins of these pyramid-shaped stupas to northern India (Sirisena 1978).

Interestingly, the design of the stupa known as Satmahal Prasada in Polonnaruwa (dated to the twelfth century, Fig. 3.2f), north-central Sri Lanka, also resembles the Hariphunchai stupas. This unique stupa was constructed inside the royal Buddhist temple complex, and no other matching monuments have been found in Sri Lanka (Sakai 2012). Although the number of niches on each side is different from its counterpart in Hariphunchai, the shared style illustrates that the link between Sri Lanka and the Hariphunchai Kingdom was particularly close at the time. Sirisena (1978) thus further considered Satmahal Prasada a rare example of Southeast Asian influence on Sri Lanka.

The textual evidence of Buddhism in Southeast Asia is so scarce that archaeological and art historical studies are critical. By tracing elements from

54 · Ellen Hsieh and Takashi Sakai

a single stupa, such as Borobudur, and identifying shared characteristics of monuments with bell/cylindrical/pyramid forms from various locations, the complex connections among the Buddhist world are at least partially revealed.

Cenotaphs, Wall Tiles, and the Islamic World: Fifteenth Century

The Gujarat-Style Cenotaph

While the Theravada movement took place in mainland Southeast Asia, Islam was introduced into insular Southeast Asia through the filter of India, accompanying the active commercial development among port cities (Reid 1993). In contrast to the architecture of the local traditional mosques blended with the Javanese and Hindu-Buddhist holy mountain idea, the Gujarat-style cenotaphs are one of the best examples for demonstrating the connection across the Indian Ocean during the early process of Islamization.

Although cenotaphs or tombs are usually considered non-movable structures in archaeology, they were constructed with portable artifacts that were sometimes ordered or traded from particular places. About a century ago, J. P. Moquette (1912) had observed the similarity between the marble cenotaph of Nahrasiyah, the sultana of Samudera-Pasai in Aceh (dated 1428 CE, Fig. 3.3a), and the marble cenotaph of Malik Ibrahim, an Islamic introducer, in Gresik (dated 1419 CE). The style of the cenotaphs could be traced back to Gujarat, northwest India. Besides Arabic inscriptions, both cenotaphs are composed of several panels decorated with reliefs of mosque lamp motifs (Lambourn 2003).

Besides these two famous cenotaphs, most royal family tombs in the Samudera-Pasai region were decorated with similar marble materials ordered from Gujarat during the first half of the fifteenth century, revealing the origin of the Muslim elites in these areas. The same kind of cenotaph is commonly found in the Gujarat region, especially Ahmadabad, the early capital of the Gujarat Sultanate (Lambourn 2004; Yajima 2006). The latest example from the royal family might be the tombs of Ahmad Shah and his queen (dated 1442 CE), while the earliest example of this kind of cenotaph belongs to Umar bin Ahmad al-Kazaruni (dated 1334 CE, Fig. 3.3b) in the Jami Masjid at Khambhat (Cambay), a port city on the Arabian Sea. Umar bin Ahmad al-Kazaruni, a businessman from Kazerun, contributed to the mosque's construction in 1325 CE after Alauddin Khalji, the emperor of the Delhi Sultanate, invaded the city and destroyed many Hindu and Jain temples; part of the mosque then became his mausoleum.

Figure 3.3. Islamic tombs in Aceh and their origins in India: (*a*) cenotaph of Nahrasiyah, Aceh, Indonesia; (*b*) Cenotaph of Umar bin Ahmad al-Kazaruni, Cambay, India; (*c*) tombstone of Malikussaleh, Aceh, Indonesia; (*d*) exterior of the Sidi Saeed Mosque, Ahmadabad, India. Credit: (*a*) Tu Shih-Yi; (*b–d*) Takashi Sakai.

However, the earliest tombstone with the title of sultan in Southeast Asia was not an import: the tombstone of Malikussaleh (dated 1297 CE), the ancestor of Nahrasiyah, was designed with a particular two-wing shape (Fig. 3.3c). Called "Aceh stone," the two-wing style was widely copied by the later Muslim rulers in the Indonesian Archipelago. More research is needed to determine whether this style is an example of Islam compromising with local pre-Islamic beliefs or based on other sources in the Indian or Arabic world. According to preliminary observations from one of the authors, the wing motifs decorating the exterior of the Sidi Saeed Mosque in Ahmadabad might shed light on an early connection between Pasai and Gujarat (Fig. 3.3d).

Vietnamese Glazed Wall Tiles on Early Mosques in Southeast Asia

The adoption of Islam in Southeast Asia was gradual, and it was not until the fifteenth century that the activities of Muslims were materially evident in East Java. Interestingly, some unique tiles produced in Vietnam shed light on such religious development. Northern Vietnam is usually not considered part of Indianized or Islamized Southeast Asia due to the long history of Chinese occupation since the Han Dynasty. Regarding the ceramic industry, potters in this region traditionally made wares that resembled Chinese products in terms of glaze, motifs, and shapes. Around the fifteenth century, Vietnamese blue-and-white wares occupied a certain portion of the regional overseas market, while the Chinese products declined due to the maritime ban (Brown 2004). Meanwhile, a kind of blue-and-white tile with a particular shape was produced. Of neither Chinese nor Vietnamese tradition, these new products were characterized by intricate geometric forms and wide projective belts surrounding them. Tracing the style's origin and the primary consumption contexts of these tiles yields a connection between Islamic and non-Islamic Southeast Asia in the middle of the second millennium.

Such tiles have been found only in two sites in Vietnam (i.e., Van Don port and Thang Long royal citadel), while Java seems to be the primary destination of the goods: in the Great Mosque of Demak, the earliest extant mosque on the island, sixty-four glazed tiles with various shapes remain on the outer wall of the prayer hall and inside the mihrab (Fig. 3.4a). The same kind of tiles are also visible at nearby monuments, such as the Minaret Mosque of Kudus and the mausoleum of Sunan Bonang, a legendary Islamic saint in Tuban, the port of Majapahit Kingdom. Furthermore, numerous sherds of tiles were discovered in the kingdom's capital, Trowulan (Fig. 3.4b) (Miksic 2009; Sakai 2015). The ceramic trade between Vietnam and Java might follow the earlier commercial relationship documented in the Javanese text *Nagarakretagama* (1365 CE) and may have been triggered by the decline of the Chinese ceramic trade (Miksic 2009).

At Trowulan, other than the tiles from northern Vietnam, several sherds of Persian tiles with projective belts were found (Fig. 3.4c). They resemble the decorative tiles used in Central and West Asia during the Timurid Dynasty. Furthermore, the tiles can be found in a few constructions in northwest India by the fifteenth century, such as the Cini Mahal of Fort Daulatabad, Maharashtra. The evidence, although only suggestive, makes it possible to propose

Figure 3.4. Islamic tiles of Southeast Asia and Central Asia: (*a*) tile decoration at the Great Mosque of Demak, Java, Indonesia; (*b*) Vietnamese tile shards found at Trowulan, Java, Indonesia; (*c*) Persian tile shards found at Trowulan, Java, Indonesia; (*d*) tile decoration at the mausoleum of Khoja Ahmed Yasawi, Turkestan, Kazakhstan. Credit: Takashi Sakai.

that the Muslim elites in Trowulan, the capital of the declining Hindu-Buddhist kingdom, ordered the Vietnamese tiles with references from Persian materials, which might have been transported via India (Sakai 2015).

It is worth noting that the connection between Persia and Java via India is both material and spiritual, considering that Islam in India and Java was influenced by Sufism (Johns 1995). Malik Ibrahim, one of the Nine Saints in Java, was indeed a member of Kubrawiya (a Sufi order) and originally from Kashan (or Samarkand). At the mausoleum of Najm-ad-Din al-Kubra (1145–1221 CE), the founder of the Kubrawiya order, at Konye-Urgench, and that of Khoja Ahmed Yasawi (1093–1166 CE), a Sufi mystic, in Turkestan, cobalt-blue glazed tiles were found (Fig. 3.4d). From Gujarat marble to local Aceh stone, from Persia- to Vietnam-exported tiles, regardless of missing links, archaeological evidence associated with Islam reflects sophisticated networks where the religious and non-religious met each other.

Persian Wares, Anping Jars, and the Asian Trade: Sixteenth to Eighteenth Centuries

Safavid and Iznik Wares toward the East

Asian traders actively conducted long-distance maritime trade against the backdrop of European exploration. Various ceramics uncovered in Asian waters reveal details of trade networks not told in documents. Instead of using typical trade ceramics such as Kraak porcelain as examples, we select two unique types of ceramics—late Persian wares and Anping jars—to address the transfer of knowledge and the movement of people and goods across the Indian Ocean and beyond.

Persian wares, a tin-glazed, low-fired stoneware originating in Mesopotamia and Egypt, have been produced in the western Islamic world since the ninth century. The ceramic trade in Asian waters led to a technology exchange in ceramic manufacture. The creation of Chinese blue-and-white porcelain, which can be seen as a mixture of the Chinese white porcelain technique with the Persian white stoneware slipped with cobalt-blue pigments, was a milestone in this interaction. During the Yuan Dynasty, many pieces of so-called Zhizheng-style blue-and-white porcelain were brought to the western Islamic world as popular goods. As in other parts of the world, the Persian potters tried to copy the design of Chinese blue-and-white porcelain. By the first half of the fifteenth century, the potters in the Timurid Empire produced underglazed cobalt-blue stoneware that was closely similar to Chinese products. After the fall of the Timurid, this technology was further developed in the Safavid and Ottoman empires, becoming the Safavid blue-and-white ware and the Iznik polychrome ware, respectively.

During the middle of the seventeenth century the Dutch East India Company ordered Safavid ware as a substitute when the supply of Chinese blue-and-white porcelain was unstable. Such products were also found in some places with connections with the Dutch, including Indonesia and Japan. However, a Safavid stoneware sherd with blue decoration found in Banten Lama, the ruin of the Banten Sultanate's capital, is dated earlier than the flourishing of the trade already mentioned (Sakai and Ohashi 2017: 70; Fig. 3.5a). The piece decorated with a continuous three-leaves motif has little similarity to the Chinese blue-and-white products. Instead, the blue tone of the sherd is closer to the Timurid ware than the Chinese one. It was therefore identified as an early Safavid product, dated around the sixteenth century. A related sample is in the Reza Abbasi Museum, Tehran, Iran (Fig. 3.5b).

Figure 3.5. Persian wares: (*a*) a sherd found at Banten Lama, Java, Indonesia; (*b*) a ceramic ware at Reza Abbasi Museum, Tehran, Iran. Credit: Takashi Sakai.

Although these late Persian ceramics could not match their Chinese counterpart, they might have been taken to Southeast Asia as part of Islamic cultural and economic exchange. When the Dutch landed in Banten in 1596, they noted that many Asian traders, including Persians, came to this vital port for the pepper trade. Although not all Persian traders were directly associated with the Safavid Empire, there is some evidence of active Safavid Persians in Southeast Asia. Sheikh Ahmad Qomi (1543–1631 CE), a merchant and Islamic teacher from Qom who later held an official position in Ayutthaya, might be the best example. His descendants retained high rank in Siamese society until the nineteenth century. Other Persians visiting Southeast Asia might have come from the Mughal Empire in India, where Persians were a major ethnic group. People also moved in the other direction: pilgrims from Southeast Asia, including Fatahillah, the founder of the Banten Sultanates and a Muslim scholar, consistently traveled westward to the Ottoman Empire to complete the Hajj to Mecca. Other than the Safavid ware, small amounts of Iznik ware dated to the first half of the seventeenth century, found in the ruin of the residence of the Kaga lord in Tokyo, may also have found their way to East Asia via similar channels. Such finds remind us that the Ottoman Empire still competed with the Europeans on maritime trade routes during the early modern period.

Anping Jars toward the West

The Anping jar is a kind of whitish-gray, shouldered ceramic made for containing trade goods. It was mass-produced in Shaowu and Shunchang, northern Fujian, China, but was named after Anping in Taiwan, where a considerable amount of it was first found. The trace of the wheel technique, angular shoulder, thick base, junction line between the upper and lower parts at the inner side, and the mouth rim's particular shape make it relatively easy to identify archaeologically. Sherds of Anping jars are commonly found in seventeenth- and eighteenth-century port cities in Southeast Asia and Japan (Fig. 3.6a). The earliest example is a set of complete jars from the *San Diego* shipwreck near Manila, dated 1600 CE.

There are several theories regarding the original use of Anping jars. Shaped simply and without decoration, Anping jars are believed to have functioned as containers of valuable goods rather than commerce articles (Hsieh 2017). First identified in European forts, they were believed to be gunpowder containers and have a strong connection with European colonialism in Asia in early research. However, based on the vast archaeological findings at an indigenous site of northeast Taiwan, Lee (2021) argues that Anping jars were traded before the arrival of the Europeans. Moreover, as to the original function, Chen (2004) suggested that Anping jars were made for transporting Chinese wine. However, Sakai (2020) disagrees with this hypothesis, since many Anping jars have been found in Muslim sites in Southeast Asia. Instead, he argues that Anping jars may have been made for shipping Oolong tea from Wuyishan, a tea production area in northern Fujian, even though the jar dates to a period before Chinese tea was exported overseas in tremendous amounts (Sakai 2020, 2021). Aside from these ideas, Anping jars are considered to be associated with the activities of Hokkien traders from southern China.

A completed sample and two big sherds of Anping jars identified from Galle, Sri Lanka, are rare examples of this kind of ware being carried across the Indian Ocean (Fig. 3.6b). Although the sherds are held in a private collection and their original archaeological contexts were not precisely recorded, it is believed that they were collected around the old port city occupied by the Portuguese and the Dutch in 1505 CE and 1640 CE, respectively. The two thin glazed sherds resemble an early form of the Anping jar, which might be associated with the Portuguese trade route. In contrast, the complete one with a thick glaze could be of a later date and most likely related to the Dutch (Sakai 2020). These samples thus remind us that the direct collaborations between the Hokkien Chinese and the Europeans might expand to the Indian Ocean region during these periods.

The late Persian wares and Anping jars associated with West and East Asian traders, respectively, piece together the long-distance networks before and after the participation of the Europeans, providing a counter-Eurocentric perspective of the regions.

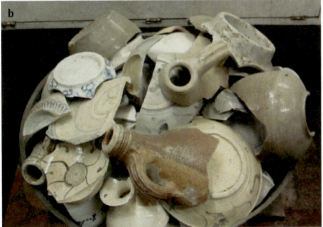

Figure 3.6. Anping jars: (*a*) an Anping jar discovered in Minamishimabara, Nagasaki, held at Arima Christian Heritage Museum, Japan; (*b*) two shards of Anping jars on a pile of ceramics, Galle, Sri Lanka. Credit: (*a*) Ellen Hsieh; (*b*) Takashi Sakai.

Art Nouveau Tiles and Double-Happiness Bowls in the Age of Imperialism: Nineteenth to Early Twentieth Century

Decorative Glazed Tiles in Asia

Since the nineteenth century, European ceramics, including transfer-printed ware and polychrome spongeware, have come to replace Chinese porcelain and symbolize wealth and power in Asian households. Aside from tableware, architectural elements based on the fashion of Art Nouveau, including colorful glass windows and metal rails as well as wall and floor tiles, were fashionable in public and private buildings. Among these decorative materials, glazed wall tiles with vibrant colors, sometimes named Victorian tiles, were the most popular commodity that testified to the dynamics of trade and cultural exchange during the age of imperialism in Asian waters.

Glazed tiles for walls or floors were not common products in China historically, except when produced for a few overseas orders. For example, Jingdezhen used to produce blue-and-white porcelain tiles for Batavia during the seventeenth century. Eighteenth-century Jingdezhen tiles were not only used in a church in Manila and mosques in Java but also shipped across the Indian Ocean, reaching a synagogue in Cochin as well as palaces in Rajasthan and Istanbul (Sakai 2015; Hsieh 2021). A century later, decorative wall tiles were shipped in the opposite direction and became even more popular than where they came from, mainly Britain. The initial spread of Victorian decorative tiles to India and Southeast Asia was associated with British trading networks, and the tiles could be found in various corners of the British colonies. Later, when the tiles were introduced to Japan, the Japanese began to imitate the products by the 1910s–20s and sold them to its Asian colonies and other Southeast Asian countries. The Chinese trade diasporas in Southeast Asia also brought the tiles to their hometowns, such as Kinmen and Chaozhou, as a symbol of their successful overseas enterprises (Fig. 3.7a). Similar products from the far sides of Eurasia thus created a colorful trend.

The Victorian tiles have two shapes: square ones were used for filling the central space, and rectangular ones for borders. Instead of applying these tiles in kitchens, bathrooms, or around fireplaces for practical reasons, they were used mostly for decorating the interior and exterior of buildings such as palaces, temples, mosques, gardens, and shophouses (stores opening onto the sidewalk and also serving as residences). They were also found on furniture and even tombs (Fig. 3.7b). Exceptional patterns were produced for specific orders, such as deities for Hindu temples, while some other motifs were cross-culturally appreciated, such as peacocks in India and East Asia.

A Thousand Years of Connections: The Indian Ocean Region and Southeast Asia · 63

Figure 3.7. Art Nouveau tiles in different contexts: (*a*) outdoors, on a house at Kinmen Island; (*b*) indoors, as panels of a bed made in the 1930s, private collection, Hsinchu, Taiwan. Credits: (*a*) Ellen Hsieh; (*b*) Eugene Chuang.

In general, however, the majority of the tile motifs are plants or simple geometric designs, making them easily accepted by people of different cultural backgrounds. The tiles were not only used in newly constructed buildings but also popular materials for the renovation of old monuments, such as the Shri Varun Dev Mandir at Karachi. Other than tiles themselves being a symbol of wealth and beauty, the ways tiles were placed brought additional meanings in some cases. For example, Ahmad and Mujani (2015) noted that the tiles in the Kampung Kling Mosque in Malacca, a mosque characterized by elements from India, China, and Indonesia, composed swastika motifs.

64 · Ellen Hsieh and Takashi Sakai

Regardless of their foreign origins and transcultural applications, the colorful glazed tiles are celebrated as local heritage in some places today. Called "Peranakan tiles" and "vintage flora tiles" in Singapore and Taiwan, respectively, the foreign tiles nowadays carry local memories and are placed in the spotlight of conservation issues (Kang 2015; Lim 2020).

"Double-Happiness" on Global Tables

Although the Chinese porcelain trade decreased in the Asian ceramic market due to the introduction of European industrial ware, some particular products were continually shipped overseas. Aside from a small number of Bencharong and Peranakan porcelains made for upper socioeconomic groups in Southeast Asia (Hsieh 2023), a vast amount of inferior tableware made in Fujian or Guangdong was shipped to various corners of the world. Among these ceramics, blue-and-white porcelain bowls decorated with the Chinese character 'Xi' (meaning double-happiness, associated initially with weddings) and an arabesque background are identifiable. Except for the seals on the bottom of the ware, it was not until the sixteenth century that Chinese characters were found painted on the surface of ceramics. The double-happiness motif was created in Jingdezhen around the 1820s and was quickly copied in Fujian and Guangdong until the 1880s. After the 1850s the quality of most Fujian and Guangdong products degraded with respect to raw materials and the neatness of the handwriting. Nevertheless, the distinct Chinese character and background make this type of ware easy to identify and thus become a good dating reference.

Rather than selling to non-Chinese foreigners, the double-happiness bowls, among other types of inferior wares, were exported overseas mainly for the Chinese migrant workers. In the Malay Peninsula and Singapore, these bowls were called tin-miners' bowls, implying that their primary consumers were coolies working in tin mines, among other harsh working environments (Barry 2000: 55; Fig. 3.8a). In the Americas they were also associated with Chinese migrant workers (Nogami and Terreros 2016; Voss et al. 2018). At Pulau Saigon, a place used to house trade goods en route to Saigon in the middle stream of the Singapore River, double-happiness porcelain ware is the most common type of ceramic find (Miksic and Gek 2005; Barry 2000). Considering the context of the site and the role of Singapore in the regional maritime trade, the double-happiness bowls found at this site were perhaps to be redistributed to other ports in Southeast Asia.

Nevertheless, Chinese migrant workers were not the only consumers of the double-happiness bowls. The rough calligraphic pattern interwoven with the abstract floral design makes the double-happiness bowls potentially popular

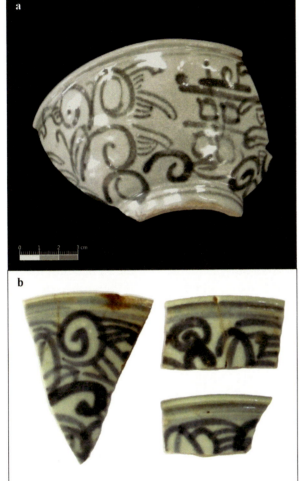

Figure 3.8. Double-happiness wares: (*a*) a sherd excavated from Siaboey, Penang, by George Town World Heritage Incorporated and Centre for Global Archaeological Research, Universiti Sains Malaysia; (*b*) sherds from Khor Fakkan, UAE. Credit: (*a*) Ellen Hsieh; (*b*) Yuzankaku.

in the Arabic world. On the right bank of the Singapore River, about ninety meters upstream of Pulau Saigon, an area called Al Kaff Quay used to host the famous Hadhrami Arab family, who conducted trade between Singapore and the Arabic world. Part of the findings in the Pulau Saigon site might belong to this particular group of people since the double-happiness bowls have been discovered in diverse places, including South India, the Persian Gulf, and East Africa (Sakai 2019; Sasaki and Sasaki 2006, 2015; Nogami 2006; Hansman 1985) (Fig. 3.8b). During the nineteenth century the trade route might have followed the British imperial network. However, considering that a sizable number of the Chinese inferior porcelain sherds have been dated to earlier than the establishment of British control in the region, the maritime trade conducted by the Hadhrami Arabs from East Yemen began earlier.

Even without taking into account the original concepts of Art Nouveau and double-happiness, the diverse applications of Victorian decorative tiles in Asia and the wide spread of Chinese blue-and-white bowls lead us to see faces of different ethnicities and classes during the age of imperialism. In addition to the networks related to dominant colonial empires, archaeological evidence indicates the presence of the overseas Chinese and Arabs, who still thrived in Asian waters.

Concluding Remarks

This chapter addresses the *longue durée* connection between the Indian Ocean region and Southeast Asia via cross-regional comparative studies in four cultural/historical contexts: Indianization, Islamization, European colonization, and imperialism. We start from Borobudur, the well-known Buddhist monument in Java. The monument's local and foreign architectural characteristics make it the best example of Indianization as well as localization. Considered with the connectivity among stupas at Bodh Gaya, Bagan, Lamphun, and Polonnaruwa, a complex Buddhist network among north India, Sri Lanka, and mainland and insular Southeast Asia is presented. Compared with the locally made stupas, the marble cenotaphs shipped directly from Gujarat and the wall tiles shipped from northern Vietnam and Persia during the introduction of Islam (and probably Sufism) in insular Southeast Asia reveal a stronger trade connection inherited from the previous period, and one that might have given local Muslim elites more power. The making and distribution of colorful Persian ware and plain Anping jars remind us that Asian ceramics were not merely exported goods for the West; the regional trade networks of the East were reinforced during the period of European exploration. Finally, in the nineteenth century and even the twentieth, we see an intensified globalization phenomenon through the wide usage of colorful glazed wall tiles for the rich and the double-happiness blue-and-white bowls for the poor. Again, non-European agents, such as the Arabs and the Japanese, played significant roles in these trade networks. The networks between the Indian Ocean region and Southeast Asia include economic, political, and religious aspects, which were interwoven together. Due to the characteristics of the materials, some cases highlight religious links while others present insight into trade or power. Nonetheless, these studies enrich our understanding of the dynamics of interactions in Asian waters over time.

Acknowledgments

We thank Shih-Yi Tu and Eugene Chuang for providing the figures of the cenotaph of Nahrasiyah and the bed with decorative tiles, respectively.

Note

1 For this reason, when the British colonial government tried to reconstruct the Mahabodhi Temple of Bodh Gaya during the nineteenth century, they used the Bagan temple as a reference.

Bibliography

Ahmad, Anisah Bahyah, and Wan Kamal Mujani. 2015. "Interior Motifs and Designs of the Malacca Mosque: A Discussion of the Kampung Kiling Mosque." *Journal of Islam and Science* 2(1): 39–51.

Amrith, Sunil S. 2013. *Crossing the Bay of Bengal: The Furies of Nature and the Fortunes of Migrants.* Cambridge, Mass.: Harvard University Press.

Barry, Jennifer. 2000. *Pulau Saigon: A Post Eighteenth Century Archaeological Assemblage Recovered from a Former Island in the Singapore River.* Stamford, U.K.: Rheidol Press.

Bellina, Bérénice, and Ian Glover. 2004. "The Archaeology of Early Contact with India and the Mediterranean World, from the Fourth Century BCE to the Fourth Century AD." In *Southeast Asia: From Prehistory to History,* edited by Ian Glover and Peter Bellwood, 68–88. London: Routledge.

Brown, Roxanna Maude. 2004. *The Ming Gap and Shipwreck Ceramics in Southeast Asia.* PhD diss., Art History, University of California, Los Angeles.

Capistrano-Baker, Florina H. 2015. *Philippine Gold: Treasures of Forgotten Kingdoms.* New York: Asia Society.

Chen, Kuo-tung. 2004. Anping Jars and Sanshao Liquor (「安平壺」與「三燒酒」Anpinghu yu sanshaojiu). *Taiwan Historica (台灣文獻)* 8: 2–9.

Cœdès, George. 1968. *The Indianized States of Southeast Asia.* Honolulu: University of Hawai'i Press.

Hansman, J. 1985. *Julfar: An Arabian Port.* London: Royal Asiatic Society of Great Britain and Ireland.

Hsieh, Ellen. 2017. *Early Spanish Colonialism in Manila, the Philippines: An Historical Archaeological Viewpoint.* PhD diss., Archaeology, University of California, Los Angeles.

———. 2021. "Decorative Tiles in Southeast Asia after the Age of Exploration." In *Port City, Exchange and Porcelain: Studies of Southeast Asian Archaeology,* edited by the Committee of the Festschrift for Retirement of Prof. Seiichi Kikuchi and Prof. Takashi Sakai, 225–35. Tokyo: Yuzankaku.

———. 2023. "China for Asia: Bencharong and Peranakan Porcelains in the Eighteenth and the Nineteenth Centuries." In *Ritual and Economy in East Asia: Archaeological Perspectives*, edited by Anke Hein, Rowan Flad, and Bryan K. Miller. Los Angeles: Cotsen Institute of Archaeology Press.

Johns, A. H. 1995. "Sufism in Southeast Asia: Reflections and Reconsiderations." *Journal of Southeast Asian Studies* 26(1): 169–83.

Kang, Nuo-xi. 2015. *The Architectural Memory of Old Colorful Tiles in Taiwan (台灣老花磚的建築記憶)*. Taipei: Maotouing.

Knapp, Ronald G. 2010. *Chinese Houses of Southeast Asia: The Eclectic Architecture of Sojourners and Settlers*. Tokyo: Tuttle.

Lambourn, Elizabeth. 2003. "From Cambay to Samudera-Pasai and Gresik: The Export of Gujarati Grave Memorials to Sumatra and Java in the Fifteenth Century C.E." *Indonesia and the Malay World* 31(90): 221–84.

———. 2004. "Carving and Communities: Marble Carving for Muslim Patrons at Khambhāt and around the Indian Ocean Rim, Late Thirteenth–Mid-Fifteenth Centuries." *Ars Orientalis* 34: 99–133.

Lee, Chun. 2021. *A Research of Anping Jars from the Ki-wu-lan Site, I-lan: The Sea Trade Route between East Asia and South East Asia (從淇武蘭出土安平壺看十七世紀東亞與東南亞間海上貿易網絡 Cóng qí wǔ lán chūtǔ ānpíng hú kàn shíqī shìjì dōngyà yǔ dōngnányà jiān hǎishàng màoyì wǎngluò)*. MA thesis, Art History, National Taiwan University.

Lim, Jennifer. 2020. "Singapore Heritage Tile Project: An International Mosaic of Love." Accessed January 20, 2021. https://jenniferlimart.com/singaporeheritagetiles

Manguin, Pierre-Yves. 2010. "Pan-Regional Responses to South Asian Inputs in Early Southeast Asia." In *50 Years of Archaeology in Southeast Asia: Essays in Honour of Ian Glover*, edited by Bérénice Bellina, Elisabeth A. Bacus, Thomas Oliver Pryce, and Jan Wisseman Christie, 171–82. Bangkok: River Books.

Miksic, John N. 1990. *Borobudur: Golden Tale of the Buddhas*. Singapore: Pepiplus.

———. 2009. "Research on Ceramic Trade, within Southeast Asia and between Southeast Asia and China." In *Southeast Asian Ceramics: New Light on Old Pottery*, edited by John N. Miksic, 70–99. Singapore: Southeast Asian Ceramic Society.

Miksic, John, and Cheryl-Ann Low Mei Gek (eds.). 2005. *Early Singapore 1300s–1819: Evidence in Maps, Text and Artefacts*. Singapore: Singapore History Museum.

Miksic, John N., and Geok Yian Goh. 2017. *Ancient Southeast Asia*. London: Routledge.

Moquette, J. P. 1912. "De grafsteenen te Pasé en Grisse vergeleken met dergelijk monumenten uit Hindoestan," *Tijdschrift van het Bataviaasch Genootschap voor Kunsten en Wettenschappen* 54: 536–48.

Nogami, Takenori. 2006. "The Dating of Chinese Underglaze Cobalt-Blue Porcelain found in Fort Masafi through Data of Wrecked Ship Cargoes (沈没船資料からみたマサフィ砦出土の中国染付の年代 Chinbotsu-sen shiryō kara mita masafi toride shutsudo no Chūgoku shimitsu no nendai)." *Kindai Archaeology (金大考古 Kindai-Koko)* 53: 17–21.

Nogami, Takenori, and Eladio Terreros. 2016. "Japanese Porcelain Carried to Peru (ペルーに渡った日本磁器 Perū ni watatta Nihon jiki)." *Bulletin of the Yokohama Museum of EurAsian Cultures (横浜ユーラシア文化館紀要 Yokohama yūrashia bunka-kan kiyō)* 4: 1–17.

Reid, Anthony. 1993. "Islamization and Christianization in Southeast Asia: The Critical Phase, 1550–1650." In *Southeast Asia in the Early Modern Era: Trade, Power, and Belief*, edited by Anthony Reid, 151–79. New Haven, Conn.: Yale University Press.

A Thousand Years of Connections: The Indian Ocean Region and Southeast Asia · 69

Revire, Nicolas. 2015. "Re-Exploring the Buddhist 'Foundation Deposits' at Chedi Chula Prathon, Nakhon Pathom." In *Buddhist Dynamics in Premodern and Early Modern Southeast Asia,* edited by Dietrich Christian Lammerts, 172–217. Cambridge, U.K.: Cambridge University Press.

Sakai, Takashi. 2012. "A Preliminary Study for Ancient High-Rise Buildings in Southeast & South Asia (東南アジア・南アジアの古代高層建築について Tōnan ajia minami ajia no kodai kōsō genchiku ni tsuite)." *Journal of Southeast Asian Archaeology (東南アジア考古学 Tōnan ajia kōkogaku)* 32: 85–97.

———. 2014. "The Monumental Origin of Borobudur: A Study for Buildings in the Relief Panels (ボロブドゥール遺跡の起源―レリーフ中建造物の研究)." *Journal of Southeast Asian Archaeology (東南アジア考古学)* 34: 31–46.

———. 2015a. "Tiles Excavated at the Trowulan Site, Indonesia (インドネシア、トロウラン遺跡出土のタイル Indoneshia, torouran iseki shutsudo no tairu)." *Oriental Ceramics (東洋陶磁 Toyo-Toji)* 44: 63–83.

———. 2015b. "Jingdezhen Interior Tiles in Asian Waters: Indonesia, India and Turkey in the 18th Century (アジア海域を走る景徳鎮インテリア・タイル―インドネシア・インド・トルコの18世紀―Ajia kaiiki o hashiru Keitokuchin interia・ tairu — Indoneshia・ Indo・ Toruko no 18 seiki —)." In *Archaeology of Ceramics from Middle Age and Early Modern Period 1 (中近世陶磁器の考古学Chūkinsei tōjiki no kōkogaku 1),* 303–20. Tokyo: Yuzankaku.

———. 2019. "The Trade of Fujian Inferior Porcelains: Concentrated on the Double Happiness Bowl (福建産粗製陶磁器の貿易―双喜文碗を中心に Fukken-san sosei tōjiki no bōeki — sōkimon wan o chūshin ni)." In *Archaeology of Ceramics from Middle Age and Early Modern Period 10 (中近世陶磁器の考古学 Chūkinsei tōjiki no kōkogaku 10),* edited by Tatsuo Sasaki, 281–304. Tokyo: Yuzankaku.

———. 2020. "The Mystery around Anping Jars (安平壺をめぐる謎 Anpingko o meguru nazo)." In *Archaeology of Ceramics from Middle Age and Early Modern Period 12 (中近世陶磁器の考古学 Chūkinsei tōjiki no kōkogaku 12),* edited by Tatsuo Sasaki, 171–94. Tokyo: Yuzankaku.

———. 2021. Addendum: The Mystery around Anping Jars (補遺: 安平壺をめぐる謎 Hoi: Anpingko o meguru nazo). In *Archaeology of Ceramics from Middle Age and Early Modern Period 14 (中近世陶磁器の考古学 Chūkinsei tōjiki no kōkogaku 14),* edited by Tatsuo Sasaki, 203–26. Tokyo: Yuzankaku.

Sakai, Takashi, and Ohashi Koji. 2017. *Hizen Wares Excavated from Royal Capital Sites in Indonesia—Trowulan and Other Sites,* Tokyo: Yuzankaku.

Sasaki, Tatsuo, and Hanae Sasaki. 2006. "Excavation and Renovation of the Masafi Fort (マサフィ砦の発掘と保存修復 Masafi toride no hakkutsu to hozon shūfuku)." *Kindai Archaeology (金大考古 Kindai-Koko)* 53: 6–17.

———. 2015. "Excavation at Heart of Sharjah: Bank Street Archaeological Survey—2012/13 Season (シャルジャ港町の発掘 Sharuja Minatochō no hakkutsu)." *Archaeological Bulletin Kanazawa University (金沢大学考古学紀要 Kanazawav daigaku kōkogaku kiyō)* 36: 103–19.

Sirisena, W. M. 1978. *Sri Lanka and South-East Asia: Political, Religious and Cultural Relations: From A.D. c. 1000 to c. 1500.* Leiden: Brill.

70 · Ellen Hsieh and Takashi Sakai

Voss, Barbara L., J. Ryan Kennedy, Jinhua (Selia) Tan, and Laura W. Ng. 2018. "The Archaeology of Home: Qiaoxiang and Nonstate Actors in the Archaeology of the Chinese Diaspora." *American Antiquity* 83(3): 407–26.

Wolters, O. W. 1999. *History, Culture, and Region in Southeast Asian Perspectives.* Singapore: Cornell Southeast Asia Program Publications.

Yajima, Hikoichi. 2006. *History Seen from Sea: The Exchange History between the Indian Ocean and the Mediterranean Sea* (海域から見た歴史—インド洋と地中海を結ぶ交流史 Kaiiki kara mita rekishi—indoyō to chichūkai o musubu kōryū-shi). Nagoya: Nagoya University Press (名古屋大学出版会 Nagoya daigaku shuppankai).

4

Connectivity and Small Island Historical Archaeology in the Indian Ocean

KRISH SEETAH, STEFANIA MANFIO, AND AKSHAY SARATHI

Introduction: Challenges for Historical Archaeology in the Indian Ocean World

In this chapter we navigate the complex process of decentralizing Europe without eschewing existing frameworks that could help with the development of an Indian Ocean historical archaeology. We respond by introducing and applying the theoretical framing of *connectivity* to island archaeology, specifically of Mauritius and Zanzibar. Decentralizing Europe is here observed as a positive effort to provide further recognition to the cultural and ethnic richness that characterizes this expansive oceanic basin. We seek to emphasize the role Indigenous and diasporic communities played for millennia in shaping trade, networks, and social development, and in the future to move beyond historicization, which has invariably favored the achievements and influence of specific groups of people and certain academic approaches. Given the central role of European imperial elites, alongside the soldiers, convicts, and craftspeople of European descent with their attendant material culture, and the long-standing interactions between Europeans, Africans, Arabs, Bengalis, Indians, and a host of other groups, knowledge of "Europeans" is crucial to developing an understanding of the broader Indian Ocean World in the last 500 years—and, moreover, of archaeology as a discipline developed in Europe. Hence there is a benefit and necessity to adopt, adapt, and utilize the wealth of theoretical and practical resources that have developed within a European framework.

Scholars of the Indian Ocean World (IOW) recognize the ways in which research from this region offers unique perspectives on topics of major global significance: enslavement, colonization, Europeanization, climate change, epidemic disease, and the development of heritage. This opens many opportunities for comparative analysis with the Atlantic and Pacific oceans (Miller

2003; Hofmeyr 2007; Wilson and Hauser 2016; Oas and Hauser 2018). However, the practice and conceptualization of historical archaeology in the Indian Ocean are not without challenges (Seetah and Allen 2018: 5; see also contributions in Seetah 2018). Indeed, even the use of this term has been a point of contention within IOW and African contexts (Connah 2007; Seetah and Allen 2018). When considering the nature of history and prehistory in this region, it is necessary to emphasize oral tradition as well as the textual record. One also needs to account for the chronological flux between literate and preliterate societies (Connah 2007) and the fact that Western academic traditions tend to elevate the written over the spoken word. With these points in mind, there is clearly a need to develop specificity regarding the practice, and theory, of historical archaeology in this region.

Numerous approaches have been forwarded that respond to the needs of historical archaeologists working in the IOW. *Triangulating* between archival sources and cultural materials was used by Kirkman as early as the 1950s to understand the dynamics of the East African coast, and to enhance understanding of the precolonial past, now increasingly referred to as "the Swahili coast" (Kirkman 1957; Lane 2018: 146–47). Another measure has been to eschew periodization based on Eurocentric division (Schmidt and Walz 2007). Campbell's recent effort to centralize African peoples in shaping trade and cultural features in the IOW demonstrates the utility of moving beyond existing periodization. He explains the dynamic nature of socioeconomic development against a backdrop of climatic and environmental stability and instability, rather than chronological divisions such as prehistory, or early medieval, which have tended to be superimposed onto African and IOW contexts (Campbell 2019).

Periodization has obvious utility, especially within comparative frameworks, and for the near future, we will remain dependent on existing chronological divisions (Cooper 2002). Moreover, avoiding traditional periodization is one avenue to improve historical archaeology in this region (Kusimba 2004; Schmidt 2016; Wilson and Hauser 2016; Walz and Gooding 2021). However, reconsidering Eurocentric approaches to the production of knowledge forms part of a much wider endeavor to decolonize academic disciplines (Fleisher and LaViolette 2013; Lane 2018: 162). Given the recent social upheavals the world has witnessed, this is one route for archaeologists and historians to respond to contemporary issues surrounding social justice and to help tackle the negative legacies of colonialism. Thus, in addition to providing important comparative dimensions, historical archaeology in this region should seek to explore and reveal the unique interconnections between communities in the Indian Ocean.

The focus on islands provides a way to bring different sub-regions into a cohesive scaffold. Islands have invariably played a central role as entrepôt and nodal points within wider networks. Simultaneously, our comparative analysis between two connected but vastly different islands helps illustrate how small island communities develop unique features in their own right (Hauser 2011). While we emphasize the relationships between islands and the unique developments that took place upon them, we seek to understand better how they were *connected* to each other, the IOW, and the rest of the world. Ultimately, the unique role played by islands, as we argue later, stems from the way in which their geographies influence human behavior.

Connectivity in the Indian Ocean World

This particular disposition for islands to serve as nodes underpins our use of connectivity as a framing mechanism. As a concept, *connectivity* has its origins in graph theory (Pettegrew 2013) and has been applied mainly, though not exclusively, to studies of the Classical world. The concept has been used to evaluate the extended historical process of globalization (LaBianca and Scham 2006) or to situate the relationship between technology and social development (Pitts and Versluys 2014). Connectivity can thus help us to think about the interconnectedness that governs trade and commerce. At the same time, it has an obvious affinity with network theory concepts and, more recently, with the expanding field of the digital humanities and digitization itself. As such, it aligns well with ideas of *communication*. Scham applies connectivity within a discourse on colonialism, a topic that has been at the core of the concept since its early use in the Mediterranean world. Similarly, as the concept was popularized in Horden and Purcell's *The Corrupting Sea* (2000) to underscore the inherent mobility of the Mediterranean seascape, it has garnered a strong association with ecological forces.

As connectivity amalgamates ideas on technology (a point we revisit in the discussion), mobility, globalization, communication, and environment, it has vibrant applicability to historical archaeology in the IOW (Douglass and Cooper 2020; see Schnepel and Alpers 2018 for a historical and social science treatment of these concepts for the region). Indeed, connectivity has been implicitly engaged to link the creation of cultural practice and its subsequent cascading transformative re-creation (Seetah 2016), changing landscapes, and colonial enterprise within this region (see case studies in Sarathi 2018b; Seetah 2018). However, connectivities in the IOW differ fundamentally from those occurring elsewhere in their near-absolute reliance on the monsoon, which was only partially lifted with the advent of the Age of Steam

(Chaudhuri 1985). The Indian Ocean monsoon cycle serves to unify a vast swathe of the planet through its predictability and the sheer magnitude of its effects. In this context, connectivity represents a means of interrogating the phenomenon whereby social decision making is inherently dependent on, indeed controlled by, an ecosystem's functional characteristics or "landscape affordances" (Kempf 2020).

To illustrate the applicability of connectivity to IOW contexts: the dependence that Mauritian plantation economies had on the Zanzibar slave market is attested to by the fact that the majority of the enslaved people arriving in Mauritius from the 1770s had been purchased from Zanzibar and East Africa (Sheriff et al. 2016: 4). This trade in human lives was largely conducted along new maritime routes that were themselves an extension of well-established monsoon-driven networks of exchange. This example epitomizes how connectivity may in the future help to frame the commercial, ideological, ecological, and cultural lines that intersected around a topic of particular importance for regional historical archaeology, namely, enslavement.

The Archaeology of Islands

Before discussing our case studies, we briefly summarize and situate existing perspectives on the archaeology of islands, aligning these with research from the IOW where appropriate. This provides a basis from which we can then discuss the potential benefits of studying Indian Ocean islands as part of comparative historical archaeology.

> An island is for all seasons and for all tastes. An island can be both paradise and prison, both heaven and hell. An island is a contradiction between openness and closure, between roots and routes, which islanders must continually negotiate. (Baldacchino 2007: 165)

Baldacchino summarizes the duality that underscores the scholarship on islands. Island archaeology is an ideal example of why decentralizing Europe and Eurocentric concepts can be beneficial in broadening and deepening academic discourse on a given topic. Notions of being bounded spaces, insular and isolated, have characterized western scholarship on islands, islanders, and island archaeology (Boomert and Bright 2007). These ideas partly stem from the development of Darwin's original thesis on the evolution of species. Indeed, contemporary studies of islands, including island archaeology, have largely been framed from biogeographical concepts (Berg 2010). However, looking back further into antiquity, one observes that Christianity engendered a vision of islands as desolate and remote, ideas concretized into western culture by Shakespeare, DeFoe, and Stevenson (Smith 2009). Negative connotations have also been attributed since at least the 1300s in connection to the spread of epidemic disease in Europe and the use of islands for quarantine and containment.

For at least the last two decades, archaeologists working in the Mediterranean (Broodbank 2000) and beyond European waters (Rainbird 2007) have called into question this ideological stance. Isolation is relative, after all, not absolute (Anderson 2004; Broodbank 2008; Erlandson 2008). The view of islands as insular, peripheral, sequestered, and cloistered spaces exemplifies a non-islander perspective. This can undermine the agency of islanders either to promote, encourage, and utilize isolation (Eriksen 1993) or to develop and maintain networks and links for their own benefit. Unsurprisingly, islands may appear more isolated to the external, as opposed to the local, point of view.

Rainbird's (2007) seminal book represented a milestone in terms of overturning notions of marginality and insularity; Broodbank (2008: 72) suggests that this change—exploding "the myth of primitive isolation"—is likely irrevocable. Another key achievement of this conceptual reevaluation of islands has been to decenter the terrestrial context and refocus on "an archaeology of the sea to match that of the land" (Broodbank 2000: 34). This stance proposes an engaged and connected relationship between humans and the ocean, viewed from the maritime rather than land context. In turn, new ideas have been promoted that center on how maritime communities around the IOW have developed over time and the connections that exist between them (see cases in Sarathi 2018b). It has also led to new assessments of the way that maritime and terrestrial heritage contexts intersect (Seetah and Leidwanger, in press). There is thus reason to question notions of islands as cul-de-sacs of culture or as places where cultural influences spread and remain unchanged until acted upon again.

As the subdiscipline of island archaeology has developed, the geographic and social *emplacement* of islands themselves has forced reappraisal and a more sympathetic approach to their study. The biogeographic underpinnings have continued to be a central guiding framework in the practice of island studies more generally; however, social dimensions have, in turn, had a greater influence on how we view anthropogenic influence. As such, rather than regarding them as cultural laboratories, Vitousek (2002) suggests we consider islands to be "model systems," locations that illustrate a confluence of the various grand interacting phenomena, and subsystems of larger systems. These model systems need not necessarily be ecological in nature but include, for example, diaspora (Seetah 2016). Thus, while islands may not necessarily be inherently different from larger landmasses, it should be remembered that environmental and cultural forces may be viewed in sharper relief and be more evident within an island context (Dawson 2019).

A Comparative Historical Archaeology: Zanzibar and Mauritius

Fixing the spotlight on the IOW specifically, islands in this region were critical to the specific mode of commerce that developed in antiquity. Due to diverse and discrete climatic and environmental conditions, different parts of this oceanic basin produced distinct goods. The unique commodities, in the form of spices, hemp, and sugar, to name a few, meant that a flourishing trade developed to exchange these goods, giving rise to long-distance commercial enterprise.

Our comparative framework draws on work from Zanzibar and Mauritius, islands sharing this oceanic space, but each with its own role. These two islands formed critical nodal points within much wider interregional and intercontinental networks. They were each enmeshed in the monsoonal cycle, but this weather system had quite different influences on each island. They were also incredibly salient as part of the wider colonial enterprise in the IOW. Zanzibar's long history of habitation contrasts with the relatively short period of human settlement in Mauritius; both played distinctly important roles in the movement of enslaved peoples and commodities such as spices and sugar. Similarly, the particular form of a plantation shaped the economic and social history, as well as the landscape, that developed on each island. The archaeological context is also distinctive. Zanzibar has a long sequence of human activity as well as numerous large, well-developed projects (LaViolette and Norman, this volume; Juma 2004; Chami 2009; Croucher 2014; Kourampas et al. 2015; Shipton et al. 2016; Prendergast et al. 2016, 2017; Fitton 2017, 2018; Faulkner et al. 2018; Sarathi 2018a; Baužytė 2019; Sulas et al. 2019; Alders 2020; Rødland 2021, 2022; Rødland et al. 2020; Wynne-Jones et al. 2021; Sarathi et al. 2022). The archaeology of Mauritius is relatively nascent, though much has been achieved over the last decade (Seetah 2015b; see also cases in Seetah 2018). Indeed, local perception has transitioned from one suggesting that "there is no archaeology in Mauritius" (Seetah 2015c) to large numbers of visitors attending commemorative heritage sites (Calaon and Forrest 2018). In brief, these two islands present many opportunities to draw comparative appraisals that consider geographic and geological, linguistic, religious, socioeconomic, and historical dimensions.

After a brief outline of the archaeo-historic background of our study locations, we focus on the plantation economies and the laboring peoples forming the backbone of the clove and sugar industries that developed in Zanzibar and Mauritius.

Zanzibar

The Archipelago of Zanzibar consists of two main islands: Unguja (also known as Zanzibar) to the south and Pemba to the north. Of the two, excavations at Unguja have yielded evidence for human presence on the island that has been claimed to date to c. 20,000 years ago at the site of Kuumbi Cave (Chami 2009), but it should be noted that there exists some disagreement between Chami (2009) and Shipton et al. (2016) about the earliest date at which this site was occupied. A more conservative dating of c. 17,000 years ago is more reasonable given the evidence at hand. It should be noted that at this early date Unguja was still connected to the mainland. Occupation at Kuumbi Cave disappears with the rise of sea levels at the end of the Pleistocene. Kuumbi Cave was reoccupied in the middle of the first millennium CE, along with sites like Unguja Ukuu (Fitton and Wynne-Jones 2017) and Fukuchani (Fitton 2017; Kessy 2003; Shipton et al. 2016). Pemba was occupied in roughly the seventh century (LaViolette and Fleisher 2009).

The twelfth century was marked by the conversion of at least some of the local East Africa population to Islam. The earliest surviving mosque in Zanzibar was constructed in 1106 at Kizimkazi Dimbani (Chittick 1960; Kleppe 2001), behind which a cemetery was discovered in 2018 (Sarathi, in press). Trade seems to have directed the location of settlements. On Tumbatu, an island just off the northwestern shores of Unguja, a city grew in the thirteenth and fourteenth centuries (Rødland 2021) that resembled coral limestone "Stone Towns" that sprouted in dozens along the coast of East Africa. The material culture of these cities consisted of both local and imported goods (Kusimba and Kusimba 2017; Kusimba 1999). A common architectural style was present along the East African coast, and cities shared a common town plan. Limestone was used to construct mosques, houses, civic structures, and pillared tombs located near mosques (Garlake 1966). The East African coast from Somalia to Mozambique, in the eleventh through fifteenth centuries, was characterized by limestone architecture, gradual conversion to Islam, and a shared ideology.

The sixteenth through twentieth centuries marked the gradual rise of Omani and Portuguese colonialism (until 1698; see LaViolette and Norman, this volume) and a decline in Indigenous political power. During these centuries, however, exchange networks of all types—economic, ideological, and cultural—intensified, and the cities of the East African coast were integrated into a world economy (Declich 2018; Kusimba et al. 2013; Perkins 2015).

Mauritius

The islands of the Mascarenes, Rodrigues, Réunion, and Mauritius were uninhabited at the time of European colonialism. In the 1502 map of Cantino, the Mascarene Islands are mentioned for the first time, their discovery attributed to the Portuguese (Toorawa 2007: 50). The first settlers of Mauritius were the Dutch, who, after landing in 1598, then abandoned and subsequently recolonized in 1638–58 and 1664–1710, respectively (Moree 1998: 3). In 1710 the French claimed and settled the island (Vaughan 2005), playing a defining role in shaping the socioeconomic dimensions to the present day. The British seized Mauritius in 1810, retaining the island until independence in 1968. The impacts of colonialism on the island's "pristine" ecosystem have been investigated through climate proxy evidence (de Boer et al. 2014) alongside the devastating effects of introduced species (Cheke 2010). Complementing this broader ecological research are studies focused on the Dutch fortification of Vieux Grand Port at Mahebourg (Floore and Jayasena 2010), strategically important enclaves such as Île de la Passe (Summers and Summers 2008; Summers 2021), and the role of illegal slave traders using specially designed vessels to circumvent British Naval patrols (Manfio and von Arnim 2020; Metwalli et al. 2007). Together, these archaeological studies have served to enrich the historical narrative that has tended to dominate accounts of the island's colonial past.

As archaeological studies have evolved, emphasis has been placed on sugar estates, including Trianon (Calaon et al. 2012; Seetah et al. 2015) and Bras d'Eau (Haines 2019, 2020). Research from burial grounds such as Bois Marchand and Le Morne Old Cemetery supplements work on the economic role of laboring peoples, providing direct evidence from human remains as well as features of social practice (Seetah 2015a, 2015b). These lines of evidence have helped to deepen our knowledge of religion and syncretism (Čaval 2018, in press), foodways of enslaved and indentured peoples (Lightfoot et al. 2020), and demography (Fregel et al. 2014). Overall, the flourishing archaeology of Mauritius offers an important opportunity to study the lifeways of the laboring class and to improve our understanding of the connectivity between different laboring communities.

Labor Diasporas Connected through Cloves, Sugar, and Gun Powder

Zanzibar's location has made it strategically central to connections between East Africa, the Gulf region, and India. This particular position generated enormous interest from Europeans, Arabs, and other maritime powers (Breen et al. 2016). Mauritius, on the other hand, uninhabited before the arrival of the Europeans, was created as a mercantile economy. Initially, extractive processes for hardwood by the Dutch gave way to mixed agriculture, mainly of exportable goods by the French. Under British rule, the island was transformed into a sugar colony after preferential taxes on Caribbean sugar were lifted in the early nineteenth century. Mauritius produced close to 7 percent of the world's supply by the 1850s (Allen 2008: 152). A similar scenario occurred in Zanzibar when, with Omani domination in the nineteenth century, the island became the central hub for the production and distribution of cloves in the Indian Ocean.

Mauritius and Zanzibar needed increasing numbers of workers to cultivate the plantations. This need was exacerbated by the high death toll during transport; historical sources emphasize that the percentage of deaths among enslaved people on relatively short journeys between IOW islands was as high as on the much longer Atlantic crossings (Clarence-Smith 2013: 15). The urge to transport many captives resulted in smaller rations of food and water stowed on board and a reduction in the space allocated per enslaved person (Manfio and von Arnim 2020: 501–3).

As a result of geopolitical developments and the high attrition rate, acquiring labor became increasingly complicated. Both islands were under British control, but they were governed differently. Mauritius was a Crown Colony under direct rule but with a plantocracy that remained French. Christianity served as the overarching religious belief system, heavily influencing the enactment of enslavement, as seen in the *Code Noir*, for example. Zanzibar was a Protectorate, indirectly governed by an Arab sultan, who defended the interests of the predominantly Muslim former slave-owning class (Sheriff et al. 2016). With the Abolition Act coming into effect in 1807, the legal slave trade to islands under British control was no longer possible. The acquisition of enslaved peoples would technically be legal in those areas controlled by the Zanzibari Sultanate, but the slave trade continued into those British-controlled areas where the trade was illegal. The acquisition of captured people was easier for Zanzibar due to its proximity to the Swahili coast and the different approach to enslavement practiced by the Arabs for Mauritian landowners; the situation caused increasing anxiety.

Although a significant number of captured people continued to enter Mauritius illegally, the increased vigilance and suppression of slave trading by the Royal Navy led to unprecedented concern among plantation owners (Anderson 2019: 212). Attention shifted to India as a source of labor, targeting and exploiting many of the same populations in northeastern India who had been subject to enslavement in the eighteenth century (Carter 2006). Consequently, under the specter of pending labor shortages, the British government decided to test the importation of Indian workers to the sugar plantations of Mauritius in the 1820s, starting "The Great Experiment" (Mahmud 2012: 230)—discussed later.

No archaeological or historical information has yet been found concerning how enslaved people were transitioned from ship to plantation; certainly, as of now, there is no evidence of a slave market in Mauritius. By comparison, one of the most active slave markets was in Zanzibar. Captured men, women, and children had been exported from the East African coast to Zanzibar for centuries. By the seventeenth century, Stone Town had become the main center for human trafficking in the Indian Ocean, reaching international importance during the Sultan of Oman's hegemony. The market remained active until 1873, when it was finally closed after decades of effort by abolitionists (Hazell 2011).

Archaeological evidence of the illegal slave trade, and the connection that existed between Zanzibar and Mauritius, emerged with the investigation of the *Coureur* wreck. In 2005, at Pointe aux Feuilles on the east coast of Mauritius, underwater excavations discovered the wreck, which sank in 1821 due to the captain's error (Manfio and von Arnim 2020; Metwalli et al. 2007). The *Coureur,* a lugger built in 1818 in Grand Port, Mauritius, was authorized to trade with Madagascar and Réunion. However, commanded by Captain Dorval and under false cover as a merchant ship, the ship made six voyages between Mauritius, Madagascar, and Zanzibar to purchase enslaved people illegally from 1820 to 1821. On her last voyage the *Coureur* had to divert from Madagascar to purchase enslaved people in Zanzibar, since King Radama I of Madagascar had decided to honor the terms of a treaty with Governor Farquhar of Mauritius, ending the slave trade between Mauritius and Zanzibar. Dorval illegally purchased enslaved people for 40 barrels of gunpowder, which had been produced in Mauritius at least a decade earlier. Mauritius was the only French colony in which gunpowder was produced (Teelock 2017). Gunpowder was a desirable commodity, and Mauritian merchants used it to trade for goods as well as enslaved people.

Archival records indicate that between 70 to 120 enslaved people were embarked. The discrepancy probably derives from the difference between the numbers of captured people purchased and those who survived the journey. On its return from Zanzibar, the *Coureur* was spotted by a British patrol that was surveilling Mauritian waters after receiving information of illegal activity led by Captain Dorval. The captain steered the vessel through the lagoon, attempting to escape; the *Coureur* struck a rock outcrop in the notoriously difficult to navigate reef, causing the ship to sink. The enslaved people were immediately disembarked and made to hide in the forest, while the ship was set on fire to conceal any trace of illegal activity.

While our existing understanding of the deeply enmeshed labor exchange between Zanzibar and Mauritius has been constructed largely from historical sources, archaeological research could concretize these connections through material analysis. The *Coureur*'s ballast was composed of irregular and oval-shaped stones, and the significant quantity recovered has helped confirm its activity as a slave ship. Specifically for the Indian Ocean, ships were engaged in an itineraries trade. Enslaved peoples and goods were purchased and disembarked at the various ports, as were the rocks used for the ballast. Since human cargo is relatively light, large quantities of ballast had to be added to the hull to maintain the ship's stability. Studying the composition and petrography of the different rock types could help determine where the ship had docked. This would reveal the network and the connectivity between different ports and people needed to carry out human trafficking, helping us to understand better the illegal slave trade, which remains poorly documented due to the obvious clandestine nature of this activity.

Additionally, lost and discarded artifacts are often recovered from within the ballast assemblage, having fallen to the bottom of the hull. A poignant example of this comes in the form of two lead tags, typical for the identification of the enslaved people, which were recovered from the *Coureur*. Similar tags were recovered from the Moulin à Poudre complex, at Pamplemousse (Teelock 2017). Although this facility was closed in 1810 when the British took over the island, the Moulin à Poudre had produced a considerable amount of gunpowder, which continued to supply Mauritius and be sold in the Indian Ocean for many years to follow (Kimberley and Nidhi 2018; Teelock 2017). As this was the only site producing gunpowder, we can be sure that the powder used to purchase the human cargo from Zanzibar was derived from Moulin à Poudre.

Plantation Economies in Zanzibar and Mauritius

Oral histories, texts, and archaeology have contributed to our understanding of enslaved peoples working on clove plantations in the Zanzibar archipelago in the nineteenth and twentieth centuries. The foundations of the clove plantation economy on the islands of Zanzibar and Pemba were laid during the Omani conquest of the islands in the nineteenth century. The Sultanate of Zanzibar rapidly developed a clove plantation economy worked by slaves imported from the mainland. While a primarily Arab landed class controlled the plantations, the Sultanate's commerce began to be dominated by South

Asian traders (Bishara 2017; Glassman 2011; Nicolini 2018; Nicolini and Watson 2004). The evolution of the clove plantation system and its physical attributes in the Zanzibar archipelago was determined by the political economy of the Sultanate of Zanzibar, tensions between "Arab" and "African" identities, and Islam. The establishment of clove plantations on Zanzibar, meant to participate in a capitalist world market, marked a significant break from earlier forms of engagement with labor, markets, and the landscape. At the same time, earlier cultural practices indigenous to the island and to the homelands from which enslaved peoples were taken found ready expression.

The establishment of the Sultanate, with its plantations and markets, drove the expansion of trade networks in East Africa, bringing enslaved peoples and material goods to Zanzibar. The vast majority of enslaved people were non-Muslim, which meant that according to the Qu'ran, the Muslim Omani plantation owners were tasked with their conversion and manumission (Croucher 2014; Glassman 2011). Oral and written histories coupled with archaeology suggest that the conversion to Islam by enslaved peoples on plantations was complicated and contingent. First, not all plantation owners sought to convert—and thus manumit—their slaves (Glassman 2011). Second, enslaved plantation workers themselves converted over time, usually through interaction with Sufi mystics or recent converts. As Croucher (2014) and Glassman (2011) note, this self-conversion allowed enslaved people from the mainland to incorporate some of their ancestral religions into their practice of Islam, such as the use of drums and dancing.

This reinterpretation of Islam by new converts was frowned upon by traditional Muslim authorities residing in centers of Islamic learning, like Zanzibar City. But Islam was merely one avenue by which competing and complementary identities formed in the rapidly changing social landscapes of Zanzibar's plantations in the nineteenth century. Omani landowners consciously sought to emulate Middle Eastern architecture, but enslaved peoples themselves often drew on coastal architectural forms and burial practices associated with Islam and social mobility (Croucher 2014). This, as Glassman (2011) notes, was an active choice to participate publicly in Swahili notions of *Uungwana* ("civilization") and to announce their conversion to Islam. Thus the conversion of enslaved peoples to Islam and their incorporation into coastal Islamic society ultimately seems to have been the choice of enslaved peoples rather than of plantation owners. While Omani plantation owners worked to distinguish themselves in their architecture from coastal East Africa, enslaved peoples did quite the opposite.

Beyond architectural forms, Croucher's (2014) work on the spatial layout of plantations emphasizes the role of built environments in reinforcing hierarchies of power and gender. The prominence of clove-drying floors in plantation structures allowed male plantation owners to emphasize their dominance in a social structure that favored paternalism and patron-client relations. Yet the significant number of women plantation owners suggests that systemic paternalism did not require patrons or those controlling plantations to be male. Social relations between plantation owners and enslaved peoples were thus defined in masculine terms but made room for women to practice paternalism with their enslaved laborers and clients. The role of concubines on plantations, who were still enslaved but enjoyed a higher standard of living than other enslaved people on the plantation, highlights the complex and gendered nature of power on plantations. Finally, the distribution of local and imported ceramics on plantations suggests that access to foreign goods was one marker of social status. The circulation of imported ceramics through lending and gifting chains was one expression of patron-client relationships present on plantations.

The creation of a "Swahili" identity in the early twentieth century was itself a product of the tensions of identity and power inherent in the plantation system. The conversion of enslaved peoples to Islam and their self-incorporation into the coastal Zanzibari culture, and the efforts made by Omani landowners to remain distinctly Middle Eastern, led to the broad division of Zanzibari society into Arabs and the Swahili, with small populations of South Asians and Europeans. While the term Swahili is now projected historically to describe precolonial coastal civilization, its roots lie fundamentally in the agency of enslaved peoples working on plantations in the Zanzibar archipelago. Their negotiation of bondage, religion, and ethnicity led to the creation of new social forms in Zanzibar (Glassman 2011).

The Mascarene islands were transformed into plantation economies similar to the Caribbean islands of the Atlantic. Mauritius, in particular, provided favorable environmental and topographical conditions for the development of large-scale mono-crop agriculture (Seetah et al. 2022). The plantations that came to dominate the landscape required a large workforce. This need, but also its status as an entrepôt along maritime trade routes, meant that the island also played a prominent historical role in the movement of enslaved people (Allen 2008). By 1811 the island became the destination for some 90,000 enslaved people (Allen 2010: 68).

Following the abolition of the trade in slaves, Mauritius then served as the crucible for the Great Experiment undertaken by the British to find a new, cheap workforce for an expanding sugar market. The indentured system was the outcome of this experiment, leading to the mobilization of some 451,000 laborers to Mauritius from 1834 to 1910 (Allen 1999: 16) and over two million laborers around the world (Allen 2012: 2–3). Through archaeological research we are starting to understand better how the transition to indentured shaped the way labor was organized and how indentured laborers contributed to the plantation economy. Investigation of the Immigration Depot at Aapravasi Ghat, a UNESCO World Heritage Site commemorating indenture in Port Louis harbor, reveals a complex site (Summers 2011; Mungur-Medhi 2016). The depot had several annexes, a hospital, dormitories, and offices, all of which demonstrate the central role that Mauritius played in the new system of labor.

Important new information is being uncovered from colonial enclaves. Although we are still in the early stages of developing archaeological knowledge on the functioning and organization of plantations and estates, important features are coming to light. The number of estates increased during British rule, and sugar became the main export commodity. The architecture of sites such as Antoinette, the first estate to utilize indentured labor, and Belle Mare (Fig. 4.1) emphasizes the extensive exploitation of basalt as well as an organizational structure that shares similarities with the plantations of the Atlantic. The Trianon Sugar Estate typifies the "Big House and Slave Quarters" model of landscape organization. The site retains the "Old Laborer's Barracks" and was listed as a national monument in 1974. The barracks reflect British colonial military architecture (Home and King 2016), the cantonment model, where structures are arranged following functional principles but also to emphasize hierarchy. Although we have little information on how enslaved people lived and worked on this site, it seems that by the period of indenture, the need to accommodate the laborers' desires led to changes in the site's overall organization, at least within the context of dwelling construction. The laborers preferred to live in hut-type units with straw roofs, structures with which they were more familiar and which they considered to be healthier than buildings made of stone (Frere and Williamson 1875). Estate owners allowed the laborers to gather raw materials from around the estate to construct their dwellings. To a certain extent, the laborers were permitted to site and group their new dwellings in relation to work and social needs; from this, "camps" formed. While the central zone of the estate retained a clear organizational hierarchy, with the growth of the camps, a degree of distance and independence—physical and metaphorical—began to emerge between the plantation elite and workers. The camps served as the model for proto-villages that ultimately led to incipient urbanization (Seetah et al. 2018: 155–59).

The most detailed study of an estate and plantation has been undertaken on Bras d'Eau Sugar Estate. The aim of work on Bras d'Eau has been to situate the evolution of the estate within broader diachronic developments, focused

Figure 4.1. Belle Mare Sugar Estate; arches forming part of the main sugar-making infrastructure, with chimney in the background (Credit: Krish Seetah).

on landscape, social, and economic changes, and the enduring impacts in the modern day (Haines 2021). The physical work of enslaved and indentured peoples, within the context of agricultural production but also in reshaping the landscape to connect the estate to local logistical networks, forms a major focus of the study at Bras d'Eau (Haines 2019). Haines (2019) likens the plantation to a factory, reflecting capitalist motivations and manipulating social space, landscape, and even soundscapes to maximize productivity.

However, it is the sheer scale of landscape transformation revealed by archaeological surveys and excavations that provides direct evidence of the physical work of laboring peoples on this site (see also Haines and Hauser, this volume, on water infrastructure at Bras d'Eau). Initial walking reconnaissance undertaken in 2014 signaled the extent of the internal road networks, walls, and dwellings, all fabricated using basalt (Seetah et al. unpub.). Detailed surveys and mapping have since revealed some 35.5 km of roadways, constructed from basalt and, in some cases, elevated on basalt platforms to accommodate changes in elevation, ranging from 4 to 8 meters in width (Haines 2019). The roadways were heavily used over many decades, as evidenced by deep rutted grooves from cartwheels. Carts pulled by beasts of burden moved goods around the site. The vast majority, ~90 percent, of the site is plantation land, with the remaining 10 percent being used for domestic and industrial space. Due to the nature of the underlying soil, which was volcanic and rocky, plantation workers were required to break into the ground using crowbars and form long furrows with basalt fieldstones—only then could cane be planted. Thousands of these furrows exist on the site (Haines 2019), a testament to the backbreaking work that laboring peoples endured. The road network on the estate was connected to the main thoroughfares of the island, demonstrating that the site was deeply integrated into the local trade network. The ceramic finds recovered from the domestic quarter illustrate that Bras d'Eau was well connected to wider Indian Ocean trade networks, and global markets, but also that indentured laborers were able to bring some of their own material culture (Haines 2020). Research on Bras d'Eau has been instrumental in shedding light on the work regime of indentured peoples.

Evidence of the varied tasks of enslaved people within the colonial milieu is also emerging from Moulin à Poudre (Mungur-Medhi, in press). The process of creating gunpowder is dangerous, as attested by the fact that the island's first gunpowder mill in Balaclava exploded in 1756. The work was also highly skilled. Moulin à Poudre engaged a large number of enslaved men, women, and children, individuals who were housed on the site. As excavations proceed, there is an opportunity to understand better how the singular task of gunpowder production, one that was critical to broader colonial endeavors in the region, was organized at a site level and how this ostensibly compared with the type of organizational structure in place on sugar estates such as Bras d'Eau.

Discussion: *Connectivity* and Island Archaeology

Connectivities are clearly dynamic: links between nodes in a network must be renewed, and new types of connections open the possibility of new forms of behavior. Connectivities tend to lie outside human control and are the consequences of the past and the arbiters of the future. The Sultanate of Zanzibar was successful in creating an economy dependent on clove plantations and trade because it tapped into histories of connectivity—political, religious, and economic—the effects of which preceded its conquest of the island.

Islands force us to confront the limits of our categories and the universality of their applicability. The perception of islands as isolated stems in no small part from connectivity seen as a technological achievement and a fulfillment of Judeo-Christian sentiments of achieving mastery over nature. Notions of connectivity are in turn linked to notions of cultural passivity, in which agency is denied to certain cultures. As Said (1979) and Bhabha (1994) note, colonial perceptions of technology and culture were rooted in reductionist categories—the West vs. East, male vs. female, etc. The "superior" in reductionist dualities was almost always assigned to the colonial power. The "male," for instance, was seen as the colonial power who actively sought out new lands and peoples. The "female" were those people they met who were perceived to be unable or unwilling to take the initiative or had fallen into decadence after a glorious age of civilization. Connectivity, technology, and the colonial gaze are thus linked inextricably. Sub-Saharan Africans were deemed incapable of change without the aid of outsiders possessing technological superiority (Adas 1989). Adas was not discussing island cultures when he wrote his seminal work on ideologies purporting to explain Western ascendance in the late second millennium; however, much of his analysis is applicable. Island isolation after initial colonization was ascribed to technological backwardness or a racial inability to progress or explore (Sen 2010). With these caveats in mind, connectivity as a concept offers immense potential for viewing the IOW as a united whole while acknowledging the unique historical trajectories of individual regions. Breaking the chains of colonial thought that bind our views on connectivity and islands requires us to move away from teleologies of technology and focus more thoroughly on human and non-human actors that formed the world(s) of the Indian Ocean.

A de-emphasis of technology in historical narratives of connectivity brings attention to non-human actors and human actors who were stripped of their agency. We have acknowledged non-human historical agents whose effects cannot be ignored, such as the monsoon winds and commensals. Yet many human actors have themselves been marginalized in the narrative of the IOW and its islands. Here, we ask: connectivities *of* whom? And connectivities *for* whom? It is easy enough to slip into facile narratives emphasizing technologies of seafaring and commerce while discussing island connectivities. This is in large part due to the nature of the evidence available to us for our analyses. Some materials preserve better than others, and elite narratives tend to drown out the historical din of other actors. Yet some of these other actors themselves are critical if we are to understand connectivity in its entirety and write a more comprehensive and accurate narrative of the past.

Viewing islands and people denied agency as key to shaping connectivities and historical processes has multiple advantages. It allows us to examine how island geographies powerfully influenced the shape of human activity. Misguided notions of isolation aside, humans are biologically limited in certain ways. Islands and their surrounding waters exert a presence on historical landscapes that emphasize biological limitations and cultural creativity. As earlier noted, the bounded nature of islands modulates certain types of behavior and offers opportunities and risks absent in land-locked or coastal regions. In the narratives we present here, island geographies served oppressive institutions of enslavement. In the IOW, the agency of island geographies (or, indeed, the agency of any actor) gains additional meaning due to the constant environmental and cultural effects of the monsoon cycle. As bound as they are, then, islands in the IOW participate in cultural worlds on continental and oceanic scales. The human institutions built on islands like Zanzibar and Mauritius were based on ideologies and cultural forms developed elsewhere.

Our narrative discusses enslaved peoples brought to novel island geographies. Enslaved men, women, and children in nineteenth-century Zanzibar and Mauritius were not part of the same institution as their Roman counterparts millennia ago. Nor were they part of the brutal institutions of the American South and the Caribbean. The institutions that served the Atlantic slave trade differed significantly from the multiple institutions used to control the bodies and activities of people within the long history of the IOW. The status of an enslaved person was, in many instances, negotiable, which allowed enslaved people to exercise agency in specific ways (Alpers et al. 2007; Campbell 2013, 2018; Stanziani 2014). The brutality of institutions of servitude was contingent on the degree to which enslaved men, women, and children could, individually and collectively, engage in cultural negotiations concerning their status. This is vastly different from the institutions of chattel slavery with their roots in racism that developed in the Atlantic World (Campbell 2003: x; Mbeki and van Rossum 2017: 96). Religious laws, such as those in Islam, dictated who could and could not be enslaved, the conditions for enslaved persons, and manumission (Campbell 2004: xv). Slave communities rapidly absorbed and deployed the ideologies of their captors. The Abbasid Caliphate's mass importation of Zanji (East African) enslaved individuals to build cities and public works led to the Zanj Revolt (869–883 CE). The revolt took place within the context of Islamic ideology. Ali ibn Muhammad, a leader of the rebellion, took the title of Sahib al-Zanj ("Leader of the Zanj") and adopted a Kharijite saying that asserted that "even an Abyssinian slave" was capable of being the caliph if he were qualified (Popović 1999; Talhami 1977).

The unique geological conditions of Mauritius, as shown, for example, at Bras d'Eau, had a major impact on laboring peoples' work. Through an incredibly arduous process, the very fabric of the island had to be broken, reshaped, and reconfigured before a "plantation" could be created. The same process was necessary for the development of infrastructure such as roads and dwellings. These "landscape affordances" played a role in how laboring peoples responded to the treatment they endured.

A form of resistance developed in Mauritius that has been termed *petit marronage*; that is, absconding for less than a month (Allen 2002). Geograph-

Connectivity and Small Island Historical Archaeology in the Indian Ocean · 89

ical limitations and local conditions, such as the terrain and availability of resources, likely prevented slaves from absconding for protracted periods of time. Efforts to recapture enslaved people may also have limited the duration of marronage. Incidences of *petit marronage* increased over time (Allen 2002). The specificities of French enslavement may have forced runaway slaves to seek other avenues to abscond. In this system, *gens de color libre,* free or freed people of color, owned land and were engaged in various tasks by the colonial elite. J. Baptiste was one such person. Originally from Mozambique, he and his wife owned 30 ha of land at Bras d'Eau. Although Baptiste was alleged to be a member of the slave-hunting retinues, he and his wife may also have helped runaways, many of whom were also from Mozambique (Haines 2019). Ecological factors played an important role in determining how enslaved people escaped the plantations. Runaways could not seek refuge in forested and remote terrain in Mauritius, which had been heavily deforested to create plantations, so they likely sought escape in urban centers, possibly escaping on ships or seeking work as free labor (Vaughan 2005: 265). In the context of our discussion of islands, we ask: how did island geographies in the IOW affect the agency of enslaved populations? Diasporic slave communities discovered avenues other than rebellion to rise to power in their new homelands. Indian Ocean island geographies shaped the available avenues.

In addition to our cases revealing different iterations of the plantation economy, other examples suggest how ideas of connectivity and landscape affordance could enrich and broaden the scope of historical archaeology in the region. The Siddis of Janjira demonstrate how enslaved populations can use island geographies to their advantage. Descendants of Africans brought to South Asia as enslaved people over the centuries (Jayasuriya 2009) are a threatened and marginalized community today. The Siddis enjoyed success in South Asia in the past, even establishing policies of their own. A prominent Siddi, Malik Ambar (1548–1626), rose to become the virtual ruler of the Ahmadnagar Sultanate in the Deccan. Likely enslaved somewhere in East Africa, Malik Ambar was placed in a system of servitude that allowed for some social mobility based on exceptional talent. The Siddi community credits him with the acquisition of the island of Janjira (near modern Mumbai) and its fortification. Janjira's fortifications rendered it practically impregnable. Its Siddi rulers created a navy that challenged and cooperated with the British, Portuguese, Mughals, and Marathas (Ali 2016; Oka and Kusimba 2008; Toledano 2011).

The Siddis thus used their island as a base from which they projected power and influence over much of the western coast of India (Jasdanwalla 2015).

The Siddis of Janjira retained a collective identity based on their African roots but also absorbed and deployed ideologies of rulership that they encountered in South Asia. Out of deference to the Mughal emperor and the Ahmadnagar sultans, the ruler of Janjira took the title of *wazir* ("minister"). The *wazir* cooperated with the Mughals in campaigns against the Marathas and received ships, supplies, and money in return. While they were adept at posing as Muslim allies to the Mughals, they also took pains to patronize Hindu shrines and holy men (Sadiq Ali 1996). The island's fortifications and cannons, in no small part, allowed this community to rise as it did, serving as the active canvas on which the Siddi agency was painted.

Connectivities centered on enslavement show how people in diaspora over time can develop roots deep enough to empower despite their marginalized status. Focusing on technologies of connectivity rather than human agency does not allow us to explain the historical contexts under which people like Malik Ambar rose to positions of power. Admittedly, we often do not have historical records of the thoughts, feelings, and activities of marginalized groups. However, the archaeological record, as demonstrated in this chapter, often contributes these perspectives in ways that other records do not. The success of Malik Ambar and the Siddi community, however, does force us to consider the historical processes and actions enabling a dramatic rise from enslavement to rulership.

Conclusion

Islands are places where stories of people with "European, African, and Asian traditions have been violently brought together" (Hofmeyr 2007: 9). This characterizes the Indian Ocean basin. Island geographies and their landscape affordances provide a way to move beyond historicization and situate the broader human assemblage within the socio-ecological and political landscape. As Hauser (2021) illustrates, the everyday difficulties of enslaved people in Dominica can be mapped through the way water has been managed and perceived. Indeed, the study of "water, as a political, economic, and cultural matter" helps shed light on how enslaved people coped with the challenges of security, mobility, and belonging (Hauser 2021: 190; Haines and Hauser, this volume). Connectivity, viewed through the practical medium of water, can provide a means to illustrate fluidity between vastly different scales of human interaction—with each other and with a broad overarching phenomenon, such as politics, climate, and ecology.

Bibliography

Adas, Michael. 1989. *Machines as the Measure of Men: Science, Technology, and Ideologies of Western Dominance*. Cornell Studies in Comparative History. Ithaca: Cornell University Press.

Alders, Wolfgang. 2020. Preliminary Results of a 2019 Survey in Inland Zanzibar, Tanzania. *Nyame Akuma* 94: 38–45.

Ali, Omar H. 2016. *Malik Ambar: Power and Slavery across the Indian Ocean*. The World in a Life. New York: Oxford University Press.

Allen, Richard B. 1999. *Slaves, Freedmen and Indentured Laborers in Colonial Mauritius*. Cambridge, Mass.: Cambridge University Press.

———. 2002. "Maroonage and Its Legacy in Mauritius and in the Colonial Plantation World." *Outre-Mers. Revue d'histoire* 89(336): 131–52.

———. 2008. "The Constant Demand of the French: The Mascarene Slave Trade and the Worlds of the Indian Ocean and Atlantic during the Eighteenth and Nineteenth Centuries." *Journal of African History* 49(1): 43–72.

———. 2010. "Satisfying the 'Want for Labouring People': European Slave Trading in the Indian Ocean, 1500–1850." *Journal of World History* 21(1): 45–73.

———. 2012. "European Slave Trading, Abolitionism, and 'New Systems of Slavery' in the Indian Ocean." *PORTAL Journal of Multidisciplinary International Studies* 9(1): Indian Ocean Traffic.

Alpers, Edward A., Gwyn Campbell, and Michael Salman. 2007. *Resisting Bondage in Indian Ocean Africa and Asia*. Routledge Studies in Slave and Post-Slave Societies and Cultures 2. London: Routledge.

Anderson, Atholl. 2004. "Islands of Ambivalence." In *Voyages of Discovery: The Archaeology of Islands*, 251–73.

Anderson, Clare. 2019. "Convicts, Commodities, and Connections in British Asia and the Indian Ocean, 1789–1866." *International Review of Social History* 64 (S27): 205–27.

Baldacchino, Godfrey. 2007. "Islands as Novelty Sites." *Geographical Review* 97(2): 165–74.

Baužytė, E. 2019. "Making and Trading Iron in the Swahili World: An Archaeometallurgical Study of Iron Production Technologies, Their Role, and Exchange Networks in 500–1500 CE Coastal Tanzania." Unpublished PhD, Aarhus University.

Berg, Ina. 2010. "Re-Capturing the Sea: The Past and Future of 'Island Archaeology' in Greece." *Shima* 4(1): 16–26.

Bhabha, Homi K. 1994. *The Location of Culture*. London: Routledge.

Bishara, Fahad Ahmad. 2017. *A Sea of Debt: Law and Economic Life in the Western Indian Ocean, 1780–1950*. Asian Connections. Cambridge, U.K.: Cambridge University Press.

Boomert, Arie, and Alistair J. Bright. 2007. "Island Archaeology: In Search of a New Horizon." *Island Studies Journal* 2(1): 3–26.

Breen, Colin, Wes Forsythe, and Daniel Rhodes. 2016. "A Maritime Archaeological Survey of Stonetown, Zanzibar." *International Journal of Nautical Archaeology* 45(1): 191–99.

Broodbank, Cyprian. 2000. *An Island Archaeology of the Early Cyclades*. Cambridge, U.K.: Cambridge University Press.

———. 2008. "Not Waving but Drowning." *Journal of Island and Coastal Archaeology* 3(1): 72–76.

Calaon, Diego, and Corin Forrest. 2018. "Archaeology and the Process of Heritage Construction in Mauritius." In *Connecting Continents: Archaeology and History in the Indian Ocean World,* edited by Krish Seetah, 253–90. Athens: Ohio University Press.

Calaon, Diego, Krish Seetah, Jacob Morales, and Saša Čaval. 2012. "Archaeological Insights of the 'Indenture Experience': The Case of Trianon Barracks." In *Angajé: Explorations into the History, Society and Culture of Indentured Immigrants and Their Descendants in Mauritius,* vol. 2, 121–38. Port Louis, Mauritius: Aapravasi Ghat Trust Fund.

Campbell, Gwyn. 2003. "Introduction: Slavery and Other Forms of Unfree Labour in the Indian Ocean World." *Slavery and Abolition* 24(2): ix–xxxii.

———. 2004. "Introduction: Slavery and Other Forms of Unfree Labour in the Indian Ocean World." In *Structure of Slavery in Indian Ocean Africa and Asia,* edited by Gwyn Campbell, vii–xxxi. London: Routledge.

———. 2013. *Abolition and Its Aftermath in the Indian Ocean Africa and Asia.* London: Routledge.

———. 2018. *Bondage and the Environment in the Indian Ocean World.* 1st edition. New York: Nature America.

———. 2019. *Africa and the Indian Ocean World from Early Times to circa 1900.* Cambridge, U.K.: Cambridge University Press.

Carter, Marina. 2006. "Slavery and Unfree Labour in the Indian Ocean." *History Compass* 4(5): 800–13.

Čaval, Saša. 2018. "Archaeology and Religious Syncretism in Mauritius." In *Connecting Continents: Archaeology and History in the Indian Ocean World,* edited by Krish Seetah, 230–52. Athens: Ohio University Press.

———. In press. "Layering Segregation in Life and Death: The Social and Environmental Role of the Bois Marchand Cemetery." *International Journal of Historical Archaeology.*

Chami, Felix. 2009. *Zanzibar and the Swahili Coast from c. 30,000 Years Ago.* Dar es Salaam: E&D Vision Pub.

Chaudhuri, Kirti N. 1985. *Trade and Civilisation in the Indian Ocean: An Economic History from the Rise of Islam to 1750.* Cambridge, U.K.: Cambridge University Press.

Cheke, Anthony. 2010. "The Timing of Arrival of Humans and Their Commensal Animals on Western Indian Ocean Oceanic Islands." *Phelsuma* 18: 38–69.

Chittick, H. Neville. 1960. "Preliminary Report on the Excavations at Kizimkazi Dimbani, Zanzibar." Annual Report for 1960. Division of Antiquities, Tanganyika.

Clarence-Smith, William Gervase. 2013. "The Economics of the Indian Ocean and Red Sea Slave Trades in the 19th Century: An Overview." In *The Economics of the Indian Ocean Slave Trade in the Nineteenth Century,* edited by William Gervase Clarence-Smith, 9–28. London: Routledge, Taylor & Francis Group.

Connah, Graham. 2007. "Historical Archaeology in Africa: An Appropriate Concept?" *African Archaeological Review* 24(1): 35–40.

Cooper, Frederick. 2002. "Decolonizing Situations: The Rise, Fall, and Rise of Colonial Studies, 1951–2001." *French Politics, Culture & Society* 20(2): 47–76.

Croucher, Sarah K. 2014. *Capitalism and Cloves: An Archaeology of Plantation Life on Nineteenth-Century Zanzibar.* New York: Springer.

Dawson, Helen. 2019. "Island Archaeology." In *Encyclopedia of Global Archaeology,* 1–8. Cham, Switzerland: Springer.

de Boer, Erik J., Rik Tjallingii, Maria I. Vélez, Kenneth F. Rijsdijk, Anouk Vlug, Gert-Jan Reichart, Amy L. Prendergast, et al. 2014. "Climate Variability in the SW Indian Ocean from an 8000-Yr Long Multi-Proxy Record in the Mauritian Lowlands Shows a Middle to Late Holocene Shift from Negative IOD-State to ENSO-State." *Quaternary Science Reviews* 86 (February): 175–89.

Declich, Francesca. 2018. *Translocal Connections across the Indian Ocean: Swahili Speaking Networks on the Move*. African Social Studies Series, vol. 37. Leiden: Brill.

Douglass, Kristina, and Jago Cooper. 2020. "Archaeology, Environmental Justice, and Climate Change on Islands of the Caribbean and Southwestern Indian Ocean." *Proceedings of the National Academy of Sciences* 117(15): 8254–62.

Eriksen, Thomas Hylland. 1993. "In Which Sense Do Cultural Islands Exist?" *Social Anthropology* 1(1b): 133–47. https://doi.org/10.1111/j.1469-8676.1993.tb00246.x

Erlandson, Jon M. 2008. "Isolation, Interaction, and Island Archaeology." *Journal of Island and Coastal Archaeology* 3(1): 83–86.

Faulkner, Patrick, Matthew Harris, Abdallah K. Ali, Othman Haji, Alison Crowther, Mark C. Horton, and Nicole L. Boivin. 2018. "Characterising Marine Mollusc Exploitation in the Eastern African Iron Age: Archaeomalacological Evidence from Unguja Ukuu and Fukuchani, Zanzibar." *Quaternary International* 471: 66–80.

Fitton, Tom. 2017. *Pushing the Boat Out: A Study of Spatial Organisation and Harbour Spaces in the Early Swahili Ports of the Zanzibar Archipelago, 550–1100 CE*. PhD diss., University of York.

———. 2018. "Zanzibar." In *The Swahili World,* edited by Adria LaViolette and Stephanie Wynne-Jones, 239–44. London: Routledge.

Fitton, Tom, and Stephanie Wynne-Jones. 2017. Understanding the Layout of Early Coastal Settlement at Unguja Ukuu, Zanzibar. *Antiquity* 91(359): 1268–84.

Fleisher, Jeffrey, and Adria LaViolette. 2013. "The Early Swahili Trade Village of Tumbe, Pemba Island, Tanzania, AD 600–950." *Antiquity* 87(338): 1151–68.

Floore, Pieter M., and Ranjith M. Jayasena. 2010. "In Want of Everything? Archaeological Perceptions of a Dutch Outstation on Mauritius (1638–1710)." *Post-Medieval Archaeology* 44(2): 320–40.

Fregel, Rosa, Krish Seetah, Eva Betancor, Nicolás M. Suárez, Diego Calaon, Saša Čaval, Anwar Janoo, and Jose Pestano. 2014. "Multiple Ethnic Origins of Mitochondrial DNA Lineages for the Population of Mauritius." *PloS One* 9(3): e93294.

Frere, William Edward, and Victor Alexander Williamson. 1875. *Report of the Royal Commissioners Appointed to Enquire into the Treatment of Immigrants in Mauritius: Presented to Both Houses of Parliament by Command of Her Majesty, 6th February 1875.* London: Printed by William Clowes and Sons. https://catalog.hathitrust.org/Record/001755360

Garlake, Peter S. 1966. *The Early Islamic Architecture of the East African Coast*. British Institute of History and Archaeology in East Africa Memoir, no 1. Nairobi and London: Published for the Institute by Oxford University Press.

Glassman, Jonathon. 2011. *War of Words, War of Stones: Racial Thought and Violence in Colonial Zanzibar*. Bloomington: Indiana University Press.

Haines, Julia Jong. 2019. "Landscape Transformation under Slavery, Indenture, and Imperial Projects in Bras d'Eau National Park, Mauritius." *Journal of African Diaspora Archaeology and Heritage* 7(2): 131–64.

———. 2020. "Mauritian Indentured Labour and Plantation Household Archaeology." *Azania: Archaeological Research in Africa* 55(4): 509–27.

———. 2021. "Shaping Landscapes: Environmental History, Plantation Management and Colonial Legacies in Mauritius." *International Journal of Historical Archaeology*, October 1. https:doi.org/10.1007/s10761-021-00629-0

Hauser, Mark W. 2011. "Routes and Roots of Empire: Pots, Power, and Slavery in the 18th-Century British Caribbean." *American Anthropologist* 113(3): 431–47.

Hauser, Mark. 2021. *Mapping Water in Dominica: Enslavement and Environment under Colonialism.* Seattle: University of Washington Press.

Hazell, Alastair. 2011. *The Last Slave Market: Dr. John Kirk and the Struggle to End the East African Slave Trade.* London: Constable.

Hofmeyr, Isabel. 2007. "The Black Atlantic Meets the Indian Ocean: Forging New Paradigms of Transnationalism for the Global South—Literary and Cultural Perspectives." *Social Dynamics* 33(2): 3–32.

Home, Robert, and Anthony D. King. 2016. "Urbanism and Master Planning: Configuring the Colonial City." In *Architecture and Urbanism in the British Empire,* edited by George Alexander Bremner, 51–85. Oxford: Oxford University Press.

Horden, Peregrine, and Nicholas Purcell. 2000. *The Corrupting Sea: A Study of Mediterranean History.* Hoboken, N.J.: Wiley-Blackwell.

Jasdanwalla, Faaeza. 2015. "The Invincible Fort of the Nawabs of Janjira." *Journal of African Diaspora Archaeology and Heritage* 4(1): 72–91.

Jayasuriya, Shihan de Silva. 2009. "African Identity in Asia: Cultural Effects of Forced Migration." *African Diaspora Archaeology Newsletter* 12(3): 14.

Juma, Abdurahman. 2004. *Unguja Ukuu on Zanzibar: An Archaeological Study of Early Urbanism.* PhD diss., Afrikansk och jämförande arkeologi, Uppsala University, Sweden.

Kempf, Michael. 2020. "From Landscape Affordances to Landscape Connectivity: Contextualizing an Archaeology of Human Ecology." *Archaeological and Anthropological Sciences* 12(8): 1–12.

Kessy, Emanuel T. 2003. "Iron Age Settlement Patterns and Economic Change on Zanzibar and Pemba Islands." In *East African Archaeology: Foragers, Potters, Smiths, and Traders,* edited by Chapurukha Kusimba and Sibel Kusimba, 117–32. Philadelphia: University of Pennsylvania Museum of Archaeology and Anthropology.

Kimberley, Therese, and Banka Nidhi. 2018. "Moulin à Poudre—Cultural Landscape." Heritage Trail-Story Map, ESRI (May 25, 2018). https://www.arcgis.com/apps/MapTour/index.html?appid=16b32eb0447546f8b1263e5d58c03739

Kirkman, James. 1957. "Historical Archaeology in Kenya 1948–56." *Antiquaries Journal* 37(1–2): 16–28.

Kleppe, E. Johansen. 2001. "Archaeological Investigations at Kizimkazi Dimbani." In *Islam in East Africa, New Sources: Archives, Manuscripts and Written Historical Sources, Oral History, Archaeology, International Colloquium, Rome 2–4 December 1999,* edited by Biancamaria Scarcia Amoretti, 361–84. Rome: Herder.

Kourampas, Nikos, Ceri Shipton, William Mills, Ruth Tibesasa, Henrietta Horton, Mark Horton, Mary Prendergast, et al. 2015. "Late Quaternary Speleogenesis and Landscape Evolution in a Tropical Carbonate Island: Pango La Kuumbi (Kuumbi Cave), Zanzibar." *International Journal of Speleology* 44(3): 293–314.

Kusimba, Chapurukha M. 1999. *The Rise and Fall of Swahili States*. Walnut Creek, Calif.: AltaMira Press.

———. 2004. "Archaeology of Slavery in East Africa." *African Archaeological Review* 21(2): 59–88.

Kusimba, Chapurukha M., and Sibel B. Kusimba. 2017. "Mosaics: Rethinking African Connections in Coastal and Hinterland Kenya." In *The Swahili World*, edited by Stephanie Wynne-Jones and Adia LaViolette, 403–18. London: Routledge.

Kusimba, Chapurukha M., Sibel B. Kusimba, and Laure Dussubieux. 2013. "Beyond the Coastalscapes: Preindustrial Social and Political Networks in East Africa." *African Archaeological Review* 30(4): 399–426.

LaBianca, Øystein Sakala, and Sandra Arnold Scham (eds.). 2016. *Connectivity in Antiquity: Globalization as a Long-Term Historical Process*. Approaches to Archaeology. London: Equinox Publishing, 2006.

Lane, Paul J. 2018. "The Archaeology of Colonial Encounters in Coastal East Africa: Recent Developments and Continuing Conceptual Challenges." In *Connecting Continents: Archaeology and History in the Indian Ocean World*, edited by Krish Seetah, 143–70. Athens: Ohio University Press.

LaViolette, Adria, and Jeffrey Fleisher. 2009. "The Urban History of a Rural Place: Swahili Archaeology on Pemba Island, Tanzania, 700–1500 AD." *International Journal of African Historical Studies* 42(3): 433–55.

Lightfoot, Emma, Saša Čaval, Diego Calaon, Joanne Appleby, Jonathan Santana, Alessandra Cianciosi, Rosa Fregel, and Krish Seetah. 2020. "Colonialism, Slavery and 'The Great Experiment': Carbon, Nitrogen and Oxygen Isotope Analysis of Le Morne and Bois Marchand Cemeteries, Mauritius." *Journal of Archaeological Science: Reports* 31: https://doi.org/10.1016/j.jasrep.2020.102335

Mahmud, Tayyab. 2012. "Cheaper than a Slave: Indentured Labor, Colonialism, and Capitalism Symposium." *Whittier Law Review* 34(2): 215–44.

Manfio, Stefania, and Yann von Arnim. 2020. "Maritime Archaeology of Slave Ships: Reviews and Future Directions for Mauritius and the Indian Ocean." *Azania: Archaeological Research in Africa* 55(4): 492–508.

Mbeki, Linda, and Matthias van Rossum. 2017. "Private Slave Trade in the Dutch Indian Ocean World: A Study into the Networks and Backgrounds of the Slavers and the Enslaved in South Asia and South Africa." *Slavery and Abolition* 38(1): 95–116.

Metwalli, Ibrahim A., Nicolas Bigourdan, and Yann von Arnim. 2007. "Interim Report of a Shipwreck at Pointe Aux Feuilles, Mauritius: 'Le Coureur' (1818), an Illegal Slave Trader?" *Journal of the Australasian Institute for Maritime Archaeology* 31: 74–81.

Miller, Joseph C. 2003. "A Theme in Variations: A Historical Schema of Slaving in the Atlantic and Indian Ocean Regions." *Slavery and Abolition* 24(2): 169–94.

Moree, Perry J. 1998. *A Concise History of Dutch Mauritius, 1598–1710: A Fruitful and Healthy Land*. Studies from the International Institute for Asian Studies. London: Kegan Paul International.

Mungur-Medhi, Jayshree. 2016. "The Reconstitution of Aapravasi Ghat, a Nineteenth-Century Immigration Depot in the Capital City of Port Louis, Mauritius, through Archaeology." *International Journal of Historical Archaeology* 20(4): 781–803.

———. In press. "Archaeological Evidence of Landscape and Environmental Changes Due to Iron and Gunpowder Production in Mauritius." *International Journal of Historical Archaeology.*

Nicolini, Beatrice. 2018. *The Historical Relations between Oman and Balochistan in the Indian Ocean.* Milano: EDUCatt.

Nicolini, Beatrice, and Penelope-Jane Watson. 2004. *Makran, Oman, and Zanzibar: Three-Terminal Cultural Corridor in the Western Indian Ocean, 1799–1856.* Islam in Africa, no. 3. Leiden: Brill.

Oas, Sarah E., and Mark W. Hauser. 2018. "The Political Ecology of Plantations from the Ground Up." *Environmental Archaeology* 23(1): 4–12.

Oka, Rahul, and Chapurukha M. Kusimba. 2008. "Siddi as Mercenary or as African Success Story on the West Coast of India." In *India in Africa, Africa in India: Indian Ocean Cosmopolitanisms,* edited by John C. Hawley, 203–30. Bloomington: Indiana University Press.

Perkins, John. 2015. "The Indian Ocean and Swahili Coast Coins, International Networks and Local Developments." *Afriques,* no. 06. https://doi.org/10.4000/afriques.1769

Pettegrew, David K. 2013. "Connectivity." In *The Encyclopedia of Ancient History,* edited by Roger S. Bagnall, Kai Brodersen, Craige B. Champion, Andrew Erskine, and Sabine R. Huebner, 1st edition, 1708–11. Malden, Mass.: Wiley-Blackwell.

Pitts, Martin, and Miguel John Versluys. 2014. *Globalisation and the Roman World: World History, Connectivity and Material Culture.* Cambridge, U.K.: Cambridge University Press.

Popović, Alexandre. 1999. *The Revolt of African Slaves in Iraq in the 3rd/9th Century.* Princeton Series on the Middle East. Princeton, N.J.: Markus Wiener Publishers.

Prendergast, M. E., E. M. Quintana Morales, A. Crowther, M. C. Horton, and N. L. Boivin. 2017. "Dietary Diversity on the Swahili Coast: The Fauna from Two Zanzibar Trading Locales." *International Journal of Osteoarchaeology* 27(4): 621–37.

Prendergast, M. E., H. Rouby, P. Punnwong, R. Marchant, A. Crowther, N. Kourampas, C. Shipton, M. Walsh, K. Lambeck, and N. L. Boivin. 2016. "Continental Island Formation and the Archaeology of Defaunation on Zanzibar, Eastern Africa." *PLoS One* 11(2): e0149565.

Rainbird, Paul. 2007. *The Archaeology of Islands.* Cambridge, U.K.: Cambridge University Press.

Rødland, Henriette. 2021. *Swahili Social Landscapes: Material Expressions of Identity, Agency, and Labour in Zanzibar, 1000–1400 CE.* PhD diss., Department of Archaeology and Ancient History, Uppsala University, Sweden.

———. 2022. "Crafting Swahili Beads: Exploring a New Glass Bead Assemblage from Northern Zanzibar, Tanzania." *African Archaeological Review,* March 2022: 1–22.

Rødland, Henriette, Stephanie Wynne-Jones, Marilee Wood, and Jeffrey Fleisher. 2020. "No Such Thing as Invisible People: Toward an Archaeology of Slavery at the Fifteenth-Century Swahili Site of Songo Mnara." *Azania* 55(4): 439–57.

Sadiq Ali, Shanti. 1996. *The African Dispersal in the Deccan: From Medieval to Modern Times*. New Delhi: Orient Longman.

Said, Edward W. 1979. *Orientalism: Western Conceptions of the Orient*. New York: Vintage.

Sarathi, Akshay. 2018a. "Shellfish Exploitation at Kuumbi Cave, Zanzibar (c. 11kya–20th Cen. CE): A Preliminary Study." In *Early Maritime Cultures in East Africa and the Western Indian Ocean: Papers from a Conference Held at the University of Wisconsin-Madison (African Studies Program), 23–24 October 2015, with Additional Contributions*, edited by Akshay Sarathi, 171–84. Oxford: Archaeopress.

Sarathi, Akshay (ed.). 2018b. *Early Maritime Cultures in East Africa and the Western Indian Ocean: Papers from a Conference Held at the University of Wisconsin-Madison (African Studies Program), 23–24 October 2015, with Additional Contributions*. Oxford: Archaeopress.

———. In press. *A Preliminary Report on the 2018 excavations of Kizimkazi Dimbani, Zanzibar*.

Sarathi, Akshay, Jonathan Walz, and Laure Dussubieux. 2022. "Glass Beads at Unguja Ukuu in the Late 1st Millennium CE: Results from the 2018 Excavation in Zanzibar." In *Glass Bead Technology, Chronology, and Exchange: LA-ICP-MS Glass Compositions from the Field Museum's Elemental Analysis Facility*, edited by L. Dussubieux and Heather Walder, 287–304. Studies in Archaeological Sciences. Leuven, Belgium: University of Leuven Press.

Schmidt, Peter R. 2016. "Historical Archaeology in East Africa: Past Practice and Future Directions." *Journal of African History* 57(2): 183–94.

Schmidt, Peter R., and Jonathan R. Walz. 2007. "Re-Representing African Pasts through Historical Archaeology." *American Antiquity* 72(1): 53–70.

Schnepel, Burkhard, and Edward A. Alpers (eds.). 2018. *Connectivity in Motion: Island Hubs in the Indian Ocean World*. Palgrave Series in Indian Ocean World Studies. Palgrave Macmillan.

Seetah, Krish. 2015a. "Objects Past, Objects Present: Materials, Resistance and Memory from the Le Morne Old Cemetery, Mauritius." *Journal of Social Archaeology* 15(2): 233–53.

———. 2015b. "The Archaeology of Mauritius." *Antiquity* 89: 346.

———. 2015c. "'The Minister Will Tell the Nation': The Role of the Media for Archaeology in Mauritius." *World Archaeology* 47(2): 285–98.

———. 2016. "Contextualizing Complex Social Contact: Mauritius, a Microcosm of Global Diaspora." *Cambridge Archaeological Journal* 26(2): 265–83.

Seetah, Krish (ed.). 2018. *Connecting Continents: Archaeology and History in the Indian Ocean World*. Athens: Ohio University Press.

Seetah, Krish, and Richard B. Allen. 2018. "Interdisciplinary Ripples across the Indian Ocean." In *Connecting Continents: Archaeology and History in the Indian Ocean World*, edited by Krish Seetah, 1–29. Athens: Ohio University Press.

Seetah, Krish, Thomas Birch, Diego Calaon, and Saša Čaval. 2015. "Colonial Iron in Context: The Trianon Slave Shackle from Mauritius." *Archaeological and Anthropological Sciences* 9(3): 419–30.

Seetah, Krish, Diego Calaon, Saša Čaval, Alessandra Cianciosi, and Aleksander Pluskowski. 2018. "The Materiality of Multiculturalism." *The Mauritian Paradox: Fifty Years of Development, Diversity and Democracy,* 155–90. Réduit: University of Mauritius Press.

Seetah, Krish, Saša Čaval, Alessandra Cianciosi, and Diego Calaon. Unpub. Bras d'Eau Interim Report: Report Covering the 2014 Season of Work.

Seetah, Krish, and Justin Leidwanger. In press. *Across the Shore: Integrating Perspectives on Heritage.* When the Land Meets the Sea (series). Berlin: Springer Science and Business Media.

Seetah, Krish, Stefania Manfio, Andrea Balbo, R. Helen Farr, and F. B. Florens. 2022. "Colonization during Colonialism: Developing a Framework to Assess the Rapid Ecological Transformation of Mauritius's Pristine Ecosystem." *Front. Ecol. Evol.* 10:791539. doi: 10.3389/fevo.2022.791539.

Sen, Satadru. 2010. *Savagery and Colonialism in the Indian Ocean: Power, Pleasure and the Andaman Islanders.* Routledge/Edinburgh South Asian Studies Series. London: Routledge.

Sheriff, Abdul, Vijayalakshmi Teelock, Saada Omar Wahab, and Satyendra Peerthum. 2016. *Transition from Slavery in Zanzibar and Mauritius.* Dakar, Senegal: Council for the Development of Social Science Research in Africa (CODESRIA).

Shipton, Ceri, Alison Crowther, Nikos Kourampas, Mary E. Prendergast, Mark Horton, Katerina Douka, Jean-Luc Schwenninger, et al. 2016. "Reinvestigation of Kuumbi Cave, Zanzibar, Reveals Later Stone Age Coastal Habitation, Early Holocene Abandonment and Iron Age Reoccupation." *Azania: Archaeological Research in Africa* 51(2): 197–233.

Smith, Frederick H. 2009. Review of *The Archaeology of Islands,* by Paul Rainbird. *American Antiquity* 74(3): 591–92.

Stanziani, Alessandro. 2014. *Sailors, Slaves, and Immigrants: Bondage in the Indian Ocean World, 1750–1914.* New York: Palgrave Macmillan.

Sulas, Federica, Søren Munch Kristiansen, and Stephanie Wynne-Jones. 2019. "Soil Geochemistry, Phytoliths and Artefacts from an Early Swahili Daub House, Unguja Ukuu, Zanzibar." *Journal of Archaeological Science* 103 (March): 32–45.

Summers, Geoffrey D. 2011. Excavated Artifacts from the Aapravasi Ghat World Heritage Site. Unpublished report commissioned by Aapravasi Ghat Trust Fund, Port Louis, Mauritius.

———. 2021. "Landscapes, Seascapes, and Coastal Defenses: A Case Study from Southeast Mauritius." *International Journal of Historical Archaeology,* July. https://doi.org/10.1007/s10761-021-00607-6

Summers, Geoffrey D., and Françoise Summers. 2008. "A Note on the Rockcut Ditch on Ile de La Passe, Mauritius." *Azania: Journal of the British Institute in Eastern Africa* 43(1): 124–32.

Talhami, Ghada Hashem. 1977. "The Zanj Rebellion Reconsidered." *International Journal of African Historical Studies* 10(3): 443–61.

Teelock, Vijayalakshmi. 2017. "A Unique Site in the Former French Colony of Isle de France: The Powder Mill Complex." *Entreprises et Histoire,* no. 2: 76–87.

Toledano, Ehud R. 2011. *African Communities in Asia and the Mediterranean: Identities between Integration and Conflict.* Trenton, N.J.: Africa World Press.

Toorawa, Shawkat (ed.). 2007. "The Medieval Waqwaq Islands and the Mascarenes." In *The Western Indian Ocean: Essays on Islands and Islanders*, 49–66. Port Louis, Mauritius: Hassam Toorawa Trust.

Vaughan, Megan. 2005. *Creating the Creole Island: Slavery in Eighteenth-Century Mauritius*. Durham, N.C.: Duke University Press.

Vitousek, Peter M. 2002. "Oceanic Islands as Model Systems for Ecological Studies." *Journal of Biogeography* 29(5–6): 573–82.

Walz, Jonathan, and Philip Gooding. 2021. "Reality and Representation of Eastern Africa's Past: Archaeology and History Redress the 'Coast-Inland Dichotomy.'" *African Studies Quarterly* 20(4): 56–85.

Wilson, Brian C., and Mark W. Hauser. 2016. "Toward a South Asian Historical Archaeology." *Historical Archaeology* 50(4): 7–21.

Wynne-Jones, Stephanie, Federica Sulas, Welmoed A. Out, Søren Munch Kristiansen, Tom Fitton, Abdallah K. Ali, and Jesper Olsen. 2021. "Urban Chronology at a Human Scale on the Coast of East Africa in the 1st Millennium AD." *Journal of Field Archaeology*, 46(1): 21–35.

5

Healthcare Inequality and Reticence in the Mascarenes

The Contribution of Historical Archaeology

Saša Čaval and Alessandra Cianciosi

Archaeology at the Intersection of Labor Migration, Health, and Gender

This chapter reconstructs and analyzes the management of health primarily for women, and men who, either forcibly or voluntarily, emigrated from their place of origin to the islands of Réunion (Île de Bourbon) and Mauritius (Île de France) in the centuries between 1639 and 1920.[1] Understanding how health management and public healthcare developed in policy and practice during historical periods, characterized by a massive movement of people in the Indian Ocean World, provides insight into this region's cultural and political characteristics.

Social anthropologists identify five intertwined dimensions of modern migration infrastructure: commercial, regulatory, technological, humanitarian, and social. Their entanglement is key to understanding the infrastructure of historical and modern migrations (Xiang and Lindquist 2014). While social scientists within modern migration studies call for research on broader societal transformations, archaeologists focus on migrants or migration as behavior as the primary subject (van Dommelen 2014). The experience of labor migration, with all its infrastructure, has always been gendered. In modern times female labor migration waves have been larger than those of males (Xiang and Lindquist 2014), but that was not the case historically, especially since the initiation of contract-based servitude in the 1830s and 1840s (Allen 2004: 58). This positioning chapter presents a historical and archaeological perspective on predominantly unfree women's involvement in and exposure to healthcare (or lack thereof) as well as their engagement in health issues, such as well-being, prevention, and protection. It also explores the gendered dimensions of a specific health management infrastructure, that of quarantine stations (see Cianciosi et al. 2022). This analysis aims to highlight the value of historical archaeology and offer a distinct perspective on gendered healthcare in the colonial world.

Modern health policymaking in the context of migration is generally viewed in terms of the threat posed to public health or from a rights-based approach focusing on health hazards and the associated service challenges that migrants face. Both public health and human rights perspectives stem from our past, the most recent from shared historical labor immigration experiences (Schrover et al. 2008; Guchteniere and Pécoudet 2009; Ambrosini and Van der Leun 2015; see also Seetah et al., this volume). The health control and disease prevention measures introduced in the medieval period and used in European colonies throughout the early modern period remain in effect today. They have either been used continuously or practiced periodically as necessity dictated (Gushulak and MacPherson 2011; Tognotti 2013). The medieval quarantine practices prioritized public health security and communicable disease control, relying heavily on monitoring and disinfection, especially of wares transported by ships. The rights-based perspective is more recent and grounded in medical ethics. It recognizes migrants' vulnerability to interpersonal and occupational hazards, social exclusion, and discrimination as well as the importance of universal access and culturally competent healthcare services (Zimmerman et al. 2011). Fundamental human rights pertaining to medical care in the labor world emerged from the abuse that enslaved and indentured people endured during the age of modern colonialism (CESCR 2000; Stanziani 2012; UN General Assembly 2015).

Health Conditions in the Mascarenes

Slavery and the Post-Emancipation Period

Sketching healthcare conditions in the Mascarenes during slavery (1639–1833) is challenging for several reasons. The neighboring islands of Réunion and Mauritius are the largest within the archipelago. Their roles in the colonial past were quite different due to dissimilar spheres of European influence: continuous French rule for the former and a transition from French to British rule for the latter. Nevertheless, divergences between these sister islands' colonial social structures (Pomfret 2009) and decolonization processes (Smith 1978) have been emphasized more than differences in their public health management (Boodhoo 2019: 57–62).

Opposite to the slave period in the British Caribbean, where plantation hospitals existed from the early 1700s on (Wright 1966: 29; Sheridan 1985:

272; Veit et al. 2022), in the Mascarenes, healthcare was a private affair except for rare dispensaries dedicated mainly to free people, if not exclusively to Europeans. The enslaved and the lowest free social classes were almost entirely excluded from sanitary and health inspections. Plantation owners had slaves primarily for economic development, and the latter's health depended on individual owners' motivation and compassion (Boodhoo 2019: 20–32). Economically, it was more convenient to obtain new slaves than to maintain the health of those already owned, and the growing demand for sugar made captive people endure even harder work (Blonigen 2004).

Comparative studies in the Caribbean and North American colonies demonstrate that relentless work leading to high mortality and undesired procreation were a primary inhibitor of increased exploitation. The lives of enslaved women on Mascarenes plantations were probably comparable to the harsh conditions of enslaved women on Atlantic colonial sugar plantations. Captive women opposed reproduction; thus, a new pool of labor could not be generated (Bush 1993; Wood 1997; Burnard 2004: 181). Apart from women not owning their own bodies, the resistance stemmed from the smaller number of women than men and the poor physical condition of women, who often could not bear a pregnancy. In the West Indies, especially on the Jamaican sugar plantations, women were constantly subjected to harsh plantation work and sexual exploitation (Bush 1993: 85; Ross and Solinger 2017; Turner 2017; Barnes 2021; Veit et al. 2022). The complex and hierarchical division of labor on large plantations valued men more than women because of the perception that men had crafts skills and ability to work in the sugar mill's semi-industrial environment. The main work for women outside an estate's household was in the sugar cane fields, where they formed close to half the workforce. Women faced the same backbreaking work, miseries, and punishments as men, with obvious implications for their well-being, particularly during pregnancy. Similar practices can be assumed in Mauritius, where contemporary sources reveal a high rate of miscarriages and abortions among enslaved women. The nineteenth-century essayist Eugène Bernard (1834) reports that enslaved Malagasy were apt to use birth control and abortion to prevent pregnancies (see also Kuczynski 1949: 869; Turner 2017; Barnes 2021). Such actions already existed during French governance and presented such a big problem that in 1778 an edict of the Île de France's colonial government dispensed the death penalty for women who concealed their pregnancies (Vaughan 2000: 420–21). The government assumed that by doing so, women sought to abort the child, and they punished the women (Kuczynski 1949: 869; Benedict 1980: 140).

Obtaining enslaved people after the prohibition of the slave trade in the

British Empire in 1807 was not problematic because the illegal trade ensured their continuing availability (Allen 2001, 2014). Demographic studies of the transitional period between the slave trade (1807) and the abolition of slavery (1833) in Mauritius and its dependencies reveal no improvement in the health conditions of slaves and formerly enslaved people. Despite inaccuracies in statistical data, resulting from the illegal importation of enslaved people, the data reveal a decline in the enslaved population, probably a result of precarious nutritional conditions and the spread of diseases, such as cholera in 1819 and smallpox in 1820 (Parahoo 1986; Reddi and Sookrajowa 2019: 1754–57). Shifting to an indentured labor system seemed a suitable and innovative way to counter the diminishing number of enslaved people. Because indentured laborers had to renew their work contracts periodically, plantation owners retained the possibility of continued exploitation. This transition resulted in the implementation of transportation for South and Southeast Asian immigrants and, hence, a profound change in trade routes (Amrith 2011).

Indenture Period: Female Health between Prevention and Contagion

Although after the abolition of slavery, the labor world changed, immigration remained prevalent in the labor market. In the mid-nineteenth century intercontinental transportation of indentured laborers from the Indian Ocean rim and beyond escalated. Indentured immigrants, primarily from India (Calcutta, Madras, Bombay), were brought to work on Mauritian sugar estates, while in Réunion the number of workers from Africa remained substantial (Stanziani 2013: 1230–36). The indenture system's recruitment infrastructure was initially nonexistent, with informal agents drafting laborers by any means. The Indian investigation of the Mauritian labor trade in 1838–39 uncovered misrepresentation, coercive recruitment, exploitation, and abuse of laborers, which led to the suspension of all Indian overseas labor migration (Northrup 1995: 62). A call for better regulations and appropriate legislation around worker mobility was enacted (Stanziani 2013, 2015). In 1842 for Mauritius and 1849 for Réunion, after the end of the ban on Indian emigration, the government-based recruitment system was established. Verifying agencies were placed at every stage, from the district level to the port of embarkation, overseeing the free-will migration (Northrup 1995: 62; Mishra 2009). At the port of embarkation, indentured laborers were subjected to a physical medical examination by the port's depot surgeon. They had to be healthy, disease-free, and vaccinated against smallpox. After being vaccinated and certified not to have any "bodily and mental disease," women were issued a *Woman's Emigration Pass,* which included personal details such as their name, father's name, name of next-of-kin, marital status, caste, district, taluq (an Indian estate), village, age, height, and bodily marks (Boodhoo 2010: 79–82; Deb Roy 2017: 107–9).

The earliest laborers from India were primarily male farmers searching for a better life (Dey 2014; Boodhoo 2010). Later, family groups migrated, increasing the proportion of women in Mauritius (Carter and Ng Foong Kwong 1997: 81–82). The gender disparity in the indentured labor population was high in the beginning (Fig. 5.1). In 1839 the ratio of males to females was 56:1. In 1857 Mauritius set up an immigrant family policy and introduced recruitment laws specifying that at least 35 percent of immigrants had to be women. The percentage increased to 40 percent in 1858, and 50 percent from 1859 to 1865 (Allen 1999: 162). Réunion set up a similar policy much later (Marimoutou-Oberlé 2015: 329). During the indenture period, the number of women in the Mascarene islands increased, and their social roles were gradually recognized (Allen 2011; Sénèque and De Montille 2021).

The geographical and structural span of the system of indentured labor was wide, involving immigrants' land of origin, port of embarkation, transport ship, landing port in the destination colony, and, ultimately, the estate. A range of actors were involved. Planters, with the collaboration of the local administration, were responsible for workers' transportation. Emigration agencies—initially individuals (*sirdars, duffadors, maistries, arkattias*) and later government licensed agencies—recruited workers who were principally from Bengal.[1] Infrastructure, such as dispensaries, hospitals, depots, and stations through which the immigrants had to pass, embodied and manifested colonial power. Newly appointed officials oversaw regulations surrounding the voyage as well as those concerning health institutions. These regulations, often only theoretical, concerned space, mobility, the supply of food and water, ventilation, disinfection of buildings, the use of drugs, and the management of cures (Desai and Vahed 2010: 19–35).

The colonial state viewed workers' bodies as a crucial part of progressive and advantageous production processes (Hurgobin 2016: 4). Since workers' health determined productivity, standardized medical care to prevent the spread of disease, which predominantly affected the working classes, was organized and soon became an instrument to control laborers' mobility within the island. At the embarkation ports, men were subjected to a thorough inspection, where the sickliest were rejected. Women received a more superficial examination, even when infected with cholera, typhoid, and venereal disease (Tinker 1974: 38).

Each ship had an appointed, qualified doctor on board to examine emigrants before embarkation and to oversee their health during the voyage. They subjected immigrants to a medical inspection twice daily and attended

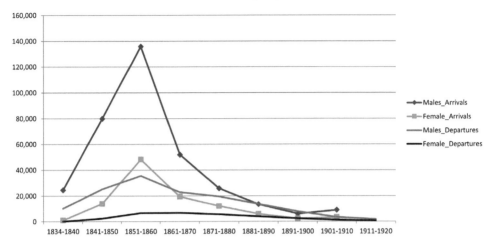

Figure 5.1. Arrivals and departures of Indian immigrants to Mauritius, from 1834 to 1920 (elaborated by A. Cianciosi from Hazareesingh 1966: 248).

to their medical needs (Anderson 2009). Crammed conditions on the ships allowed each immigrant about six by two feet of space.[2] People were divided as per their civil status: single women housed in the afterpart of the ship, married couples at the center, and single men at the ship's forepart. Men and women had different bathing days, during which sails partitioned off separate places on the ship (about South Africa, see Meer 1980: 347). The latrines were also gender-divided. To use the latrine on the deck, a married woman was accompanied by her husband, while single women generally went in groups, two or three together. Indentured women were subjected to sexual assault, discrimination, and ill-treatment (see Mishra 2009 regarding Mauritius; for Natal, South Africa, see Meer 1980: 118–69; Hiralal 2016: 47). When the number of indentured women increased, some gender-based measures were introduced. For example, because men occasionally complained about or rejected a doctor's inspection of women, a female immigrant was selected and paid to act as a nurse to help the medical officer take care of women on board some ships (Meer 1980: 343, 370–71).

Cemeteries as a Qualitative and Social Reflection of Life

Archaeological research on cemeteries in Mauritius provides essential insight into the health conditions and physical stress laborers endured in the past and a colonial infrastructure in handling the deceased, particularly during high mortality events. Investigations of the Le Morne Old Cemetery (Fig. 5.2a), a post-emancipation cemetery in Mauritius, indicate that it was a burial ground for emancipated slaves and their descendants, organized in family groups, and used during the first few decades of the nineteenth century (Seetah 2010, 2015). The cemetery is dated by the four silver coins from an adult grave (gr. 7) into the first third of the nineteenth century; however, there is a strong possibility that the cemetery was also in use during the eighteenth century.

Quantitative data from the cemetery reveal high mortality rates in children. Fifty percent of the 28 individuals excavated were juveniles, predominantly infants (newborns) and children under seven. Most of the adults were women of 18–35 years—the most fertile period of a woman's life. These demographics suggest that the primary health risks for this community were pregnancy and childhood. Although a high rate of mortality among women (Stone 2016) and children (Corruccini et al. 1985; Scott 1999) is the norm in most archaeologically investigated cemeteries, especially in preindustrial communities, the mortality rate for young adult females and children of Le Morne seems particularly high when considering the low number of women documented in the community. Though this cemetery represents a free(d) community, we assume that the gender imbalance of the enslaved population directly correlates to the demographics during the first few years of the post-emancipation period. For example, the 1826 tax registration of the Le Morne Brabant estate lists five enslaved females and 27 men (Seetah 2010: 256; Argot-Nayekoo 2011). In Mauritius between 1811 and 1826, enslaved men outnumbered women by two to one; after that, the proportion of females began to increase (Kuczynski 1949: 760, 768). However, bioarcheological data from the cemetery offer a more comprehensive picture: the osteological and isotope analyses of eleven skeletons have demonstrated that the Le Morne population had been reasonably well nourished and fitted well into the expected stature of the Mauritian colonial population. The presence of caries and abscesses in the mouth suggests a highly cariogenic diet and poor dental hygiene, probably due to the consumption of maize and manioc—less likely sugar cane—as suggested by a carbon isotope analysis of tooth enamel (Appleby et al. 2014). Nevertheless, some pathological conditions include periosteal bone lesions, frequent in individuals with compromised immunity, and chronic illnesses, such as malnutrition and immune-deficiency diseases (Lightfoot et al. 2020; Santana 2012).

In mid-nineteenth-century Mauritius, following the abolition of slavery and the subsequent apprentice system, and due to the introduction of indentured labor, emancipated slaves or *gens de couleur libre* abandoned sugar estates. They preferred the towns, working as market gardeners, charcoal burners, small traders, and artisans, or they settled in remote uncultivated areas, where they became smallholders, guardians of cattle, and fishermen (Benedict 1980: 142; Allen 1999). The lack of evidence of stress and nutri-

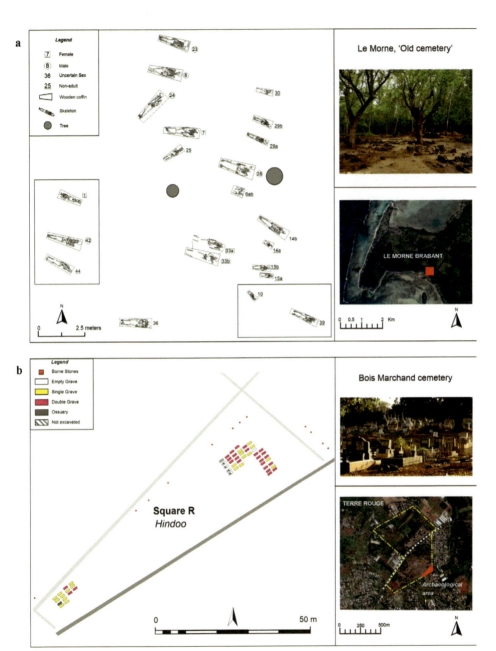

Figure 5.2. (*a*) Localization and plan of Le Morne Old Cemetery and (*b*) Bois Marchand cemetery with excavated graves (author: A. Cianciosi).

tional inadequacy in the community buried at Le Morne may suggest that the community sustained itself by farming and raising livestock, augmented by hunting and fishing. Despite an adequate diet, the high rate of mortality of non-adults would indicate that they died from infectious diseases, such as dysentery or cholera, which were constantly present on the island (Appleby et al. 2014; Lightfoot et al. 2020). Additionally, pregnancy continued to be the most critical moment in women's lives. Generally, adequate health conditions exhibit that although women toward the end of pregnancy may not have been required to do the most demanding work, they could still have suffered from general ill health related to the lack of a public health system.

Another lens is provided when comparing the birth rate of Indian and African female workers in Réunion Island in 1861–1862. The proportion of Indian women and newborn children is almost twofold that of African women and their newborn infants. Despite the absence of specific statistics, especially on birth mortality, this suggests that South Asian women had better health conditions than the descendants of enslaved individuals, at least during the first period of Indian immigration (De Nanteuil 1863; Marimoutou-Oberlé 2015: 510), which may have stemmed from better nutrition or social support from the community. Indentured workers self-organized into associations, such as *baitka* for Hindu communities and *jamma* (or madrassah) for Muslim communities (Benoit 1985; Čaval, in press). Such community associations were not uncommon among indentured diaspora (Hoefte 1987; Reddock 1994: 29; Jenkins 2005; Atta-Poku 1996; see Chand 2020 for Fiji).

The Bois Marchand cemetery in Mauritius is where mainly indentured workers found their last resting place (Fig. 5.2b). It was established in 1867 as a central burial ground during a malaria epidemic that wiped out over 72,000 people in three years (Pike 1873: 110). The cemetery served a population of a much wider area than Le Morne, including those who died at the civil hospital in Port Louis. It therefore contains a cross section of the island's population. Bois Marchand is a systematically organized public burial ground, sectioned into plots according to religious denomination. Apart from a few vocational plots (police, military), neither gender nor social classifications were used to allocate the grave (Čaval 2023). Due to the extraordinary ability of red ferritic soil to destroy biological material, including human remains, the osteological analysis is limited and likely biased. However, preserved remains do evince osteoarthritis of the axial skeleton, hip, and knee, squatting facets on long bones, infectious diseases like osteomyelitis or syphilis, and a high prevalence of dental caries and calculus (Santana and Cabrera 2016; Lightfoot et al. 2020). The poor preservation of human remains also impacts collagen isotope analysis, as diagenesis could cause changes in the stable isotope ratios of bone and dentine collagen. Indeed, dentine samples were taken partly as a precaution against poor collagen preservation since teeth tend to show better preservation than bone (Lightfoot et al. 2020). Thus, contrary to the analysis of the Le Morne cemetery, the bioarchaeological data from the Bois Marchand cemetery does not reveal much about health management or gender-related health conditions in Mauritius in the second half of the nineteenth century; however, unlike Le Morne, detailed records were maintained and archived for Bois Marchand. The Bois Marchand Cemetery Archive (1867–present) is a near-complete set of burial records of people interred here. These records contain personal information of the deceased, including the cause of their death, and provide a unique source of demographic and disease data that can bridge historic, archaeological, and anthropological concerns (Čaval 2023). No other such archive is known to exist for the entire region of the Indian Ocean. This repository of health conditions for thousands buried in the Bois Marchand cemetery can reconstruct a health situation for the indenture period in the Indian Ocean and serve as a comparison with the Atlantic. The impartiality of the records on gender, religious, or ethnic differentiation or social structuring is the outcome of the British colonial administrative system. It allows us to create an objective overview of the society in nineteenth-century Mauritius.

Quarantine Stations as Institutions of Segregation

After centuries of slavery and a prevailing indifference to preventive healthcare in the colonies, new procedures, institutions, and policies for quarantine inspection and detection from the 1860s onward accompanied the rise and regulation of indentured labor, particularly in the Indian and Pacific oceans. For a brief period in places where indentured laborers settled, quarantine stations became compulsory, especially to combat recurring outbreaks of cholera during the 1850s. Some quarantine practices had already been adopted during the French occupation of both Réunion and Mauritius; these were primarily reactive, ad hoc regulations. Contagious diseases had been monitored and contained through maritime quarantines, wherein the crew and passengers spent time in confinement directly aboard the ship anchored outside the disembarkation port. Sick people occasionally landed in special hospitals, but these were usually provisional and hardly adequate settings close to the port. After the detrimental malaria epidemic in Mauritius in the second half of the nineteenth century, the quarantine system was reorganized entirely and made permanent. The British colonial government was the leading promoter of creating a system countering mostly cholera but also other diseases carried by convoys from South Asia. On the other side, the French progressively tightened quarantine practices, already used during the slave period. On Réunion they enforced isolation for vessels transporting indentured laborers from Africa, especially Madagascar, and Asia (Marimoutou-Oberlé 2008: 28–35).

The quarantine stations served as a filter between the ocean and Mascarene islands through which thousands of people were forced to pass. By looking at the regulations surrounding quarantining and how these were manifested in the landscape, we can outline which individuals or goods were subjected to inspection, examination, and involuntary confinement and which spaces were reserved for them. Isolated from the rest of the population and often surrounded by water, quarantine places were internally differentiated. They were multi-partitioned spaces or sites of social classification, internal separation, and spatial and bodily ordering (Bashford 2004: 48). The social classification was achieved through spatiality and various means of enforcement, often combined, for example, in the natural topography of the station, the positioning of administrative buildings for surveillance, and the use of built barriers such as fences or forced paths. As these were residential facilities, gendered relations shaped quarantines. Strict control over mobility and the body's condition amplified gender segregation and differential treatment among laborers and European or non-European populations. Although research into this topic in the Indian Ocean World is relatively new, some preliminary data suggest the potential of a comparative approach to studies of quarantine sites and their internal spatial ordering (Longhurst 2017: 182–85). We employ a gendered lens using Réunion and Mauritius case studies, where in the same decade, in the 1860s, new quarantine stations were built. These comparative cases also provide the opportunity to examine differences in French and British quarantine practices and their impact on non-European unfree laborers.

Réunion (Île de Bourbon)

In Réunion, as in other Mascarene islands, the risk of contagion from epidemic diseases grew after the mid-nineteenth century with increasing influx of indentured laborers. Because the island had a rugged coastline, but there were no small islands around it, the French colonial government arranged for isolated places on the mainland to examine and monitor immigrants' and travelers' health and sanitary conditions. In 1852–1853 at least five depots in the capital, Saint-Denis, were used to survey the health of passengers at disembarkation. Each depot focused on one ship at a time, ensuring the health of newcomers. Women from countries outside Europe were examined upon arrival to confirm that they were free of venereal diseases, despite having been examined at their point of embarkation (Tinker 1974: 138). Those with contagious diseases or other health problems were taken to a hospital or the Lazaret of La Ravine à Jacques.

The Lazaret of La Ravine à Jacques, built at the end of the eighteenth century and renovated in 1840, was possibly one of Réunion's first permanent quarantine stations (Fig. 5.3). With increasing numbers of indentured laborers in the 1850s, the lazaret was complemented by the nearby Lazaret de La Grande Chaloupe, which kept newcomers under medical surveillance and isolated groups of people from the rest of the population. This new lazaretto was reconditioned into a quarantine station at the beginning of the 1860s (Marimoutou-Oberlé 2015: 214–28). Under the aegis of the colonial government and overseen by the chief medical officer, the quarantines were separated from other facilities on the island and surrounded by high walls. The buildings included dormitories and infirmaries and had a single point of access to be effortlessly and regularly monitored; the only point of contact or exchange with the outside world involved the food supply. Quarantine station maps displayed colonial principles directing the organization and spatial layout of each site. For example, the 1857 plans of the Pointe des Galets lazaretto (Fig. 5.3), though never constructed, demonstrate how dormitories, hospitals, and infirmaries were separated by gender and race. Men's health facilities were divided into white and black sections, with set routes to prevent any contact between different gender and social groups.

The new lazaretto at La Grande Chaloupe seems to replicate the original design of the Pointe de Galets. The narrow space allowed for two groups of buildings, built during the last quarter of the nineteenth century and called Lazaret no. 1 and Lazaret no. 2 (Fig. 5.3). The two double structures had the same types of buildings but were arranged differently due to the topography of their location: the first by the sea, the second by the river Grande Chaloupe. The main stone buildings were dormitories of 40 × 6 m, which could house about 400 people each. They were internally divided into open rooms on two levels: the ground floor for the refectories and the first floor for the dormitories. Multiple windows provided adequate ventilation (Marimoutou-Oberlé 2015: 262–63). Contemporary to the station's final use at the dawn of the twentieth century, the latrines and lavatories in Lazaret no. 2 are still well preserved today. The hospital is not identified because it was made from wood (Marimoutou-Oberlé 2015: 281–92). While the original plan of Lazaret no. 1 has not been preserved, a letter to the director of Internal Affairs dated August 20, 1860, provides some structural information: the buildings for migrants were divided into rooms for paying passengers and big dormitories to house indentured workers, coming primarily from the Indian subcontinent. The hospitals were segregated by gender and race. Whether black women fell

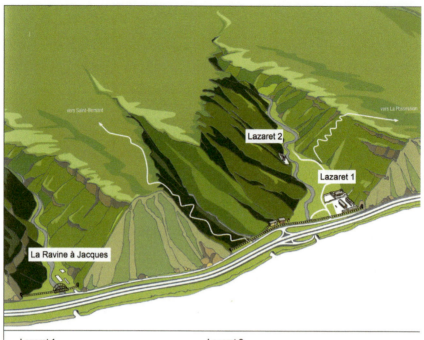

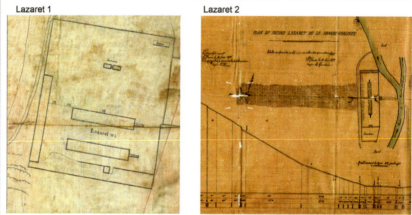

Figure 5.3. Composition of the general plan of Lazaret no. 1 and Lazaret no. 2 de la Grande-Chaloupe in the 1870s (composed by A. Cianciosi from Marimoutou-Oberlé 2008: 47, 54, 58).

under the generic definition of "women" is unclear. They were not mentioned, perhaps because their numbers were scarce in this period. Each lazaretto also had a cemetery, separated from the living space by a high wall. The old plans and historical documents show that the Euro-western medical ideology of the time was well present in the Indian Ocean colonies. However, these documents do not necessarily reflect how the sites were constructed and, more critically, how they were used in real life. Recent archaeological investigations of a portion of the graveyard in Lazaret no. 2 disclose a systematically ordered cemetery where the deceased were buried in rows and aligned in a north-south direction. Paleogenetic analyses attest that all were of Asian origin. Material culture reveals that quarantine communities used objects of European (France, Italy) and extra-European origin, particularly some ceramics from Africa and South Asia (Dijoux 2012).

Mauritius (Île de France)

Large-scale outbreaks of cholera, smallpox, malaria, and remittent fevers across the largest colonial empire forced the British to recognize the need for public health management and to introduce quarantine into the Indian Ocean World. Beginning in 1810 the Mauritian government followed British imperial regulations and established a few quarantines for the incoming ships. In contrast to Réunion's lazarets on the mainland, quarantine stations in Mauritius were located on small islets close to the main ports. The contemporary medical theory and environmental factors were crucial in planning a quarantine station; its position was carefully considered, focusing on the orientation and ventilation of buildings, since until the 1880s miasmas were considered to cause infectious diseases (Geltner 2013: 401; Beattie 2012; Cianciosi et al. 2022). Regularly alternating epidemics of smallpox and cholera between 1771 and 1862 led to the establishment of maritime quarantines for urgent cases (Boodhoo 2010; Reddi and Sookrajowa 2019). Planned in 1855 and built in the following years, the main permanent quarantine station was on Flat Island (Île Plate), north of the main island, expressly built to combat cholera epidemics (Fig. 5.5 and Table 5.1). An ongoing archaeological investigation by the Mauritian Archaeology and Cultural Heritage (MACH) project group, in collaboration with Aapravasi Ghat UNESCO World Heritage Site, has thus far included multiple archaeological reconnaissance actions to locate, identify, and record the distribution of standing structures, in addition to geophysical surveys and a general mapping of the historical archaeology of this quarantine station. During the 2018 and 2022 campaigns, the research focused on indentured laborers' quarters, specifically the indentured camp and hospital quarters.

Infected or suspected ships were diverted here from the 1850s on, even if initially, the station only had temporary and precarious shelters without proper medical infrastructure. These were built in the 1860s and operational until the 1920s. The exact number of people quarantined at Flat Island is unknown, and only some brief, fragmentary, and unsystematic details about the ships exist. For example, the list of quarantined ships between 1850 and 1855

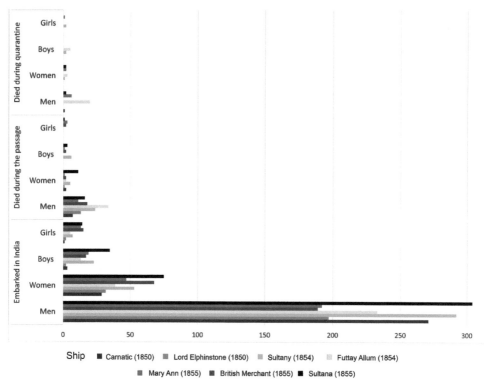

Figure 5.4. Return of seven ships with immigrants from quarantine at Flat Island and Gabriel Island between 1850 and 1855. Data from the Port Louis Immigration office, May 26, 1856 (by A. Cianciosi from Miao Foh 2018b: 48–49, table 1).

specifies the number of men-women and boys-girls (Fig. 5.4). However, between 1857 and 1877 the list of ship passengers ignores gender, reporting only the number of indentured laborers. In the later records the captain's wife is the only gendered individual mentioned (Miao Foh 2018b: 51–58). Even from 1888 on, when the colonial government started to record personal information of laborers disembarking on Flat Island, they did not document women (Marimoutou-Oberlé 2015: 316). Photographs from that time are of men exclusively. In the last quarter of the nineteenth century and early 1900s, the arrival of women was not recorded, even though this was a standard procedure at the Immigration Depot in Port Louis (Peerthum 2017: 98).

All planned architecture and infrastructure designs for this quarantine station are dated between 1855 and 1877; unfortunately, the drawings of buildings designated for women are less detailed than those in Réunion. The government's land surveyor, Thomas Corby, drew a plan of the quarantine station in 1857 and recorded most of the structures identifiable today (Cianciosi et al.

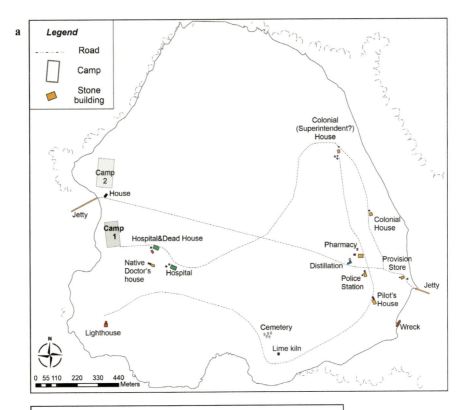
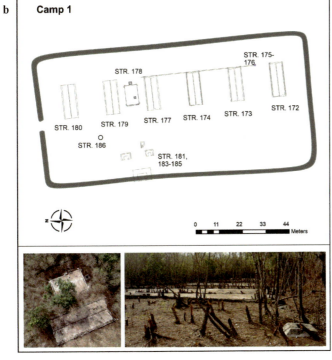

Figure 5.5. (a) Map of Flat Island showing (b) quarantine structures, and the barrack platforms uncovered in Camp 1 during the MACH team's fieldwork in 2018 (drawn by A. Cianciosi).

2022: fig. 7). The station was divided into two parts that were logistically connected by a straight road between the two landing piers (jetties) (Fig. 5.5a). One part was for Europeans, and the other was for indentured laborers. The European part had stone buildings and was positioned on the island's eastern side, where doctors and officials, such as the health superintendent, ships' pilots, police, and other medical assistants, were accommodated. The quarantine camp was located along the western coast on the opposite side of the island and consisted of two oblong enclosures, each with six large rectangular wooden barracks (Cianciosi et al. 2022). The military-inspired barrack-style dormitories offered little privacy. Some may have been reserved for married couples and families and separated from single men. Each barrack could accommodate up to fifty people, which often made them overcrowded. In discussing Australian sites, Foley (1995: 38) reasons that the standard of accommodation provided to incoming laborers in quarantine had been like the quarters they occupied on board a ship. The archaeological excavation at Palisade Bay, in Camp 1, identified and revealed six rectangular, screed-and-concrete platforms for wooden huts, a freshwater pipe system leading from the platforms to a large water tank, two built structures that served as latrines, a possible kitchen, a round pit, and a basalt drywall that surrounded the camp (Fig. 5.5). All six platforms were alike, and there was no architectural indication that the huts hosted different social groups (families or singles, men or women). Archival records indicate that over the years, some improvements were introduced: in 1873, a request was made for six additional huts in the camp (called Camp 2), for water cisterns, cookhouses, latrines, and lavatories, to accommodate immigrants from at least two ships. In Camp 1, a complex water supply system provided storage of rainwater and the disposal of dirty water and waste, which was critical to the successful functioning of the quarantine station. Other improvements in the living conditions at the laborers' camps included paving the ground within the surrounding wall with wood and constructing the roof of the barracks with a higher pitch to allow for better ventilation (Miao Foh 2018a: 13–15). Despite these efforts, in 1875 the Indian government expressed concern that immigrants' accommodation was insufficient, particularly when more than one ship arrived (Deerpalsingh and Carter 1996: 236–37).

Further development followed soon after. In 1877 gendered latrines were built (Fig. 5.6). Architectural drawings from the National Archives of Mauritius in Coromandel reveal plans for a building with six rooms for women and another with twelve internal divisions for men to be installed in both camps. The latrines for women suggest that they were a cutting-edge improvement over those at Cannoniers Point, another Mauritian quarantine station in the

Table 5.1. Return of immigrants landed in quarantine at Flat and Gabriel Islands in 1850, 1854, and 1855

Year	Ship's Name	Presidency	From What Disease	Period of Time in Quarantine
1850	*Carnatic*	Madras	Cholera	41 Days
1850	*Lord Elphinstone*	Madras	Cholera and Dysentery	34 Days
1854	*Sultany*	Calcutta	Cholera, Dysentery and Fever	21 Days
1854	*Futtay Allum*	Calcutta	Cholera and Typhus Fever	71 Days
1855	*Mary Ann*	Calcutta	Cholera and Dysentery	20 Days
1855	*British Merchant*	Calcutta	Cholera and Fever	50 Days
1855	*Sultana*	Calcutta	Cholera and Fever	19 Days

Embarked in India				Died during the passage				Died during quarantine			
Men	**Women**	**Boys**	**Girls**	**Men**	**Women**	**Boys**	**Girls**	**Men**	**Women**	**Boys**	**Girls**
271	29	3	1	7	2			1			
197	32	2	2	13	1						
292	53	23	7	24	5	6			1	2	2
233	39	13	5	34	2			20	3	5	
189	68	17	15	18	2	2	2				
192	47	19	13	11	1	1	3	6	2		1
304	75	35	14	16	11	3	1	2	2		

Source: Immigration Office, Port Louis 26th May 1856—T. Hugon, Protector of Immigrants. (Rapport des Coolies mis en quarantaine à l'Ilot Gabriel et à l'Ile Plate en 1850, 1854 et 1855) in Mauritius National Archives, rapport du comité nommé par son Excellence le Gouverneur pour rechercher et constater la cause ou les causes probables de la dernière invasion de choléra à l'Ile Maurice en mars 1856, Publié par H. Plaideau, Imprimeur du Gouvernement, Port-Louis, 1857, p. 101 (cited in Marimoutou-Oberlé 2015: I:231).

northwestern mainland. A medical and sanitary report by Andrew Balfour in 1921 describes the conditions of the latrines, criticizing their absence and unsatisfactory arrangements for water supply in third-class quarters (Balfour 1922: 115–16).

Following Corby's map, we located the hospital quarter with other buildings slightly off the main road south of the camps. The archival architectural drawings attest that at least two hospitals were planned: one was built from basalt stones and the other from wood, without any indication showing to which group of people they would be allocated (Indian hospital MA D6A A57 No. 2 Mauritius National Archives D Series plan of FI, No. 1 and 41). However, in the 1866 Report on the Civil Hospital (MNA, RA1850–year 1866, c. 3r), the superintendent of the quarantine station requested folding screens for the female hospital, officially documenting a specific building for women. During the 2022 archaeological investigation we located not only the basalt

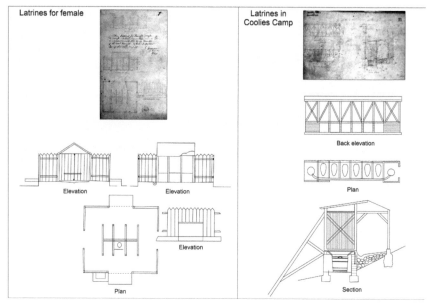

Figure 5.6. Original architectural drawings and copies of "Latrines for females—Plan & Elevation" and "Latrines in Coolies Camp" (by A. Cianciosi after Mauritius National Archives MA/D6A/A57/No.2/7 and 2/11).

stone hospital with the morgue but also a second hospital with stone foundations and wooden walls and floors, the one possibly reserved for women. Halfway between the two hospitals was the doctor's house, also with unpreserved wooden walls and a water cistern and basalt stone kitchen.

Despite the intensive use of the quarantine station, written sources about the conditions of life, subsistence activities, and the treatment of the sick and dead are quite brief. The permanent and increasing use of quarantine during the second half of the nineteenth century led to the formation of a permanent settlement for indentured laborers and convicts. They cultivated vegetables, raised animals (cows, sheep, deer), helped maintain the station, and loaded and unloaded ships (Miao Foh 2018b: 43). It is unclear whether they lived in one of the two laborers' camps on the island's western side or somewhere outside the camps.

Conclusion

The paucity of information makes understanding gender in labor migration in the Indian Ocean World during the eighteenth and nineteenth centuries challenging. However, when investigated through the archaeological lens, some crucial sites offer new data on different gendered presences and roles.

The combination of written sources and material data related to healthcare, such as quarantine stations, provides insight into the colonial mindset and how the value of humans as a labor force decisively changed due to epidemics (Cianciosi 2023).

Although written sources, especially during slavery, are largely silent about women, material evidence demonstrates how gender impacted their experience. Drawing on archaeological investigations of Le Morne cemetery, we can reflect on women's roles in slave communities. The gendered dimensions of the labor milieu in colonial Mauritius after the abolition of slavery differed from that in other colonies, like Réunion. Agricultural labor has traditionally been considered a male occupation. The invisibility of female labor in plantation farming has created huge lacunae in understanding the specificity of the experience of female indentured workers. A comparative analysis points to the root of different family policies for indentured communities between the Atlantic and the Indian oceans as well as within the Indian Ocean's colonies. In the indentured communities of the Atlantic Ocean, women were contracted to work in the plantation fields, while in the Mascarenes, women worked in the fields only during the height of harvest season and at a cheap rate. The nature of their indenture allowed them to be engaged in other sectors and focused on various aspects of social life (Chakraborty 2020).

The decade-long transition between slavery and indentured labor in the Mascarenes featured the declining health of unfree people due to extraordinary increases in the workload on sugar plantations, low rates of natural reproduction, and the mortality and morbidity associated with multiple epidemics in the nineteenth century (Parahoo 1986; Stanziani 2013; Seetah 2018; Seth 2018; Reddi and Sookrajowa 2019). The outbreaks of epidemic diseases also led to a shift in the employment of masses of indentured workers. As in other colonies, epidemics in Mauritius and Réunion revealed the poor health conditions of the population, especially the working class.

Quarantine spaces were introduced due to the protocols arising from these negative experiences. Apart from their function as strategic health management facilities, quarantines restrict migrations and impose unique conditions on migrants. As residential facilities, quarantines did shape and were shaped by gendered relations and influenced how those relations changed over an individual's life history. When analyzing quarantine regulations and spaces, it is crucial to focus on which individuals (or goods) were subject to inspection, examination, involuntary confinement, segregation, or unequal treatment.

A quarantine occupied a liminal space, constituting not an arrival but rather a continuation of, or pause within, their journey (Longhurst 2017: 60). Some of these spaces conformed to the spatial organization of the ship, playing a preparatory role in immigrants' arrival at Mauritius and the new settlement in sugar estates. In Réunion, surveillance measures were theoretically applied to all travelers: Europeans and non-Europeans, white and black, men and women, workers and non-workers, while only indentured laborers were subjected to social confinement. However, the topography and buildings within the lazarettos appear to be generally similar to comparable institutions of earlier ages, where the main concern was to separate the healthy from the sick and to use the medical institution as a treatment center for immigrants, ensuring vaccination against smallpox (Marimoutou-Oberlé 2008: 58–64). From its first construction, the lazaret La Grande Chaloupe had latrines, a kitchen, and a water supply system. Furthermore, the establishment of a cemetery was mandatory, and the archaeological investigation proved that laborers who died during the quarantine period were mainly buried there.

By contrast, in Mauritius, the Flat Island quarantine station was designed exclusively for indentured workers from South Asia suspected of carrying cholera. Their segregation was accentuated by the institution's complex topographical and architectural organization, in which the separation of European officials and quarantined people was spatially and visually evident. Comparing the European quarter and the quarantine camps, the gap in the quality of buildings and facilities is visceral. The harsh living conditions at this remote site were relieved for the officials, who lived in solid stone buildings with verandas, stocked kitchens, and water cisterns. At the same time, the immigrants were forced into crowded barracks, often lacking bare essentials. Some improvements were introduced in the last decades of its use, such as latrines, kitchens, and a proper water supply system. The location and future excavation of a graveyard in Flat Island might provide crucial bioarchaeological data on the health conditions of newly arrived labor communities from India, representing a decisive comparison with cemeteries on the mainland as well as with a similar context in Réunion or other colonies in the Indian Ocean.

Considering health and gender together provides us an essential view into the organizational development of a society and the progress of public health concerns and actions. More broadly, this research shows how colonial gender binaries defined landscapes, daily life, and people's experiences of those landscapes. Female labor migration has been largely ignored since women were seen as "associational migrants," dependent on male immigrants as their parents, daughters, or partners. However, archaeological research reveals that women's agency within the health space was not peripheral or cloistered to private niches of life. To undermine the agency of women is to disregard a significant component of the developing healthscape in a premodern world.

Notes

1 *Duffadors* and *arkattias* were native recruiters from the Calcutta region, while *maistries* were recruiters from Madras and Bombay (Nemchand 2012: 125). *Sirdars* were foremen, recruiters, and labor leaders who acted as important intermediary figures between employers and workers in both India and in colonial-period sugar colonies.
2 The same dimensions were assigned for graves at the Bois Marchand cemetery in Mauritius (Čaval 2023).

Bibliography

Allen, Richard. 1999. *Slaves, Freedmen, and Indentured Laborers in Colonial Mauritius.* Cambridge, U.K.: Cambridge University Press.

———. 2001. "Licentious and Unbridled Proceedings: The Illegal Slave Trade to Mauritius and the Seychelles during the Early Nineteenth Century." *Journal of African History* 42(1): 91–116.

———. 2004. "The Mascarene Slave-Trade and Labour Migration in the Indian Ocean during the Eighteenth and Nineteenth Centuries." In *The Structure of Slavery in Indian Ocean Africa and Asia,* edited by G. Campbell, 33–50. London: Frank Cass.

———. 2010. "Satisfying the 'Want for Labouring People': European Slave Trading in the Indian Ocean, 1500–1850." *Journal of World History* 21(1): 45–73. https://www.jstor .org/stable/20752925

———. 2011. "Marie Rozette and Her World: Class, Ethnicity, Gender, and Race in Late Eighteenth- and Early Nineteenth-Century Mauritius." *Journal of Social History* 45(2): 345–65.

———. 2014. "Slaves, Convicts, Abolitionism and the Global Origins of the Post-Emancipation Indentured Labour System." *Slavery & Abolition* 35(2): 328–48.

Ambrosini, Maurizio, and Joanne Van der Leun. 2015. "Introduction to the Special Issue: Implementing Human Rights: Civil Society and Migration Policies." *Journal of Immigrant & Refugee Studies* 13(2): 103–15.

Amrith, Sunil S. 2011. *Migration and Diaspora in Modern Asia.* New Approaches to Asian History. Cambridge, U.K.: Cambridge University Press.

Anderson, Clare. 2009. Convicts and Coolies: Rethinking Indentured Labour in the Nineteenth Century, *Slavery and Abolition* 30(1): 93–109.

Appleby, Joanna, Krish Seetah, Diego Calaon, Saša Čaval, Anwar Janoo, and Vijaya Teelock. 2014. "The Juvenile Cohort from Le Morne Cemetery: A Snapshot of Early Life and Death after Abolition." *International Journal of Osteoarchaeology* 24: 737–46.

Argot-Nayekoo, Yola. 2011. "Trou Chenille: L'histoire d'une famille descendant d'esclaves." In *Truth and Justice Commission Report, Vol. 3: Contemporary History, Culture and Society,* 201–20. Port Louis, Mauritius: Government Printing.

Atta-Poku, Agyemang. 1996. "Asanteman Immigrant Ethnic Association: An Effective Tool for Immigrant Survival and Adjustment Problem Solution in New York City." *Journal of Black Studies* 27(1): 56–76.

Baker, Anthony. 1996. *Slavery and Antislavery in Mauritius, 1810–33: The Conflict between Economic Expansion and Humanitarian Reform under British Rule.* Basingstoke, U.K.: Palgrave Macmillan.

Balfour, Andrew. 1922. *Report on Medical and Sanitary Matters in Mauritius, 1921.* London: Waterlow & Sons. https://search.wellcomelibrary.org/iii/encore/record/C__Rb3134762

Barnes, Jodi. 2021. Behind the Scenes of Hollywood: The Archaeology of Reproductive Oppression at the Intersections. *American Anthropologist* 123(1): 9–35.

Bashford, Alison. 2004. *Imperial Hygiene: A Critical History of Colonialism, Nationalism and Public Health.* Basingstoke, U.K.: Palgrave Macmillan.

Bates, Crispin, and Marina Carter. 2017. "Sirdars as Intermediaries in Nineteenth-Century Indian Ocean Indentured Labour Migration." *Modern Asian Studies* 51(2): 462–84.

Beattie, James. 2012. "Imperial Landscapes of Health: Place, Plants and People between India and Australia, 1800s–1900s." *Health and History* 14(1), 100–20. https://www.jstor.org/stable/10.5401/healthhist.14.1.0100

Beebeejaun-Muslum, Zareen Nishaat. 2020. "The Experiences/Struggles of Indian Indentured Women in Nineteenth-Century Mauritius." In *Indentured and Post-Indentured Experiences of Women in the Indian Diaspora,* edited by Amba Pande, 125–35. Singapore: Springer.

Benedict, Burton. 1980. "Slavery and Indentured in Mauritius and Seychelles." In *Asian and African Systems of Slavery,* edited by James L. Watson, 135–68. Oxford: Blackwell.

Bernard, E. 1834. *Essai sur les nouveaux affranchis de l'île Maurice 1834.* Port Louis, Ile Maurice: Imprimerie du Mauricien.

Blonigen, Beth. 2004. *A Re-Examination of the Slave Diet.* PhD diss., College of St. Benedict/St. John's University, New York City.

Boodhoo, Raj. 2010. *Health, Disease and Indian Immigrants in Nineteenth-Century Mauritius.* Port Louis, Mauritius: Aapravasi Ghat Trust Fund.

———. 2019. *Infectious Disease and Public Health Mauritius 1810–2010.* Port Louis, Mauritius: ELP Publications.

Burnard, Trevor. 2004. *Mastery, Tyranny, and Desire: Thomas Thistlewood and His Slaves in the Anglo-Jamaican World.* Chapel Hill: University of North Carolina Press.

Bush, Barbara. 1990. *Slave Women in Caribbean Society 1650–1838.* Bloomington: Indiana University Press.

———. 1993. "Hard Labour: Women, Childbirth and Resistance in British Caribbean Slave Societies." History Workshop no. 36, *Colonial and Post-Colonial History* (Autumn, 1993): 83–99.

Carter, Marina. 1994. *Lakshmi's Legacy: The Testimonies of Indian Women in 19th Century Mauritius.* Stanley, Rose-Hill, Mauritius: Editions de l'Océan Indien.

Carter, Marina, and James Ng Foong Kwong. 1997. *Forging the Rainbow: Labour Immigrants in British Mauritius.* Port Louis, Mauritius: Alfran.

Čaval, Saša. 2023. "Layering Segregation in Life and Death: The Social and Environmental Role/Character of the Bois Marchand Cemetery, Mauritius." *International Journal of Historical Archaeology,* July. https://doi.org/10.1007/s10761-023-00705-7.

———. In press. "Opium Collaterals and the Voyage of the *Ibis*: Home Far from Home." In *Imperial Addictions: Collateral Histories of Opium from the Indian Ocean to the China Seas, 1750–1900,* edited by Neil Price. Oxford: Oxbow Books.

CESCR. 2000. *General comment no. 14. The right to the highest attainable standard of health (article 12 of the International Covenant on Economic, Social and Cultural Rights)*. United Nations, Committee on Economic, Social and Cultural Rights, Geneva. https://digitallibrary.un.org/record/425041

Chakraborty, Nabanita. 2020. "Writing the 'Stigmatext' of Indenture: A Reading of Gaiutra Bahadur's Coolie Woman." In *Indentured and Post-Indentured Experiences of Women in the Indian Diaspora*, edited by Amba Pande, 55–66. Singapore: Springer Nature.

Chand, Rajni. 2020. "Under the Shadows of Girmit Era." In *Indentured and Post-Indentured Experiences of Women in the Indian Diaspora*, edited by Amba Pande, 139–52. Singapore: Springer Nature.

Cianciosi, Alessandra. 2023. "The Landscapes of Disease and Death in Colonial Mauritius." *International Journal of Historical Archaeology*, July. https://doi.org/10.1007/s10761-023-00707-5

Cianciosi, Alessandra, Saša Čaval, Diego Calaon, and Krish Seetah. 2022. "Integrated Remote Sensing to Assess Disease Control: Evidence from Flat Island Quarantine Station, Mauritius." *Remote Sensing* 14(8): 1891.

Claveyrolas, Mathieu. 2015. "The 'Land of the Vaish'? Caste Structure and Ideology in Mauritius." *South Asia Multidisciplinary Academic Journal* [Online], Free-Standing Articles, online since May 27, 2015, accessed July 15, 2021. https://doi.org/10.4000/samaj.3886

Corruccini, Robert S., Jerome S. Handler, and Keith P. Jacobi. 1985. "Chronological Distribution of Enamel Hypoplasias and Weaning in a Caribbean Slave Population." *Human Biology* 57(4): 699–711.

Cousin, Sandy. 2016. *Les lazarets à La Réunion de 1860 à 1920: Épidémies, médecins et pratique médicale . . . Quel intérêt sanitaire?* Masters thesis, Université de Bordeaux. https://dumas.ccsd.cnrs.fr/dumas-01360575

Deb Roy, Rohan. 2017. *Malarial Subjects: Empire, Medicine and Nonhumans in British India, 1820–1909*. Cambridge, U.K.: Cambridge University Press. https://library.oapen.org/handle/20.500.12657/28423

Deerpalsingh, Saloni, and Marina Carter. 1996. Select Documents on Indian Immigration, Mauritius, 1834–1926. Volume 3. Living And Working Conditions Under Indenture. Mauritius, Moka: Mahatma Gandhi Institute.

De Nanteuil, D. 1863. *Législation de l'île de la Réunion*, 2nd ed., vol. 6. Paris, Imprimerie J-B Gros.

Desai, Ashwin, and Goolam H. Vahed. 2010. *Inside Indenture: A South African Story, 1860–1914*. Cape Town, South Africa: Human Sciences Research Council Press.

Dey, Debasmita. 2014. "Indentured Laborers and the Native Women in Mauritius: The Colonial Perspectives." *Proceedings of the Indian History Congress* 75: 989–95. https://www.jstor.org/stable/44158483

Dijoux, Anne-Laure. 2012. "Saint-Denis. La Grande Chaloupe. Lazaret no. 2." *Bilan scientifique de l'Île de La Reunion 2011–2015* (Direction des affaires culturelles—Océan Indien la Réunion): 42–51.

van Dommelen, Peter. 2014. "Moving On: Archaeological Perspectives on Mobility and Migration." *World Archaeology* 46(4): 477–83.

Foley, Jean Duncan. 1995. *In Quarantine: A History of Sydney's Quarantine Station 1828–1984*. Kenthurst, New South Wales: Kangaroo Press.

Geltner, Guy. 2013. "Healthscaping a Medieval City: Lucca's Curia Viarum and the Future of Public Health History." *Urban History* 40(3): 395–415.

Guchteniere, Paul de, and Antoine Pécoud. 2009. "Introduction: The UN Convention on Migrant Workers' Rights." In *Migration and Human Rights: The United Nations Convention on Migrant Workers' Rights*, edited by Cholewinski Ryszard, Paul de Guchteniere, and Antoine Pécoud, 1–44. Cambridge: Cambridge University Press.

Gushulak, Brian D., and Douglas W. MacPherson. 2011. "Health Aspects of the Pre-Departure Phase of Migration." *PLoS Med* 8(5). e1001035.

Hazareesingh, K. 1966. "The Religion and Culture of Indian Immigrants in Mauritius and the Effect of Social Change." *Comparative Studies in Society and History* 8(2): 241–57.

Hiralal, Kalpana. 2016. "Gendered Migrations: A Comparative Study of Indentured and Non-Indentured Immigrants to South Africa 1860–1930." *Diaspora Studies* 9(1): 41–52.

Hoefte, Rose Marie Adelheid Leonie. 1987. *Plantation Labor After the Abolition of Slavery: The Case of the Plantation Marienburg (Suriname) 1880–1940*. PhD diss., University of Florida.

Hurgobin, Yoshina. 2016. "Making Medical Ideologies: Indentured Labor in Mauritius." In *Histories of Medicine and Healing in the Indian Ocean World*, Vol. 2: *The Modern Period*, edited by Anna Winterbottom and Facil Tesfaye, 1–26. Basingstoke, U.K.: Palgrave Macmillan.

Jenkins, William. 2005. "Deconstructing Diasporas: Networks and Identities among the Irish in Buffalo and Toronto, 1870–1910." *Immigrants & Minorities* 23(2–3): 359–98.

Kuczynski, Robert René. 1949. *Demographic Survey of the British Colonial Empire*. Vol. 2: *East Africa*. Oxford: Oxford University Press.

Lightfoot, Emma, Saša Čaval, Diego Calaon, Joanna Appleby, Jonathan Santana, Alessandra Cianciosi, Rosa Fregel, and Krish Seetah. 2020. "Colonialism, Slavery and 'The Great Experiment': Carbon, Nitrogen and Oxygen Isotope Analysis of Le Morne and Bois Marchand Cemeteries, Mauritius." *Journal of Archaeological Science: Reports* 31: 102335. https://doi.org/10.1016/j.jasrep.2020.102335

Longhurst, Peta. 2017. *Materialising Contagion: An Archaeology of Sydney's North Head Quarantine Station*. PhD diss., University of Sydney.

Maglen, Krista. 2014. *The English System: Quarantine, Immigration and the Making of a Port Sanitary Zone*. Manchester: Manchester University Press.

Marimoutou-Oberlé, Michèle. 2008. *Le Lazaret de La Grande Chaloupe, quarantaine et engagisme*. Saint-Denis, La Réunion: Département de La Réunion.

———. 2015. *Engagisme et contrôle sanitaire: Quarantaine et lazarets de quarantaine dans les mascareignes aux XIXe siècle et début du XXe siècle*, I–II. PhD diss., Université de Nantes.

Meer, Y. S. 1980. *Documents of Indentured Labour: Natal 1851–1917*. Durban: Institute of Black Research.

Miao Foh, Christelle. 2018a. *Progress Report on Research January 2018–May 2018*. Port Louis: Aapravasi Ghat Trust Fund.

———. 2018b. *Flat Island: A History of Quarantine in Mauritius*. Port Louis: Aapravasi Ghat Trust Fund.

Miller, Joseph C. 2007. "Introduction: Women as Slaves and Owners of Slaves." In *Women and Slavery,* vol. 1: *Africa, the Indian Ocean World,* edited by Gwyn Campbell, Suzanne Miers, and Joseph Calder Miller, 1–40. Athens: Ohio University Press.

Mishra, Amit Kumar. 2009. "Indian Indentured Labourers in Mauritius: Reassessing the 'New System of Slavery' vs. Free Labour Debate." *Studies in History* 25(2): 229–51.

Moriarty, Cpt. H. A. 1891. *Islands in the Southern Indian Ocean Westward of Longitude 80 Degrees East, Including Madagascar.* London: Hydrographic Office of the Admiralty.

Nemchand, Ashveen. 2012. "The Recruitment and Voyage of Indentured Labourers from India." In *Angaje: Explorations into the History, Society and Culture of Indentured Immigrants and Their Descendants in Mauritius,* vol.1, edited by Vijaya Teelock, 123–42. Port Louis: Aapravasi Ghat Trust Fund.

Northrup, David. 1995. *Indentured Labor in the Age of Imperialism, 1834–1922.* Cambridge, U.K.: Cambridge University Press.

Pande, Amba. 2020. *Indentured and Post-Indentured Experiences of Women in the Indian Diaspora.* Singapore: Springer Nature.

Parahoo, Kader A. 1986. "Early Colonial Health Developments in Mauritius." *International Journal of Health Services* 16(3): 409–23.

Peerthum, Satyendra. 2017. '*They came to Mauritian shores': The Life-Stories and the History of the Indentured Labourers in Mauritius (1826–1937).* Port Louis: Aapravasi Ghat Trust Fund.

Pike, Nicholas. 1873. *Sub-Tropical Rambles in the Land of the Aphanapteryx: Personal Experiences, Adventures and Wanderings in and around the Island of Mauritius.* New York: Harper & Brothers Publishers.

Pomfret, David. 2009. "Raising Eurasia: Race, Class, and Age in French and British Colonies." *Comparative Studies in Society and History* 51(2): 314–43.

Reddi, Sadasivam Jaganada, and Sheetal Sheena Sookrajowa. 2019. "Slavery, Health, and Epidemics in Mauritius 1721–1860." In *The Palgrave Handbook of Ethnicity,* edited by Steven Ratuva, 1749–65. Singapore: Palgrave Macmillan.

Reddock, Rhoda. 1994. *Women, Labour and Politics in Trinidad and Tobago: A History.* London: Zed Books.

The Right to Health, Fact Sheet No. 31. Office of the United Nations High Commissioner for Human Rights, World Health Organisation. https://www.ohchr.org/en/publications/fact-sheets/fact-sheet-no-31-right-health

Ross, Loretta, and Rickie Sollinger. 2017. *Reproductive Justice: An Introduction.* Berkeley: University of California Press.

Santana, Jonathan. 2013. Osteological report on human remains from archaeological excavations at Le Morne, Mauritius, season 2012. Unpublished report, Mauritian Archaeology and Cultural Heritage (MACH) Archive.

Santana, Jonathan, and Ricardo Cabrera. 2016. Bois Marchand: Report on Human Remains. Unpublished osteological report. Las Palmas, Canary Islands.

Schrover, Marlou, Joanne Van der Leun, Leo Lucassen, and Chris Quispel. 2008. "Introduction: Illegal Migration and Gender in a Global and Historical Perspective." In *Illegal Migration and Gender in a Global and Historical Perspective,* edited by Chris Quispel, Leo Lucassen, Marlou Schrover, and Joanne van der Leun, 9–38. Amsterdam: Amsterdam University Press. https://www.jstor.org/stable/j.ctt46mwss.3

Scott, Eleanor. 1999. *The Archaeology of Infancy and Infant Death*. BAR International Series 819. Oxford: Archaeopress.

Seetah, Krish. 2010. Le Morne Cemetery: Archaeological Investigations. Unpublished report commissioned by and prepared for the Truth and Justice Commission, Port Louis, Mauritius. From reports by D. Calaon, S. Čaval, J. Appleby, and E. Lightfoot.

———. 2015. "The Archaeology of Mauritius." *Antiquity* 89: 922–39.

———. 2018. "Climate and Disease in the Indian Ocean: An Interdisciplinary Study from Mauritius." In *Connecting Continents: Archaeology and History in the Indian Ocean World*, edited by Krish Seetah, 291–316. Athens: Ohio University Press.

Sénèque, Steve, and James De Montille. 2021. "12. Les Femmes de Confiance: The Laverdure Sisters—1. Trusted Women and Secret Wives." In *Women in the Making of Mauritian History: A Collaborative Project through the Centre for Research on Slavery and Indenture*, edited by Vijaya Teelock, Christelle Collet, James De Montille, and Steve Sénèque, vol. 1: 95–108. Reduit: Centre for Research on Slavery and Indenture, University of Mauritius.

Seth, Suman. 2018. *Difference and Disease: Medicine, Race, and the Eighteenth-Century British Empire*. Cambridge, U.K. Cambridge University Press.

Sheridan, Richard. 1985. *Doctors and Slaves: A Medical and Demographic History of Slavery in the British West Indies, 1680–1834*. Cambridge, U. K.: Cambridge University Press.

Smith, Tony. 1978. "A Comparative Study of French and British Decolonization." *Comparative Studies in Society and History* 20(1): 70–102.

Stanziani, Alessandro. 2012. "Labor, Rights, and Immigration: A Comparison between Mauritius and Réunion, 1840–1880." *Le Mouvement Social* 241: 47–64.

———. 2013. "Local Bondage in Global Economies: Servants, Wage Earners, and Indentured Migrants in Nineteenth-Century France, Great Britain, and the Mascarene Islands." *Modern Asian Studies* 47(4): 1218–51.

———. 2015. "L'immigration indentured à l'île Maurice, 1840–1870: Conditions, abus et résistance." *Afriques* [Online], online since December 21, 2015, accessed July 1, 2021. https://doi.org/10.4000/afriques.1770

Stone, Pamela. 2016. "Biocultural Perspectives on Maternal Mortality and Obstetrical Death from the Past to the Present." *American Journal of Physical Anthropology* 159: 150–71.

Teelock, Vijaya. 2021a. "Enslaved Women in Mauritius 1721–1835: An Overview." In *Women in the Making of Mauritian History*, edited by Vijaya Teelock, Christelle Collet, James de Montille, and Steve Sénèque, 31–40. Reduit: University of Mauritius.

———. 2021b. "Women in the Indentured System." In *Women in the Making of Mauritian History*, edited by Vijaya Teelock, Christelle Collet, James de Montille, and Steve Sénèque, 67–74. Reduit: University of Mauritius.

Tinker, Hugh. 1974. *A New System of Slavery: The Export of India Labour Overseas, 1830–1920*. Oxford: Oxford University Press.

Tognotti, Eugenia. 2013. "Lessons from the History of Quarantine, from Plague to Influenza A." *Emerging Infectious Disease* 19(2): 254–59.

Turner, Sasha. 2017. "The Nameless and the Forgotten: Maternal Grief, Sacred Protection, and the Archive of Slavery." *Abolition and Slavery* 38(2): 232–50.

UN General Assembly. 2015. *Transforming Our World: The 2030 Agenda for Sustainable Development.* UN General Assembly, October 21, 2015, UN Doc. A/RES/70/1. https://sdgs.un.org/2030agenda

Vaughan, Megan. 2000. "Slavery, Smallpox, and Revolution: 1792 in Île de France (Mauritius)." *Social History of Medicine* 13(3): 411–28.

Veit, Richard, Nicola Kelly, Sean McHugh, and Timothy Dinsmore. 2022. "Not Unmindful of the Unfortunate: Finding the Forgotten through Archaeology at the Orange Valley Hospital for the Enslaved." *International Journal of Historical Archaeology,* January. https://doi.org/10.1007/s10761-022-00652-9

Volcy, Elodie Laurent. 2021. "L'exploitation sexuelle de la femme esclave." In *Women in the Making of Mauritian History,* edited by Vijaya Teelock, Christelle Collet, James de Montille, and Steve Sénèque, 41–54. Reduit: University of Mauritius.

Wood, Betty. 1997. "Some Aspects of Female Resistance to Chattel Slavery in Low Country Georgia, 1763–1815." *Historical Journal* 30(3): 603–22.

Wright, Philip. 1966. *Lady Nugent's Journal of Her Residence in Jamaica from 1801 to 1805.* Kingston: Institute of Jamaica.

Xiang, Biao, and Johan Lindquist. 2014. "Migration Infrastructure." *International Migration Review* 48 (S1): 122–48.

Zimmerman, Cathy, Ligia Kiss, and Mazeda Hossain. 2011. "Migration and Health: A Framework for 21st Century Policy-Making." *PLoS Med* 8(5): e1001034.

6

The Archaeology of Portuguese Agricultural Outposts in the Seventeenth-Century Zanzibar Countryside

ADRIA LAVIOLETTE AND NEIL NORMAN

We present here results of the Later Zanzibar Archaeology Project (LZAP) carried out at two Portuguese colonial sites, Fukuchani and Mvuleni, on Unguja Island (Zanzibar), Tanzania (Fig. 6.1). Our contribution to Swahili archaeology of the late sixteenth and seventeenth centuries adds an archaeological dimension regarding Portuguese intention, practice, and interactions with Swahili people. Eastern African coastal communities have been active in the Indian Ocean over more than two millennia: from hunter-foragers and farmers, who interacted with merchants in Roman vessels (Casson 1989); to agro-fishing communities of the mid-first millennium CE, who maintained contact with Arabian Peninsula and Persian Gulf traders (Horton and Chami 2018); to later Swahili, who expanded such ocean-based interactions (Fleisher et al. 2015). The East African settler-colonial period, beginning with Portuguese and later Arab, German, and British colonizers, is less explored archaeologically than earlier periods.

In a review of the relative paucity of post-1600 CE historical archaeology in East Africa, Lane (2018) suggests that a framework on the "Swahili coast" rather than "East African coast" has tended to bound a generation of archaeologists within the years 750–1500 CE in their research. They created a focus on internal (Swahili and African) vs. external (Arab, Persian, Indian Ocean) factors underlying regional social change. Though a much-needed inquiry, such a binary excluded alternative and continuous historical narratives of regional history. As other chapters in this volume argue as well, colonialism in the Indian Ocean World needs a historical archaeology that transcends arbitrary temporal boundaries of pre- and post-colonization and that begins with a concern for effects of, and responses to, entanglements with non-African peoples (see also Hauser and Haines, Seetah et al., Sakai and Hsieh, this

The Archaeology of Portuguese Agricultural Outposts in Seventeenth-Century Zanzibar · 129

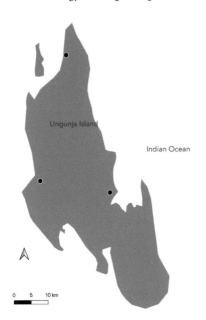

Figure 6.1. Map of Unguja Island with project area.

volume). Archaeologists and heritage managers working in the region have shown increased interest in this era (e.g., Wynne-Jones 2010; Marshall 2012; Croucher 2014; Abungu et al. 2018), and its archaeological potential is great. It is also critical to situate the region's colonial era in the global archaeological literature. In this chapter we present our recent efforts in Zanzibar to address these very points.

LZAP is a collaboration with the Zanzibar Ministry of Museums and Antiquities and a contribution to site conservation and interpretation efforts that are underway. The project has focused on detailed mapping and photogrammetry, shovel-test pit (STP) survey, and excavations in and around two Portuguese agricultural outposts: sites contemporary with larger Portuguese settlements in more urban areas, as reviewed later in the chapter. We address primarily the dynamics inside Portuguese living and work spaces seen through the archaeological record and some implications for interactions with Swahili people living nearby. Our study revealed an apparent disjuncture in the archaeological data. Architectural findings suggest that "the Portuguese" imperial effort—or Portuguese individuals—invested considerably in two settlements in northwest Unguja. Artifacts recovered from Fukuchani and Mvuleni suggest that they were occupied only briefly, perhaps never seeing the successes in commercial cultivation and plant processing for which they were likely built. We explore these findings in terms of the uneven nature of the Portuguese colonial project in the Indian Ocean World, and especially on the Kenyan and Tanzanian coasts. This research builds on pioneering archaeology on the Portuguese in East Africa (e.g., Chittick 1974; Kirkman 1974; Sassoon 1981, 1982); critical historical archaeology of East Africa informed by oral histories, traditions, and ethnohistoric evidence (e.g., Schmidt 1978; Pawlowicz and LaViolette 2013; Coppola 2018); and growing attention to the archaeology of colonial processes (e.g., Fleisher 2004; Biginagwa and Mapunda 2018; Marshall and Kiriama 2018).

Background

The Swahili coast bounds the western Indian Ocean from Mogadishu to southern Mozambique. Portuguese exploration began in 1498 as Vasco da Gama's fleet sailed northward along this coast, seeking to expand commercial shipping, profitable cultivation, and perhaps religious conversion as they visited Swahili ports and secured a route to India (Axelson 1973; cf. Prestholdt 2001; Wilson, this volume). Swahili leaders in urban-based polities responded differently in this first wave of interactions, with strategies that spanned a range from pragmatic political engagement to open hostility. Within a few years of Portuguese contact, after episodes of military violence, military threat resulting in tribute-paying arrangements to the Portuguese, and establishment of some less coercive relationships, the Swahili polities along the coast were under patchy and unstable Portuguese control. The Portuguese had already colonized African regions farther south—for example, the Zambezi valley—for access to gold mines, with their leaders encouraging Portuguese settlement through land grants and other arrangements including intermarriage with local people and enslavement (Pearson 1998; Prestholdt 2001; Pikirayi 2009; Ribeiro da Silva 2015).

On the northern Swahili coast the strategy differed; the primary goal was to support a route to India rather than exploit interior resources. While the Portuguese did not settle in large numbers in what are now Tanzania and Kenya, they nonetheless made large investments. Over the sixteenth and seventeenth centuries they built fortifications, factories (customs houses), churches and missions, and clusters of houses. They tended to construct enclaves that referenced plans and aesthetics of European urban spaces, and established bases mostly in existing urban Swahili settlements, which they experienced as familiar in terms of their architecture and aesthetics (Prestholdt 2001: 390). They built fortifications on a model designed to counter medieval European warfare, often much different from the kinds of violence they might encounter or inflict in East Africa (Fonseca 2017: 646).

Portuguese colonizers entered a Swahili society organized around its own urban centers, some already 400 years old with roots in the mid-first millennium CE (Kusimba 1999; Horton and Middleton 2000). By the late fifteenth century, different types of towns (referred to as stone towns, city-states, or states) were thriving, each including a bespoke mix of stone-built (mortared coral/limestone) mosques and other public buildings, houses, and funerary architecture as well as abundant earth-and-thatch dwellings, drawing on a set of shared coastal aesthetics and practices (Wynne-Jones 2016). Farmers and fishers lived in these towns with artisans, religious specialists, and regional and long-distance merchants (Sinclair and Håkansson 2000; Wynne-Jones 2018). Some towns, as Fleisher (2010) notes, expanded through synoecism: villagers immigrated into them from the countryside but remained active in food production in their new settings. When Portuguese entered the region, most urban and rural Swahili had been practicing Muslims for at least three centuries—some, as at Shanga on the Kenyan coast, for 750 years—with little eagerness to embrace Christian practices (Horton 1998). As we would expect based on comparative colonialism studies (e.g., Dietler 1997; Prestholdt 2001; Gosden 2004), some leaders chose to align with Portuguese leaders while others did not, producing political stress between different Swahili centers (Fleisher and LaViolette 2007).

Portuguese colonial presence in Kenya and Tanzania lasted through the sixteenth and seventeenth centuries until expulsion from Mombasa by Omani Arabs and Swahili in 1698. Ongoing if altered Swahili urban growth eventually overlaid many Portuguese structures, as did Omani investments. The Omanis had come to the military aid of the Swahili several times, after liberating their own capital Muscat in 1650 from more than a century of Portuguese occupation. Omani retaliatory raids were thus significant in the colonial history of the coast. Once the Portuguese departed, the Omanis sought colonial influence themselves. Their efforts came to a head in the early nineteenth century, when the Omani capital shifted from Muscat to Zanzibar Stone Town and effectively brought the coast into the Omani Empire (Horton and Middleton 2000). Oman held influence, if unevenly, over the Swahili coast for nearly a century until Germany and Britain took control, ending in the 1960s (Sheriff 1987). Portugal's colonial presence is thus arguably as notable for marking the beginning of European and Arab colonization of the coast as it is for its own impact.

Fukuchani and Mvuleni provide us an opportunity to investigate Portuguese colonial efforts away from the centers in which Portuguese leaders interacted most frequently with Swahili people. We suggest scenarios about what local Portuguese elites designed these settlements to do, and what took place in them. In *Ethiopia Oriental,* Fr. João dos Santos mentions Portuguese residing at unspecified locations outside town on Unguja (cited in Freeman-Grenville 1989). While we cannot yet bring archival sources to bear on these two particular settlements, Portuguese countryside enterprises add nuance to what we know from archaeological research in Swahili centers.

We conducted two four-week field seasons at Fukuchani and Mvuleni in 2015 and 2017. Although non-urban in scale, their architecture resonates with houses found in many stone towns. We argue that the two settlements functioned as comfortable but hardly luxuriously appointed houses, as well as workstations and warehouses, with tobacco growing, processing, and shipping as a main purpose. They were built when Unguja was dotted with Swahili towns and villages, but when urban settlements concentrated in the southern half of the island (see Alders 2022). The northwest was rural; the closest town to Fukuchani and Mvuleni was Zanzibar Stone Town itself, 45 km south, where Portugal placed an important settlement in the sixteenth and seventeenth centuries. A question, therefore, was what if any archaeological evidence from these sites linked them to Portuguese settlements elsewhere and to the surrounding Swahili landscape? Can they be fitted into Swahili culture history and used to help theorize this era of the Swahili colonial experience?

To address these questions, we review some other Portuguese-related settings in the Tanzania/Kenya region and then discuss Fukuchani and Mvuleni in this expanded context.

A Brief Archaeology of Portuguese Settler-Colonial Activity in Tanzania and Kenya

While explorations of Portuguese structures have been relatively infrequent, the last 50–70 years have produced dramatic evidence of Portuguese activity on the coast. Starting in the north is Malindi, Kenya, once a Portuguese stronghold. The most conspicuous relic is a stone pillar (*padrão*)—first erected in 1499 on the waterfront, destroyed, and replaced in the early 1500s (Kirkman 1964). Malindi leaders' relatively welcoming response to the Portuguese was in the hope that an alliance would increase the town's fortunes; here and elsewhere, the Portuguese upset delicate inter-town power dynamics from the turn of the sixteenth century onward (Moorthy 2010, cited in Rosa 2015: 151). Da Gama hired an Arab navigator in Malindi to guide him to India, with the town remaining a base for Portuguese sailing and actions taken against rival towns until their relocation to Mombasa (Bennett 1978). Historically, a church, customs house, and residences are noted on the waterfront (Bennett

1978), evidence for which has recently been explored archaeologically (C. Bita, pers. comm.). An open-air chapel purportedly built by da Gama stands today beside some historic Christian graves (Freeman-Grenville 1989).

Fort Jesus towers over the waterfront of Mombasa, 100 km south of Malindi. The Portuguese constructed it in the 1590s after more than a century of interest in Mombasa's superior harbor, and it remains the largest example of Portuguese architecture in the Indian Ocean World. Like Malindi, Mombasa's waterfront hosted other Portuguese structures—churches, another factory, a residential quarter of some 70 houses (Boxer and de Azevedo 1960: 30), and at least one redoubt outside town. James Kirkman (1974) carried out archaeological research at Fort Jesus between 1958 and 1971. The fort never provided political stability for the Portuguese, changing hands some ten times in its first century and captured decisively by the Omanis in collaboration with Mombasa-based Swahili leaders in 1698. Like Ghana's Elmina, it was an impressive edifice but understaffed, a condition that plagued many Portuguese colonial institutions (DeCorse 2001). Local townspeople lived closely around Fort Jesus and overran it multiple times. Unlike at Elmina, however, there has not yet been an archaeological investigation inside or outside the fort of long-term interactions and impacts of colonization. Apart from Kirkman's painstaking work at Fort Jesus there has been little archaeology carried out in the historic stone town of Mombasa itself.

The 1698 fall of the fort marked the unraveling of Portuguese efforts in the region; the building served later Omani and British colonization strategies and became a UNESCO World Heritage Site in 2011. During the two-year siege before its fall, the *Santo Antonio de Tanna*, a Portuguese frigate sent from Goa to provide relief to the fort's inhabitants, sank in Mombasa harbor. Hamo Sassoon (1981, 1982), Kenya coastal archaeologist, oversaw archaeological research on the shipwreck from 1977 to 1979 with the Institute of Nautical Archaeology and National Museums of Kenya. The excavations shed light principally on Portuguese regional naval culture.

Moving south, the Swahili settlement of Mkama Ndume (Pujini) on the east coast of Pemba Island (LaViolette 2004, 2018) has associations with a Portuguese attack. It comprises a major stone and earth rampart surrounding several Swahili stone houses and 1.5 hectares of open-air space. Pemba had close ties with Mombasa, and its multiple leaders mostly shared Mombasa's hostility to Portuguese efforts. Portuguese sailors likely sacked Mkama Ndume in 1520, according to documentary evidence (Strandes 1989), which aligns with archaeological indications of a sudden abandonment. Aspects of the site—luxurious main house, ramparting, and brief occupation—index increasing intracoastal political tensions in the years just before and certainly after the Portuguese arrival (Fleisher and LaViolette 2007). The settlement's apparent wealth likely attracted Portuguese attack, and it was probably deserted just prior to the raid (Strandes 1989: 9; Gray 1962: 56). Raiding on Pemba continued throughout the next century; the Portuguese were said to have "terrorized the local inhabitants . . . stealing or confiscating anything that took their fancy" (Boxer and de Azevedo 1960: 32).

On Unguja, after an initial military encounter off the coast of the town of Unguja Ukuu and subsequent treaty, the Portuguese built major structures on the waterfront in Stone Town: a church, mission, and factory. All have been located archaeologically within the enclosed open area of an Omani fort built after the 1699 expulsion of the Portuguese (Horton and Clark 1984–85; Power et al. 2020). Recent excavations by Power et al. (2020) re-exposed the church foundations and showed its consistency in size with Portuguese mission churches in the Americas. Multiple interments included a woman wearing a sacred heart pendant and another buried with a small crucifix and ring. Power and colleagues (2020) link evidence of a violent episode there to an Omani raid in 1651. Swahili people living around the settlement and the local leadership were likely less threatening to Portuguese efforts than were such attacks by Omanis raiding from ships and by other European powers in the Indian Ocean at the time.

Historical sources note other Portuguese locations in the region. For example, a small fort, now ruined, was built in 1505 at Kilwa in southern Tanzania and occupied briefly, as well documented by Chittick (1974: 219–23; and see Pradines 2016); another on Mafia Island has apparently washed away (P. Lane, pers. comm.). Together, such places anchored Portuguese plans to colonize Swahili people, maintain a foothold in the western Indian Ocean en route to India, and explore commercial opportunities, including raiding wealthy Swahili settlements. The historical accounts of a century of strife at Fort Jesus, the sacking of Mkama Ndume among many other such events (Vernet 2004), and violence revealed in Stone Town draw attention to skirmishes and battles characterizing Portuguese occupation of the northern Swahili coast. As in many colonial situations, however, actual violence was intermittent; states of tension and the threat of violence did not preclude day-to-day relationships with local people, which, as Prestholdt (2001: 385) notes, included "economic partnerships, military and political alliances, and even marriages." Study of Fukuchani and Mvuleni provides an opportunity to look inside colonial outposts to show that colonizers there existed in tension with their surroundings, simultaneously maintained a relationship with local people, and ultimately failed along with Portugal's larger efforts on the northern Swahili coast.

The Colonial Countryside: Fukuchani and Mvuleni

The Fukuchani ruins (Fig. 6.2a) sit over earlier sites, the first occupied around 600 CE and the second in the fourteenth and fifteenth centuries, located on a cove with a view of Tumbatu channel (Fitton 2017; Horton, in prep.). Although not deep enough for European ocean-going vessels, the cove and channel could accommodate deep-draft launches (Fitton 2017). This feature undoubtedly drew Portuguese looking to connect their settlements to the sea. The eleven-room structure is surrounded by a mortared coral-rag wall with ~50 loopholes for guns or crossbows, allowing for a nearly 360° line-of-sight around the compound (Fig. 6.3a). Guarded doorways through this wall include one facing the water, one in the rear, and a probable third on the south. Fitton (2017) identified remnants of low earthen berms at the shoreline that may have related to a dock. A small storeroom or guard space stands in the enclosure's southwest corner.

In 2019 the Zanzibar Department of Antiquities and Museums carried out reconstruction without altering the original house floorplan. The latter is Iberian (see Niell and Sundt 2015), although very likely designed by Swahili masons and executed with local labor (see Meier 2016); the European footprint had been noted previously (Horton and Clark 1984–85). It resonates well with elite European residences, although smaller due to room-size limitations determined by mangrove-pole spanning joists. Fukuchani was single-story with mangrove-pole and mortar ceilings; evidence along the ceiling line suggests a usable open space under roof thatching held aloft by two columns. The main door faces seaward and is accessed from a wide veranda; it allows passage into a wide front room, additional rooms behind, and a central hallway straight through the house to a rear door. Rooms extend left and right off that hallway. Entrance into six rooms of the house was possible only from the surrounding veranda. Earlier conservation resulted in removal of interior deposits, which made discerning specific activity areas difficult. Nonetheless, the courtyard-entry of some rooms suggested that they were used for processing or storing of agricultural goods, and/or as living spaces for servants or lower-rank soldiers. This last possibility draws from the organization of Portuguese sailing vessels, where officers quartered separately from seamen (Candido 2010).

We mentioned at the outset the possibility that Fukuchani and Mvuleni related to tobacco growing. A room in Fukuchani's southeast corner off the back veranda bears evidence that may support this idea. In the walls are several opposing mortise holes, large enough to hold wooden racks that could relate to drying tobacco. Such racks could have been for other purposes, and additional free-standing ones could have been situated elsewhere, including

Figure 6.2. (*a*) Drone image of Fukuchani (M. Horton); (*b*) drone image of Mvuleni (M. Horton); (*c*) defended entrance to shallow cave and pool below Mvuleni (2017).

among the rafters following the model of English tobacco farms (Deetz 1993). Some location names and oral traditions (Horton, in prep.) associated with this part of the island and other indirect evidence support the sites' connection to tobacco. Tobacco is known to have been on Portuguese ships headed to China by the 1520s (Benedict 2011: 19) and to have been introduced to East Africa c. 1560 by Spanish and Portuguese merchants. In the sixteenth century it was exported to southern and West Africa (Alpern 2008; see also Vernet 2017: 56). Županov and Xavier (2014: 514–19) suggest that the Portuguese used a Roman idea of land tenure as they entered early modern globalization, looking for places to grow wheat and cereals as well as more exotic plants such as cinnamon and pepper. Indeed, Strandes (1989: 277) noted that tobacco (mentioned in 1698) was among the crops the Portuguese introduced along with cassava, maize, and pineapples. This suggests its cultivation was not mainstream, making the possibility of experimentation with it here intriguing. It seems unlikely that settlers lavished defensive architecture (including around agricultural fields, as we will see) on growing staples and crops with a short shelf-life. Sugar cane is another cash-crop possibility, yet we found no evidence of the necessary processing infrastructure. While not definitive, we think there is circumstantial evidence for an intent to grow tobacco here, with Fukuchani and Mvuleni working together to make it happen.

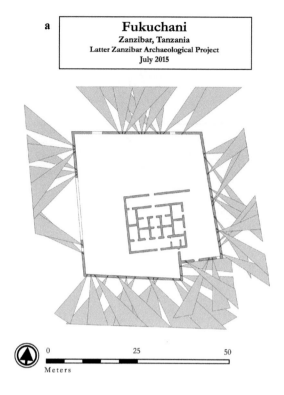

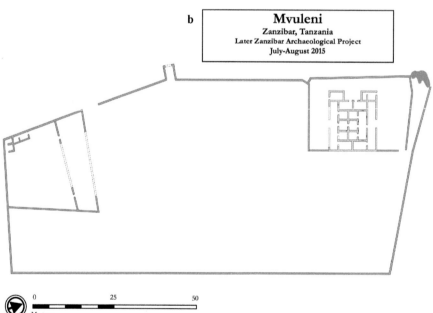

Figure 6.3. (*a*) Plan of redoubt at Fukuchani illustrating loop-hole views (H. Bassett); (*b*) plan of redoubt at Mvuleni (H. Bassett).

The Archaeology of Portuguese Agricultural Outposts in 17th-Century Zanzibar · 139

In such a scenario Fukuchani would have functioned as a reasonably secure residence and storehouse where agricultural products would be prepared for shipping. No larger fortification stood on Unguja at this time to which residents under threat could quickly retreat. The mission church and other buildings in Stone Town, though stoutly built, were 45 km away. Meanwhile, the architectural investment in these smaller settlements was not accompanied by a dense artifact record. Our systematic STP survey and excavation units within the enclosure recovered few locally made sixteenth-century artifacts. At the seaside, we recovered a piece of lead shot and a sherd of glazed European stoneware. We also found bits of iron slag, more likely from the sixth-century iron-producing village documented by Baužytė (2019). We recovered some glass beads and food remains but little pointing to prolonged activity at the Portuguese-period site. Fukuchani may have been built with the expectation of a long and profitable occupation despite little evidence of this happening. Supplies of European goods, available in the Portuguese settlement in Mombasa (Kirkman 1974) and at the Portuguese settlement in Stone Town (Power et al. 2020), were in short supply at Fukuchani.

Moving some 750 m inland we find Mvuleni at the base of an escarpment; on top of the escarpment is a modern village of the same name. A mortared coral-rag wall surrounds the house and a two-hectare plot of farmable land; a wall divides the house yard from the field (Fig. 6.2b). The surrounding wall here, too, has loopholes clustered on the north and south ends of the western wall and in a few other places, plus a small bastion jutting outward from the center of the western, seaward wall. Large sections of that wall have fallen.

The house has a long central corridor as at Fukuchani, a comparable floorplan, and a similar assortment of small rooms for living, processing, and storage (Fig. 6.3a). On the west side, twin latrines and other rooms are accessed directly from the yard. The northern, front yard's underlying coralline substrate sits at ground level. This exposed coral may have led to the house placement here, leaving the rich agricultural soil south of the structure available for cultivation. Beneath the house extends a shallow limestone cave fed by a spring; although the water is now brackish, modern residents of Mvulani village remember that within their lifetimes the water was fresh. Accessed via six squared-off steps cut into coral just north of the house (improved recently for safety), the pool remains in use by Mvuleni villagers who swim there, and tourists brought by local guides. The pool entrance was itself fortified: preventing outside access, and walled off from the house, a configuration suggesting control by the residents (Fig. 6.2c). Positioning a fortified structure atop a natural water source was a classic medieval European architectural feature, supporting the proposition that Portuguese planners considered raids on this space a possibility. In imagining how this might have worked in its original context, house residents' exchange relationships with Swahili villagers may have included access to this water source in exchange for fish, shellfish, or other local provisions as would have been consistent with coastal practices (Prestholdt 2001). However workable the relationship between local Swahili and the interlopers was, the presence of two major defensive structures at Mvulani and Fukuchani, including the taking and control of this water source, created a new colonial imprint on the landscape (see Haines and Hauser, this volume, on water access).

The absence of soil on the north side of the house eliminated the opportunity for archaeological deposits. The space immediately south, however, has areas with topsoil where we placed shovel-tests. One spot adjacent to the southeast section of the veranda would have been an appropriate location for an outdoor kitchen in the absence of an inner courtyard. The large exposure excavated there yielded an assemblage that allows us to suggest cautiously that it was a gendered workspace. In addition to local sixteenth–seventeenth-century sherds we retrieved glass beads, two earthenware spindle whorls, a small copper ring, and a worn copper coin. One spindle whorl was incised in a style represented in Chittick's (1974) typology from Kilwa; while he suggests a pre-sixteenth-century date for the style, here we consider this locally made and broadly contemporary with the site's occupation. Finding local artifacts inside Mvuleni's defensive wall suggests the presence of Swahili people and particularly women, a situation comparable to evidence from Elmina, for example, where local women were vital to the European colonial effort (DeCorse 2001; also Prestholdt 2001; Polónia and Capelão 2017).

A striking difference between Fukuchani and Mvuleni is the sizable agricultural space enclosed by the latter's defensive walls. STPs and excavations revealed a concentration of local artifacts and daub: evidence of some earth-and-thatch structures or features once standing inside the walled area, perhaps to provide shelter for workers. There is a question as to who these workers were. Some may have been local people. Otherwise, ship crews were drawn from all stations of Portuguese society, and it is entirely possible that men with agricultural backgrounds could have been brought here to work. Crew lists show that sixteenth-century Portuguese ship crews in the Indian Ocean were multi-ethnic and even primarily Muslim, adding the possibility of diverse workers employed in the countryside on Portuguese plantations (al-Salimi and Staples 2015).

As noted, in other Portuguese colonial situations—including in southeastern Africa—taking captives for enslaved labor was part of the colonizing model (Candido 2010). Slavery was also present on the coast before Portuguese arrival (Vernet 2017; Seetah et al., this volume), and we do not rule out the presence of enslaved people living and working at Mvuleni. Archaeological testing did not recover evidence for domestic life near the latrines, but earthenwares and small finds are scattered across most of the enclosed agricultural area, which would be consistent with plantation housing for captive or free workers. Our evidence suggests an overall small number of workers present, perhaps a mix of local Swahili farmers and others drawn from around the Indian Ocean.

We surface-collected and shovel-tested extending outward in all directions from the walled enclosure and located a light scatter of local earthenware that continued over some hectares now densely planted with coconut, banana, cassava, and other vegetation. It is possible that additional farmland extended beyond the enclosing walls, and that the secured area was maintained in case of the need for defense, and/or for the most commercially valuable crop(s), such as tobacco.

The small bastion on the west side of Mvuleni's enclosing wall provided the densest archaeological deposits from either site. We recovered European ceramics, a round gaming token fashioned of lime plaster and incised with an X, a blue glass marble, and a great deal of burned mussel and crab shell. Together these finds suggest that while men stood lookout in the bastion, they passed the time cooking and playing games. We also found an iron knife blade and an iron crossbow bolt. The greatest defensive concern, again, was likely against other Europeans or Omanis who might have arrived by ship. Day-to-day interaction with Swahili living nearby, however, may have been— really must have been—the norm. The assemblage from the agricultural field indicates that if the sites were places of heightened defensive preparedness, they were also characterized by routine, and boredom, resembling finds from colonial redoubts elsewhere (e.g., Spanish Colonial St. Augustine, Florida; Halbirt 2004).

We sought evidence of Portuguese activity extending beyond the confines of the two sites and found one important example. On the escarpment behind Mvuleni, we documented unmortared coral-rag walls—c. 3 m high, 0.6 m thick—which might be connected to Portuguese occupation of the area (Fig. 6.4). The cleared walls measured at least c. 170 linear m, including small rooms and enclosures. We expect that further clearing and mapping will reveal additional wall segments.

We see the walls' connection to Mvuleni (and Fukuchani) in two ways. First, it would have been only a short hike up the escarpment to gain a commanding view of ships coming and going in Tumbatu channel. Having an accessible redoubt there would make great sense. We cannot yet date this

Figure 6.4. Views of stone walling on escarpment above Mvuleni (2017).

walling; it could have been built by Swahili villagers earlier or later than the Portuguese occupation, although it is an atypical Swahili construction; Wolfgang Alders (2022) notes numerous unmortared low walls around agricultural fields in other parts of the island, however. Mvuleni elders suggested that ancestral villagers built the walls to keep feral pigs out of their gardens; indeed, the Portuguese transported pigs during their colonial expansions (Reitz and Waselkov 2015). In a Swahili setting in which the local population was predominantly Muslim, invasive pigs and their descendants would have been highly undesirable on the landscape. The location of these walls on the escarpment crest, however, and not everywhere there would have been gardens—where wooden fencing is a common response to animal pests—suggests that these began as an artifact of the Portuguese presence. The reference to feral pigs on the escarpment may recall an actual problem but may also be a collective memory of Portuguese use of the escarpment. Villagers could certainly have repurposed the walls later. By comparison, Pikirayi (2009: 175–77) records some 20 stacked stone enclosures on a ridge fitted with loopholes on Mt. Fura, Zimbabwe, thought to be of Portuguese construction. Those are more extensive than what we see above Mvuleni, but we can say minimally that placing walls along high landforms was a known Portuguese strategy for redoubts in the greater region.

Discussion

We have argued that agriculture, at least some of it protected, was the main function of Mvuleni, with Fukuchani acting as its partner for housing, processing, storage, and shipping. Where were Swahili people living in this area? Many currently inhabited villages in this part of Unguja are centuries old; we think it likely there was at least one contemporary Swahili settlement nearby. Mvuleni village, on the escarpment, may have been settled early enough to have coexisted with the Portuguese occupation, or sited atop an abandoned earlier village. Our test units there, limited to spaces away from currently inhabited houses, produced only undecorated ceramics that have not contributed to dating. From a Portuguese perspective, locating themselves near such a village for labor and trade/exchange would make sense. Swahili people likely held the literal high ground; we see the potential for partnership, whatever tensions pertained between the groups. The low ground has richer soil, such that we see the Portuguese as having chosen and appropriated a water source and some good fields over a more defensible location, but also maintaining a lookout on the escarpment.

There is much we did not find at these sites despite extensive testing: no large quantities of European or even more common Indian Ocean imports, such as Chinese and Middle Eastern ceramics. There were few beads, no smoking pipes (as a commercial crop tobacco would have been forbidden for local consumption), few personal items, and no evidence for violence or destruction. We were also hoping for more evidence of interactions with Swahili people. We think overall that we are seeing a failure to make a commercial enterprise work, and then abandonment when the Portuguese deserted the Stone Town in 1699. Although we have not been specific about the chronology of Fukuchani and Mvuleni, it makes most sense that they were constructed after Fort Jesus was completed in 1596, when confidence in regional settlement would have been growing. Meier (2016) notes that Portuguese construction incorporated verandas beginning in the seventeenth century; we have verandas at both sites. Based on the relatively thin deposits, we think occupation was likely for some years in the seventeenth century, and no later than the collapse of the Portuguese Stone Town settlement in 1699.

The land was certainly cultivated again by Swahili farmers. The stone buildings may have been reoccupied or reused for short periods; there is a light scatter of later cultural material, as often found around stone-built Swahili ruins, but we found no local memory of their reuse. Well constructed by local craftsmen, they nonetheless did not meet with Swahili practice or aesthetics. For the last 700–800 years, Swahili stone houses have featured an attention to privacy in their floorplans (Donley-Reid 1987), with front rooms to welcome guests (including foreign traders) but shield other parts of the house from view. Open inner courtyards brought in sunlight and a place for activities away from the public view. None of these principles is evident at Fukuchani or Mvuleni, which nonetheless must have been erected with extensive local expertise. Wilson (this volume) notes that Portuguese settlers in Goa, India, created an "integrated urban-agricultural system" that resonates potentially with Fukuchani and Mvuleni as elite, trade-oriented agricultural residences. However, Wilson also notes that archaeological reconstructions of Portuguese Goa align more closely with local settlement practices than with typical Portuguese colonial configurations, differing substantially from descriptions of Goa in Portuguese archives as well. Comparing colonial settlement patterns highlights Portuguese colonizers' need to localize their settler efforts and provides opportunity to examine local responses to the colonial presence.

The buildings now serve a purpose of attracting local and foreign visitors. Fukuchani is easily visible from the main north-south road on this side of Unguja, and visitors receive a welcome from the local schoolmaster, whose school is adjacent. At Mvuleni, visitors walk through the ruins, perhaps swim

The Archaeology of Portuguese Agricultural Outposts in Seventeenth-Century Zanzibar · 145

in the cave pool, and trek up the escarpment for the view and to visit Mvuleni village. The so-called Portuguese period is not well understood in Zanzibar culture history, especially with the intervening Omani period looming so large. We hope that collaboration to construct a more accessible history of the sites and the period they represent will enhance their local value intellectually and economically. A visitor center has been built by the Zanzibar government, and we have helped craft an accessible narrative for local and foreign visitors.

Conclusion

Massive stone structures bristling with cannon and those associated with notable European figures drew historical archaeologists of the colonial period to Africa. But the kind of research conducted to understand colonialism in West Africa, for example, has not been carried out to the same extent on the continent's eastern shores, nor in more rural settings. Kirkman's investigations at Fort Jesus were aimed at understanding life inside the garrison in a historical context, to tell a European story built on an older Eurocentric body of scholarship. The LZAP project draws inspiration from DeCorse's (2001) work at Elmina, trained not only on ways that European politics and economy converged on the Gold Coast, but also on how local people incorporated Europeans into local processes and negotiations. Pikirayi's (2009) research at Portuguese *feiras* and other non-urban Portuguese sites situates colonists in their interactions with local communities in Zimbabwe. Fukuchani and Mvuleni operated in a perhaps quieter corner of the Portuguese colonial world but were nonetheless affected by current political machinations. There is much to understand still, not only about European disruptions but about how ordinary Swahili—beyond sultans, queens, and kings of important stone towns—made sense of their entanglements with Portuguese, used them (in places) for access to power relations and perhaps certain goods, and ignored them when interests did not align, as we see happen in many colonial situations. Indeed, this is also true for the subsequent Omani colonial period, where shared religious practice created a different colonial context for Swahili (Seetah et al., this volume). We are also cognizant that while impressive stone structures—from Fort Jesus all the way down in scale to Fukuchani and Mvuleni—represented tremendous outlays of European capital, they were monuments to European fragility at a local level (DeCorse 2001; al-Salimi and Staples 2015: 325). Indeed, European accounts frequently mention the inability to maintain resident staff due to illness and costs, and the resulting reliance on local populations for trade in foodstuffs, administrative and military support, and farming. Most colonial efforts that failed went unnoticed for years, if not centuries, because of their modest architectural footprints and material residue (e.g., the "Lost Colony of Roanoke" [Lawler 2018]; Columbus's La Navidad in Haiti). We have quite the opposite here: stout standing architecture in the countryside, with a less developed narrative around them. In terms of the artifact signature, we see past that to a colonial failure, or at best only a short-term commercial enterprise.

The Portuguese agitated their way through the Indian Ocean World with both marked successes and disasters, disrupting centuries-old networks but not fully prepared to capitalize on the disruptions. A fuller understanding of the global forces that came to bear on local micro-economies and how those entanglements played out in the Swahili world could emerge through increased archaeological attention to the last five centuries of coastal history. The archaeology of colonialism is a productive subfield in our discipline, although the Indian Ocean region has only begun to benefit from such interest (see Seetah 2018). The watershed 1980s historiographic understandings of Swahili recontextualized it as an indigenous, cosmopolitan society, in which stone towns were not evidence of colonial settlement, but rather centers tied to local and regional populations and networks. Recent research further complicates this narrative (Brielle et al. 2023). We look forward to a continued blossoming of contextualized archaeological research that takes us more seamlessly from the best-known centuries on the East African coast through the colonial period and into the most recent past.

Acknowledgments

Thank you to Julia Jong Haines and Mark Hauser for their invitation to be in this volume and for their editorial input. Adria LaViolette presented a version of the chapter in the Anthropology Graduate Students Organization (AGSO) Speaker Series, Syracuse University, in November 2020. We thank the AGSO for that opportunity and the generous feedback provided by audience members at the Zoom talk. We thank Jeffrey Hantman, Rhiannon Stephens, and Jeffrey Fleisher for comments on earlier drafts; Caesar Bita and Paul Lane for their consultation; and the anonymous reviewers for their responses, all of which improved the clarity of the chapter.

For research permission we thank Dr. Amina Issa and the current leadership of the Zanzibar Ministry of Museums and Antiquities. We thank particularly the Head of Zanzibar Antiquities, Abdallah K. Ali, for his vision and collegial collaboration during this project and over many years. The British Institute in Eastern Africa, University of Dar es Salaam, College of William &

Mary, University of Virginia, and Springer/Nature provided essential financial and material support. We thank Mark Horton for his invitation to our 2017 crew to participate in excavations on the Portuguese deposits in Stone Town, for access to his research records on Fukuchani and Mvuleni, and his generous drone photography.

We thank Zanzibar Antiquities archaeology and heritage staff Ali V. Juma and Ally Ussi for their invaluable leadership and participation. Historian Jema Halfan contributed generously to our 2015 field season. We are grateful to our Later Zanzibar Archaeology Project field and lab assistants for their hard work and good cheer: Wolfgang Alders, Miza Alex, Nassor Ali, Stephen Armstrong, Madeleine Bassett, Irtefa Binte-Farid, Phoebe Fisher, Maria Gajewska, Kelly Hoag, Jackson Kimambo, Jack LaViolette, Zachary McKeeby, Hamad Suleiman, and Issa Zuberi. Hayden Bassett provided expertise in photogrammetry, mapping, and architectural history. Finally, we are grateful to the Nungwi and Mvuleni leadership and residents who supported aspects of our work.

Bibliography

Abungu, George Okello, Mohamed Mchulla Mohamed, Abdallah Allausy, and Abdallah Khamis Ali. 2018. "The Future of Swahili Monuments." In *The Swahili World,* edited by Stephanie Wynne-Jones and Adria LaViolette, 642–50. London: Routledge.

Alders, Wolfgang A. 2022. *Uneven Ground: The Archaeology of Social Transformation in Zanzibar, Tanzania.* PhD diss., University of California–Berkeley.

Alpern, Stanley B. 2008. "Exotic Plants of Western Africa: Where They Came From and When." *History in Africa* 35: 63–102.

Axelson, Eric. 1973. *Portuguese in South-East Africa 1488–1600.* Johannesburg: C. Struik.

Baužytė, Ema. 2019. *Making and Trading Iron in the Swahili World: an Archaeometallurgical Study of Iron Production Technologies, their Role, and Exchange Networks in 500–1500 CE Coastal Tanzania.* PhD diss., Aarhus University, Denmark.

Benedict, Carol. 2011. *Golden-Silk Smoke: A History of Tobacco in China, 1550–2010.* Berkeley: University of California Press.

Bennett, Norman R. 1978. *A History of the Arab State of Zanzibar.* New York: Harper Collins.

Biginagwa, Thomas J., and Bertram B. B. Mapunda. 2018. "The Kilwa-Nyasa Caravan Route: The Long-Neglected Trading Corridor in Southern Tanzania." In *The Swahili World,* edited by Stephanie Wynne-Jones and Adria LaViolette, 541–54. London: Routledge.

Boxer, C. R., and Carlos de Azevedo. 1960. *Fort Jesus and the Portuguese in Mombasa, 1593–1729.* London: Hollis & Carter.

Brielle, E. S., J. Fleisher, S. Wynne-Jones, K. Sirak, N. Broomandkhoshbacht, K. Callan . . . and C. M. Kusimba. 2023. "Entwined African and Asian Genetic Roots of Medieval Peoples of the Swahili Coast." *Nature* 615: 866–73.

Candido, Mariana P. 2010. "Different Slave Journeys: Enslaved African Seamen on Board of Portuguese Ships, c. 1760–1820s." *Slavery and Abolition* 31(3): 395–409.

Casson, Lionel. 1989. *The Periplus Maris Erythraei: Text with Introduction, Translation, and Commentary.* Princeton, N.J.: Princeton University Press.

Chittick, H. Neville. 1974. *Kilwa: An Islamic Trading City on the East African Coast.* Vol. I. Nairobi: British Institute in Eastern Africa.

Coppola, Anna Rita. 2018. "Swahili Oral Traditions and Chronicles." In *The Swahili World,* edited by Stephanie Wynne-Jones and Adria LaViolette, 147–55. London: Routledge.

Croucher, Sarah K. 2014. *Capitalism and Cloves: An Archaeology of Plantation Life on Nineteenth-Century Zanzibar.* New York: Springer.

DeCorse, Christopher. 2001. *An Archaeology of Elmina: Europeans and Africans on the Gold Coast, 1400–1900.* Washington, D.C.: Smithsonian Institution Press.

Deetz, James F. 1993. *Flowerdew Hundred: The Archaeology of a Virginia Plantation, 1619–1864.* Charlottesville, Va.: University Press of Virginia.

Dietler, Michael. 1997. "The Iron Age in Mediterranean France: Colonial Encounters, Entanglements, and Transformations." *Journal of World Prehistory* 11(3): 269–358.

Donley-Reid, Linda W. 1987. "Life in the Swahili Town House Reveals the Symbolic Meaning of Spaces and Artefact Assemblages." *African Archaeological Review* 5: 181–92.

Fitton, Tom. 2017. "Pushing the Boat Out: A Study of Spatial Organisation and Harbour Spaces in the Early Swahili Ports of the Zanzibar Archipelago, 550–1100 CE." PhD diss., University of York.

Fleisher, Jeffrey. 2004. "Behind the Sultan of Kilwa's 'Rebellious Conduct': Local Perspectives on an International East African Town." In *African Historical Archaeologies,* edited by Andrew M. Reid and Paul J. Lane, 91–123. New York: Kluwer Academic/Plenum Publishers.

———. 2010. "Swahili Synoecism: Rural Settlements and Town Formation on the Central East African Coast, AD 750–1500." *Journal of Field Archaeology* 35(3): 265–82.

Fleisher, Jeffrey, Paul Lane, Adria LaViolette, Annalisa Christie, Mark Horton, Edward Pollard, Eréndira Quintana Morales, Thomas Vernet, and Stephanie Wynne-Jones. 2015. "When Did the Swahili Become Maritime?" *American Anthropologist* 117(1): 100–15.

Fleisher, Jeffrey, and Adria LaViolette. 2007. "The Changing Power of Swahili Houses, Fourteenth to Nineteenth Centuries A.D." In *The Durable House: House Society Models in Archaeology,* edited by R. A. Beck Jr., 175–97. Carbondale: Southern Illinois University.

Fonseca, L. A. 2017. "Portuguese Maritime Expansion from the African Coast to India." In *The Sea in History: The Medieval World,* edited by Michel Balard and Christian Buchet, 642–53. New York: Boydell Press.

Freeman-Grenville, G.S.P. 1989. "The Portuguese on the Swahili Coast: Buildings and Language." *Studia* 49: 235–54.

Gosden, Chris. 2004. *Archaeology and Colonialism: Cultural Contact from 5000 BC to the Present.* Cambridge, U.K.: Cambridge University Press.

Gray, Sir John. 1962. *History of Zanzibar from the Middle Ages to 1856.* Oxford: Oxford University Press.

Halbirt, Carl. 2004. "La Ciudad de San Augustin: A European Fighting Presidio in Eighteenth-Century 'La Florida.'" *Historical Archaeology* 38(3): 33–46.

Horton, Mark. 1998. "The Portuguese Encounter with the Swahili Towns of the East African Coast." In *Cultures of the Indian Ocean,* edited by J. Hallet and C. Amaral, 373–84. Lisbon: Comissão Nacional para as Comemorações dos Descobrimentos Portugueses.

———. In prep. *Zanzibar and Pemba: The Archaeology of an Indian Ocean Archipelago.*

Horton, Mark, and Felix Chami. 2018. "Swahili Origins." In *The Swahili World,* edited by S. Wynne-Jones and A. LaViolette, 135–46. London: Routledge.

Horton, Mark, and Catherine Clark. 1984–85. *Zanzibar Archaeological Survey 1984/5.* Zanzibar: Ministry of Information, Culture, and Sports.

Horton, Mark, and John Middleton. 2000. *The Swahili: The Social Landscape of a Mercantile Society.* Oxford: Blackwell.

Kirkman, James S. 1964. *Men and Monuments on the East African Coast.* London: Lutterworth Press.

———. 1974. *Fort Jesus: A Portuguese Fortress on the East African Coast.* Oxford: Clarendon.

Kusimba, Chapurukha M. 1999. *The Rise and Fall of Swahili States.* Walnut Creek, Calif.: AltaMira.

Lane, Paul J. 2018. "The Archaeology of Colonial Encounters in Coastal East Africa: Recent Developments and Continuing Conceptual Challenges." In *Connecting Continents: Archaeology and History in the Indian Ocean World,* edited by Krish Seetah, 143–70. Athens: Ohio University Press.

LaViolette, Adria. 2004. "Swahili Archaeology and History on Pemba, Tanzania: A Critique and Case Study of the Use of Written and Oral Sources in Archaeology." In *African Historical Archaeologies,* edited by Andrew M. Reid and Paul J. Lane, 125–62. New York: Kluwer Academic/Plenum Publishers.

———. 2018. Pemba Island, *c.* 1000–1500 CE. In *The Swahili World,* edited by Stephanie Wynne-Jones and Adria LaViolette, 231–38. London: Routledge.

Lawler, Andrew. 2018. *The Secret Token: Myth, Obsession, and the Search for the Lost Colony of Roanoke.* New York: Doubleday.

Marshall, Lydia Wilson. 2012. "Spatiality and the Interpretation of Identity Formation: Fugitive Slave Community Creation in Nineteenth-Century Kenya." *African Archaeological Review* 29: 355–81.

Marshall, Lydia Wilson, and Herman Kiriama. 2018. "The Legacy of Slavery on the Swahili Coast." In *The Swahili World,* edited by Stephanie Wynne-Jones and Adria LaViolette, 566–76. London: Routledge.

Meier, Prita. 2016. *Swahili Port Cities: The Architecture of Elsewhere.* Bloomington: Indiana University Press.

Moorthy, Shanti. 2010. "Abdulrazak Gurnah and Littoral Cosmopolitanism." In *Indian Ocean Studies,* edited by Shanti Moorthy and Ashraf Jamal, 73–102. London: Routledge.

Niell, Paul B., and Richard Sundt. 2015. "Architecture of Colonizers/Architecture of Immigrants: Gothic in Latin America from the 16th to 20th Centuries." *Postmedieval: A Journal of Medieval Cultural Studies* 6: 247–53.

Pawlowicz, Matthew, and Adria LaViolette. 2013. "Swahili Historical Chronicles from an Archaeological Perspective: Bridging History, Archaeology, Coast, and Hinterland in Southern Tanzania." In *The Death of Prehistory,* edited by Peter R. Schmidt and Stephen A. Mrozowski, 117–40. Oxford: Oxford University Press.

Pearson, Michael N. 1998. *Port Cities and Intruders: The Swahili Coast, India, and Portugal in the Early Modern Era*. Baltimore: Johns Hopkins University Press.

Pikirayi, Innocent. 2009. "Palaces, *Feiras* and *Prazos:* An Historical Archaeological Perspective of African-Portuguese Contact in Northern Zimbabwe." *African Archaeological Review* 26: 163–85.

Polónia, Amélia, and Rosa Capelão. 2017. "Connecting Worlds: Women as Intermediaries in the Portuguese Overseas Empire, 1500–1600." In *Cooperation and Empire: Local Realities of Global Processes*, edited by Tanya Bührer, Flavio Eichmann, and Stig Förster, 58–89. New York: Berghahn Books.

Power, Timothy, and Mark Horton (with Omar Salem al-Kaabi, Mohamed Matar al-Dhaheri, Myriam Saleh al-Dhaheri, Noura Hamed al-Hameli, Henry Webber, and Rosie Ireland). 2020. "Excavations at the Old Fort of Stone Town, Zanzibar: New Evidence of Historic Interactions between the Swahili Coast and Arabian Gulf." *Proceedings of the Seminar for Arabian Studies 50: Papers from the 53rd Meeting of the Seminar for Arabian Studies, University of Leiden, July 11–13th, 2019*. Havertown, Pa.: Casemate Academic.

Pradines, Stéphane. 2016. "Portuguese Fortresses in East Africa." *Fort* 44: 50–75.

Prestholdt, Jeremy. 2001. "Portuguese Conceptual Categories and the 'Other' Encounter on the Swahili Coast." *Journal of Asian and African Studies* 36(4): 383–406.

Reitz, Elizabeth J., and Gregory A. Waselkov. 2015. "Vertebrate Use at Early Colonies on the Southeastern Coasts of Eastern North America." *International Journal of Historical Archaeology* 19(1): 21–45.

Ribeiro da Silva, Filipa. 2015. "Portuguese Empire Building and Human Mobility in São Tomé and Angola, 1400s-1700s." In *Mobility Makes States: Migration and Power in Africa*, edited by Darshan Vigneswaran and Joel Quirk, 37–58. Philadelphia: University of Pennsylvania Press.

Rosa, F. 2015. *The Portuguese in the Creole Indian Ocean*. New York: Palgrave Macmillan.

al-Salimi, Abdul Rahman, and Eric Staples. 2015. "Reflections of a Muslim-Portuguese Maritime World in a Sixteenth-Century Portuguese Source." *Proceedings of the Seminar for Arabian Studies* 45: 321–27.

Sassoon, Hamo. 1981. "Ceramics from the Wreck of a Portuguese Ship at Mombasa." *Azania* 16: 98–130.

———. 1982. "The Sinking of the *Santo António de Tanná* in Mombasa Harbour." *Paideuma* 28: 101–8.

Schmidt, Peter R. 1978. *Historical Archaeology: A Structural Approach in an African Culture*. Westport, Conn.: Greenwood Press.

Seetah, Krish (ed.). 2018. *Connecting Continents: Archaeology and History in the Indian Ocean World*. Athens: Ohio University Press.

Sheriff, Abdul. 1987. *Slaves, Spices and Ivory in Zanzibar*. London: James Currey.

Sinclair, Paul, and Thomas Håkansson. 2000. "The Swahili City-State Culture." In *A Comparative Study of Thirty City-State Cultures*, edited by M. Hansen, 463–82. Copenhagen: The Royal Danish Academy of Sciences and Letters.

Strandes, Justus. 1989 [1899]. *The Portuguese Period in East Africa*, translated by Jean F. Wallwork, edited by James S. Kirkman. Nairobi: Kenya Literature Bureau.

Vernet, Thomas. 2004. "Le territoire hors les murs des cités-états swahili de l'archipel de Lamu, 1600–1800." *Journal des Africanistes* 74(1–2): 381–411.

———. 2017. "The Deep Roots of the Plantation Economy on the Swahili Coast: Productive Functions and Social Functions of Slaves and Dependents, circa 1580–1820." In *Changing Horizons of African History,* edited by Awet T. Weldemichael, Anthony A. Lee, and Edward A. Alpers, 51–100. Trenton, N.J.: Africa World Press.

Wynne-Jones, Stephanie. 2010. "Remembering and Reworking the Swahili Diwanate: The Role of Objects and Places at Vumba Kuu." *International Journal of African Historical Studies* 43(3): 407–27.

———. 2016. *A Material Culture: Consumption and Materiality on the Coast of Precolonial East Africa.* Oxford: Oxford University Press.

———. 2018. "The Social Composition of Swahili Society." In *The Swahili World,* edited by Stephanie Wynne-Jones and Adria LaViolette, 293–305. London: Routledge.

Županov, Ines G., and Angela Barreto Xavier. 2014. "Quest for Permanence in the Tropics: Portuguese Bioprospecting in Asia (16th–18th Centuries)." *Journal of the Economic and Social History of the Orient* 57(4): 511–48.

7

Sources for Analyzing the Social and Economic Contexts of the Diaspora on the Coromandel Coast

V. Selvakumar and Mark William Hauser

One of the most profound material legacies of European colonial efforts in Asia is in South Asia, which includes the modern-day countries of Bangladesh, Bhutan, India, Pakistan, Nepal, and Sri Lanka. India is one of the largest postcolonial states in the world and home to nearly 1.42 billion people. Equally profound is the scale and extent of the South Asian Diaspora and its material legacies throughout the world (see Haines and Hauser; Čaval and Cianciosi, this volume). If we take just one chapter of that history, the movement of indentured laborers in the wake of slavery's abolition, approximately 1.6 million people were transported to the Atlantic, the Pacific, and other parts of the Indian Ocean. In those places, community members left indelible impressions on the tangible and intangible heritage–shaping landscape, language, and culinary practices. Understanding the contexts from which those communities came is important in documenting those transformations. In this chapter, we explore the varied sources required to understand and situate the South Asian diaspora in South India. The combination of archaeological and textural sources from Chennai to Nagapattinam explored here provides one means through which to document how local economic, social, and political dynamics contributed to the South Asian diaspora.

There is considerable potential for an archaeology of the South Asian diaspora and the contexts from which people originated in South India. Understanding the more recent past through the archaeological record surrounding colonial enclaves is not without its challenges. In South Asia, there has been a traditional tendency by the archaeological community to focus on prehistoric and early historical periods, with only some attention paid to medieval and colonial phases. Furthermore, the built heritage related to the European colonial era is rich, especially in former colonial enclaves, and archaeological attention in these enclaves has traditionally focused on fortifications and commercial buildings. Focus on such monuments can have the unintended consequence of reinforcing dominant narratives about the past. Such focus has also come at the expense of examining contemporary settlements in the hinterland. This is a shame since historians and anthropologists have shown the role that these settlements played in transforming regional economies, developing craft industries, and human migration (Arasaratnam 1986; Ramaswamy 1985; Subrahmanyam 1987, 2009; Subrahmanyam and Bayly 1988; Kanakalatha Mukund 1999; Om Prakash 2007; Fihl 2009; Fihl and Venkatachalapathy 2009; Roy 2014; Stephen 2014, 2018; Allen 2014a, 2014b, 2017; Sunil Amrit 2015; Mbeki and van Rossum 2017; Stanziani 2020). More recently scholars have been challenging this tendency by showing how archaeology can contribute to understanding the changing contours of the Indian Ocean World through the archaeological record (see Varma, this volume). Indeed, as has been demonstrated elsewhere, there is ample scope for undertaking historical and archaeological research on settlements (Hauser and Selvakumar 2021), urbanization (Wilson this volume), craft networks (Selvakumar 2017), and commerce (Selvakumar 2019).

In this chapter, we make three interrelated points. First, to conflate the various diasporic communities solely with labor migration is to overlook some of the commercial dynamics that led South Asians to live in varied parts of the world, especially in the precolonial period. Rice cultivation, long a staple for local and regional economies, provides a mechanism through which to view political arrangements and the consolidation of a burgeoning commercial class. Textile weaving was also a crucial expanding industry, feeding local, regional, and global markets. While debt bondage and other forms of servitude existed in precolonial South India and could form a basis for agricultural labor, such workers were rarely transported overseas. Rather, Tamil-speaking merchant communities dotted the Indian Ocean, facilitating trade in textiles and foodstuffs. Such engagement did not come without a political, economic, or ecological cost.

Second, there is an archaeological record that documents the long-term contexts and conditions which prompted marginalized people to enter into indenture contracts in the nineteenth century--a significant component of the South Asian diaspora. Archaeological survey shows how settlements geared toward commercial agriculture and rural industry increased in number or enlarged during the early colonial period, recruiting workers from other parts of the subcontinent and spurring a system of intra-regional migrations. Beginning in the 17th century, Europeans purchased large quantities of textiles

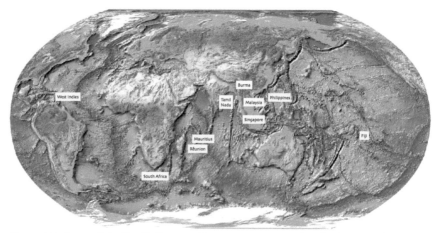

Figure 7.1. Areas of the Tamil diaspora. Base map courtesy of Michael Schmeling.

that became implicated in the trans-Atlantic slave trade either as sumptuary goods or as currency in the trade of humans. At the same time, people became more dependent on regional trade for food staples, such as rice. Many of the settlements established or expanded in the early colonial period show some abandonment in the nineteenth century. Many of the agricultural workers cultivating rice and servicing weaving centers became potential conscripts for human trafficking during periods of famine and warfare that characterized the eighteenth and nineteenth centuries.

Third, we show how sources comparable to those used in the historical archaeology of the Atlantic, such as European documents and material culture from commercial, domestic, and factory contexts, provide only a limited glimpse into contexts in which diasporic communities originated. Such studies are profoundly enriched by incorporating a more diverse array of sources. These include traditional archaeological sources highlighting the political and economic contours of settlements devoted to rural industry and commercial agriculture in the longue durée. They also include temple inscriptions that help situate the commercial and legal arrangements facilitating commercial agriculture and rural industry. They also include literary sources, such as Cindu (poems), which provide compelling accounts of the lived experience of laborers transported to distant shores.

Geographic and Historical Context

The Coromandel coast in South India traditionally refers to the southeastern coast of the Indian subcontinent, which now includes the modern states of Karnataka and Tamil Nadu and the union territories of Pondicherry. Of India's seven major rivers, two, the Krishna and the Kaveri, flow into the Coromandel coast, directly linking hinterland economies with Indian Ocean trade networks. These southernmost states contain settlements and port towns that have engaged in sustained interoceanic commerce over the centuries. It is not surprising, therefore, that the Coromandel coast occupied a pivotal position in the political and commercial activities of the Indian Ocean region from the sixteenth to the early twentieth century.

Long focused on this region, overseas mercantile companies and the maritime enterprises of colonial powers impacted not only the history of South India in general but, more specifically, the trajectory of certain enclaves in coastal areas along the Coromandel coast. Between the sixteenth and nineteenth centuries, the Coromandel coast could also be defined by the dense cluster of European-commissioned fortifications and port towns. These fortified ports and commercial centers relied on rural industry, commercial agriculture, and merchant networks forged after the twelfth century. That being said, colonial engagements created precarities that agricultural workers and craft producers would encounter.

Enticed by colonial developments, lower middle-income groups, small landholders, warriors, and poorer and marginalized sections of society migrated to port towns and coastal areas. People willingly also migrated to foreign lands as a result of political instability in South India from the twelfth century onward. In this location of commercial agriculture and rural industry people were conscripted as laborers from the coastal and hinterland regions of South India and brought to Indian Ocean ports. The terms of labor varied from debt bondage to indentureship, but their conscription invariably resulted from numerous factors, including an increase in population density, competition for available resources, higher taxation on land and commodity production, and famines (Fig. 7.1).

The colonial capitalist system needed labor and service classes to support the production systems around tobacco, sugar cane, tea, rubber, coffee, and rice cultivation in various European colonies. New forms of economic production associated with commercial agriculture, such as growing cash crops on plantations, required cheap labor. As a result, colonial powers fostered the slave trade (Gøbel 2016; Izquierdo Díaz 2019) and later facilitated indentured labor migrations, as discussed in several chapters in this volume. One of the hunting grounds for such labor was Asia and India. Colonial powers relied on racial stereotyping to identify particular communities deemed to be "suitable" laborers, such as the Tamils, who were known for being "non-belligerent," and "amenable" workers. People in need of subsistence became victims of this system. By 1931 roughly 1.5 million Tamils from South India worked in various British colonies (Guilmoto 1993). Although the precolonial labor employment system was unequal—aligned along communities of difference—a cocktail of colonialism, merchant capitalism, and commercial agriculture intensified exploitation and played a powerful role in South Indian lives and in the South Asian diaspora from the colonial period to twentieth-century global decolonization.

Contextualizing Sources for Diaspora in South India

Considering the combination of classical Tamil literary sources, excavated settlements, and the distribution of contemporary material culture at Arikamedu and Kaveripumpattinam (Poompuhar) suggests the presence of Indian Ocean port towns and production centers since the second century BCE, if not earlier (Rajan 2019). By the tenth century, the Coromandel coast and its hinterland settlement network had an active role in long-distance trade activities. Copper plates and temple inscriptions from between the tenth and sixteenth centuries show a florescence of ports and productions centers at Sadras (Sadurangapattinam) (Karashima 2001: 171) and Tharangambadi (Subramanian 2003: 4). Copper plates also reveal a series of ports most closely associated with Muslim traders, including Nagore, in the tenth century as well as Parangipettai, Kilakkarai, Periyapattinam, Kunimeddu, and Korkai after the twelfth century (Mohamad 2004; Hassan, Mydin and Saidumasudu 2018).

By the seventeenth century, these ports were geographically clustered in three regions: the North including Santhome (Portuguese), Madras (English), and Pulicat (Portuguese, Dutch); Central, including Sadras (Dutch), Pondicherry (Danish then French), Cuddalore (English); and the South, including Porto Novo (Portuguese, Swedish, English), Tharangambadi (Danish), Karaikkal (French), and Nagapattinam (Portuguese, Dutch) (Stephen 2014; n.d.) (Fig. 7.2). Another group of ports existed in the pearl fisher coast of Southern Tamil Nadu but is outside the scope of this paper.

One of the challenges for historical archaeologist is the fact that, in the sources available, many ports are identified by various names. In some instances, this is the result of changing identifications, shortening, or transliteration. For example, Sadras, a factory closely associated with the Dutch in the seventeenth century, was called "Rajanarayanan pattinam" in the fourteenth century (Baliga 2000: 118). Over the next three centuries, its name became Sadiravasagan Pattinam, then Sadurangapattinam and was later abbreviated to Sadras by Europeans (Karashima 2001: 171). Other port names changed over time, reflecting the nationalities of merchant colonies located within their quarters. Pulicat was known as Anandarayanpattinam before becom-

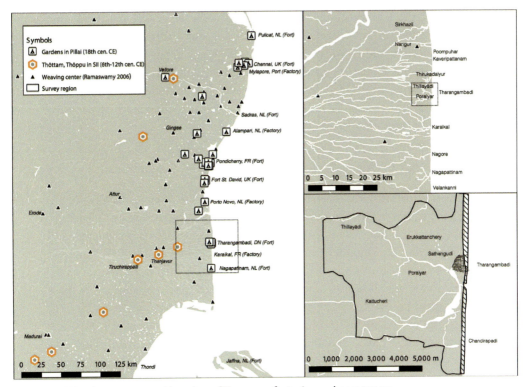

Figure 7.2. Weaving centers and location of European factories and port towns.

ing a Portuguese, and then a Dutch, commercial center (SII 17: 679). Pulicat (or Anandarayanpattinam) was already a major port and textile center with Armenian, Arabic, and Telugu Chetti traders when the Portuguese arrived in 1517 (Subrahmanyan 1990: 96; Teles E Cunha 2007). Simple miscommunication also contributed to the evolution in names. For example, during their control of the location between 1620 and 1845, the Danish called Tharangambadi, Tranquebar. The Danes appear to have attached the Arabic suffix -bar for land to a transliterated and shortened version of Tharangambadi, which was variously identified as Kulasekaranpattinam (SII 4: 399) and Sadanganpadi (SII 4: 401).

Inscriptions found on temples have been useful in studying commercial dynamics. For example, several temple-centric towns and villages along the Coromandel coast appear to have been in continuous existence since the seventh century, if not earlier. They functioned as regional political headquarters (*naadu*), commercial centers (*nagaram*), and religious centers (sacred temples of Saiva and Vaishnava origins). These centers and the associated settlements were also areas of agrarian and commodity production. From the seventh century, these centers linked one of two ports on the coast (Arikamedu and Kaveripattinam) with hinterland markets, and supplied human and material resources for trade. Inscriptions on temples speak about land grants as well as the establishment of rural industries, including weavers who produced commodities meant for long-distance trade. Communities of lower income groups and those from the dry regions beyond the Coromandel, attracted by the labor service trade, also existed.

Precolonial Craft and Agricultural Production and Circulations

The foundation for all subsequent developments in the expansion of commerce began before the thirteenth century, when the number of villages in the interior of the Coromandel Coast tripled, the number of people living in towns grew, the amount of metal-based currency circulated between different hamlets increased, and villages and towns mushroomed. Settlement survey and toponyms allow us to document evidence for the materialization of these changes in the landscape. Formal records manifest in palm leaves and temple inscriptions enable us to count the number of weaving centers, the dispensation of garden lands (*Thottam* and *Thoppu*), trade and exchange of commodities, as well as mortgages and debts contracted by individuals from institutions such as temples and mosques. Guilds, or *nagarams*, and temple boards, or *sabha*, played important investment roles in local rice and cloth production. Guilds in and around towns established close contact with temples. As assemblies received gold or grain (in the form of rice paddy), temples not only performed functions of receiving gifts but also made sure that they received returns, in cash or in kind, on their investments. The *sabha* invested donations in a productive enterprise, such as weaving, and utilized interest accrued from the investment for a stipulated endowment. Some inscriptions reveal that money deposited with residents of a village in turn reinvested accrued interest in paddy. The growth of these temple towns was associated with, and dependent on, an increase in agriculture manufacturing and commercial activities.

Explaining this change in archaeological settlement pattern requires some contextualization. From the seventh through the twelfth century CE, agrarian and craft production, temple-centric activities, and long-distance interactions grew (Nilakanta Sastry 1955; Champakalakshmi 1996; Hall 1980; Karashima 2002; Subbarayalu 2012). Merchant guilds maintained their own armies to respond to various agencies' interference in their activities. They did not, however, have either the aspiration or the power for political control. Moreover, the nature of their activities and their insistence on ethical codes and welfare measures reveal the conflict-ridden conditions in which they had to undertake commercial activities. Nevertheless, some guilds, such as the Manigramattar and Tisayirattuainurruvar guilds, extended their reach as far as Southeast Asia and China. Hinterland participation in Indian Ocean trade prior to the twelfth century is best known from temple inscriptions that show the sale of quantities of rice as well as the considerable strength and power of guilds (Karashima 2002) and maritime networks (Selvakumar 2019). The prevalence of inscriptions detailing commodity transactions and assigned values suggests the changing nature of political and economic fortunes.

The frequency of inscriptions declined dramatically beginning in the last quarter of the twelfth century, leading to what appears to be a sudden disappearance of these guilds. While it appears that the merchants began to operate as individual agents, guilds continued to exert some influence in commerce until the seventeenth century, when European power began to form joint stock companies with South Indian merchants in order to gain greater access to the hinterland and markets (Stephen 2014: 352). The merchants' voluntary contributions to the temples (*Pattanpa gudi*) continued to be one measure through which guilds distributed commodities (Shanmugam 2002). These contributions also reveal the continued relevancy of guilds despite their absence in other temple inscriptions.

The growth of the weaving industry is an especially striking feature during this period, with an increase in the number of production centers, the arrangements of their charters, and the volume of their output (Ramaswamy 2006). In a comprehensive review of South Indian temple inscriptions, Vijaya Ramaswamy (2006) identified weaving communities that emerged between the tenth century C.E. and the sixteenth century C.E. When mapped in relation to physical geography and port towns through the archaeological and documentary record, we can make the following observations. The 132 weaving centers documented on temple inscriptions were located throughout South India close to the tributaries or main branches of the region's major river systems (Krishna, Pennar, Palar, Pennaiyar, Kaveri, and Vaippar rivers). The densest cluster of weaving centers was located between the Palar and Kaveri rivers in Medieval India. Port towns associated with these drainages were not located on the Arabian Sea, but on the Bay of Bengal, suggesting that overseas textile trade originated on the eastern coast of South India.

Crucial transformations in the political arena of South Asia from the twelfth century CE greatly influenced all spheres of society (Karashima 2001; Appadorai 1936; Tschacher 2018). The expansion of West-Central Asian political powers into South Asia and the Indian Ocean region added to preexisting political conflicts for territorial control (Mukund 1999: 53–58). In South

Figure 7.3. Weaver's pit loom, Thilyaidi, 2019 (photo by Hauser).

India, new political regimes began to replace the old orders of the Cholas, Pandyas, Chalukyas, and Hoysalas. These new powers emerged from the Deccan region—Andhra Pradesh, Karnataka, and Maharashtra—and expanded in the extreme south and along the Coromandel coast (Mukund 1999).

Historians focusing on South India between the twelfth and sixteenth centuries stress that weaving was an industry geared to both local and overseas markets and required artisan weavers, merchants, and finance. Most weavers were full-time specialists, but a small, yet significant number of South Indians started weaving in order to supplement their income (Parthasarathi 2001; Subrahmanyam, 1990). Agriculturalists, cobblers, barbers, and scavengers, weaving part-time, tended to produce coarse cloth for local markets. Some of these weaving centers still exist (Fig. 7.3). Professional weavers worked full-time weaving and were drawn from one of four castes: kaikkolar, devangar, saliyar, and seniyar. Typically weaving required a full-time specialist, involved the whole family, and employed a pit loom. Merchants advanced the capital to purchase yarn, and in some instances, maintain the physical structure required to weave cotton, to weavers. The pit loom allowed long periods of work, helped control climate conditions such as humidity, and was portable,

Figure 7.4. Nangur, Tamil Nadu, with location of temple, tank, and weaver's street; Trench 1a, possible pit loom (map by Hauser).

allowing for a degree of mobility on the part of weaving communities (Parthasarathi 2001). At least one-third of the capital was used to supply and support the family. Moreover, the weavers typically maintained control over all production decisions (Ludden 1996).

Hamlets and isolated farmsteads dating to this time period are insufficiently excavated, but large-scale work has been conducted near Nangur. Nangur, like many villages in the Kaveri basin, belongs to the type of nucleated settlements that include Brahmanical temples, merchants' quarters, and quarters with weavers from the Kaikkolar community (Fig. 7.3). While the central mound appears to have been occupied as early as the third century CE, the elaborate community pattern of temple streets, *nagarams,* and weaving colonies appear only after the thirteenth century, when the town became a political center in the region (Selvakumar et al. 2021). Excavations reveal that increasingly dense and elaborate structures associated with weaving developed by the sixteenth century (Fig. 7.4). Finds from the excavations also reveal that such producers were also consuming regional and Indian Ocean trade goods. For example, while the pottery remains are mostly from local producers, in at least in one case, the pottery was from southwest Asia. The inhabitants also used metal implements and terracotta objects, adorning themselves with beads and bangles attributable to the time period. As documented through surface finds of single Chola and Vijayanagra period coins circulating in the centuries before, during, and after the thirteenth century, they operated in an increasingly monetized economy (Selvakumar et al. 2021).

Other Precolonial Cultural Transformations

The importance of this period lies not just in the socioeconomic transformations discussed above, but in durable changes in ways of life and outlook. Take, for example, attitudes to clothes and dressing between the twelfth and eighteenth centuries. Stone sculptures and bronze statuary that detail poorly clad figures prior to the twelfth century contrast sharply with later bodies adorned with elaborate textiles in paintings commissioned by Nayaka courts beginning in the seventeenth century. While it is always dangerous to assume that such representations act as ethnographic detail of everyday life, these changes in representative art align with new cultural formations and the arrival of different ideologies and perspectives. Beginning in the twelfth century, women of certain sections began to wear long textiles, the *pudavai*. At the same time, images of princely figures depict greater and more elaborate textiles. It must be noted that in some areas of Kannyakumari, women of certain castes were not allowed to cover their upper part. New cultural formations and the arrival of different ideologies and perspectives from about the twelfth century likely contributed to these changes in outlook.

Simultaneously the increased use of currency characterized commerce, rent payments, and other economic interactions. This is evident, for example, in increasing references to the *kasaya varkam* (craftspersons offering tax in cash) in Vijayanagara inscriptions. Commercialism coincided with sustained, but uneven, demographic growth. During this period, people from various communities and professional and service groups moved into the extreme South. Elites and craftspeople from present-day Andhra Pradesh and Karnataka migrated to the hinterland of the Coromandel coast as did subordinated communities. This movement spanned the spectrum of social strata from elites to subalterns, thereby increasing demographic diversity and the material production capacity of the Coromandel coast and its hinterlands (Ludden 1985; Karashima 2001).

Of the various communities identified with the land, commoners' influence is evident in their payments of rents and taxes and in the restitution of debts. Their provision of small scale, but cumulatively valuable, goods, such as fruits, vegetables, cotton, honey, poultry, pulses, and grains like rice and millet, was central to temples and markets and shaped the region's commercial agriculture. Commoner communities involved in rural industry, such as specialists crafting pottery, weaving textiles, smelting iron, and smithing gold,

Table 7.1. Select inscriptions and palm-leaf documents referencing enslavement

Village	Period CE	Nature and Content of the Document	Reference
Tiruvidanthai	1003	Stone inscription; slave-like assignment to a temple of 12 families of fisher-folk	ARE 274 of 1910; Nilakanta Sastry 1955: 555
Tiruvalangadu	1175	Sale of four women to the temple for 700 *kasus* (coins)	ARE 80 of 1913; Nilakanta Sastry 1955: 556
Tiruvalangadu	Medieval period	Punishment of slaves for defying orders	Nilakanta Sastry 1955: 556
Kurukkai	1235	100 slaves purchased and donated to a temple	Sridharan et al. 2004: 203
Velliyankunram, Madurai District	1448	Palm leaf document; sale of 7 children of untouchable Toti community for 37 coins	Senthalir 2017; Muthukumar 2018
Kanniyakumari District	1458	Slaves sold themselves because of poverty	Kolappan 2017
Kanniyakumari District	1459	"The severe drought has left us with nothing, not even gruel. Our legs and calf muscles have become swollen and we are not able to walk. So as suggested by the head of our family, we sold ourselves to Raman Iyappan."	Kolappan 2017
Kanniyakumari District	1472	Sale of a man and his daughter because they could not repay the loan	Kolappan 2017
Kumarakoil	1679	Donation of agricultural land and slaves to temple	Natarajan et al. 2011
Sirkazhi Region	sixteenth–eighteenth centuries	Thiyagaraya Mudaliyar sells a Paraiya Adimai to Subramania Mudaliyar for 10 gopala chakkram Kuligai pon (a type of gold coin)	Krishnamurthy 1984
Sirkazhi Region	sixteenth–eighteenth centuries	Ramachandra Nayakar sells four slaves for 14 coins	Krishnamurthy 1984
Sirkazhi Region	sixteenth–eighteenth centuries	Several slaves are sold for 80 *pon* (coins)	Krishnamurthy 1984

also provided goods central to the regional economy. Inscriptions from the time reveal that whether engaged in commercial agriculture or rural industry, commoners shared an important predicament—precarity. To be a commoner meant vulnerability to the vagaries of everyday life—drought, warfare, or changes in regional demands for specific goods.

Debt Bondage and Wage Labor between the Twelfth and Sixteenth Centuries

Another very specific kind of transaction occurred: debt bondage, wherein people placed themselves or family members under contract with temples or other agencies for a defined time period. Ninth-century CE Terisapalli copper plates reveal such transactions in Kerala (Sreedhara Menon 2008: 178; Yates 2018: 178). While there is some debate as to whether the system detailed was slavery or bonded labor, the system of servitude, in which landless agricultural laborers were embedded, imposed conditions with some superficial similarities to conditions of enslavement (cf. Gulimoto 1993: 117). For example, during Chola rule in the tenth century, unfree communities of laborers were "owned" by landowners and temples, required to labor in domestic or predial contexts, and sold for currency (Ali 2006: 45).

Palm-leaf documents datable to seventeenth to twentieth centuries similarly document slavery, and the Digital Archive of Tamil Agrarian History (1650–1950) of IFP, Pondicherry, records some of these cases (Muthukumar 2018) (Table 7.1). An inscription of 1235 CE dated in the reign of Rajaraja III records the purchase of roughly one hundred people who were then donated to a temple in the Thanjavur region (Sridharan et al. 2004: 203). These temple servants, *Devaradiyars,* should not be equated with enslaved workers laboring in predial or domestic contexts. Foreign accounts also speak to conditions of servitude. The Moroccan traveler Ibn Batuta described being accompanied by enslaved servants when he visited South India. Letters from the Genziah in Cairo also document merchants who conducted business in India who were accompanied by an enslaved companion (Goitein 1962, 18).

That being said, using the words slave, slavery, and enslaved should be done with some caution. In discussing and comparing diaspora within and beyond South India across the precolonial and colonial eras, it is critical to consider the terminology denizens used regarding status and labor relations. The practice of keeping slaves was not new to colonial India (Hjejle 1967; Patil 1973; Srivastava 1978; Sharma 1990; Ali 2006; Upinder Singh 2008). In the medieval period, a slave trade, including an African slave trade (Collins 2006), already existed within Asian contexts in the Indian Ocean World (Bano 1997, 2001); however, this does not suggest the terms of enslavement were equivalent to those under European colonial slavery. Using ancient and medieval texts, inscriptions, and paintings as archaeological sources, we reveal that servitude and slave labor were a central part of the primary production system of medieval South India's temple-centric society.

On the Coromandel coast, the term *adimai* is most closely associated with enslavement. This Tamil term refers to a subordinated worker who is obligated to an institution or individual and whose products belongs to the institution or individual. Several inscriptions refer to the sale and transfer of *adimai* to the temples and other agencies. An important question concerns whether Tamil notions of *adimai* would have fit the practice of bound labor—wage workers and indentured laborers—in medieval times. Although the term translates as "slave," its meaning, usage, and nature in medieval times could differ substantially from that in colonial times. Furthermore, it would be misleading to refer to all the individuals employed in European and missionary households, establishments, and business enterprises as slaves; some worked as voluntary or free labor. The perception of the observer is important. For example, S. Jeyaseela Stephen (1998) reports that in 1729, three hundred carpenters were taken to Mauritius from Pondicherry to work, whereas Allen (2014a) saw them as slaves.

Rather than slaves in the strict sense of the term, Indian workers prior to the seventeenth century may have been free laborers, bonded laborers, or wage workers. Poverty among the poorer classes drove them into systems of bondage that resembled enslavement. Distinct from slaves during the colonial period, it seems more appropriate to refer to them as attached laborers rather than slaves, even though some may have been in a kind of debt bondage and servitude. By the seventeenth century, when European merchants began to engage workers through debt bondage as well, these labor relations began to have the appearance of slavery. Specifically, pushed by socioeconomic conditions, workers, traders, and people from lower middle-class and poorer sections may have been engaged as wage laborers or debt bondage, but the very real possibility of transportation to distant shores in the Indian Ocean in which there was no opportunity for return made such human trafficking effectively a form of slave trade.

Colonial Interactions and Diaspora Formation

Historians note that Asian merchants continued to hold the central role in trade between weaving centers, company stores, and ports within and beyond the Indian Ocean (Subrahmanyam 1990: 81). South Indian traders established trading quarters in Southeast Asia and presumably employed workers in this period. Complex patterns of investment and debt as well as interregional patterns of trade in surplus foodstuffs, such as rice, existed before European engagement. As settlement increased in port towns on the Coromandel coast, rice, which had been part of regional commercial agriculture, became increasingly important. Areas of surplus production, such as the area north of the Godavari River delta, became bread baskets for urban areas facing a deficit. In 1719 Chennai, for example, required 4,000 garce (approx. 16,000 tonnes) per annum to feed its population (Arasaratnam 1986: 201). Ports located in the Lower Kaveri exported rice within the region to Madurai and beyond to places like Malacca, Aceh, Sri Lanka, and Malabar.

Local merchants largely controlled these networks throughout the colonial period (Subrahmanyam 1990). For example, Sunku Rama, a member of the Komati merchant community, was a textile trader providing calico textiles sometimes referred to as "guinea cloth," "Madras," or "salempouris." He advanced cash to bleachers and washers in order to purchase rice for making *conjee* (rice starch). His ship traded annually with Manila in the Philippines, exporting textiles and importing silver (Stephen 2014: 149). When the Danish attempted to enter the lucrative Manila trade, they relied on a ship formerly registered to a Muslim merchant with cargo provided by a Chettiyar Hindu (Mukherjee 2020). Entrepreneurs operating in Tamil countryside and port towns between the sixteenth and nineteenth centuries could be described as capitalists. Although capitalism is always a difficult term to define, for the purpose of this chapter we consider it in terms of the values assigned to commodities and to labor within market conditions. The scale of production in both rural industry and commercial agriculture was great enough to yield profits for investors and future investment funds.

In these trade networks rice was not only a food commodity in regional markets but an important component of the textile industry. Rice fed the many different specialist communities involved in rural industry, such as weavers, washers, bleachers, and dyers, and was an important component of *conjee* (rice gruel) used to starch textiles (Pillai 1904: I, 217). Rice was so important that it took on characteristics of a currency. The terms of the agreement between the Vijayanagara ruler Venkatapathi Devaraya II and the Dutch, which allowed the Dutch East India Company to establish a port at Pulicat, imposed a 2 percent duty on all goods save gold and rice (Stephen 2014: 191). In some instances weavers demanded that company agents provide "cotton yarn and rice to support their families, money, or both" (Chaudhuri 1974: 158). By the eighteenth century the French East India Company used rice to pay cloth bleachers and washers in the Pondicherry textile industry (Stephen 2014: 94).

Slavery and Indentureship between the Seventeenth and Nineteenth Centuries

Precolonial developments in South India on the Coromandel coast provided an ideal basis for the trafficking of humans through either slavery or indenture contracts. It is well documented that agents encouraged indentureship

Sources for Analyzing the Diaspora on the Coromandel Coast · 167

in the nineteenth century in order to meet the demands for labor within new forms of production surrounding plantation agriculture (Gøbel 2016; Izquierdo Díaz 2019; Bates 2017). Prior to that company agents and brokers were involved in very brisk and enormously profitable slave trade to the colonial agencies in the Indian Ocean World (Pinkston 2018; Teelock and Sheriff 2016). Colonialism, merchant capitalism, and commercial agricultural practices from the colonial period until decolonization in the twentieth century were powerful and exploitative developments that contributed significantly to South Asian diaspora formation.

Agricultural workers from the hinterland facing precarity brought about by famine or warfare migrated and settled in newly emerging ports (Stephen 2018: 53). At the same time, famines and internal clashes also forced fisher folk from coastal regions to migrate to emerging ports (Stephen 2018: 139). These agricultural workers and fisher folk facing few other options would enroll to contract themselves or family members into limited terms of service to pay off their debts. These bonded laborers would fill a variety of roles, in domestic service, the craft industries, and agricultural labor on the Coromandel coast and beyond. The condition for those transported throughout the Indian Ocean World effectively became that of an enslaved laborer since the cost of return was rarely written into the initial agreements of their bondage (Carter 2006; Arasaratnam 1986). Thus debt bondage became a form of slave trade, though insufficient attention has been paid to it (Allen 2014b: 328–29; Alam 2007).

Beginning with the Portuguese in the sixteenth century, slaves were traded, employed, and maintained at places such as San Thome (Shngreiyo 2016). The Dutch succeeded the Portuguese in an extensive slave trade (Alam 2007; Linda and van Rossum 2017). One hundred and thirty-one Dutch ships transported 38,441 slaves acquired through Pulicat-based brokers between 1621 and 1665 (Allen 2017; Keen 2020: 251). During the nineteenth and early twentieth centuries, the British and the French took a large volume of contracted laborers and skilled workers to various places. They also sent rebels and convicts to colonies. Europeans, including the Danes, developed commercial traffic in the Indian Ocean and beyond, including the trafficking of conscripted labor. The Danes actively sought to acquire slaves to work as servants in aristocratic homes in Denmark. When identified as Moors, slaves traded in the Indian Ocean World conferred prestige on their putative owners and legitimacy to their trade (Izquierdo Díaz 2019). Private trade among the company's officers was largely responsible for the commerce in humans.

Enslavement must be distinguished as a relation of labor from indentureship that became pervasive in the nineteenth century. Examining correspondence, ship manifests, and legal contract documents provides some insight into the structure of human labor trafficking. For example, the two major embarkation ports of indentured labor to British colonies between 1860 and 1911 were Kolkata and Chennai. Those emigrating from Chennai came from South Arcot and North Arcot (Bhana 1987: table 11). The largest caste groups represented were Pariahs and Vannias, constituting 14.6 and 14.3 percent, respectively, of Madras passengers (Bhana 1987: table 16). It also gives us a sense of these documents' limitations. For example, a digitized data set for those who migrated to South Africa includes 15,002 migrants who arrived in the 1860s and 1870s. These entries note the various caste names and villages of origin of individual migrants, interestingly revealing the groups of people who migrated. There is some difficulty identifying caste names due to misspelling or unintelligibility. The groups of laborers included washermen, huntsmen, weavers, and potters, Chakkliyars (working on leather), blacksmiths, and Oddars. Among these, there are more Vanniyars and Vellalars: 70 plus. In this data set, the Brahmins who migrated are mainly from the northern part of India. No Brahmins of South Indian origin migrated. The Chettis are very limited in number (4). The record notes another large group of individuals (2,643) from Malabar. Yet the names and villages of those recorded with Malabar as their source region suggest that they came from different parts of South India, perhaps due to misidentification or misreporting (Bhana 1987: 82). The data also reveal that not only marginalized communities migrated, but agrarian Vellalars as well. This indicates that some of the Vellalars were also economically in weaker condition. The category of Vellalar implies that small landholders among them might have chosen to migrate, perhaps because of the limited agricultural income.

Archaeological insights into indentureship on the Coromandel coast can be gleaned from the numerous hamlets that began to emerge as European colonial enclaves gave way to European imperial administrative efforts in the nineteenth century. For example, Sathangudi is a small settlement that appears to have increased in population and size during the last quarter of the eighteenth century, when commercial and agricultural interests in the region attracted a community of washer people to migrate. Both the presence of a cemetery marking the deceased of those who converted to Christianity and the dense artifact scatters dating to the last three-quarters of the nineteenth century detail the temporality and extent of this settlement. Housing, discussed in Hauser and Haines (this volume) highlights that architecture was informed both by long-standing notions of class and difference and also by the availability of resources. Vernacular housing built in the last quarter of the nineteenth century and the first quarter of the twentieth century suggest that such housing was infused with wealth generated from the diaspora.

Numerous other sources also provide insight into the context for diaspora in Sathangudi. Palm leaves record the sale of animal skin and paddy, the mortgage of bullock and cart, farm labor contracts, and purchases of bricks and tiles. While some of these documents have been curated in state or district archives, many are still in the hands of those who initiated contracts. For example, descendants of a money-lending family still have original palm leaves recording various transactions (Ramachandran 2005: 21, 32). In general, these record loans, mortgages, and deeds of properties that were transacted in the nineteenth century and first half of the twentieth century and reveal that people sought money on loan or mortgage to meet the expenses related to weddings, housewarming ceremonies, and festivals. Some refer to individuals who have engaged in contracts of indenture, such as Ayirandu Sinnaiya Nayakkar (Ramachandran 2005: Record 50, p. 44). Others refer to individuals who entered contracts with an advance of money and worked on the farms to repay the advance. One person, named Nettai Subramanian, went to Mauritius (Moris), forcing his wife, Ramayi, to repay the loan taken out by her husband (Ramachandran 2005: Record 26, p. 31). The records document landless laborers, of lower middle-class and poorer sections of society, in need of resources to fulfill their existential requirements. These documents also reveal conditions of the middle and lower strata of society who perhaps chose to migrate to work in the plantations despite such difficult conditions.

The lived experiences of such historical subjects are poorly revealed in such documents. While colonial archives and documents provide statistical information on the migration of the indentured laborers, literary sources about the diaspora are an important alternate source revealing the conditions of migrations, empathies, subjective feelings, and sufferings of the migrants. For example, C. V. Velupillai's "Tea Garden," published in 1956, portrays the conditions of the Tamils working in the tea gardens of Sri Lanka. In one poem, Velupillai narrates the wretched conditions in which the indentured laborers worked and lived—without any time limits, proper food, proper facilities, or medical aid. One poem, "Kappalerrum Kankaniccindu," published in 1913, narrates the condition of the indentured laborers. It presents popular and poetic perception of the migration and the role of *kankanis* (supervisors who recruit laborers).

Cindu is a folk poetic tradition that became popular in the Tamil region in the nineteenth century and conveys the conditions of the diaspora population (Minaṭcicuntaranar 1976: 53; Venkatachalapathy 2000). This literary genre is a folk poetic tradition that became popular in the Tamil region in the nineteenth century. This simple literary medium covers all aspects of life and became a popular means whereby people remarked upon important events and expressed their ideas, recording and documenting historical events. With the emergence of the printing press, these types of texts were published and exported for the pleasure of laborers. The folk song "Kappalerrum Kanganic-cindu" ("Cindu genre on the kankani or agent who ships people abroad"), published in 1913, narrates the condition of the indentured laborers.

Following are translations of parts of the poems and some select ideas presented in the *Cindu* genre of poetry. *Cindu* follow a scheme. They have an opening prayer to God, often to Lord Ganesa, and then the main poem:

> *Oh Lord Ganesha I am glad to sing the chaning*
> *minds of the rich migrants to Singapore and Penang!*
> *Ragam: Natha Namgiriyai; Rupagam Talam*

It became a popular medium for expressing ideas, and it was part of folk literature. It was a form of recording and documenting historical events.

> *Do not get cheated*
> *Do not long to go to Mauritius*
> *Do not get cheated due to excessive greed for money*
> *Do not go with excessive desire ignoring the word of elders*

> *There exist some frauds who recruit people [laborers]*
> *They call you elder and younger brothers with love and care!*
> *They select the youngsters and serve as if god sent them*
> *They hold an umbrella in the front*
> *with the one-cubit-long tassel of the turban behind*

> *Do not trust the wastrels who taunt and cheat you stating:*
> *"Why were you born as humans?*
> *Why do you remain as a burden to the earth?*
> *Follow my word and follow me"*

> *Do not get cheated*
> *Do not long to go to Mauritius*
> *Do not get cheated due to excessive greed for money*
> *Do not go with excessive desire ignoring the word of elders*

> *Singapore Penang is here*
> *In the famous Kuala Lumpur live Sinhalar [Sri Lankan Tamils?]*
> *Rangoon is there to earn a livelihood*
> *Poverty have overtaken you*

Coffee in the morning with Appam
Koppi in the evening

This *cindu* describes the viciousness and the *modus operandi* of the supervisors or *kankanis*. It was composed by Nettappakkam Narayanasamy Goundar, and it was published in 1913 at Nellikuppam near Cuddalore.

The ship arrives at Nagapattinam tomorrow [in the near future]
If we walk we can reach there in four days
It is better if you bring your wife
Claim these cheats who indulge in Prostitution
Do not trust them
Do not get cheated
Do not long to go to Mauritius
Do not get cheated due to excessive greed for money
Do not go with excessive desire ignoring the word of elders

They invite you stating
"I have two young daughters
They remain unmarried
Want them to get married in this country"
They attract you like a magnet attracting iron
They offer you a bag of betel nut and leaves
And silk handkerchief and spectacles [?]
Protector God would never leave you
They would talk as if they witnessed it
Do not trust these frauds
Do not get cheated
Do not long to go to Mauritius
Do not get cheated due to excessive greed for money
Do not go with excessive desire ignoring the word of elders

The ship is not bad
Do not get cheated because of greed
Do not long to go to Mauritius
Do not ignore the word of elders

"God would help you once you board the ship
You would see the port after tough 6 days voyage
You leave this birth and reach the foot of lords"
Claim these twice bord [meaning upper castes or Brahmins?]
Traveling by ship is no sin

Nothing wrong if you board the ship
Board the ship and earn plenty of wealth
You can close the gate on the creditors/ usurers
You can wander freely"
These sinners, lowlifes would convince you nicely.
There are people who trust them
They invite them home and treat them with food
They offer prostitutes;
The cheaters of the Kaliyuga are revered as gods
Fools are those who trusted their words now!

We are not presenting the poem in full, just some of the ideas:

"They take people like cattle and
Lock them in the sheds and chain/handcuff them
They are offered a 5 year contract"
"People borrow jewels from neighbours,
Abandon their wives, parents and family
Sell milking animals and leave for abroad
Marry women and leave."

"Earlier people were happy without going to Mauritius
They treat people like cattle in the markets
Stuff them like cattle in the steamers
They work hard and are squeezed and had to
Wake up at 5 a.m."
"Diseases afflict them" [venereal diseases]
Pearl headed prostitutes"
"Nattukkottai Chettiyar
Tonsure [shave] their heads and talk like saints"
They charge 6 percent per month interest = 72 percent per year

This poem clearly reveals the condition of indentured laborers and the sufferings they incurred from the *kankanis*.

From these sources it is clear that a new form of human trafficking developed, and people were selling their skills for a price. New classes of laborers, such as washer men, good loaders, and port workers moved to the cities. The colonial capitalist regime required laborers and service classes to support the production system involving tobacco, tea, and rice cultivation in various colonies. The policy of recruiting non-local workers as indentured laborers was a mechanism that served the needs of European empires and local merchants.

The commerce in humans contributed to the dispersal of the Tamil diaspora far beyond the Indian Ocean region.

Beginning in the sixteenth century, but reaching an apogee in the nineteenth century, South Asians of multiple religions, genders, and castes circulated as enslaved and indentured laborers in administrative, manufacturing, domestic, and agrarian contexts within the Indian, Pacific, and Atlantic oceans. This South Asian/Indian diaspora evolved throughout the precolonial and colonial, shaping the social, economic, and political landscapes of the places they came to inhabit and call home. Historians and archaeologists have begun to map this diaspora through material and textual sources but have paid little attention to the South Asian contexts in which these migrants, forced or otherwise, originally lived. We argue that understanding the political and economic landscapes that migrants called home—whether they were forced or compelled to migrate or did so in some other way—illuminates some of the long-term local processes shaping the diaspora.

Conclusion

The success of colonial enterprises starting in the seventeenth century was contingent upon the political and socioeconomic context; the support and cooperation of local rulers, agents, and elites; and the precarity of agricultural work and rural craftspeople. Although colonial powers conflicted with political powers, they negotiated with local population groups at different levels. Traders and money lenders proliferated as part of the system of mercantile capitalism, and greedy intermediary agents traded the deprived class as commodities—initially as part of servitude and later as indentured laborers. The movement of large volumes of laborers was not a direct force but arose from indeterminacies such as famine and warfare, made more precarious through colonial arrangements.

While to equate the indentured labor system with slavery provides both anachronisms and stereotypes, comparison does allow three crucial elements. In addition to European colonial and imperial impositions, indentureship also has genealogies that look to commercial interests and legal arrangements in South Asia. Second, from the perspective of the lived experience of those laborers, the system was undeniably harsh on indentured laborers and was exacerbated by transportation to distant locales. Finally, policies established in the eighteenth and nineteenth centuries continue to reverberate today for migrants and their descendants in a region once identified as the Coromandel coast.

Bibliography

Ali, Daud. 2006. "War, Servitude, and the Imperial Household: A Study of Palace Women in the Chola Empire." In *Slavery and South Asian History*, edited by Indrani Chatterjee and Richard M. Eaton, 44–62. Bloomington: Indiana University Press.

Alam, Ishrat. 2007. "Indian Ocean Slave Trade: The Dutch Enterprise." *Proceedings of the Indian History Congress* 68(2): 1178–1190.

Allen, Richard B. 2014a. *European Slave Trading in the Indian Ocean, 1500–1850*. Athens: Ohio University Press.

———. 2014b. "Slaves, Convicts, Abolitionism and the Global Origins of the Post-Emancipation Indenture Labor System." *Slavery and Abolition* 35(2): 328–48.

———. 2017. "Ending the History of Silence: Reconstructing European Slave Trading in the Indian Ocean." *O Tráfico de Escravos Africanos: Novos Horizontes* 23(2): 295–313.

Amrit, Sunil S. 2015. *Crossing the Bay of Bengal: Furies of Nature and Fortunes of the Migrants*. Cambridge, Mass.: Harvard University Press.

Appadorai, A. 1936. *Economic Conditions in Southern India (1000–1500 A.D.)*. 2 vols. Madras: University of Madras.

Aranha, Paolo. 2011. "From Meliapor to Mylapore, 1662–1749: The Portuguese Presence in São Tomé Between the Qut B Sha Hi Conquest and Its Incorporation into British Madras." In *Portuguese and Luso-Asian Legacies: The Making of the Luso-Asian World: Intricacies of Engagement*, 7–82. Paper presented at the conference "Portuguese and Luso-Asian Legacies in Southeast Asia, 1511–2011," held in Singapore and Malacca, September 28–30, 2010.

Arasaratnam, Sinnappah. 1986. *Merchants, Companies and Commerce on the Coromandel Coast, 1650–1740*. Delhi: Oxford University Press.

Baliga, B. S. 2000. *Madras District Gazetteers: Kancheepuram and Tiruvallur districts (erstwhile Chengalpattu District)*. Madras: Government Press.

Bates, Crispin. 2017. "Some Thoughts on the Representation and Misrepresentation of the Colonial South Asian Labor Diaspora." *South Asian Studies* 33(1): 7–22.

Bano, S. 1997. "India's Overland Slave Trade in the Medieval Period." *Proceedings of the Indian History Congress* 58:315–21.

———. 2001. "Slave Acquisition in the Mughal Empire." Professor J. S. Grewal Prize essay. In *Proceedings of the Indian History Congress* 62: 317–24.

Bhana, Surendra. 1987. *Indenture Indians in Natal, 1860 to 1902: A Study Based on Ship's Lists*. https://www.sahistory.org.za/archive/indenture-indians-natal-1860-1902-study-based-ships-lists-surendra-bhana-october-1987

Bredsdorff, Asta. 2009. *The Trials and Travels of Willem Leyel: An Account of the Danish East India Company in Tranquebar, 1639–48*. Copenhagen: Museum Tusculanum Press.

Carter, Marina. 2006. "Slavery and Unfree Labour in the Indian Ocean." *History Compass* 4(5): 800–13.

Champakalakshmi, R. 1996 *Trade, Ideology and Urbanization: South India 300 BC to AD 1300*. Delhi: Oxford University Press.

Chaudhuri, K. N. 1974. "The Structure of Indian Textile Industry in the Seventeenth and Eighteenth Centuries." *Indian Economic & Social History Review* 11(2–3): 127–82.

Fihl, E. 2009. "Shipwrecked on the Coromandel: The First Indo-Danish Contact, 1620." *Review of Development and Change* 14(1–2): 19–40.

Sources for Analyzing the Diaspora on the Coromandel Coast · 175

Fihl, E., and A. R. Venkatachalapathy (eds.). 2009. *Indo-Danish Cultural Encounters in Tranquebar: Past and Present. Review of Development and Change* 14(1–2): 1–317.

Gøbel, Erik. 2016. *The Danish Slave Trade and Its Abolition.* Leiden: Brill.

Guilmoto, Christophe Z. 1993. "The Tamil Migration Cycle, 1830–1950." *Economic and Political Weekly* 28 (3–4): 111–20.

Hall, Kenneth. 1980. *Trade and Statecraft in the Age of the Colas.* New Delhi: Abhinav Publications.

Hassan Mydin, S., and M. Saidumasudu. 2018. "The Changing Identities of the Tamil Muslims from the Coromandel Coast to Malaysia: An Etymological Analysis." In *Proceedings of the 7th International Conference on Multidisciplinary Research* (ICMR 2018), 650–56.

Hauser, Mark, and V. Selvakumar. 2021. "Gardens of the Coromandel Coast: Landscape Considerations of Commercial Agriculture in Tamil Nadu, South India." *International Journal of Historical Archaeology* 25(4): 1113–41.

Hjejle, Benedicte. 1967. Slavery and Agricultural Bondage in South India in the Nineteenth Century. *Scandinavian Economic History Review* 15(1–2): 71–126.

Izquierdo Díaz, Jorge Simón. 2019. "The Trade in Domestic Servants (Morianer) from Tranquebar for Upper Class Danish Homes in the First Half of the Seventeenth Century." *Itinerario* 43(2): 194–217.

Karashima, Noboru. 2001. *History and Society in South India: The Cholas to Vijayanagar (comprising South Indian History and Society and Towards a New Formation).* New Delhi: Oxford University Press.

Karashima, N. (ed.). 2002. *Ancient and Medieval Commercial Activities in the Indian Ocean: Testimony of Inscriptions and Ceramic-Sherds.* Tokyo: Taisho University.

Keen, Caroline. 2020. *A Judge in Madras: Sir Sidney Wadsworth and the Indian Civil Service, 1913–47.* London: C. Hurst & Company.

Kolappan, B. 2017. "When Dalits Were Also Landowners and Vellalas Slaves." *The Hindu*, May 8, 2017. https://www.thehindu.com/news/national/tamil-nadu/once-dalits-were -landowners-vellalas-slaves/article18405606.ece

Krishnamurthy, S. 1984. "Adimai Virapanaiyai Kurikkum Al Olaikal." *Kalvettu Quarterly* 17: 1–7. Chennai: Journal of Tamil Nadu State Archaeology Department.

———. 2005 *Tarangampadi Olai Anvangkal.* Madras: Tamil Nadu State Archaeology Department.

Ludden, David. 1985. *Peasant History in South India.* Princeton, N.J.: Princeton University Press.

———. 1996. "Archaic Formations of Agricultural Knowledge in South India." In *Meanings of Agriculture in South Asia: Essays in South Asian History and Economics.* SOAS Studies on South Asia. Oxford: Oxford University Press.

Mbeki, Linda, and Matthias van Rossum. 2017. "Private Slave Trade in the Dutch Indian Ocean World: A Study into the Networks and Backgrounds of the Slavers and the Enslaved in South Asia and South Africa." *Slavery and Abolition* 3(1): 95–116.

Minaṭcicuntaranar, Te. Po. 1976. *Tamil: A Bird's-Eye View.* Makkal Nalvaalyu Manṟam.

Moosvi, Shireen. 2011. "The World of Labor in Mughal India (c. 1500–1750)." *Internation-aal Instituut voor Sociale Geschiedenis* (IRSH) 56, Special Issue: 245–61.

Mukherjee, Rila. 2020. "Global Networks in Maritime Worlds 1400–1800." In *The Rout-*

ledge Companion to Marine and Maritime Worlds 1400–1800, edited by Clare Jowitt, Craig Lambert, and Steve Mentz, 125–50. London: Routledge.

Mukund, Kanaklatha. 1999. *The Trading World of the Tamil Merchant.* Hyderabad: Orient Longman.

Muthukumar, V. 2018. Records of Slavery in Palm Leaf Manuscripts [Kallar Nadu]. https://clac.hypotheses.org/datah-working-papers-2/records-of-slavery-in-palm-leaf-manuscripts

Natarajan, S. Sundaram, Rajukmar, A. K. Perumal, and Selvadaran. 2011. "Kumarakoil puthiyakalvettukal." *Avanam Journal of Tamil Nadu Archaeological Society* 22: 156–58.

Nilakanta Sastry, K. A. 1955. *The Colas.* Madras: University of Madras.

Parthasarathi, P. 2001. *The Transition to a Colonial Economy: Weavers, Merchants and Kings in South India, 1720–1800.* Cambridge Studies in Indian History and Society no. 7. Cambridge, U.K.: Cambridge University Press.

Patil, Sharad. 1973. "Problem of Slavery in Ancient India." *Social Scientist* 1(11): 32–48.

Peebles, Patrick. 2001. *The Plantation Tamils of Ceylon.* London: Leicester University Press.

Pillai, Ananda Ranga. 1904. *The Private Diary of Ananda Ranga Pillai*, Vol. 1: *Dubash to Joseph François Dupleix, a Record of Matters Political, Historical, Social, and Personal, from 1736 to 1761.* Madras: Government Press.

Pinkston, Bonnie. 2018. "Documenting the British East India Company and Their Involvement in the East Indian Slave Trade." *SLIS Connecting* 7(1), article 10. DOI: 10.18785/slis.0701.10.

Raja Mohamad, J. 2004. *Maritime History of the Coromandel Muslims: A Socio- Historical Study on the Tamil Muslims 1750–1900.* Chennai: Government Museum.

Ramachandran, S. 2005. *Tarangampadi Olai Avanankal.* Chennai: Tamil Nadu State Archaeology Department (in Tamil).

Ramaswamy, V. 1985. *Textiles and Weavers in Medieval South India.* Delhi: Oxford University Press; repr. edition 2006 .

Rohini Krishnan, R. 2016. "Groves, Gods and Slaves: A Study on Agrestic Slavery in Medieval Malabar." *Journal of Indian History and Culture* 22(2016): 152–77.

Roy, T. 2014. "Trading Firms in Colonial India." *Business History Review* 88(1): 9–42.

Selvakumar, V. 2017. "Ancient Tamizhagam, Urbanization and the Cultural Interactions in the Afroeurasian World." Sectional presidential address, Archaeology, Art and Cultural History Section. In *Tamil Nadu History Congress Proceedings (Twenty-Fourth Session), Tamil Nadu Historical Congress*, 345–66.

———. 2019. "Trading Ports and Maritime Routes: Tamil Network with Southeast Asia." In *Sojourners to Settlers: Tamils in Southeast Asia*, edited by Arun Mahizhnan and Nalina Gopal, 97–115. Singapore: Indian Heritage Centre.

Selvakumar, V., M. Hauser, S. Gowrishankar, and R. Karthikeyan. 2021. *Excavations at Nangur: A Historical Settlement in the Lower Kaveri Valley.* Report Submitted to the Archaeological Survey of India. Thanjavur: Tamil University.

Senthalir, S. 2017. "Chilling Evidence of Slave Trade." *The Hindu*, March 18, 2017. https://www.thehindu.com/news/national/tamil-nadu/chilling-evidence-of-slave-trade/article17529447.ece

Shanmugam, P. 2002. "Pattanappagudi: A Voluntary Impost of the Trade Guilds." In *Ancient and Medieval Commercial Activities in the Indian Ocean: Testimony of Inscriptions and Ceramic-Sherds*, edited by N. Karashima, 72–78. Tokyo: Taisho University.

Sharma, R. S. 1990. *Sudras in Ancient India: A Social History of the Lower Order Down to Circa A.D. 600.* Delhi: Motilal Banarasidas.

Shngreiyo, A. 2016. "The Portuguese Settlement on the Coromandel Coast, a Case Study of San Thome and Nagapattinam in the Seventeenth Century." *IRA, International Journal of Management and Social Sciences* 5(2): 367–84.

Sridharan, K., A. Padmavathy, and R. Vasanthakalyani. 2004. *Tamilna ttuk Kalvettukal 2004.* Madras, Tamil Nadu State Archaeology Department (in Tamil).

Srivastava, O. P. 1978. "Slave-Trade in Ancient and Early Medieval India." *Proceedings of the Indian History Congress* 39, Vol. I: 124–36. https://www.jstor.org/stable/44139343

Stanziani, Alessandro. 2020. "Slavery and Post Slavery in the Indian Ocean World." ff-hal-02556369. https://hal.archives-ouvertes.fr/hal-02556369/document

Stephen, S. Jeyaseela. 1998. *Portuguese in the Tamil Coast: Historical Explorations in Commerce and Culture, 1507–1749.* New Delhi: Navajothi Publishing House.

———. 2018. *Kalaniya Valarcikkalam; Pulampeyarnthaarkalin Vaazhkkai.* Chennai: New Century Book House (in Tamil).

———. n.d. Nagapattinam in the Colonial Map of India: Urban Growth of Town and City under Portuguese, 1525–1658. https://www.academia.edu/29683513/urbanization_og_nagapattinam_under_Portuguese

Stephen, S. Jeyaseela (ed.). 2014. *Oceanscape: Tamil Textiles in the Early Modern World.* Delhi: Primus Books.

Subbarayalu, Y. 2012. *South India under Cholas.* New Delhi: Oxford University Press .

Subrahmanyam, Sanjay. 1989. "The Coromandel Trade of the Danish East India Company, 1618–1649." *Scandinavian Economic History Review* 37(1): 41–56.

———. 1990. *Improvising Empire: Portuguese Trade and Settlement in the Bay of Bengal, 1500–1700.* New Delhi: Oxford University Press.

Subrahmanyam, S., and C. A. Bayly. 1988. "Portfolio Capitalists and the Political Economy of Early Modern India." *Indian Economic and Social History Review* 25(4): 401–24.

Subramanian, T. 2003. *Tarangampadi (Tranquebar) Excavation & Conservation Report, 2001–2002.* Chennai: Tamil Nadu State Archaeology Department .

Teelock, Vijayalakshmi, and Abdul Sheriff. 2016. "Slavery and the Slave Trade in the Indian Ocean Transition from Slavery in Zanzibar and Mauritius," edited by Abdul Sheriff, Vijayalakshmi Teelock, Saada Omar Wahab, and Satyendra Peerthum, 25–44. Dakar, Senegal: Council for the Development of Social Science Research in Africa (CODESRIA).

Teles E Cunha, João. 2012. "Armenian Merchants in Portuguese Trade Networks in the Western Indian Ocean in the Early Modern Age." In *Les Arméniens dans le commerce asiatique au début de l'ère moderne [en ligne].* Paris: Éditions de la Maison des Sciences de l' Homme, 2007 (online since May 1, 2021).

Tschacher, T. 2018. "Coromandel Coast." In *Islam, Judaism, and Zoroastrianism: Encyclopedia of Indian Religions*, edited by Z. R. Kassam, Y. K. Greenberg, and J. Bagli, 192–94. Dordrecht: Springer.

Upinder Singh. 2008. *A History of Ancient and Early Medieval India: From Stone Age to the 12th century.* New Delhi: Pearson.

Venkatachalapathy, A. R. 2000. *Anthakkaalatthil Kaappi Illai.* Chennai: Kalachuvadu (in Tamil; *In Those Days There Was No Coffee*, Yoda Press, 2006).

8

Diaspora in the Domestic

A Comparative Approach to Tamil Nadu and Mauritius

JULIA JONG HAINES AND MARK WILLIAM HAUSER

Recent archaeological research in the Atlantic and Indian Oceans has focused on post-emancipation communities in agrarian contexts, providing insight into everyday life of indentured laborers and the emergence of a modern South Asian diaspora (Armstrong and Hauser 2004; Seetah et al. 2018; Haines 2019a, 2019b, 2020, 2021; Allen 2021). However, the material record in South Asia has not been as integrated into this discussion, especially in terms of the recruitment and transportation of laborers, their conditions of everyday life, and how returnees might have contributed to those landscapes in meaningful ways.

In this chapter we compare the effects of commercial agriculture on architecture and settlement organization using two archaeological cases with connected histories and populations, and with contrasting ecologies and economies. In both cases, laborers who immigrated to these regions experienced and were a part of increasing population density of settlements, intensification of hydrological manipulation, and amplification of subsistence and political economies, world colonization, and changing environmental values. Specifically, we examine residential architecture and settlement organization in two settlements occupied between the late eighteenth and twentieth centuries: Sathangudi outside Tranquebar on the lower Coromandel coast of India and Bras d'Eau Sugar Plantation in Mauritius. These settlements were chosen not because there are direct links but because they were both commercial agricultural enterprises and represent two of the many endmembers in the circulation of indentured laborers in the Indian Ocean.

While there is a long-term history of human circulation throughout the Indian Ocean and beyond, our comparison is largely restricted to movements of people from South Asia between the eighteenth and twentieth centuries.

Diaspora in the Domestic: A Comparative Approach to Tamil Nadu and Mauritius · 179

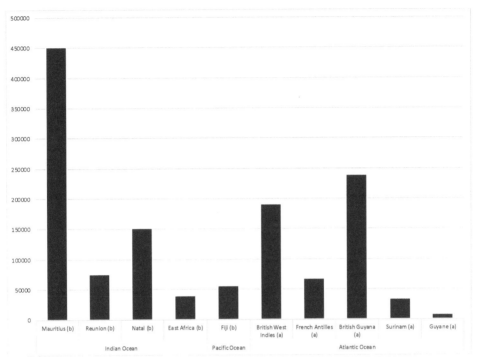

Figure 8.1. Movement of Indian indentured laborers. Data sources: Singaravelou 1987, vol. 1: 144; Northrup 1995: 159–61.

During this period this movement was far from even. Migration came from two distinct regions: the Gangetic plain, from which Calcutta was the major port of embarkation (approximately 79 percent), and the Coromandel coast (approximately 16 percent), with the remainder originating from a variety of port cities along South Asia's western coastline (Northrup 1995; Singaravelou 1987: 60–62). Those caught up in this migration found themselves in disparate and distinct geographies including the Caribbean, Sri Lanka, South Africa, Fiji, Mauritius, and Réunion (Fig 8.1). While there does appear to have been some structure to this trade—for example, many laborers in Malaysia, Singapore, and Fiji came from the south, and those in the English-speaking Caribbean came from the north—such easy distinctions are not possible throughout the diaspora. Mauritius was the single largest locale to receive people from South Asia and became home to southern and northern South Asians alike.

In this chapter we argue that the economic and symbolic roles of water during this time period are crucial. Landscapes were manipulated to capture, move, and store water so that rice along the Coromandel coast and sugar in Mauritius could be cultivated. These thirsty crops were grown to meet regional food needs and global markets and as such created a condition in which the metabolic needs of labor and the metabolic needs of capital were put in competition. Studies of who gets what kind of water enable subtle understandings of power in the context of colonial enclosure (Hauser 2021). Water also plays important symbolic roles. Laborers, recruited to modify these landscapes and cultivate these crops, carried varying ideas about water, including the way it can both delineate and transform social identities such as caste. For example, in India the water with which one cooks, bathes, and drinks is famously part of a complex of purity and pollution upon which many social identities are predicated. Similarly, *kala pani*, literally "black waters," was a concept used to describe how people who crossed the ocean were stripped of their caste identity (Bates and Carter 2021). As has been noted in a variety of places and times, such economic and symbolic impulses are connected.

Because our two areas of study are only a sample of the places of departure and destination in the South Asian diaspora, the discussion that follows is not meant to be exhaustive or exemplary. Rather we use these two regions to make three interrelated points. The first is that the structure of the diaspora defies easy transoceanic analogies—that is, it may not work to use domestic space in Mauritius to infer domestic space use in South Asia or vice versa. Second, even within specific regions, a large variety of spatial practices suggests that greater attention should be paid to local particularities than to broader trends. Finally, with these caveats stated, there do seem to be important trends that can be documented, though seeking the "origins" of specific cultural practices is a flawed endeavor, given the duration of historical flows, movements, and exchanges within the Indian Ocean. Our emphasis is therefore on comparing local particularities through a perspective that has come to define historical archaeology within the Indian Ocean (see also Cianciosi and Čaval, Seetah et al., this volume). Rather than seeking origins we show how these case studies are both distinct and intra-regionally connected within the oceanic sphere and colonial contexts. We begin by positioning our chapter within a larger body of scholarship on indentureship and diaspora. In the following sections we begin our comparison through a consideration of structure of migration in both locations. We build on this contextual data through a comparison of architecture and water infrastructures and conclude with a discussion of its implications.

Indentureship and the South Asian Diaspora

The historiography of indentureship in the South Asian diaspora has produced two—and at first glance, opposing—accounts of labor, identity, and the

South Asian diaspora. On one hand scholarly accounts stress powerful legal and social intuitions where the strictures of the indenture contracts and the indignities associated with transportation and living circumstances combine to "imprison" the indentured laborer to the micro-world of the plantation (Schœlcher 2008: 205; Anderson 2009). For example, discussion of indentureship as a "new system of slavery," a phrase common in the British liberal press, was first coined by the colonial secretary Lord John Russell. He suspended the practice of transporting indentured labor to British Guiana from India, stating, "I am not prepared to encounter the responsibility of a measure which may lead to a dreadful loss of life on the one hand, or, on the other, to a new system of slavery" (House of Commons 1840). This top-down approach equates challenges of indentured laborers with those of enslaved laborers who had little or no legal opportunity to challenge the institutionalization of status (Tinker 1974). Even when indentured South Asians did author formal challenges to their indenture contract, they could only expect to become marginal beneficiaries through hard work and savings, land acceptance and settlement, or final repatriation to their homeland (Look Lai 1993; Laurence 1995; Hoefte 1998).

On the other hand, scholars (Shephard 2002; Bose 2015) have adopted a bottom-up approach by positioning the indentured laborer as a kind of peasant with the capacity to enact everyday forms of resistance. For them documenting indentureship as a novel, more hidden, type of enslavement provides only a partial account of the experiences of those caught up in migration (Shephard 2002). Rather they attend to varying systems of indenture, passages of laborers from and to South Asian homelands (Bahadur 2014; Hurgobin and Basu 2015), and the high rate of voluntary re-indenture (Lal 1998; Roopnarine 2010, 2018), and returnee's roles in recruitment of new laborers (Carter 1995; Bates 2017; Kumar 2017) form a critical lens through which to investigate the plantation as a moral economy. Here the indentured laborer is constituted as part of a peasantry with the capacity to improvise everyday forms of resistance (Haraksingh 1998; Mahase 2008; Mangru 1996), navigate the predicaments of labor, and plan a better life beyond the spatial confines and temporal cycles of indenture.

In some cases this meant aligning themselves with landholding elites and imperial interests to become an "also colonizer other," as in the case of South Asian–Zulu interactions in Natal (Soske 2017). Additionally, everyday forms of resistance had their limits. In Caribbean contexts, where "the impact of racist perceptions was obviously magnified, and its principal consequence was to hold back the maturing of working class unity by offering an explanation of exploitation and oppression that seemed reasonably consistent with aspects of people's life experience" (Rodney 1981: 181), pitting labor communities against one another helped reproduce the plantation as the anchoring reality of everyday life (Munasinghe 2018).

Rather than two opposing accounts, these debates should be seen as end members in a wide range of perspectives first authored in colonial contexts that continue to shape how indentureship is framed. Through the methods of historical archaeology and our attention to the material, we pivot this historiography to define the commercial agricultural context as one in which ecology and class—along with co-constitutive social identities, especially gender, caste, race, and religion—intersected and influenced the conditions and consequences of indentureship. We make this pivot because it allows us to ask a series of questions: How and in what specific, local, and global ways does commercial agriculture differ from past agricultural intensifications? How are different people—in relation to class and other co-constituted axes of social difference such as gender, race, ethnicity, age, occupation—affected by commercial agriculture? Finally, what combinations of narratives and strategies frame commercial agriculture and the institutionalized responses to it in agrarian settings? Our two archaeological sites of study represent not only the points of departure and settlement of the South Asian indentured diaspora but two distinctive agricultural communities.

The first community, Sathangudi, is located a little over 1 km northwest of Tharangambadi, in Tamil Nadu, South India. Archaeological survey documented imported ceramics ranging from the mid-eighteenth century to the first quarter of the twentieth century (Hauser and Selvakumar 2019). Maps of the region drawn by European observers document the presence of a village (*dorf*) and three water tanks (*Teicher*) by the mid-seventeenth century (Anonymous 1650). By the turn of the eighteenth century, depictions of Sathangudi also include a Portuguese or Roman Catholic church, neighboring rice fields (*Nellu felder*), and a rest house (*Ruhehäuser*) (Seutter 1730). By 1760 the village became home to a commercial enterprise run by Moravians to fund missionary efforts in Nicobar through the sale of agricultural products including rice and grapes (Krieger 2008, see also Hauser and Selvakumar 2021). While the enterprise failed, agriculture continued under the new ownership of a Mr. Nagel after 1803. Oral histories collected by V. Selvakumar state that this settlement was inhabited by washer men who moved to this area during colonial times (Hauser and Selvakumar 2019). Described in greater detail in Selvakumar and Hauser's chapter in this volume, an oral history collected by the survey team also details a family indebted to moneylenders for a variety of household events including weddings and festivals. The family continued to be obliged to repay these loans even after members emigrated to Mauritius (see Selvakumar and Hauser, this volume). Such family stories exemplify the conditions of the middle and lower strata of the society, who perhaps chose to migrate to work in the plantations under such difficult conditions.

The second community, Bras d'Eau, was a plantation on the northeast coast of Mauritius. Bras d'Eau was under private ownership by French colonists from 1786 through 1904. Based on mean ceramic dating of excavated and surface collection artifacts, occupational deposits have been recovered only from the middle to end of the nineteenth century (Haines 2020). The soil in the northeast region of Mauritius is rich, but very rocky, and cultivating sugar cane required boring into the bedrock, altering the very fabric of the island (Haines 2021). Though the land was not ideal for agricultural use, and in acreage it was not the largest estate on Mauritius, at one point in 1847 Bras d'Eau had 545 laborers, including 414 men, 70 women, and 68 children (House of Commons 1874), giving the plantation the largest workforce in the colony, either in spite of or perhaps because of the geological nature of the land. In more typical years, Bras d'Eau had 250–300 laborers engaged to work on the estate. Therefore the social and community dynamics on a single plantation like Bras d'Eau were under processes not only of continuous renewal but also of adjustment.

While direct connections between these two sites and their inhabitants are not available, the sites can be compared through layered scales of analysis: as domestic sites rich with the materiality of everyday life; as nodes within the South Asian diaspora; and as representations of global migrations of the modern period.

Building the Comparison

Comparative analyses in the study of indenture have been difficult to realize. There have been two methodological concerns in the study of indenture from South Asia and its diaspora in the eighteenth and nineteenth centuries. To begin with, the statistics on indenture in published studies from different regions or colonies often operate at different scales of analysis and levels of resolution, making simple comparisons confusing and unreliable. Compounding these statistical challenges, the names, identified caste, perceived phenotype, and linguistic capabilities recorded in colonial documents do not speak to the active engagement in place making that occurred in the diaspora—using old ways of doing things to make things anew. Despite these difficulties, the archaeological record attached to households provides a valuable venue through which to compare related but unconnected communities.

Depending on the archive, published source, or scale of resolution, one gets contradictory information of the structure and temporality of the labor migration. According to imperial accounts about migration from the Coromandel coast, we see one particular structure to the trade. The four major ports in the south were Yanon, Madras, Pondicherry, and Karaikal, from which populations would come from Telegu-speaking districts, including Ganjam, Cuttack, Kristna, and Godavery (Yanon), as well Tamil-speaking districts, including Chingleput, North Arcot, Nellore, Cuddapah, and Bellary (Madras); Salem, South Arcot, Coimbatore, and Mysore (Pondicherry); Thanjavur, Thrinpolly, Madurai, and Tinelvy (Karaikal) (Singaravelou 1987: 62). The earliest of Tamil-speaking peoples brought to Mauritius include a series of artisans who came from Karaikal to work under contract in 1729, and by 1792 there were nearly 1,200 skilled Tamil artisans working on the island (Stephen 2019: 35–36). Between 1850 and 1861, just over 73,000 Tamils migrated to Mauritius (House of Commons 1874: 72–73). Between 1862 and 1870 that number dropped dramatically to some 20,000 (House of Commons 1874: 74).

By comparison, the statistics associated with points of departure and identity in Mauritius are much more difficult to ascertain (see also Čaval and Cianciosi, this volume, on gendered identities). Primary sources located in the Mauritius National Archives provide broad resolution, highlighting that workers embarked at the major ports of the three presidencies: Bengal, Madras, and Bombay. More detailed regional data associated with individual migrants, that might reveal caste, names, linguistic capabilities, and ports of embarkation, are available only through the Indian Immigration Archives held by the Mahatma Gandhi Institute in Mauritius, and privacy restrictions over access exist to prevent stigma associated with Mauritian families' past identities. Furthermore, island-wide migration trends are not perfect correlates for plantation demographics, particularly over shorter time scales. For example, a sample of ship records related to one settlement in our comparison, Bras d'Eau estate, from the first half of the 1840s (Table 8.1) shows that twice as many laborers who worked in Bras d'Eau came through the port of Calcutta as came through Madras. However, in early March of 1845 there were 129 laborers who came through Madras, 118 from Bengal, and 56 from Bombay (Table 8.2). Immigrant demographics on a plantation fluctuated even over the course of a single year.

That being said, we can make several important observations considering the data from Bras d'Eau in light of those from South Asia. First, the plurality of laborers migrating from Tamil Nadu to Bras d'Eau, represented by a Madras port of departure (Tables 8.1 and 8.2), especially in its earliest manifestation, would have come from the Lower Kaveri and departed through the French port of Karaikal. Major towns feeding this migration would have in-

Diaspora in the Domestic: A Comparative Approach to Tamil Nadu and Mauritius · 185

Table 8.1. Indentured immigrants who worked on Bras d'Eau arrived from different ports in South Asia

Date the Ship Landed	Proprietor and Estate	Total Laborers	Men	Women	Children	Ship Name	Port of Departure
July 4, 1841	Ulcoq, Bras d'Eau estate	10	10 "Chinese"	—	—	*Ganges*	Penang
May 1, 1843	Ulcoq, Bras d'Eau estate	54	38	13	3	*Flowers of Ugie*	Madras
October 10, 1843	Ulcoq, Flacq	1	1			*Gaugrs*	Madras
November 3, 1843	Ulcoq, Bras d'Eau estate	63	50	8	5	*Henry*	Madras
July 5, 1843	Ulcoq, Bras d'Eau estate	50	45	5	—	*August à Jossie*	Bombay
January 13, 1844	Ulcoq, Bras d'Eau estate	100	80	11	9	*Edmonstone*	Calcutta
July 22, 1845	Ulcoq and LeBigot, Bras d'Eau	7	6	1	—	*Mermaid*	Calcutta
July 14, 1846	Ulcoq, Bras d'Eau estate	60	33	12	15	*Lady Macdonald*	Calcutta
July 2, 1846	Ulcoq, Bras d'Eau estate	45	31	10	4	*Peking*	Calcutta

Source: Records in the PB series of the Mauritius National Archives, Coromandel, Mauritius.

cluded Thanjavur, Tharangambadi, Nagapattinam. In 1843 the majority of the migrants to Mauritius from the Madras Presidency would have come through Karaikal from Thanjavur district (39 percent); Trichupalli (31 percent), and other locations (5 percent). This was followed by those coming through Madras (12 percent), and Pondicherry (8 percent) (House of Commons 1874: 72–73). Between 1869 and 1873 the center of gravity for the Tamil migration to Mauritius had significantly shifted to those embarking from Madras (59 percent) (House of Commons 1874: 72–74), though Karaikal continues to play a significant role (34 percent). Second, the majority of those migrating from South India identified as Hindu. And finally, many of the communities represented in this migration were those most closely associated with agricultural work. This is in part a result of recruitment strategies, but it also represents communities that were particularly precarious (Bhatia 1963).

The second reason comparative analysis has been difficult to realize is that a discontinuity in the study of indenture from South Asia to the western Indian Ocean has produced a contradiction between the two, and as a consequence, there has been potential overemphasis of certain themes in diasporic

Table 8.2. Bras d'Eau and district demographics log showing the "Return of Indian laborers . . . on 8th March 1845 according to the last statements furnished by the masters" (Mauritius National Archives, HA series, 101)

Number of Indians Engaged from Regions in India

FIRST IMMIGRATION

ESTATE AND OWNER	BENGAL	MADRES	BOMBAY	TOTAL
Bras d'Eau, Ulcoq & Company	36	13	0	**39**
Total for Flacq district	404	335	11	**754**

BOUNTY IMMIGRATION

ESTATE AND OWNER	BENGAL	MADRES	BOMBAY	TOTAL
Bras d'Eau, Ulcoq & Company	82	116	56	**254**
Total for Flacq district	797	1996	302	**3995**

GOVERNMENT IMMIGRATION

ESTATE AND OWNER	BENGAL	MADRES	BOMBAY	TOTAL
Bras d'Eau, Ulcoq & Company	0	0	0	**0**
Total for Flacq district	1601	262	157	**2020**

literature. As mentioned earlier, Indian Ocean scholars have noted that for land-bound people, the concept of stepping aboard ships and voyaging to foreign lands was terrifying, summed up in what was referred to as the *kala pani* or "black waters," a combination of the waters themselves and the experience of dislocation. Anderson (2009: 104) argues that Indians believed the transportation and migration of indentured laborers led to "social rupture and permanent loss." The dread of the kala pani included the loss of caste and religion through forced interaction with members of other castes in the confined spaces of the ship, such as having to consume food with, or prepared by, those in other castes (see also Brown and Mahase 2009, and Kumar 2016 for the indentured experience of shipboard food and drink). However, Bates and Carter (2021) argue there were shifts in the meaning and uses of kala pani over time, including the ways in which it was reframed in the British colonial imaginary in India as a threatening punishment for colonized subjects, by Indian anti-indenture and anti-colonial nationalists, and later within political framings of diaspora heritage.

Despite the challenges of reconstructing caste data due to regional variation in the perceived status of specific castes and tribal groupings and misunderstanding or misrepresentation by colonial archivists, Carter (1995) and Lal (2004) have shown that people from the lowest to highest caste groups became indentured immigrants, though planters' preferences in recruits changed over time in favor of agriculturalists and artisan caste members. Therefore, caution is in order to avoid an overemphasis on the connection between the kala pani and caste anxiety for all indentured migrants throughout a century of indentured movements. Migrating across the ocean could also represent an escape from structural inequalities for those of the most impoverished and marginalized classes (Bass 2013: 27). Furthermore, not only did approximately 20 percent of indentured laborers return to India after the five-year contract, but many went on to encourage kin and village members to make the voyage, becoming instrumental in recruitment of new laborers through both formal and informal social networks (Carter 1995; Bates 2017; Kumar 2017). A smaller number of laborers chose to re-contract themselves to the same estate, or boarded sailing vessels bound for other colonies, such as Natal (South Africa), Guyana, and Trinidad.

Those Tamil-speaking peoples arriving in Mauritius during Bras d'Eau's early manifestation who were identified by caste on the voyages include communities associated with agriculture. Also listed were artisans, including Ambattans (barbers, 6 percent) and Dalit communities (13 percent). A range of other castes were represented, including members of smithing, weaving, and other artisanal communities. When Tamils worked in Bras d'Eau, the majority of émigrés continued to be from communities associated with agriculture, including Paraiyars, Reddiyars, Vanniyars, and Vellalars (71 percent), though the numbers of weavers (11 percent) and leatherworkers (7 percent) were also large enough to be enumerated separately (Stephen 2019: 36).

Because domestic space sits at the intersection of identity and landscape, political economy and the everyday ways people negotiate and reproduce social boundaries become useful ways to compare the changing contours of social identity, power, and daily life as people crossed the kala pani. The architecture and arrangement of domestic space has the added benefit of providing a degree of archaeological visibility that enables such comparison. The concept of the domestic is not new in the archaeology of the ancient—nor is it new to the material study of enslavement. For our discussion here we rely on Mary Moran's (1992) definition of domestic as "both the socially defined spaces associated with residential group and the meaningful practices that take place there" (98). We ask a simple question: did this symbolic boundary shape the way people organized their domestic space? In what follows, we compare villages and architecture in two locations, the Lower Kaveri and Mauritius. We pay special attention to water as a fundamental substance of everyday life tied directly with commercial agriculture (Hauser 2021), and carrying implications for social identity and power (Hauser and Selvakumar

2021). The following sections contextualize the results of our archaeological surveys and subsequent targeted excavations of domestic areas at Sathangudi and Bras d'Eau within the broader scope of local architectural and spatial practices, thus establishing a foundation from which we can compare the diasporic experiences in Mauritius with those in Tamil Nadu.

Archaeology at Sathangudi

Archaeological survey at Sathangudi documented a variety of housing plans, construction materials, and states of repair. For a partial typology of Tamil housing between the eighteenth and nineteenth centuries we can turn to several studies conducted in former colonial enclave Pondicherry (French), where "Tamil houses are strictly functional, and a series of open, semi-covered, and covered spaces with subtle levels and a through axis characterize the plan" (INTACH 2004: 60). We have also sought to establish a simple classification of plans for Tharangambadi, a former Danish colonial enclave, based on surveys conducted by Karl Pedersen (1987b) and Jens Damborg (1987a, 1987b) and on a separate study of polite architecture by Niels Jensen (2017). Though a partial typology is offered, it is important to be cognizant of Matthew Johnson's (2005) opprobrium of such endeavors in medieval England, suggesting that such typologies can be misleading, providing superficial rigor forcing buildings into a set of ideal types to which they do not belong. It is the same for Tamil townscapes, where for the period between 1600 and 1900, a variety of house types defy attempts at neat architectural classification. It is therefore important to consider using such taxonomies only as a general indication of preferred arrangements of buildings on a house plot (*ania*), whether urban or rural.

Pragmatically, Tamil housing can be classified into large, medium, and small, which align, though loosely, to upper, middle, and lower classes. According to contemporary documents, housing varied significantly in size and construction, if not in layout, in eighteenth-century Tranquebar. In 1730, in connection with the Crown's temporary takeover of Tranquebar from the East India Company, administrators enumerated the town's population. Categories employed were Indian, Danish, and Portuguese. The term "Portuguese" came to have ethno-religious connotations, though it could describe people with backgrounds from Africa, western India, Europe, and Southeast Asia. As a census, there are many elements missing from this enumeration. For example, details on many Indian households were missing, and "Portuguese" households were difficult to locate geographically. What makes this enumeration interesting are the brief building descriptions. They describe brick, stone,

Figure 8.2. Location of Sathangudi and associated water infrastructure.

straw, and earthfast houses or huts, thus adding a further dimension to housing and racialized categories used to document the population by Danish administrators. Of the 674 households documented, 66 were Danish, 38 were Portuguese, and 570 were Indian (Pedersen 1987a). The vast majority of Danish households were associated with brick architecture. Most Indian households were associated with stone architecture (68 percent) or straw huts (25 percent). The "Portuguese" community represented the most diverse range of housing: brick (16 percent), stone (29 percent), mud (5 percent), and straw (50 percent).

Large and medium Tamil houses can be found in the region and they follow vernacular patterns. Structures were built around a central room called the *mutram*. *Mutram* were meeting places for residents and honored guests but also functioned as a place for washing. Typically, the front of large- and medium-sized houses included a raised platform immediately facing the street with masonry columns supporting a roof for the veranda. Then followed the entrance to the building. At the back of these houses was an inner courtyard (*ania padappai*) that typically contained a well. It took generations for a family to acquire all the capital to purchase land large enough to build a house. Nearby examples of large houses include the "Company Garden" and the "Nadar Bungalow" in the neighboring town, Poriyar. Both were built in the second half of the nineteenth century.

Traditionally associated with the cultivation of palms and the production of toddy, the Nadar community of Tamil Nadu, took advantage of new commercial and administrative opportunities emerged when Denmark relinquished control of Tranquebar in 1845. Along with these opportunities came properties that once belonged to the crown. The large house at "Company Garden" was built by Vellaiya Nadar when the family purchased the land after the colony was transferred to British rule in 1845 (see Hauser and Selvakumar 2021 for discussion of gardens). The house is two stories and is approximately 27 by 25 meters. It is situated on an urban plot that is approximately 2 hectares in size. The plot also includes a tank that is nearly 1000 square meters. Such tanks were vital for bathing and other household activities. Drinking water was obtained through a brick-lined well.

The archaeological survey identified a variety of housing types as well as water infrastructure in Sathangudi (Fig. 8.2). That being said, there were no examples of large Tamil houses. The only evidence of a large house was a structure commissioned by missionaries who purchased land adjacent to the village in the 1760s identified as "Brother's Garden." Between 1760 and 1795, 73 Moravian "brothers" and "sisters" were sent to Tranquebar and worked as merchants, carpenters, watchmakers, tanners, boat builders, farmers, and doctors (Krieger 2008). A contemporary ground plan depicts a main structure that was cross-shaped and called "*Gemein haus und Saal*" (common house and room). Two near-symmetrical structures flanked on either side of the common hall: a single brothers' house and a family house for married couples (Karth 1763). Surface features, including house platforms, sunken fields, tanks, pillar bases, and evidence of a gate, conform to drawings depicting the polite architecture of the garden, including the "Brothers' House," the "Family House," and the "Common House" (Anonymous 1763). During the survey, the team documented platforms associated with all three residences. The team also identified a complex drainage system indicating that the structure's roofs were used to capture rainfall to fill the tanks on the complex's north, south, and west sides. These tanks were an assemblage of sluice gates, steps, and drainages commissioned by the missionaries (Fig. 8.2). Given the elaborate water system, these European-commissioned buildings most likely followed some idioms of Tamil housing.

Many elements in 18th-century ground plans were not always visible during the pedestrian survey. Some required closer scrutiny of soil and topography. A raised platform of hardened earth, artifact scatter, and a dried pond (Fig. 8.3b) provided evidence of a less durable structure some distance from the "Common" house. The only clue to this structure is an outbuilding on the ground plan describing it as the "Malabar House" for "native" employees

Figure 8.3. One of three tanks enlarged for the main buildings at Brothers' Garden, Sathangudi (*a*). Platform and dried pond for the Malabar house at Brothers' Garden, Sathangudi (*b*).

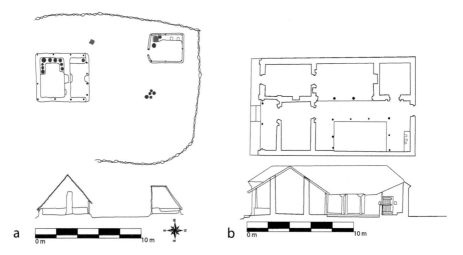

Figure 8.4. Tamil vernacular housing. (*a*) A Tamil modest house. Tamil wattle and daub housing can vary in size. (*b*) A Tamil town house, made of brick or stone plastered with clay (after Damborg 1987: 207, 209).

(Anonymous 1763). While Malabari might signify that its inhabitant came from the west coast of India, it most likely denotes that workers were from South India more generally, whether their status was enslaved, bonded, or free (Carter 2006: 808). For example, those listed in Pondicherry slave registers in the 1760s are referred to as Malabaris regardless of origin or caste. Importantly it highlights that new labor requirements brought about the need to increase the number of buildings to house them.

Scholarship (Damborg 1987a; Cooper and Dawson 1998) on housing in neighboring villages is helpful for interpreting how these houses might have been configured. Thatched-roofed houses (*kurai vidu* or *kuraikattu vidu*) can vary in size. Typically, they are 5 to 6 meters long and 3 to 4 meters wide, though some can extend up to 12 to 14 meters in length and 8 to 9 meters in width (Fig. 8.4). These houses are arranged in a linear pattern along the cross streets, which are connected to the main street of a village surrounded by agricultural fields. Unlike middle- and upper-class housing, small houses are generally detached. A typical home usually consists of a lockable multipurpose space in the interior and an accessible space in the front. The inner lockable room is used for food preservation and storing a few family possessions. House shrines are generally located in a recessed portion of the building. Pots for rice and herbs stand in recesses on a clay rise. The second room, the open porch, is used for sleeping and daycare. Most day-to-day activities occur in outdoor spaces. These houses also follow traditional principles of

Diaspora in the Domestic: A Comparative Approach to Tamil Nadu and Mauritius · 193

construction. Today, these houses are mostly self-built by family members, sometimes aided by neighbors. Small houses were made of local materials like timber, bamboo, clay, straw, cow dung, and a special variety of grass called *nanal* (Cooper and Dawson 1998). The thick walls (approximately 0.3–0.5 m) were made of mud mixed with cow dung plastering, woven twigs, and bamboo. A shallow pond near the barracks met some water needs. Precipitation would have filled this pond, especially in the wet season. It would have been less reliable as a water source during the dry season. As we will see below, nearby rivers and tanks also served as the water source for drinking, bathing, washing, and cooking.

Not all elements identified during the survey were documented on the 18th-century ground plans and maps. For example, the survey identified four tanks, one enlarged pond, and two ditches, none of which were present on the 1763 ground plan (Fig. 8.3a). According to a 1730 map of the region (Seutter 1730), these tanks predate Moravian investment in the region and were critical in the everyday life of the settlement. Also not present on the contemporary ground plan and maps are the many medium-sized houses that populate Sathangudi. The village at Sathangudi also contained buildings dating to the nineteenth century. Medium-sized houses here are made of brick, and are approximately 10 by 12 meters with two to three rooms, a veranda, and, significantly, no wells. Though additions in subsequent centuries made identifying earlier architectural elements difficult, scholarship on Tharangambadi is useful here (Damborg 1987b). Primary examples include the 18 townhouses (Fig. 8.4) on Goldsmith and Mosque streets in Tharangambadi. Midway between the stately polite bungalows and the humbler housing, properties of this size were approximately 13 by 12 meters and universally contained and contained three to six rooms. These more elaborate houses were one story and often included a *thinnai,* a veranda with wooden pillars facing the street. Though not all houses had a true inner courtyard, most had a backyard that contained a well. As noted earlier, such wells granted access to groundwater that was considered private. In contrast, Sathangudi villagers shared water sources. Three of the tanks from which villagers drew their water were named *kusinikulam, nadukulam,* and *kudiraikkulam. Kusini,* or kitchen, is probably derived from the Portuguese *cozhina* highlighting their influence. The other tanks were for watering livestock and other domestic uses.

Sara Dickey notes that Tamil housing was a "porous container of the middle- and upper-class families and their values" (2008: 249). She adds that upper- and middle-class housing values vary along two spatial dimensions: intimacy and elaboration (Dickey 2008: 232). Depending on religious ideas of purity or privacy, these dimensions regulated the placement of areas and which persons had access to them. In Hindu homes, for example, the higher the caste, the greater the anxiety for maintaining these spatial relations of purity. The purest spaces, including those devoted to cooking, food storage, and worship, are placed farthest away from a source of pollution, the entrance. At the same time, the higher the class, the greater the number of rooms and the amount of space enforcing those distinctions.

Such analyses do not take into consideration the ways in which housing associated with laborers and newcomers is incorporated into this scheme. During the early modern period, two processes affected medium-sized residences in Tamil Nadu, many of which had started off as more humble residences. There was an expansion of rural industry and trade. It is therefore common to see workshops attached to each of these residences. There was also an elaboration of social distinction beyond class boundaries to include craft distinctions.

Water Management and Everyday Use in Tamil Nadu

Today the amount of water and access to it is subject to location, formal and informal rules of distribution, and the social fields that constitute the matrixes of power. Water, as a function of architecture, is an important consideration in understanding the matrixes of power for those caught in the diaspora. It is useful to consider the role of water in examining the archaeological evidence of architecture and social divisions in Sathangudi. In Tamil Nadu today surface water from tanks and streams constitutes a commons for those who can gain access to the land on which they dwell. Groundwater, on the other hand, is a form of private property and access to it enforces distinctions between communities and classes that frame social relations.

Tanks present an important yet precarious mechanism to capture, store, and distribute water. David Mosse has argued that the South Indian water "production system . . . is inherently unstable, changeable, fluid and subject to calamity . . . local and regional institutions not only respond to the inherent uncertainty of water resources but contribute to or amplify this uncertainty" (Mosse 2003: 7). Today tank irrigation has numerous limitations. Tanks are, by definition, limited in the capacity that they can store. The ability to take advantage of that capacity is dependent on two factors: rainfall and the tank's position in interconnected irrigation systems such as those in the hinterland of Tharangambadi. During dry seasons precipitation is limited to a few millimeters of rain a month; these are times of pronounced anxiety over the community's water use, especially for those located downstream in irrigated areas. Finally tanks, as implied by their names given earlier, not only supply water to fields but are also an important source of water for people to bathe and wash and for more precarious communities to collect drinking water. In the precolonial and colonial landscape, water systems were subject to the unreliable investments of warrior overlords (Mosse 2003: 11). Indeed it is critical to understand that even if tank water formed a commons, one should not underestimate the social heterogeneity and conflicts of interest in the past landscape (Gujit and Shah 1998). Even though architecture varies, it still reflects class concerns.

Archaeology at Bras d'Eau

Historians of Mauritius have creatively used the often incomplete records of official immigrant complaints as well as colonial investigations on the conditions of indenture—often conducted to compare the living conditions of indentured people with those of the enslaved people they replaced—to provide a preliminary picture of what life was like on plantations for laborers (Carter 1995). Comprehensive studies of architectural styles in Mauritius have largely focused on wealthy houses, urban structures, and colonial institutional structures (Floore and Jayasena 2010; Summers 2021), with the notable exception of Dwight Carey (2018a, 2018b), who uses historical documents to reconstruct a historical architectural portrayal of domestic housing built for and by enslaved people during the French period. Captive or exploited laborers, including slaves and indentured laborers, had a hand in the construction of colonial architecture in Mauritius, though are rarely given credit (Carey 2018a). Oral histories and narratives also remain a largely untapped source for localized understandings of indenture in Mauritius. Archaeological investigations of sugar plantations' standing and residual structures therefore provide material weight to the study of non-elite domestic spaces. In addition, historical archaeology provides an avenue to examine critically how power and cultural constructions intersect within the ways plantation spaces are configured.

Bras d'Eau is the first plantation to be surveyed on Mauritius with surviving industrial and domestic areas, their preservation due in large part to the abandonment of the sugar mill and domestic housing in the later nineteenth century, and conversion of the sugar estate into a national forest at the start of the twentieth century, and a national park in 2011 (Haines 2021). This remarkable level of preservation, as well as the practice of constructing stone foundations for structures and features, allowed for the identification and mapping of 7 hectares of ruins using on-the-ground surface survey methods (Haines 2019a).

Stone and mortar barracks still stand on several plantations in Mauritius, and they are the most complete known examples of housing attributed to enslaved and indentured plantation workers. Barracks with vaulted stone roofs that were once part of the Trianon Sugar Estate have been examined and documented by the Mauritius Archaeology and Cultural Heritage project in collaboration with the Aapravasi Ghat Trust Fund (Seetah et al. 2018). Such structures were occupied first by enslaved, then indentured, and later free laborers after abolition of both labor regimes, but the majority of the indentured population would not have lived in stone buildings (Seetah et al. 2018: 158). As the indentured laborer population increased, larger villages were built to accommodate them. Descriptions of housing and historic photographs of indentured housing indicate that houses were made with straw thatching woven around wood-framed structures with pitched roofs. Thatching was eventually replaced by corrugated metal sheets at the end of the nineteenth century. Photos often show houses lining linear streets. The architectural style varied, including roof shape and dimensions of the houses. Some roofs extended past the walls to create a covered veranda; other thatched structures were set on stone foundations like those found at Bras d'Eau.

At Bras d'Eau two general types of housing were identified in the domestic quarter: parallel rows of line barracks, and detached, almost square houses (Haines 2019b). To the west and north of the village there are about 50 similar detached structures that may have also been used as dwellings but their function is yet to be confirmed. Despite some collapsing and rubble surrounding the walls, it is clear that the barracks at Bras d'Eau differ from the vaulted-ceiling stone barracks found on other estates; the stone walls extend up only about 1–1.5 meters. Coral-lime mortar appears to have been used to fill in cracks more than to secure the masonry. A post-hole laboriously bored 20 cm into the basalt bedrock about 2 meters from the barracks structure foundation into the yard may have been used to hold a support column for a covered veranda. A separate house for overseers and/or managers of the estate likely existed but has yet to be distinguished from or within the general laborers' village. The largely absentee estate owner is reported also to have had a 9 × 9-meter residence with four rooms and constructed entirely of stone (Mauritius National Archives 1844). The specific structure has yet to be identified, though several standing ruins close to the mill are likely possibilities.

The wall lengths of the detached dwellings range from 2.5 meters to 6 meters, though on average they are 14 square meters in size, and for the most part the structures are dispersed within the 4 ha area quarter rather than set in linear rows. These dwellings are roughly oriented on a north-south axis with more than 80 percent of the doorways facing toward the northwest, away from predominant winds (Haines 2019b). Structures nearest to the road tend to run parallel to it. Nine detached houses—possibly more had collapsed and were unidentifiable—also had a much smaller adjacent outbuilding, sometimes sharing a wall, but never with internal connecting doorways. With dimensions of ~1.5 to 2 meters by 2 to 3 meters, these outbuildings may not have been sleeping quarters and may have had another function. These outbuildings have yet to be excavated. Low stone partitioning walls further define the space around the houses in the 4 ha area quarter. Though all the structures within Bras d'Eau are rectangular, most of these walls are curved, creating rounded yard spaces, and not always following the natural topography, which undulates with dips and pillowed basalt outcrops.

For both the barracks and detached dwellings, constructing foundation walls served a dual purpose. First, they secured the frames on which thatching could be applied and saved laborers the task of boring holes into the bedrock. Second, building the foundations as well as the yard walls also cleared the land of the largest boulders and rubble, providing open and more level indoor and outdoor living surfaces. Evidence of such carefully displaced rocks is found across the entire estate, including stone walls that mark house yards in the village and rows of fieldstone in the agricultural zones. An excavation of the cross-section of one of the barracks revealed vestiges of red clay flooring layers hard packed into natural low points in the basalt bedrock. These floors would have been made with a mixture of Mauritian clayey soils and cow dung, still used for plastering house floors and walls as recently as 50 years ago and recalled through oral histories. We did not find any hearths during the excavations or survey but based on oral accounts of Mauritians, cooking over open fires both outside and indoors was typical.

As with Tamil house typologies, variation exists within the two distinct barracks and detached dwellings. Even the barracks, though in perfectly parallel rows, had variations in room size, length, and possibly in the upper story structure that no longer stands. Some barracks rooms were positioned on high sloped outcrops where it would not have been possible to have a veranda.

Wells and Water Tanks

Located 600 meters walking distance from the mill is an area subdivided into two sections by a 100-meter-long wall. The west section consists of an elaborate waterworks infrastructure in an area measuring 0.5 hectares. A well has two sets of stone steps that lead down to a small platform from which one could collect water (Fig. 8.5). The whole eastern side of the well is eroding into the well hole, but it seems to have been lined with square-cut blocks, at least along its upper 4 m. About 2 m from the well, a mortared wall with a narrow plaster channel on top slopes gently down to a 1 × 2 m plastered open tank, c. 50 m away. The sides of this small tank rise about 50 cm above the ground, and the interior extends below the surface level, though the exact depth is unknown as the base is filled in with soil. Another 40 m north, two larger

198 · Julia Jong Haines and Mark William Hauser

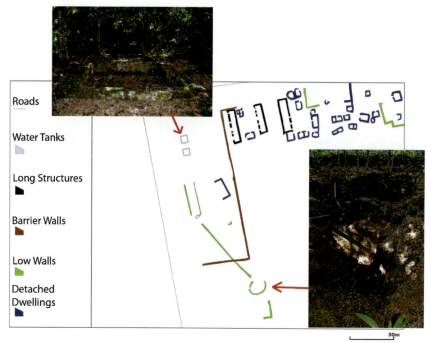

Figure 8.5. Map of Bras d'Eau water infrastructure. The well closest to the laborers' village (*photo, lower right*) was connected to three open water tanks by a series of plaster-lined channels (*photo, upper left*). (Credit: Julia Haines).

plaster-lined open tanks, each about 3.75 m by 4 m, are dug into the ground and sit side by side. Broken fragments of a mortared stone and plaster-lined channel are scattered between the small tank and the two larger tanks, indicating that all three were connected to the well at some point. Well water could have been poured or pumped into the first narrow channel next to the well and would have flowed down the chutes to fill the series of tanks, thus creating a modest aqueduct system.

On either side of the water channel stand a stone and mortar building, a plaster platform, and the remnants of several walls close to the road. The upper portions of these walls were likely dismantled by the Forestry Department in 1970 to build the large orchard enclosure walls that run alongside the roads (Archives of the Forestry Services 1970). No systematic surface collection or excavations were conducted in this area, but anecdotally the surface artifact scatter is significantly lower than among the ruins around the mill and laborers' quarter. Around the waterworks the undergrowth has been kept clear by the National Parks and Conservation Services, perhaps because the last ebony tree in the park stands between the well and the first small tank, and yet only a few ceramic and glass pieces were seen on the ground surface during the mapping process. The area itself is remarkably level ground compared with surrounding plots, suggesting that the entire area was cleared to make moving through it easier. The complexity of the infrastructure would have required planning, engineering, and resources, and its centralized location between both fields and the village perhaps indicates multiple uses.

A large amount of water would have been needed to sustain the 200–500 people living on the estate, working animals, such as horses, oxen, mules, other animals or crops people raised for food independent of the estate owners, and acres of sugarcane during dry spells. The closest dwelling in the laborers' quarter is more than 200 m walking distance from the water and well complex. The well next to the mill is about the same distance in the other direction. The aqueducts may have been put in place to avoid congestion around the well itself, for drawing water, bathing, watering animals, doing laundry, and so on. If this space was used for bathing and washing, the lack of artifacts might be more reflective of the laborers' desire to keep this area clean of the trash and refuse that is scattered around the rest of the site, than of its use as an industrial work space. In the first 10 years after Bras d'Eau became Crown land the Forestry Department reported that they were caring for a sisal-hemp plantation on the property (Archives of the Forestry Services 1908, 1909). The sisal plantations were typically a residual effect from the estate's growing, processing, and weaving fibers into gunny sacks to package sugar, and potentially to sell to other local estates to supplement income from the global sugar market. Sisal processing requires the pulpy tissues of the leaves to be beaten and washed out with water several times, leaving only the fibers. Once cleaned, fibers are hung to dry, woven into sheets, and finally sewn into sacks. As one of two wells on the property, it is reasonable to assume that the stepped well was in use during the nineteenth century. Though there is no corroborating archaeological evidence, given the volume of water required for domestic needs and water-intensive industrial activities, it is also likely that water was drawn from the entirety of the aqueduct.

Diaspora and Comparative Archaeology

In some ways, this comparison of residential configurations and architecture demonstrates the ways in which diasporic spaces, like the domestic quarter of Bras d'Eau, are a distinct amalgam of concepts and ideas transformed into creating viable livable places. In other ways, it reinforces that all Mauritian ways of doing things gesture to the broad oceanic origins of all the island's inhabitants, and it is exactly such networked practices that define the Indian Ocean more broadly, rather than specific cultural links.

The line barracks with verandas gesture to the general configuration of Tamil village streets, while the detached dwellings themselves resemble detached village houses, at least in size. References to room divisions in the written records suggest that additional house excavations will likely reveal internal walls, though no evidence of them has been found thus far. Multiple skeleton keys and padlocks were recovered during excavations in both the barracks and detached dwellings, possibly for locking interior rooms or storage boxes, as noted in Tamil houses. Yards themselves might be interpreted as one such barrier between intimate and public space.

Plantation owners perceived the transition from an enslaved to an indentured labor force as a substitution and attempted to reuse for the new workers the housing previously occupied by enslaved people. Excavations of two barracks rooms and two detached dwellings show that the barracks were occupied and abandoned before the detached dwellings (Haines 2020). The village ruins at Bras d'Eau and written colonial reports on the conditions of indentured labor suggest that despite the planters' efforts, the demographic shift from captive people mostly from East Africa to indentured people mostly from North and South India had an impact on occupational patterns throughout the plantation system. Further comparative research that extends into the period of slavery and provides solid material evidence for the landscapes enslaved people created are likely to illuminate these similarities and differences further.

An 1875 *Report of the Royal Commissioners Appointed to Enquire into the Treatment of Immigrants in Mauritius* notes that

> though the stone buildings are more lasting and, the first expenses having been incurred, are more economical, it appears better to indulge the Indians' taste and allow them to live in huts as they do in their own villages. . . . There are the ranges, whether of stone or other material, which resemble the chawls [tenement buildings] which are to be seen in Bombay and the Concan. There are the huts, much as we see them above the Ghauts and in the Mawuls; none so good as the houses of well-to-do ryots [peasant agriculturalists or tenant farmers] in Guzerat, the Deccan, and Southern Mahratta country; but still, there is nothing for the immigrants generally to complain of, for the huts are much the same, perhaps, as they would have in their own country; though the European officer traveling through the district would certainly find fault with the state of the villages, and require them to be improved. (Frere and Williamson 1875: 353–54)

European colonists clearly were interested in noting cultural differences between themselves and laborers, albeit from a position of perceived racial superiority. Furthermore, indentured laborers' preference for "huts" had to do with the architecture itself: straw thatching was preferable to stone. At Bras d'Eau, however, both the stone barracks and the individual houses were constructed with stone foundations and wood and thatch uppers, which suggests that laborers preferred detached houses for their configuration rather than just the construction material. The incredibly rocky nature of the land at Bras d'Eau likely makes this example of residential life somewhat abnormal within the larger plantation-scape of nineteenth-century Mauritius.

Indian Ocean vernacular architecture has great regional variation. Ethnohistoric photographs from the northeastern districts of India, where the majority of indentured immigrants originated, revealed architectural styles similar to those found in Mauritius: rectangular structures with peaked roofs of straw (Kolkman and Blackburn 2014). Rectangular wood-framed structures with thatched roofs are also common in Madagascar, Zanzibar, and elsewhere in East Africa, making the direct link between Indian and Mauritius architectural knowledge less remarkable (Carey 2018a: 80).

The significance of water storage features for both communities is worth noting. The waterworks at Bras d'Eau covered a large plot of land, and the complexity of such infrastructure might normally suggest that the plantation owner had a hand in directing its construction. The comparative Tamil example of the three water tanks, however, provides the alternative possibility that distinctive water tanks for different uses was something immigrants specifically negotiated for and constructed themselves. Reading the conceptual spatial frameworks of Tamil housing and water uses into the Bras d'Eau waterworks generates a private-public water map that can be traced from the purest well source to increasingly polluted tank to tank to tank.

Concluding Remarks

This discussion has contributed to the archaeology of the Indian Ocean through a comparison of village landscapes and domestic architecture in two disparate, but connected locations, the Lower Kaveri in Tamil Nadu, and Mauritius, off the coast of East Africa. It does so by taking a transregional approach—that is, not to take for granted boundaries contemporary or past, nor to limit the spaces we locate to contextualize archaeological evidence. In the case of the comparison drawn here, the boundaries are political and symbolic. They are political in that they are two distinct polities with different yet interwoven colonial histories. In one case, that of Tamil Nadu, there are millennia of trade, urbanization, and commercial agriculture. In the case of Mauritius, human exploitation of the landscape began when Europeans laid claim to it and conscripted labor from other parts of the Indian Ocean. It is symbolic in that some of the substantive boundaries imparted into the landscape, such as kala pani or black waters, shaped the articulation of social identity in the crossing.

In both Tamil Nadu and Mauritius a survey of housing, the organization of space, and the water sources are present variables in vernacular architecture that require explanation. The destabilizing effects of this migration led to novel social forms in which social identity was asserted and challenged through space and architecture. Multiple lines of archaeological evidence, including settlement location, architecture, and the everyday sources and uses of water show that hierarchy did not disappear in the crossing, but merely transformed and reasserted itself in novel modes. As such, considering the comparative and connected histories of domestic space becomes uniquely tied to how people identify themselves in the making of modern worlds.

Acknowledgments

Research in Bras d'Eau was conducted under a permit from the Ministry of Agro-Industry and Food Security of the Republic of Mauritius, through the National Parks and Conservation Services. It was supported by the American Council of Learned Societies and Andrew W. Mellon Foundation, Fulbright Association, Social Science Research Council, and National Science Foundation (grant number 1536095).

Bibliography

Allen, Richard. 2021. "The Poverty of Archival Riches: Reconstructing Eighteenth- and Nineteenth-century Mauritian History." *International Journal of Historical Archaeology*, November. https://doi.org/10.1007/s10761-021-00639-y

Anderson, Clare. 2009. "Convicts and Coolies: Rethinking Indentured Labour in the Nineteenth Century." *Slavery* and *Abolition* 30(1): 93–109.

———. 2012. *Subaltern Lives: Biographies of Colonialism in the Indian Ocean World, 1790–1920*. New York: Cambridge University Press.

Anonymous. 1650. *Den Kongelig Danske Fæstning Dansborg, Bye Tranquebaer, og dends Destrict i det Tanjoursche Riige paa Cüst Coromandel i Ost-Indien*. Frederik den Femtes Atlas, Bd. 48, Tvl. 49, Danish Royal Library.

———. 1763. *Grundriss vom Brudergarten bey Tranquebar in Ostindien*. Unitaetsarchiv, Herrnhut, Germany. LN Mp.318.4.

Archives of the Forestry Services. 1908. *Annual Reports on Forests and Gardens Department*. Les Casernes, Curepipe: Mauritius Ministry of Agro-Industry and Food Security.

———. 1909. *Annual Reports on Forests and Gardens Department*. Les Casernes, Curepipe: Mauritius Ministry of Agro-Industry and Food Security.

Archives of the Forestry Services. 1970. *Annual Report of the Forestry Service*. Les Casernes, Curepipe: Mauritius Ministry of Agro-Industry and Food Security.

Armstrong, Douglas, and Mark W. Hauser 2004. "An East Indian Laborer's Household in 19th Century Jamaica: A Case for Spatial, Chronological, and Material Analysis in Determining Ethnicity." *Historical Archaeology* 38(2): 9–21.

Bahadur, Gaiutra. 2014. *Coolie Woman: The Odyssey of Indenture*. Chicago: University of Chicago Press.

Bass, Daniel. 2013. *Everyday Ethnicity in Sri Lanka: Up-Country Tamil Identity Politics*. London: Routledge.

Bates, Crispin. 2017. "Some Thoughts on the Representation and Misrepresentation of the Colonial South Asian Labor Diaspora." *South Asian Studies* 33(1): 7–22.

Bates, Crispin, and Marina Carter. 2021. "Kala Pani Revisited: Indian Labor Migrants and the Sea Crossing." *Journal of Indentureship* 1(1): 36–62.

Bhatia, B. M. 1963. *Famines in India 1860–1945: A Study in Some Aspects of the Economic History of India*. New York: Asia House Publishing.

Bose, Sugata. 2015. "Blackbirders Refitted? The Journeys of Capitalists and Labourers in the Indian Ocean, 1830s–1930s." In *Indian and Chinese Immigrant Communities: Comparative Perspectives*, edited by Jayati Bhattacharya and Coonoor Kripalani, 3–12. London: Anthem Press.

Brown, Laurence, and Radica Mahase. 2009. "Medical Encounters on the Kala Pani: Regulation and Resistance in the Passages of Indentured Indian Migrants, 1834–1900." In *Health and Medicine at Sea, 1700–1900*, edited by Sally Archer and David Boyd Haycock, 195–212. Woodbridge, U.K.: Boydell Press.

Carey, Dwight. 2018a. "Creole Architectural Translation: Process of Exchange in Eighteenth-Century Mauritius." *Art in Translation* 10(1): 71–90.

———. 2018b. "How Slaves Indigenized Themselves: The Architectural Cost Logs of French Colonial Mauritius." *Grey Room* 71 (Spring): 68–87.

Carter, Marina. 1995. *Servants, Sirdars, and Settlers: Indians in Mauritius, 1834–1874*. Oxford: Oxford University Press.

———. 2006. "Slavery and Unfree Labour in the Indian Ocean." *History Compass* 4(5):800–13.

Cooper, Ilay, and Barry Dawson. 1998. *Traditional Buildings of India*. London: Thames and Hudson.

Damborg, Jens 1987a. "Fiskerhytter i Tranquebar." *Architectura* 9: 201–10.

———. 1987b. "Indiske Bygninger i Prins Christiansgade." *Architectura* 9: 205–7.

Dickey, Sara. 2008. "Permeable Homes, Domestic Service, Household Space, and the Vulnerability of Class Boundaries in Urban South India." In *Tamil Geographies: Cultural Constructions of Space and Place in South India*, edited by A. S. Selby and I. V. Petersen, 221–52. Albany: State University of New York Press.

Floore, Pieter M., and Ranjith M. Jayasena, R. M. 2010. "In Want of Everything? Archaeological Perceptions of a Dutch Outstation on Mauritius (1638–1710)." *Post-Medieval Archaeology* 44: 320–40.

Frere, William Edward, and Victor Alexander Williamson. 1875. *Report of the Royal Commissioners Appointed to Enquire into the Treatment of Immigrants in Mauritius: Presented to Both Houses of Parliament by Command of Her Majesty, 6th February, 1875.*

Gujit, Irene, and Meera Kaul Shah (eds.). 1998. *The Myth of Community: Gender Issues in Participatory Development.* London: ITGD Publishing.

Haines, Julia. 2019a. *Intimate Spaces and Plantation Landscapes in Nineteenth-Century Mauritius: Archaeology of Indentured Laborers in the Western Indian Ocean.* PhD diss., University of Virginia, LibraETD. https://libraetd.lib.virginia.edu/public_view/mg74qm669

———. 2019b. "Landscape Transformation under Slavery, Indenture, and Imperial Project in Bras d'Eau National Park, Mauritius." *Journal of African Diaspora Archaeology and Heritage* 7(2): 131–64.

———. 2020. "Mauritian Indentured Labour and Plantation Household Archaeology." *Azania: Archaeological Research in Africa* 55(4): 509–27.

———. 2021. "Shaping Landscapes: Environmental History, Plantation Management and Colonial Legacies in Mauritius." *International Journal of Historical Archaeology,* October. https://doi.org/10.1007/s10761-021-00629-0

Haraksingh, Kusha. 1987. "Control and Resistance among Indian Workers: A Study of Labour on the Sugar Plantations of Trinidad 1875–1917." In *India in the Caribbean*, edited by David Dabydeen and Brinsley Samaroo, 61–80. London: Hansib.

Hauser, Mark. 2021. *Mapping Water in Dominica: Enslavement and Environment under Colonialism.* Seattle: University of Washington Press.

Hauser, Mark, and V. Selvakumar. 2019. Report on Non-Intrusive Archaeological Exploration in Tharangambadi and Its Environs in March-September 2019. Report Submitted to the Archaeological Survey of India.

———. 2021. "Gardens of the Coromandel Coast: Landscape Considerations of Commercial Agriculture in Tamil Nadu, South India." *International Journal of Historical Archaeology* 25(4): 1113–41.

Hoefte, Rosemarijn. 1998. *In Place of Slavery: A Social History of British Indian and Javanese Laborers in Suriname.* Gainesville: University Press of Florida.

House of Commons. 1840. "Lord John Russell to Governor Light, 2 November 1839, Acknowledging Dispatch of 5th September." In *Hill Coolies, British Guiana,* accessed October 10, 2022. https://hdl.handle.net/2027/coo.31924078179615

House of Commons. 1874. "Report on Coolie Emigration from India." *Parliamentary Papers*, vol. 74. London: Parliamentary Papers.

Hurgobin, Yoshina, and Subho Basu. 2015. "'Oceans without Borders': Dialectics of Transcolonial Labor Migration from the Indian Ocean World to the Atlantic World." *International Labor and Working-Class History* 87: 7–26.

INTACH Pondicherry. 2004. *Architectural Heritage of Pondicherry*, 1st edition. Puducherry: Indian National Trust for Art and Cultural Heritage (INTACH).

Jensen, Niklas E. 2017. "The Most Prominent House in Town: The Architectural Lay-Out of the Building and Its Garden." In *The Governor's Residence in Tranquebar: The House and the Daily Life of Its People, 1770–1845,* edited by Esther Fihl, 88–113. Copenhagen: Museum Tusculanum Press.

Johnson, Matthew H. 2005. "On the Particularism of English Landscape Archaeology." *International Journal of Historical Archaeology* 9(2): 111–22.

Karth, I. 1763. Grund—und Aufriss der Häuser im Brüder Garten bey Tranquebar in Ostindien. Unitaetsarchiv, Herrnhut, Germany. LN Mp.317.6.a.

Kolkman, René, and Stuart Blackburn. 2014. *Tribal Architecture in Northeast India.* Leiden: Brill.

Krieger, M. 2008. "Vom 'Brüdergarten' zu den Nikobaren: Die Herrnhuter Brüder in Südasien." In *Aufgeklärter Geist und evangelische Missionen in Indien,* edited by M. Mann, 63–83. Heidelberg: Draupadi Verlag.

Kumar, Ashutosh. 2016. "Feeding the Girmitiya: Food and Drink on Indentured Ships to the Sugar Colonies." *Gastronomica: The Journal of Critical Food Studies* 16(1): 41–52.

———. 2017. "Naukari, Networks, and Knowledge: Views of Indenture in Nineteenth-Century North India." *South Asian Studies* 33(1): 52–67.

Lal, Brij. V. 1998. "Understanding the Indian Indenture Experience." *South Asia: A Journal of South Asian Studies* 21(Special Issue): 215–237.

———. 2004. *Girmitiyas: The Origins of the Fiji Indians.* Lautoka: Fiji Institute of Applied Studies.

Laurence, Keith. 1995. *A Question of Labor.* Kingston: Ian Randle.

Look Lai, Walton. 1993. *Indentured Labor, Caribbean Sugar: Chinese and Indian Migrants to the British West Indies, 1838–1917.* Baltimore: Johns Hopkins University Press.

Lowe, Lisa. 2015. *The Intimacies of Four Continents.* Durham: Duke University Press.

Mahase, Radica. 2008. "'rij, 1870–1920." *Labor History* 49(4): 465–80.

Mangru, Basdeo. 1996. *A History of East Indian Resistance on the Guyana Sugar Estates, 1869–1948.* New York: Mellon.

Mauritius National Archives. 1844. Report on the Conditions, Number, and Lodging of the Indian Labourers in the "Flacq" District. HA series: 101.

Moran, Mary H. 1992. "Civilized Servants: Child Fosterage and Training for Status among the Glebo of Liberia." In *African Encounters with Domesticity,* edited by K. T. Hansen, 98–115. New Brunswick: Rutgers University Press.

Mosse, David. 1997. "The Symbolic Making of a Common Property Resource: History, Ecology and Locality in a Tank-Irrigated Landscape in South India." *Development and Change* 28(3): 467–504.

———. 1999. "Colonial and Contemporary Ideologies of 'Community Management': The Case of Tank Irrigation Development in South India." *Modern Asian Studies* 33(2): 303–38.

———. 2003. *The Rule of Water: Statecraft, Ecology and Collective Action in South India.* New Delhi: Oxford University Press.

Munasinghe, Viranjini. 2018. "Anxieties of Belonging: East Indians and the Cultural Politics of the Nation in Trinidad." In *Göttingen Series in Social and Cultural Anthropology,* edited by Elfriede Hermann and Antonie Fuhse, 67–82. Göttingen: Göttingen University Press.

Northrup, David. 1995. *Indentured Labor in the Age of Imperialism, 1834–1922.* Cambridge: Cambridge University Press.

Pedersen, Karl Peder. 1987a. "Landstederne Omkring Tranquebar." *Architectura* 9: 211–15.

———. 1987b. "Privatejede Danske Bygninger." *Architectura* 9: 174–99.

Rodney, Walter. 1981. *A History of the Guyanese Working People, 1881–1905*. Baltimore: Johns Hopkins University Press.

Roopnarine, L. 2018. *The Indian Caribbean: Migration and Identity in the Diaspora*. Jackson: University Press of Mississippi.

Roopnarine, Lomarsh. 2010. "Repatriation and Remittances of ex-Indian Indentured from Danish St. Croix: 1868–1873." *Scandinavian Journal of History* 35(2): 247–67.

Schœlcher, Victor. 2008 [1948]. *Esclavage et Colonisation*, edited by Émile Tersin. Paris: Presses Universitaires de France.

Soske, Jon. 2017. *Internal Frontiers: African Nationalism and the Indian Diaspora in Twentieth-Century South Africa*. Athens: Ohio University Press.

Seetah, Krish, Diego Calaon, Saša Čaval, Alessandra Cianciosi, and Aleks Pluskowski. 2018. "The Materiality of Multi-Culturalism: An Archaeological Perspective." In *The Mauritian Paradox: Fifty Years of Development, Diversity and Democracy*, edited by R. Ramtohul and T. H. Eriksen, 155–74. Réduit: University of Mauritius Press.

Selvakumar, V., Mark Hauser, S. Gowrishankar, and R. Karthikeyan. 2021. Excavations at Nangur: A Historical Settlement in the Lower Kaveri Valley. Report Submitted to the Archaeological Survey of India.

Seutter, Matteus. 1730. Accurater Geographischer Entwurf der Königlichen Dänischen Auf der Küste Choromandel in Ost-Indien belegenen Stadt und Vestung Trankebar oder Tarangenbadi u: Dansburg. Frederik den Femtes Atlas, Bd. 48, Tvl. 41. Augsburg, Danish Royal Library.

Shepherd, Verene 2002. *Maharani's Misery: Narratives of a Passage from India to the Caribbean*. Jamaica: University of West Indies Press.

Singaravelou, Pierre. 1987. *Les Indiens de la Caraïbe, Tome 1*. Paris: Editions L'Harmattan.

Stephen, S. Jeyaseela. 2019. *Goodbye to Tamil Motherland: The Rise of Labour Migration Oversees and the Society, 1729–1890*. GenNext Publication.

Tinker, Hugh. 1974. *A New System of Slavery: The Export of Indian Labour Overseas, 1830–1920*. New York: Oxford University Press.

9

Approaching Past, Present, and Future Urbanisms in Goa, India

BRIAN C. WILSON

The first glance around convinced us that we were about to visit a city of
the dead, and at once swept away the delusion caused by the distant view
of whitewashed churches and towers, glittering steeples and domes. . . .
Everything that met the eye or ear seemed teeming with melancholy associations; the very rustling of the leaves and murmur of the waves sounded
like a dirge for the departed grandeur of the city.

(Burton 1851: 58–59)

This evocative description of Velha Goa written in the nineteenth century
encapsulates the dominant historical narratives written of the capital city of
the Portuguese colonial trading empire in Asia. In addition, it points toward
the reason many tourists visited the city in the nineteenth century: to see the
"white-washed churches and towers, glittering steeples and domes," to enjoy
the "rustling of the leaves and murmur of the waves" sounding like a "dirge
for the departed grandeur of the city" (Burton 1851, 58–59). The churches
rising above the palm groves are indeed impressive markers of the past glories
of a maritime trading empire that spanned much of the globe. These same
churches and the important Catholic relics they hold continue to draw numerous tourists to the city today. However, the quote also points toward the
existence of a past urban underbelly, of slum-like conditions, and the people
and semi-illicit economies that are familiar parts of so-called urban blight and
decay in today's cities.

Travelers' accounts such as Burton's ask us to reconsider what socialites
may have existed in this colonial capital after the seeming failure of the elite
population to maintain such a symbolically important urban landscape. Considering these failures, how might the historical record ignore or disguise

more quotidian, non-elite forms of spatial practice? Had the city truly become ruined and abandoned, or was it rather the European forms of spatial practice that declined, leaving a less historically visible subaltern population? My work argues for the latter and calls for a reconsideration of the heritage management practices in Goa today that perpetuate these colonial narratives. Both the colonial narratives and the heritage practices they engender provide value to only one set of urban experiences and re-create stereotypes that justified the exploitation of the socio-spatial landscape for colonial ends. The ruins of colonial projects in India (and globally) remain an integral part of the landscape in numerous urban and non-urban locales. This project thus offers an example of how analyzing these places through historical archaeology can engender a broader, more democratic understanding of our recent past.

This chapter provides an overview of archaeological evidence from Velha Goa that supports the continued existence of a vibrant population in the city of Goa after the decline of its more formal urban façade. These data are juxtaposed to heritage management practices, showing how they re-create a past view of the city that never wholly existed. Following Ann Stoler, I ask how imperial formations "persist in their material debris, in ruined landscapes and through the social ruination of people's lives" (2008: 194). By taking this approach, we find ruination becomes a critical vantage point that allows us an entrée into what counts as imperial ruins and how they can be and are appropriated into contemporary politics.

Historical Context

The state of Goa is located midway down peninsular India, several hundred kilometers south of Mumbai. Alfonso de Albuquerque conquered Goa in 1510, and the Portuguese occupied the area for over 450 years. It remained one of last vestiges of European colonial rule in South Asia, which came to end only when the new nation state of India invaded the colony and defeated the Portuguese in 1961. Thus, the Portuguese who controlled this small enclave had the dubious title of both the first and the last European power to have colonial holdings on the subcontinent. As would be expected with such a lengthy rule, the Portuguese had a substantial impact on Goa and left behind an extensive archive that historians continue to mine, working to understand better the processes of social and economic change under colonial rule. Considering it was one of the longest-lived colonial occupations of the recent past, this archive represents a unique opportunity to explore the varied interconnections created by colonial encounters during a period that saw significant shifts in economic, political, and social systems the world over. And it offers a counterpoint to the better known British colonial experience in India.

The pre-Portuguese colonial history of Goa is less well known. The earliest historical evidence of Goa as a trading center on the western coast of peninsular South Asia occurs in documents written by ancient Greeks and Romans. The best known of these is the *Periplus of the Erythraean Sea*, written in the early centuries CE. Goa's involvement in the medieval trading networks of the Indian Ocean is also well documented (Souza 1990). The earliest known rulers of Goa were the Bhojas. Copper plate inscriptions indicate that Goa was ruled by this dynasty either outright or in vassalage from as early as the third century BCE. Bhoja rule in Goa is also mentioned in the edicts of the Mauryan emperor Ashoka. The Bhojas were succeeded by other dynasties, and Goa was variously dominated by the Konkan Mauryas, the Chalukyas, and Silaharas, among others. The political situation of Goa stabilized somewhat from the tenth to the fourteenth centuries CE, when the region was ruled by the Kadamba dynasty. In the first half of the fourteenth century Goa was invaded twice by the Delhi Sultanate, first by Malik Kafur and then in 1327 by Muhammad-bin-Tughlaq. These invasions marked the beginning of Muslim political dominance in the region (Fonseca 1878; Souza 1990).

The Bahamani kingdom on the central Deccan Plateau ruled Goa after the weakening of political power in Delhi later in the century. While the Bahamani kingdom was consolidating power to the north, the kingdom of Vijayanagar was also gaining prominence farther south on the Deccan (Cruz 1998; Nayeem et al. 2002). The two kingdoms would vie for power in the region, and Goa changed hands several times in the fourteenth century because both kingdoms needed access to the excellent port, which was also the center for the importation of horses from the Arabian Peninsula. Access to horses was critical to the military successes of both the Bahamani Sultanate and Vijayanagar. By 1378 Vijayanagar consolidated its control of Goa and ruled the region until the 1470s, when the Bahamani Sultanate once more regained control of the region. Due to internal dissent, the Bahamani Kingdom soon collapsed into five autonomous sultanates, and the region fell under the rule of the Adil Shahi dynasty of Bijapur in 1488 (Pereira 1973; Kamat 1990; Correia 2006).

The primary port city of Goa was located on the island of Tiswadi between the Zuari and Mandovi rivers. While technically an island, Tiswadi is separated from the mainland only by a narrow channel, the Cumbarjua Canal, that connects these two rivers. This canal can be waded across to the north at the crossing known as the Paso Seco or dry passage. In the fourteenth or fifteenth century the original harbor located on the Zuari River became too silted to allow easy access for ships, and it was moved to the north of the island to its current location on the banks of the Mandovi River. This new port city of Goa began to gain prominence shortly after its establishment under the patronage of the Deccan Sultanate of Bijapur ruled by the Adil Shahs, and most of the wealthy traders relocated to the new, more accessible northern port.

The first Portuguese ships arrived in India at Calicut in 1498 under the command of Vasco da Gama, inaugurating the 450-year presence of the Portuguese in the Indian Ocean (see also LaViolette and Norman on Portuguese in Zanzibar, this volume). During this period the second governor of the Estado da Índia (the Portuguese state in India), Alfonso de Albuquerque, focused on establishing an extensive network of permanent naval bases in Asia. His military successes would serve to define the Portuguese presence in the region as a largely maritime enterprise with limited land holdings. This enterprise controlled the sea through superior naval power and the possession of strategic access points in the Asian trading networks, such as Ormuz (Boxer 1985). Goa's excellent port (and Muslim rulers) provided an ideal prize for Afonso de Albuquerque, and he decisively conquered the city of Velha Goa in 1510, defeating the forces of the Adil Shah.

His early military experiences in the Indian Ocean forced Albuquerque to recognize the rather precarious military and political situation of Portuguese land holdings in South Asia. Although the Portuguese were the dominant sea power in the Indian Ocean in the sixteenth century, there was a significant lack of available Portuguese personnel (military and administrative), which precluded any large-scale land-based colonies. Albuquerque's initial strategy, therefore, was to create a stable population base while establishing profitable trade, so he made strategic alliances with local Hindu leaders in order to conquer Goa (Boxer 1985; Disney 2009). After their help in successfully defeating the forces of the Adil Shah, Albuquerque largely protected Hindu temples and religious practice. This same protection, however, did not extend to the Muslim population, whose mosques were burned and whose property was confiscated. Albuquerque further encouraged the intermarriage of his soldiers with local women (albeit after they converted to Christianity). However, changing political circumstances in Europe, the Counter-Reformation, and the close association of the Portuguese Crown and nobility with the Catholic Church led to a later colonial strategy much more concerned with producing proper, Christian, colonial subjects. By the 1560s the Inquisition was established in Goa along with attempts at mass conversions of local peoples and an associated campaign of temple breaking (Alden 1996; Pearson 1987; Frykenberg 2008).

Building the Capital of Empire

The result of the Portuguese entanglement between the Crown and the Church and the nature of the geopolitical realities in the Indian Ocean led directly to a form of socio-spatial production in Goa rooted in the establishment of Goa as the capital of the Eastern Empire. After conquering the city of Goa, Albuquerque granted an initial charter of privileges to city officials that outlined the municipal organization. It is clear from this charter that city governance was modeled after its "metropolitan prototype," Lisbon (Souza 2009: 98). The charter provides for a municipal council (*Camara municipal*) through the election of aldermen (*vereadores*) and justices of the peace (*juizes ordinários*), and established the rights of the *casados* (married Portuguese settlers) in the city (Cunha Rivara 1875: fasc. 2, 4–8). In addition to the municipal council, the charter created a body to represent the guilds and artisans of the city, called the House of Twenty-Four (Casa dos Vinte e Quatro), which was organized in the same way as the identical institution in Lisbon (Cunha Rivara 1875: fasc. 2; Rego 1965: 55).

King Manuel I confirmed the charter of Albuquerque in 1518, officially raising the status of Goa to a "royal city, never to be severed from the Portuguese Crown" (Rego 1965: 54). Later these privileges and the interactions between the city and state were clarified when Goa became the official capital of the Estado da Índia and the administrative center of the Portuguese empire in Asia, taking over from Cochin in 1530. Additional decrees in 1559 by King Sebastian—and further decrees in 1577, 1582, and 1641—stated that Goa should follow the system of Lisbon "without alteration" (Souza 2009: 99–100).

Certain aspects of these laws reveal how the city of Goa was re-envisioned as a Christian and Portuguese urban space. Specifically, the 1518 proclamation by King Manuel stated that city life and finances were to be governed by a group of elected officials, which included the *vereadores* and *juizes* (Cunha Rivara 1875: vols. 2, 5). The non-heritable nature of these titles was ensured by establishing complicated election procedures meant to prevent nepotism or cronyism (Souza 2009: 101; Boxer 1966: 35–36). In addition, these official positions were reserved for Christians and undoubtedly meant for Portuguese natives. Hindus, Muslims, and converted Jews (New Christians) were specifically excluded (Priolkar 1961: 124–25).

Boxer provides a translation of a letter sent to Goa by King John III of Portugal in 1542 in which the king stipulates that in the city of Goa those "in whom the control of the city is vested, should always be drawn from among the married men and heads of household therein, who are Portuguese by nationality and birth and not from among those of any other nationality, birth, and quality whatsoever" (Boxer 1966: 154). Given the continual shortage of labor in the colony, these ordinances were likely not followed to the letter. There is evidence that various *mestiços* were allowed to serve in these offices and that they were also occasionally held by prominent New Christians and others (Boxer 1966: 30–35; Souza 2009: 101).

The charter and subsequent decrees thus mandated that the city of Goa function in the same way as Lisbon and that it should enjoy the same privileges and freedoms, placing Goa and its Portuguese denizens on par with those in the metropole (Boxer 1966; Rego 1965; Russell-Wood 2007; Souza 2009). As Pius Malekandathil states:

> The administration of the city affairs passed into the hands of the urban elite, through the mechanism of the city council with members elected from the Portuguese married settlers . . . where they decided on all matters related to urban cleanliness, sanitation, property acquisition and space management, food supply and hoarding, management of welfare institutions like misericordia, local trade, law and order within the city, matters affecting morality of the city-dwellers, etc. (Malekandathil 2009: 26–27)

In short, the city was imagined as a place that should represent a fully functioning Portuguese city recognizable as the capital of the empire.

During the period establishing Goa as the capital of the Asian empire, the historical archives (and contemporary scholarship based on these accounts) show that the physical city also grew considerably from its original pre-Portuguese configuration. According to these sources, the original small urban space of the Adil Shahi period city, built along the Mandovi River, was surrounded by a semi-circular fortification wall and moat with gates opening in the cardinal directions, walls that Albuquerque would repair and reinforce (Albuquerque 1884). Several of the larger buildings within the city (such as the palace of the Adil Shah) were appropriated by the colonial government, whereas other buildings, such as mosques, were destroyed and new edifices were built in their place. The circular patterns of streets surrounding the fortification walls and the layout of the space interior to the wall—the space that would become the urban core and civil-ceremonial center of the Portuguese city—were thus structured by this early urban form. Although almost all visible traces of the city before Portuguese occupation are now gone, archaeological survey revealed that some of this infrastructure still exists. These elements included a few preserved sections of the original Adil Shahi fortification wall, two rebuilt gates that now function as archways, streets, and the remains of the moat surrounding the old city.

Figure 9.1. Modern street overlay of Old Goa. Black: extant portions of sixteenth-century roads used today. White: modern roads.

While the Portuguese did relatively little to modify the overall design and layout of Velha Goa after its initial occupation, the urban structure was increasingly changed throughout the sixteenth century as the Portuguese rose to prominence in the region. In response to the growing population, the settlement quickly expanded beyond the original fortification walls. Construction outside the original Adil Shahi city occurred in a largely organic fashion along axes that corresponded to paths or roads leading outward from the main gates (Santos and Mendiratta 2009). The newer portions of the city also never conformed to any regular street pattern, unlike the civil-ceremonial center, in part because of its rather hasty expansion and formation around prominent topographic features (Rossa 1997: 47). These features included the hills surrounding the city and the large *lagoa* or lagoon, which stretched almost to the southeast portion of the old Adil Shahi fortification wall.

The Portuguese used these surrounding elevations to construct imposing Catholic edifices in visually dominant positions on the landscape. Some of the more prominent edifices, which are still visible today, marked the extent of the more densely occupied, truly urban areas of Velha Goa and are situated on hilltops that surround and overlook the urban core of the city. These buildings include the Convento Oratoriano da Cruz dos Milagres (Oratorian Convent of the Cross of Miracles) forming the southern boundary of the city; the Capela de Nossa Senhora do Monte (Chapel of Our Lady of the Mount) forming the eastern boundary of the city; and the Convento Agostinho de Nossa Senhora da Graça (Augustinian Convent and Our Lady of Grace) and Igreja de Nossa Senhora do Rosário (Church of Our Lady of the Rosary), both located on the Monte Santo (Holy Hill) that formed the western boundary of the city. The construction of massive churches in visually dominant locales reflected the importance of Goa as the center of Catholicism in Asia as it worked to reaffirm the power of the colonial administration (Malekandathil 2009). The areas where large religious installations or administrative buildings were constructed became focal points for additional urban development, and the city expanded through the successive articulation of these nodes of settlement (Teixeira 1990: 25). The urban elements that gave the city its underlying urban form (religious, governmental, commercial, and residential) developed around a single central axis: the Rua Direita (High or Straight Street), which along with the original Adil Shahi fortification wall occupied the low-lying flat area near the river and defined the civil-ceremonial and urban core of Velha Goa.

The size and configuration of the city at the height of Portuguese power is depicted in numerous maps and images of the city. These maps show a thriving, urbanized metropolis, the most famous being a map produced by Jan Huygen van Linschoten, a Dutch immigrant to Goa. Linschoten's depiction is one of the earliest known maps of the city of Goa, and was published in Holland as part of his well-known *Itinerario* published in 1596 (Fig. 9.2). The map was a result of Linschoten's detailed observations of his travels to India and his stay in Goa working as an accountant for the archbishop. The various descriptions and images accompanying Linschoten's map—and all the others produced in the late sixteenth and early seventeenth centuries—highlight the great wealth contained in the city along with its impressive buildings and stately homes. These accounts describe an urbanized port city with paved streets, whitewashed stone buildings with red tile roofs, grand churches rivaling any in Europe, and markets brimming with goods from around the world. These goods included Chinese porcelain, furniture, gold and silver, spices, and a range of other luxury goods (e.g., Pyrard 1619: 57). The wealth described in these accounts would contribute to growing myths concerning Goa that rendered it as *Goa Dourada* (Golden Goa) or the Rome of the East.

There is a general lack of archival documentation that directly addresses the development of what would become known as Indo-Portuguese architecture in Goa; however, an analysis of a vast number of building contracts from the late sixteenth century demonstrates the implementation of standard building techniques and architectural models in the city—models that were imported directly from Lisbon (Carita 2007: 77–89). Helder Carita argues that these contracts correspond to legislation implemented during the reign of King Manuel (1495–1521), "which established a new, rational and centralized management of public works carried out on behalf of the monarchy and

Figure 9.2. Map of Velha Goa (*a*) and accompanying market scene (*b*), published in Jan Huygen van Linschoten's *Itinerario* in 1596.

which later applied to municipal councils, the church and religious orders" (Carita 2007: 71). These laws, originating in the metropole, were directly imported to the city of Goa in 1527 when King João III ordered the Camara de Lisboa to send its own *regimento* directly to the city of Goa.

A wide range of buildings and structures in the city were encompassed by this legislation, including "walls, towers, barricades, bastions, places of refuge, subterranean works that necessitate a master-builder, as well as cisterns, wells, and ovens and mills" (Carita 2007: 86). The laws mandated specific percentages of lime and mortar and proper building techniques based on set ratios of structural walls and empty space. In addition, they detailed the best practices for construction—particularly hydraulic projects on sandy soils. All these details were then included in bids made by contractors to the Crown, who thus chose the best price but also maintained centralized oversight over the form of urban space through the management of these contracts—what Carita refers to as "contracts and instructions for work to proceed" (Carita 2007: 73). These standardized practices worked to create the idealized urban space and Portuguese-style unity depicted in so many maps and travelers' accounts.

A City in Decline

The period of urban expansion would continue into the seventeenth century. However, the Portuguese were beginning to experience significant challenges to their power in the Indian Ocean trading networks by the Dutch and English as well as by the rise of both Maratha and Mughal powers to the north (Disney 2009). The city also experienced significant episodes of plague beginning in the latter half of the sixteenth century, which continued into the seventeenth century. The plague of 1625 in Goa was particularly severe, and in 1639 even the viceroy, Pedro da Silva, succumbed to an outbreak. In addition, the Dutch began yearly blockades of the port from 1636 to 1644 (Blusse and Winius 1985). Goa was always somewhat dependent on the importation of goods, especially rice, to feed its urban population, and these blockades had serious effects on the well-being of the urban population. Starvation and famine were not uncommon during this period (Pearson 1990: 166; Souza 2009: 83).

In addition to the outbreaks of plague and problems of declining revenue, the city was nearly invaded by the Marathas in 1683. According to several accounts of this period, these events caused the "more opulent families" to leave the city, and the general ruination of private residences increased (Fonseca 1878: 173 ff.). In light of this continuing elite abandonment, a discourse developed parallel to the myth of Goa Dourada and began to suggest that the once great city of Goa was becoming abandoned and falling into ruin during the latter half of the seventeenth century. Immediately following the attack by the Marathas, the viceroy, Count of Alvor, attempted to implement a plan to move the seat of government to Mormugão (a coastal enclave several kilometers south of Velha Goa). The plan proceeded in fits and starts with some progress made on the new city, but it was finally abandoned in 1712 due to the resistance of various colonial factions, particularly the Church, which maintained several large establishments and were still firmly entrenched in the old city (Fonseca 1878: 176). The attempt to transfer the capital, however, gave many of the more affluent residents the needed justification to abandon the place fully and pull down their larger stone homes. A large number of these wealthier families had in many cases already left for suburban and country estates but were required by law to maintain their homes in the capital.

These purposeful acts of destruction had the result of contributing to a European vision of a ruined, desolate cityscape. José Nicolau da Fonseca cites numerous British, French, Dutch, and Portuguese accounts from the late seventeenth century through the late eighteenth century that remark on the decay of the more formal aspects of urban architecture, which often juxtaposed the "heap of ruins" in the capital to the more splendid villas in neighboring villages and suburbs (Fonseca 1878: 177–83). Returning to the quote that began this chapter, the city by the nineteenth century had become firmly associated with romantic notions of a beautiful ruin rising out of the jungle, a memorial to the past glories and riches of a great trading empire that spanned the globe. The colonial administration would use these romantic associations to foster an image of the city's past glories that aligned with and reinforced the symbolic importance of the space. It was during the period of decline that the tropes of Goa Dourada and the "Rome of the East" became even more common and were circulated by the colonial government. The administration used these images to try to instill a sense of loyalty to the Crown through a celebration of its past greatness and the long history of Portuguese power (Malekandathil 2009: 32).

In 1843 the capital was officially moved several kilometers down the river to its current location in Panaji. The move was made due to the large number of ruined stone homes and buildings, the insalubrious nature of its location, large-scale contamination of drinking water, and a decline in the European population. The city, however, remained an official part of the capital, with the old city included in the new capital's official boundaries. The presence of the cathedral, the Basilica of Bom Jesus (which housed the remains of St. Francis Xavier), and numerous other active churches also guaranteed that the old city would maintain its relevance for the Catholic faithful. Despite these associations and the continued symbolic importance of the city, all records suggest that by the end of the nineteenth century the city was nothing more than "a piteous spectacle of wide-spread desolation and decay" (Fonseca 1878: 189–90).

Archival Memories and the Practice of Ruin-Making

The story the archive tells is one of great, early economic successes and domination of the trading routes in the Indian Ocean and Southeast Asia followed by a precipitous decline as the Portuguese are outcompeted by the Dutch and English, face invasion from the Marathas, and generally become marginalized in the Indian Ocean. The archive and associated scholarship have certainly revealed much about the processes of rise and decline in Goa; however, they epitomize a problem with historical archives more generally. The accounts show a clear bias toward elite economic and political concerns, which from a material perspective include only the grand stone constructions comprising elite residences, ecclesiastical structures, and administrative buildings.

A focus on elite urban social spaces is not unexpected, though, as these archives are authored by and written for colonial elite populations. Of course historians and historical anthropologists have addressed these issues by becoming adept at examining the categories that create "grammars of difference" and that frame the particular, sometimes deafening, silences in the colonial archive (Stahl 2001: 37). This work of contextualizing the production of knowledge, both in the past and today, has greatly expanded our understanding of the colonial experience. The problem that remains in places like Goa, however, is that the archive remains one of the only sources of data scholars have used to examine the socio-spatial processes that resulted in Goa's current heritage landscape. That is, heritage management is completely reliant on the sources of the colonizers.

The constitution of Velha Goa as a "ruin" in its later days represents another attempt to appropriate space forcefully and violently; ruins are not just found but made (Stoler 2008: 208). When a place is established as a ruin, it becomes objectified through a process similar to the early mapping of colonial empires: the city becomes defined and codified in ways that both create a seemingly stable entity and erase other possible points of view. As a ruin undergoes this process of definition, it fixes the temporality of the place to a single point, thereby denying (or worse, criminalizing) any subsequent or current use or reuse of the space—something seen in part in the laws surrounding UNESCO World Heritage sites (Gordillo 2014). As I demonstrate for Velha Goa, this temporal fixing attempted to erase and delegitimize the non-elite social groups that remain (and were always present) in this former capital of a colonial empire.

There is abundant archaeological evidence for the formally constructed, urban elements of the city that supports the view of the previously discussed Linschoten map of the urban layout and design and its subsequent decline. While some of the grand churches and administrative buildings remain intact, numerous structures are now only partially standing or completely gone. Of the residential structures, there is only one colonial era stone house that remains standing in the city proper, known as the Casa da Bula da Cruzado.

Archaeological evidence, however, reveals that the colonial era streets were indeed lined with the rowhouse-like stone homes of the elite. This evidence includes occupational terraces, wall fall, and brick scatters; dense scatters of roof tile fragments, lime plaster, lime and mud mortar, and ceramics. Located adjacent to these structural remains were cisterns and house wells—an infrastructural element commonly associated with residential occupation in Goa. At least one of these structures existed into the late eighteenth century and was depicted on a map from that period drawn by José de Morais Antas Machada (Fig. 9.3). During the survey work, the remains of this structure were found to be exemplary of the archaeological foot print of residential architecture. All these material remains further mirror the remaining colonial era residential structure, the still standing Casa da Bula da Cruzada. It is the loss of these structures that led to the common historical narrative of urban decline. One can see the extent of this ruination in a map by José Nicolau da Fonseca from 1878, which shows a ruined city consisting almost entirely of agricultural space and fallow wasteland. Archaeological survey of the city, however, suggests an alternative narrative and warrants a reconsideration of the colonial archival sources.

First, the historical descriptions of Goa never go beyond a phenomenological, streetside view of a bustling, densely built urban port. Behind this whitewashed urban façade, however, were large tracts of agricultural space, containing a range of non-elite residences. Evidence for non-elite occupation in Velha Goa was more ephemeral than that of the larger street side homes, but numerous traces remained visible during the survey. These traces suggest that the city was not the fully built, urbanized environment written of in the archives. Instead, Velha Goa was a large, integrated urban-agricultural system. These adjacent yet historically and structurally *hidden* urban places better resemble the vernacular settlement patterns seen outside the city. In the Konkan region, the pre-Portuguese pattern of settlement was more dispersed, with homes set on high ground among the agricultural fields and plantations. This pattern created a more continuously occupied landscape that differed from the classic Iberian vision of colonial space, which imagined discrete village settlements centered around a church and plaza.

The evidence for these structures consisted of roof tile and ceramic scatters, cisterns, and one- or two-room structures built of rough, laterite bricks and mud mortar. Other evidence supporting residential occupation included the presence of grinding stones and mortar as well as small house shrines for crosses or Tulsi plants—still a common feature in front of Hindu homes in Goa today. These residential structures were also directly adjacent to agricultural infrastructure, most commonly equipment for the processing of *caju*

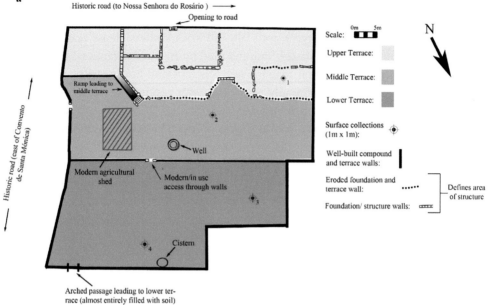

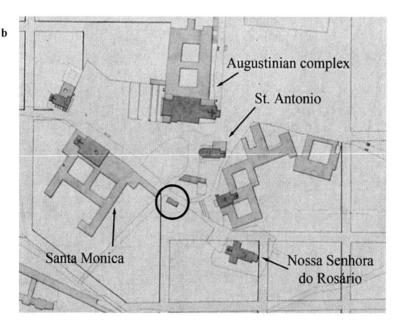

Figure 9.3. Plan view of elite structure recorded during archaeological survey (*a*). Detail of 18th-century map of Goa produced by José de Morais Antas Machada (*b*). (Figure by author, originally published in "The City as Façade in Velha Goa: Recognizing Enduring Forms of Urbanism in the Early Modern Konkan," *Medieval History Journal* [24]1: 320–52 [2021]).

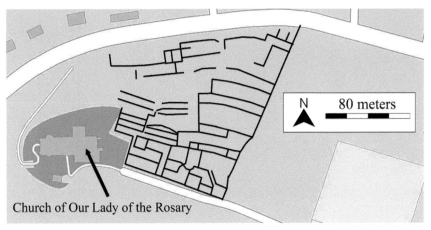

Figure 9.4. Preserved terrace walls in Velha Goa.

fruit for both the well-known cashew nut it contains and the lesser known alcoholic drink, *feni*, made from its juice. The survey evidence further made it clear that this type of more dispersed occupation continued from colonial times until today. Substantial aspects of urban infrastructure such as the system of terrace walls were continuously maintained and show evidence of rebuilding and maintenance (Fig. 9.4). There was also ample evidence for the reuse and recycling of material taken from ruined colonial buildings for the construction of small one- and two-room structures for day laborers and others uses (Fig. 9.5).

As Velha Goa's economic fortunes declined, the elite populations abandoned the city, and the larger stone homes that lined the streets fell into ruin, causing the homes and social spaces of the common, laboring population to become more and more visible. The historic record during this period shifts from descriptions of the rich, bustling port city seen in writing from the sixteenth century to writing focused on the melancholic descriptions of ruination. At the same time, the colonial administration initiated various attempts to revitalize the city due to its symbolic role as the capital of their erstwhile empire. Plans were drawn to reconfigure the city in the late eighteenth century following enlightenment ideals for urban space. They imagined straight, gridded street patterns, a more open urban plan to accommodate better forms of circulation, and the removal of an encroaching nature. The attempts to revitalize the city and reform its urban landscape into an idealized, structured space indicative of past glories lasted until the very end of colonial occupation. The last plan was drawn in 1959, two years before the nation state of India invaded Goa and ended 450 years of Portuguese rule.

Figure 9.5. Non-elite structure (*a*), with associated grinding stone (*b*) and house shrine (*c*).

Colonial Pasts and the Politics of Managing Cultural Heritage

It is this last colonial era plan that provided the basis for the later preservation efforts by the Archaeological Survey of India (ASI). However, these plans show significant changes in heritage management marked by a shift from revitalization to preservation. According to the ASI's Goa Circle website (https://asigoacircle.gov.in/about/), the ASI is "dedicated to the protection, preservation and conservation of the national monuments." Adding to this, Velha Goa was given UNESCO World Heritage status in 1986. UNESCO is also deeply committed to "protection and preservation of cultural and natural heritage" (UNESCO World Heritage Centre 2019b). Officially though, it is not the site as a whole that is recognized by UNESCO but rather specifically the churches and convents—meaning it is only the large religious monuments with a World Heritage inscription and not the urban landscape itself. Furthermore, the churches in Velha Goa remain active as part of the Catholic Archdiocese of Goa and Daman, and the Church often has differing views on heritage management from the ASI and UNESCO.

It is these new management practices that deserve further consideration. A UNESCO World Heritage inscription undoubtedly affords great benefits for a historic site. It provides global recognition and access to a range of resources, including increased revenue from tourism and an internationally accepted legal framework for preservation and protection. A UNESCO designation, however, is particularly complex in the context of a site like Velha Goa (as in many places around the globe). Despite the admirable goals of UNESCO to foster peace and intercultural understanding, the inscription of sites like Velha Goa commodifies its monuments in ways that lay bare and often exacerbate social and political tensions (Meskell 2018: 122).

Urban space is not something that is static or monolithic; urban space is a process and not simply a product (Abu-Lughod 1987). The churches and convents of Velha Goa are exceptionally important pieces of world heritage; however, they are only one facet of the urban center. The UNESCO designation works to preserve only this very specific *product* from Velha Goa's history and thereby obscures the process of urbanism. It hides much of the verve of the city—its rich diversity of thought, action, and spatial practice—in the shadow of the imposing Catholic edifices. It does so because it locks the historical perception of the city to a very particular time and set of socioeconomic relationships (those of the religious and colonial elite). This designation memorializes and gives value *only* to this version of the city. Providing value to only one set of urban experiences in this way at best unintentionally *re-creates* colonial stereotypes that justified the exploitation of both the space and its inhabitants for colonial ends. It gives the greatest value to a particular set of urban experiences, to the exclusion of others.

The UNESCO designation does identify a 300-meter buffer zone around the structures that should be kept free from development, and the ASI has gone to great lengths to try to protect these spaces. The rest of the city, however, is neglected due to a lack of political will, adequate resources, and the neoliberal capitalization of land. By focusing only on the preservation of the elite structures, the received narrative of rise and decline is therefore doubly reinforced through both written and spatial media. With this focus we continue to lose the contributions of non-elite actors to the city—mainly because evidence for these past activities falls outside the protected buffer zones in most cases. Or they are obscured by the production of a common landscape aesthetic seen in many archaeological monuments throughout India—an aesthetic that prioritizes large, architecturally significant buildings surrounded by large, well-manicured lawns.

While UNESCO does acknowledge that more needs to be done in Velha Goa to preserve the "historic urban form" and "integrity of the site as a former port town" (UNESCO World Heritage Centre 2019a), the current regime of heritage values makes it impossible to explore histories outside the hegemonic, top-down narratives, and these important aspects of the cultural landscape are fast disappearing. For example, the history of early agrarian capitalism and plantation agriculture is a compelling story that is in part told through the vast network of shaft wells, cisterns, and terrace architecture documented in the city by my research. The long history and continued artisanal production of Goa's national drink, feni, is equally neglected. In addition, the magnificent 22-km-long fortification surrounding the city is also under constant threat, and the remains of both elite and non-elite residences throughout the city are being lost beneath modern housing blocks, car parks, and the expansion of roads. This ongoing destruction is erasing our last chance to understand better the full spectrum of Velha Goa's material and cultural history and, importantly, the contributions of Goa's laboring class.

The challenges to heritage management from an official capacity (ASI, UNESCO, and the Church) are further complicated by other state interests, local landowners, heritage enthusiasts, businessmen, day laborers, and tourists. The often-conflicting aims and practices of these groups have led to a hodgepodge of current preservation, historical markers, landscaping practices, and the ability to access culturally significant areas. Much of the heritage preservation (or destruction) occurring in the city legitimizes itself by drawing on a range of conflicting tropes: one encounters ideas of nostalgia for the golden colonial era juxtaposed with anti-colonial and anti-Portuguese sentiments, nationalist ideas regarding a unified India versus the still extant desire for an independent or Portuguese Goa, economic progress versus historical or environmental preservation, simmering friction between religious and ethnic groups, language politics, etc. Regardless of the specific viewpoints of individuals concerned with Goa's future, the complex legal and political situation in Goa reminds us that tensions between domination and resistance persist in forms not unlike those in its colonial past.

One of Goa's most important industries remains tourism. Preserving the nature of the city, both the romantic aspects of its ruined structures and its history of labor and integration—despite its often violent nature—has the potential to increase, improve, and provide valuable educational experiences for the tourism industry. To accomplish this task, however, requires an approach that goes beyond the archives and includes the more quotidian aspects of city life. Historical archaeology provides material data that cut across social, religious, and class divides, revealing the rich diversity of colonial and postcolonial society. Velha Goa's archaeological and heritage futures may pose to us seemingly intractable questions of how we decolonize this history and its public engagements, and yet, the endeavor to do so and preserve this unique past remains one of the most important avenues of research to help us create an equitable and representative heritage management practice across India and the world.

Bibliography

Abu-Lughod, Janet. 1987. "The Islamic City: Historic Myth, Islamic Essence, and Contemporary Relevance." *International Journal of Middle East Studies* 19: 155–76.

Albuquerque, Afonso de. 1884. *Cartas de Affonso de Albuquerque.* Vol. 1: *Collecção de Monumentos Ineditos Para a Historia Das Conquistas Dos Portuguezes Em Africa, Asia e America*, edited by Raymundo Antonio de Bulhão Bulhão Pato. Lisboa: Academia Real das Sciencias de Lisboa. https://catalog.hathitrust.org/Record/000222637

Alden, Dauril. 1996. *The Making of an Enterprise: The Society of Jesus in Portugal, Its Empire, and Beyond: 1540–1750*. Stanford, Calif.: Stanford University Press.

Blusse, Leonard, and George D. Winius. 1985. "The Origin and Rhythm of Dutch Aggression against the Estado Da India 1601–1661." In *Indo-Portuguese History: Old Issues, New Questions,* edited by Teotonio R. De Souza, 73–83. New Delhi: Concept.

Boxer, C. R. 1966. *Portuguese Society in the Tropics: Municipal Councils of Goa, Macao, Bahia and Luanda, 1510–1800*. Madison: University of Wisconsin Press.

———. 1985. *Portuguese Conquest and Commerce in Southern Asia, 1500–1750*. London: Variorum Reprints.

Burton, Sir Richard Francis. 1851. *Goa, and the Blue Mountains: Or, Six Months of Sick Leave.* London: Richard Bentley.

Carita, Helder. 2007. "Creating Norms for Indo-Portuguese Architecture: The Livro de Acordãos e Assentos Da Câmara de Goa, 1592–1597." *Itinerario* 31(2): 71–86.

Correia, Luis de Assis. 2006. *Goa through the Mists of History from 10000 BC–AD 1958.* Panaji, Goa: Maureen Publishers.

Cruz, Maria Augusta. 1998. "Notes on Portuguese Relations with Vijayanagara, 1500–1565." In *Sinners and Saints: The Successors of Vasco Da Gama,* edited by Sanjay Subrahmanyam, 13–39. Delhi: Oxford University Press.

Cunha Rivara, J. H. da. 1875. *Archivo Portuguese Oriental.* New Delhi: Asian Educational Services.

Disney, A. R. 2009. *A History of Portugal and the Portuguese Empire,* Vol. 1: *From Beginnings to 1807: Portugal.* Illustrated edition. New York: Cambridge University Press.

Fonseca, José Nicolau da. 1878. *An Historical and Archaeological Sketch of the City of Goa.* New Delhi: Asian Educational Services.

Frykenberg, Robert Eric. 2008. *Christianity in India: From Beginnings to the Present.* Oxford: Oxford University Press.

Gordillo, Gastón R. 2014. *Rubble: The Afterlife of Destruction.* Durham, N.C.: Duke University Press.

Kamat, Pratima. 1990. "Historical Geography and Natural Resources." In *Goa through the Ages: An Economic History,* edited by Teotonio R. De Souza, 1–54. New Delhi: Concept Publishing Company.

Malekandathil, Pius. 2009. "City in Space and Metaphor." *Studies in History* 25(1): 13–38.

Meskell, Lynn. 2018. *A Future in Ruins: UNESCO, World Heritage, and the Dream of Peace.* New York: Oxford University Press.

Nayeem, M. A., Aniruddha Ray, and Kuzhippalli Skaria Mathew (eds.). 2002. *Studies in History of the Deccan, Medieval and Modern: Professor A.R. Kulkarni Felicitation Volume.* Delhi: Pragati Publications.

Pearson, M. N. 1987. *The Portuguese in India.* Vol. 1. New Cambridge History of India. Cambridge, U.K.: Cambridge University Press.

———. 1990. "Goa-Based Seaborne Trade (17th–18th Centuries)." In *Goa through the Ages: An Economic History,* edited by Teotonio R. De Souza, 146–75. New Delhi: Concept Publishing Company.

Pereira, Gerald A. 1973. *An Outline of Pre-Portuguese History of Goa.* Goa: G. Pereira.

Priolkar, Anant Kakba. 1961. *The Goa Inquisition: Being a Quatercentenary Commemoration Study of the Inquisition in India.* Bombay: Bombay University Press.

Pyrard, Francois. 1619. *The Voyage of Francois Pyard of Laval: To the East Indies, the Maldives, the Moluccas, and Brazil, 2 Vols., 3 Parts.* Repr. 2000, New Delhi: Asian Educational Services.

Rego, António da Silva. 1965. *Portuguese Colonization in the Sixteenth Century: A Study of the Royal Ordinances (Regimentos).* Johannesburg: Witwatersrand University Press.

Rossa, Walter. 1997. *Cidades Indo-Portuguesas: Contribuições Para o Estudo Do Urbanismo Português No Hindustão Ocidental.* Lisbon: Commissão Nacional para as Comemorações dos Descobrimentos Portugueses.

Russell-Wood, A. J. 2007. "Politics and Institutions: Patterns of Settlement in the Portuguese Empire." In *Portuguese Oceanic Expansion, 1400–1800,* edited by Francisco Bethencourt and Diogo Ramada Curto, 160–96. Cambridge: Cambridge University Press.

Santos, Joaquim, and Sidh Mendiratta. 2009. "Sistemas Defensivos Das Ilhas de Tiswadi e Diu (Séc. XVI–XVIII)." *CEAMA* 5: 92–106.

Souza, Teotonio R. de (ed.). 1990. *Goa through the Ages: An Economic History.* New Delhi: Concept Publishing Company.

———. 2009. *Medieval Goa: A Socio-Economic History.* 2nd ed. Goa: Goa 1556.

Stahl, Ann Brower. 2001. "Envisioning Africa's Lived Past." In *Making History in Banda: Anthropological Visions of Africa's Past,* 19–40. Cambridge, U.K.: Cambridge University Press.

Stoler, Ann Laura. 2008. "Imperial Debris: Reflections on Ruins and Ruination." *Cultural Anthropology* 23(2): 191–219.

Teixeira, Manuel C. 1990. "Portuguese Traditional Settlements, a Result of Cultural Miscegenation." *Traditional Dwellings and Settlements Review* 1(2): 23–34.

UNESCO World Heritage Centre. 2019a. "UNESCO World Heritage Centre—Decision—23 BUR IV.B.61." UNESCO World Heritage Centre. June 2019. https://whc.unesco.org/en/decisions/5736

———. 2019b. "World Heritage." UNESCO World Heritage Centre. June 2019. https://whc.unesco.org/en/about/

10

Commentary

The Swahili World and Its Global Connections

CHAPURUKHA M. KUSIMBA

A globalized world is interconnected and interdependent. Globalization implies the breaking down of boundaries of time, space, culture, and differences. It implies our awareness that we are interconnected, and our actions, whether motivated by selflessness or greed, affect those around us and those in far-off places. When did globalization in Africa begin? How did Africa and, specifically, the Swahili world become global? This volume documents strong connections between Africans and their counterparts in the Indian Ocean and the Persian Gulf during the last 500 years. The evidence from archaeology and historical documents strongly contradicts the idea that Europe initiated globalization. Rather, long-distance trade, industrialization, and mass consumption are rooted in early interactions that arose across Asia. These interactions occurred long before the rise of the Islamic Caliphate and the Chinese Tang Dynasty (Beaujard 2018; Bennison 2009; Elverskog 2011). Philippe Beaujard's remarkable two-volume study *The Worlds of the Indian Ocean: A Global History* traces this globalization to the Bronze Age (Beaujard 2019).

Two extreme views of the East African coast's medieval history have dominated the debate. Early narratives disenfranchised Africans from their accounts, preferring to credit their colonizers, whether real or imagined. Postcolonial scholarship discredited migration and colonization scenarios, arguing that the development of Swahili urbanism was an exclusively African initiative. Both perspectives have undermined progress in understanding the connections that bound communities around the Indian Ocean, creating one of the oldest examples of globalization. The consequent polarized debate over origins has neglected the process's crucial questions—how urbanism developed and its long-term implications for culture. The archaeological evidence shows that Swahili towns and southern Zambezia in present-day Zimbabwe and South Africa were built and inhabited primarily by African people. These Africans came from diverse subsistence economic backgrounds—forager, fisher, herder, and agriculturalist. Some became successful traders with regional and global connections to the interior and across the seas (Kusimba 2022). Still, most African residents remained workers, including some enslaved by fellow Africans (Middleton 2004:4; Kusimba 2006). Whether on the coast or inland, these towns were engaged in international trade and had a diasporic resident community from different regions. Like their African counterparts, non-African residents also migrated for various reasons (Haines and Hauser, this volume). Understanding the relationships across these interacting entities is crucial; it must be an inclusive process, not one that *a priori* assigns current notions of racialized understanding to the forces that shaped global interactions during the postmedieval period.

The growth in urbanism between the tenth and sixteenth centuries in the Old World is connected to regionwide political stability. It is a consequence of economic prosperity and population growth—migration for work and business molded relationships and alliances that sustained and shaped this emergent African urban landscape. Changes in the cuisine and how food was prepared and served are examples of globalization. Trade goods and the languages used between trading partners provide critical evidence for examining extra-regional connections, including long-term settlement and assimilations (Fabian 1991; Mugane 2015). Trade ceramics and glass beads recovered in coastal and interior towns dominate the conversation as evidence of the trade relationships and the dominance of Asian products vis-à-vis locally produced ones (e.g., Robertshaw et al. 2003, 2010; Wood 2012; Zhao 2012; Zhao and Qin 2018). But internal trade and local crafts remained dominant (Oteyo and Kusimba 2020). For example, the quantitative analysis of locally made earthenware and imported ceramics at Takwa in the Lamu archipelago by Henry Mutoro and Thomas Wilson showed that for every four sherds of imported pottery, there were approximately 12,500 sherds of local pottery (Mutoro 1979: 62). The quantity of imported pottery at coastal sites was small and likely restricted to elite uses. So even as this evidence depicts globalization, the context in which this took place must never be ignored.

Discerning Evidence for Globalization

Studies in archaeology, genetics, history, language, and oral accounts of the Swahili coast provide evidence of medieval connections with the rest of Africa and the Indian Ocean (Boivin et al. 2012, 2013; Mwacharo et al. 2007).

Archaeological data from rural and urban settlements reveal a rich heritage from these interactions. The coast's location made it a natural gateway and filtering house from which trade items, people, and ideas came to and left Africa. For example, Asian domesticates like the banana, successfully adopted in East and Central Africa, were introduced to these inland regions through coastal interactions (Fuller et al. 2011; Rowlands and Fuller 2018). Other items, such as imported ceramics, remained on the coast as a preserve of a few wealthy consumers. Still other items, like beads, made their way to nearly every African household, and their story is only beginning to be recognized (Dussubieux et al. 2008). Sadly, in the colonial period, the consumption of imported beads grew at the expense of local bead-making industries that sustained long-distance trade.

Therefore, the limited archaeological data recovered at inland and coastal settlements in the form of beads, ceramics, metals, and other inorganic artifacts are only a minor, visible part of these complex networks of interaction during the medieval period (Fagan 1966: 93). Inland Africa made the coast vibrate with activity and sustained its wealth during the medieval period. It was an integral part of that world. Therefore no justification should ever be made to include inland Africa in conversations about the Swahili world (Wynne-Jones and LaViolette 2018: 5).

Coastal artifacts such as glass beads and marine shells, including Conus cowrie (*Cypraea annulus*) and sea snail (*Polinices mammilla*), recovered at multiple settlements in interior Africa, provide the best evidence of long-distance exchange (Fagan 1966: 93). Direct genetic evidence for these interactions is beginning to emerge (Mwacharo et al. 2007). Work at contemporary settlements along the Red Sea, the Persian Gulf, and in South Asia reveals close regional similarities in material culture, social and structural planning, and urban space use (Seland 2014). Taken together, these data strongly support medieval globalization and demonstrate that Africa was a significant node in this globalized world (LaViolette 2008; Kusimba 2017).

Swahili Urbanism Was an Outcome of Medieval Globalization

Integrating materials produced in far-off places into every experience can be a long, arduous, and mostly unconscious process. Marine shells were integrated into ritual, economic, ornamental, and mortuary contexts in Central Africa but interlocked on a preexisting cultural and economic systems (Bisson 2000). For example, the circulation of ostrich eggshell beads in the Late Stone Age (Miller et al. 2018) points to a preexisting craft industry and a ready market for this product. The appearance of coastal marine and glass beads

Table 10.1. Commodities of trade

Africa to Asia—Goods Traded	Asia to Africa —Goods Traded
Ivory (elephant and hippopotamus)	Cloth (silk, cotton, wool)
Gold	Beads
Slaves	Porcelain
Mangrove timber	Rice
Grains	Spices (pepper, cinnamon, nutmeg, mace)
Beeswax	Paper
Turtle shell	Ink
Rhinoceros horn	Tea
Hide and skins	Wine
Ambergris	Sacred and other books
Palm leaves (roofing)	Kohl and other cosmetics
Cowrie shells	Fragrance (sandalwood and aloe)
Sisal	
Rubber	
Sugar	

in Africa's interior adds a curious but rare article to an old practice traceable to the African Middle Stone Age. Thus the appearance of coastal material culture such as marine shells, including cowrie shell (*Cypraea annulus*) that Professor Brian Fagan (1969: 9) excavated at Early Iron Age sites like Sanga and Ingombe in the Batoka plateau in Zambia, points to an elaboration on preexisting African exchange and production systems, while maintaining in situ structures evidenced by blood brotherhoods.

Among the trade items from the African heartland destined for the coast were gold, ivory, copper, and iron. Evidence for elite investment in extractive technologies, such as mining, panning, and processing, underlies the regional connectedness in this long-distance trade (Hammel et al. 2000; Miller et al. 2000). Trade items like gold, copper, iron hoes, salt, and beads (ostrich and glass) were in high demand, and their context varied as sources of wealth and symbolic status markets (Table 10.1). Their value changed situationally, and anthropology's role is to understand these shifting uses and meanings.

As Hauser and Haines state in chapter 1, disruptions caused by the slave trade and work-enforced migration complicate understandings of history, and anthropologists must resort to employing analogies drawn from oral traditions, ethnoarchaeology, and ethnohistory (see also V. Selvakumar and Mark Hauser, chapter 7, this volume). Thus inland East African trading societies such as the Nyamwezi, Giriama, and Akamba, who maintained connections with the coast in the eighteenth and nineteenth centuries, provide us

232 · Chapurukha M. Kusimba

with superb cases for reimagining the uses and meanings of medieval materiality. For example, the Nyamwezi trade networks extended beyond Lake Tanganyika to the west, Lake Victoria to the north, and the southern regions of Ufipa and Ruemba. They monopolized regional trade in copper, tobacco and its by-products, iron, and salt. Still, they constituted the largest East African trading diaspora in the Katanga copper region in the mid-nineteenth century (Thomson, 1968: 46; Roberts 1970). The trade items served many purposes, and their meaning was also situational. Salt could be consumed, but it could also be used as currency for debt or bridewealth payments. Cowrie shells were ornamental, oracle, and monetary objects. Glass beads connected the different currencies and were combined with other locally made beads to improve the "how do I look?" effect.

Towns and Caravanserais as Ports of Trade and Modes of Trade

As nodes of long-distance trade, towns provided water, food, recreation, hospitality, places of worship, and personal security to residents and traders alike (Barendse 2016). Trader networks depended upon successful brokerage. Intermediaries in Swahili towns assembled crews, sellers, and buyers, giving them financial security to make deals, find forms of credit, and provide safe storage and the means for enforcing contracts (Middleton 2004:7 9). They understood the climate of the interior and coordinated caravans' movements to avoid both the dry and wet seasons that would have disrupted trade.

The risks of trade were mitigated and safe passage to trade caravans was promoted by trade pacts, tributes, and broker networks with local leaders. Modes of exchange were based upon intimate ties of kinship, friendship, rank, and trust (Middleton 2004: 88). According to John Middleton, the method of trade on the Swahili coast (summed up in Table 10.2) was primarily between in-laws, blood relatives, friends, and their networks. Exchanges were negotiated between affines within the merchants' houses and secured places that nonfamily members could not enter unless invited—places where open disputes and arguments were forbidden (Middleton 2004: 83). These exchanges were not made at impersonal markets (which dealt mainly in foodstuffs) but through intensely personal dealings where competition was carefully controlled and limited. This mode of exchange dealt in relatively small volumes. Merchants sought to minimize open competition. Piety, charity, trust, and religious faith were the cornerstones of these transactions. The affinal nature of these transactions minimized exploitation as they were businesses between in-laws, and the beneficiaries were usually members of one's lineage. Thus the skillful manipulation of kin networks enabled the Swahili merchants and

Table 10.2. Modes of exchange on the Swahili Coast

Affinal

Visiting Asian trader married daughter of broker, becoming son in-law, matrilocal residence	On the coast, children from these unions became Swahili
Sons of the broker married daughters of inland trading partners, establishing matrilocal residences	In inland Africa, children from these unions became Swahili

Gift Exchange

Visiting trader presented gift before any trade negotiation would begin; host gave a banquet to celebrate successful business transaction; gift, usually porcelain, would never be sold but became family heirloom	Coastal trader presented gift before any trade negotiation would begin; host threw a banquet to celebrate successful business transaction; gift usually cloth fitting status of the partner

Source: Drawn from 19th-century accounts collected by Carl Velten between 1893 and 1969 and edited by Lyndon Harries (1965: 182).

intermediaries to control long-distance trade between the coast and inland and to build wide-scale and long-term heritable relationships that connected Asia and Africa.

Merchant Relationships: Blood Brotherhoods

Beyond sustained kinship relationships discussed in the preceding section, African merchants created relationships and pledged trust and fidelity through blood brotherhoods (White 1994). Men would develop relationships, trust, and reciprocity in a blood brotherhood ritual. These rituals were exceedingly common across East Africa during the historical period, as Evans-Pritchard (1933) initially noted, and created a pact of mutual assistance that involved two participants ingesting each other's blood. For example, the Zande's lifelong agreement allowed blood brothers to assure joint service and alliance against common enemies. However, the ritual was also common among travelers and traders who ventured beyond the boundaries of Zandeland to trade during periods of hunger or drought. Travelers sought out a local blood brother and relied on him for assistance whenever they were vulnerable visitors. The supernatural sanction would curse anyone who hurt his blood brother. Evans-Pritchard reports various rituals involving cutting the chest or hand and soaking a piece of wood or groundnut in the blood before eating.

In her classic review, Louise White (1994) showed that the blood brotherhood ritual allowed men to create idealized relationships with each other outside those already recognized by consanguineal kinship or marriage or forms of friendship with intimates. The blood brotherhood allowed men with little in common to form pacts of intimacy and reciprocity using the symbolic intimacy of shared bodily fluids. Among the Tatsimo of Madagascar, cloth was essential for sealing a blood brotherhood contract called *atihena*. One week after the initial atihena ceremony, the two individuals united by it exchanged personal clothes. This exchange was accompanied by a telling of the histories, *tantara*, of the respective family ancestors. The two actions combined to cement the relationship—both materially and historically—and created new kinship ties meant to endure for generations. Each piece of cloth symbolized the individual who offered it, while the clothing exchange symbolized their social relationship.

As in other regions, blood brotherhood was the primary means through which people forged trade relationships with each other in inland Kenya. The hunter gatherer Waata, who refer to themselves as elephant people and live in the coastal hinterland, were known for their excellent hunting and tracking skills (Ville 1995; Parker 2017: 33). They monopolized the trade of bushmeat, honey, beeswax, and poison supply, exchanging these goods for cowpeas, millet, and sorghum with the Taita's agricultural neighbors, the Mijikenda, Akamba, and Swahili. They were indispensable in regional trade due to their intimate knowledge of the Tsavo wilderness, their leadership in hunting and tracking skills, and their knowledge of the great long bow, *buni*, and a wide variety of medicines, chief among them that of poison making (Parker 2017: 34). So crucial were the Waata in the procurement of ivory and rhinoceros horn, giraffe, buffalo, leopard and lion skins, honey and beeswax, and other trophies in high demand for local, regional, and extra-regional markets that renowned Swahili scholar Ahmed Sheikh Nabhany credited them with the wealth that the medieval Swahili accumulated (Nabhany, interview 2001).

The Tsavo region of the Kenya coast was connected by complex systems of paths linking the region's communities to market centers. Local and regional traders regularly met at these centers to exchange agricultural products, game meat, beeswax, honey, milk, yogurt, butter, livestock, and poultry, as well as hoes, arrows, spears, bows, quivers, and leather. Other non-local products exchanged included beads, cloth, dried marine fish, ivory, and rhinoceros horn. These markets served local communities and attracted regional traders, including the Akamba, Oromo, Waata, Giriama, Duruma, Pare, Taveta, Shambaa, Chaga, and Swahili traders. Coastal traders brought beads, brass wire, cloth, and fish and returned with ivory, beeswax, honey, milk products, game meat, millet, sorghum, rice, and other products. Traders from far-off places often stayed in the homes of their blood brother relatives. In some cases the host would serve as a broker, selling the trader's articles and procuring items the seller needed. Blood brotherhoods depended on long-standing trust and reciprocity. The roles would be reversed when the host visited the coast. Oral histories chronicle a landscape of free movement of people and goods, intercommunity trust, and systems of reciprocal relationships that changed in the sixteenth century with the onset of the slave trade (Harries 1965: 182).

Brotherhoods created opportunities for strangers, competitors, and potential enemies to enter peacefully into contractual obligations legitimizing their partnership with the broader community. Membership in the organization conferred certain privileges: the freedom to exploit resources while enjoying the whole community's protection. In this sense, brotherhoods reduced tensions and suspicions arising from competition for resources while simultaneously providing opportunities for access to technical and sacred knowledge.

As Herlehey (1984: 287) writes, the social and economic links between merchants and hinterland communities were mutually reinforced through the blood brotherhood relationship, forging relationships of trust in an area of ethnic diversity: "For example, blood-brotherhood could be used by commercial partners to routinize and secure their trading relations, while local merchants could use the kinship links created by the bonds of blood brotherhood to increase the extent of their commercial activity over a large territory." Among the Saghala people of the Taita Hills, every man had a Mijikenda blood brother who served as a host when he visited the coast and other regions to trade or for pleasure. When his Mijikenda blood brother visited, the same hospitality was accorded to him, his family, and friends. He would use his brother's home as the base from which business was conducted and could expect protection on the journey. The host blood brother did this to ensure that his brother was not molested on the homeward journey, for example, by being taken into slavery. In sum, people put their bodies on the line. Their bodies were their creditworthiness, and through this system, they sustained a global chain of trade that made some extremely wealthy.

Ethnography and oral traditions create opportunities for a counterpoint to what have become traditional ways of representing those on the margins of history, whose experiences are likely to be subsumed by dominant voices. The relationships developed around blood brotherhood provide alternative ways of seeing and understanding history. Informant perspectives display the complexity, fluidity, and dynamism of ethnicity, identities, and boundaries. These boundaries stretched from Central Africa's heartland, the Persian Gulf, to South and Central Asia. Crises and conflicts from competition for access to resources created opportunities for social and economic networks sustained through gift exchange, friendship, intermarriage, alliances, blood brotherhoods, and sisterhoods. The persistence of these extra-regional networks in Taita, Giriama, Duruma, and Swahili oral traditions speaks to the coast's unique global dimensions (Kusimba et al. 2013). For example, some Swahili families I have known over the last 30 years have shared their groups' deep ancestry, which they trace to the area of Shiraz in present-day Iran. In their oral traditions these Shirazi ancestors are the putative foreign founders of many of the coast's principal settlements, a view that archaeologists and historians recounted. New genetic analysis of human remains from six medieval Swahili towns have confirmed these traditions (Brielle et al. 2023). The Shirazi identity, however, likely developed later among the early founding families of cities along the coast as a social stratification component. Social networks enabled communities to share resource exploitation risks. These interactions fostered the development of spheres of knowledge by particular ethnic groups or specific lineages within those ethnic groups. These knowledge systems provided the basis for interacting, encouraging, tolerating, and even intermarrying with people who would otherwise be enemies.

Medieval Swahili Urbanism and Global Connectivity

Undoubtedly, various communities from eastern, central, and southern Africa participated in dynamic and complex regional and interregional trade systems. As seen from the early bi-directional introduction and adoption of Asian and African domesticates, this complex economic interaction predates Islam's introduction. It illustrates the regular, continuous interaction and cross-fertilization of ideas, goods, and services among interacting partners and communities. These networks are only now beginning to be recognized and contextualized archaeologically (Kusimba and Walz 2018).

How might we reimagine how urbanism and social inequality arose from this seemingly heterarchical relationship based on affinal kinship and brokerage? Like hinterland connections, transoceanic connections were equally strong and gained prominence, especially from 800 CE onward (see Table 10.2). As interest in African products in Asia increased, the Swahili coast and its emergent intermediaries would increasingly serve as a conduit through which goods, people, ideas, and services would move into and out of Africa. Both connections were vital and brought prosperity to the participants in this transoceanic trading system. The coast's unique location was advantageous because it created opportunities for the local intermediaries to manipulate their social ties and networks. On the other hand, their positioning had a built-in disadvantage: their prosperity depended on their interior and transoceanic trade partners' willingness and compliance.

Table 10.3. Renaissance in Asia (ca. 500–1450 CE)

Political Economy and Governance	Science, Technology, Engineering, Mathematics (STEM)
Bureaucracies and tax codes unified	West Asia, South Asia, and China were major centers of innovation
Innovation in money including the use of letters of credit, insurance, and the origin of limited liability firms	Thousands of tropical plants were introduced in the more temperate regions
New legal status for conquered peoples defined	Advances in medicine including inoculation
Manual for kings developed	Mathematics and astronomy
Tax-funded development projects initiated, including irrigation, roads, and shipbuilding	Algebra and the concept of zero invented
Diverse armies—slave armies, armies based on religion, and prisoners as soldiers	A variety of geometries developed, including solutions to conic sections and even a primitive form of calculus

Today the remains of nearly 400 medieval settlements dot the coastal landscape between present-day Somalia and Mozambique. Hundreds more coeval sites are known to exist farther inland, primarily in Kenya, Mozambique, Zimbabwe, and Botswana. These settlements were diverse, ranging from hamlets to chiefdoms to prominent city-state and state capitals connected by local, regional, and extra-regional trade. Within these settlements are clear distinctions based upon differential access to wealth. The emergent elite enjoyed unfair access to more wealth-building opportunities through knowledge and access to particular local materials. For example, along the coast, elite members exploited the abundant, readily available coral, while their inland counterparts used dry stone architecture to erect their homes. Both techniques are labor-intensive and demand expertise and massive investment in time and resources. This extended beyond building permanent homes for themselves and their families. Investment in the local extractive industry can be found in all contexts. On the coast it involved coral mining and lime manufacturing, bead making, boat construction, weaving, lumbering, and commercialized fishing. Predominating in the interior were iron working; mining of gold, rock crystal, and other precious stones; professional hunting of big game for ivory, horns, skins, and meat products; and agriculture and livestock farming. All these become essential activities.

On the coast, the stone house became a symbol of stability, prosperity, and elitism (Donley-Reid 1990). Similarly, in inland Africa owning a stone house, being a successful farmer with large herds of cattle or camels, or being a successful and revered hunter, served the same purpose. Access to some trade items, such as Chinese porcelain and glazed Islamic wares, was limited by availability and affordability. However, due to their portability and affordability, other trade items like beads and cloth were distributed and consumed in the entire region. The hundreds of spindle whorls and bead grinders that abound at many sites excavated on the coast show the importance of these industries in the regional economy. Specialization and monopolization of specific tasks by region became normalized.

The medieval Swahili city-states exhibited three nodes of interaction that were crucial for their rise and sustenance: first, there was the state's relationship with nearby rural fishing and farming villages; second, partnerships with inland communities; and third, the relationship with various trading partners via Indian Ocean networks. At each of these nodes, material evidence connects the state with economic and social interactions that give us clues to the evolution and character of the Swahili civilization. Like any other state, medieval Swahili was characterized by unequal access to crucial coastal resources, such as human labor, arable land, fishing areas, and mangrove forests. As maritime trade networks overlaid these local inequalities, regional and international trade goods were incorporated into elite-controlled social and economic structures. These three nodes or levels do not have a necessary chronological relationship, and each could be paramount in any particular region at any specific time (see also Hsieh and Sakai, this volume).

The coastal trading centers were linked in urban clusters where different locations specialized in production and trade. Data from coastal and other interior sites illustrate the importance of regional, multiscalar approaches toward understanding early interactions and exchange. For example, the port of Chibuene connected individual traders from at least three networks: the southern African interior, the northern coastal trade network, and the transoceanic trade network (Sinclair et al. 2012: 735). Thus the autonomy of the ports imparted a resilience to the system that lasted until the seventeenth and eighteenth centuries. The more connection between these ports, the greater the chance that transformations in one node will dissipate and be absorbed by the system. None of these ports was a central node in the flow of goods, removal of which would cause a system collapse. For example, the period between 1300 and 1850 CE was characterized by periodic severe, unpredictable weather patterns that resulted in widespread drought, famine, and disease epidemics, including the plague (Nicholson et al. 2013). This weakened regional trade and cohesion as communities competed for declining resources. Regionwide settlement abandonment and migrations searching for food and pasture caused tensions and interregional warfare.

A Summing Up

Globalization on the Swahili coast was a product of local, regional, and international trade networks. An inclusive analytical framework adopted in this chapter provides a long-term narrative of specialized herding and agriculture alongside the rise of urbanism at local, regional, and extra-regional levels. The region's emergent elite, especially trade intermediaries on the coast, manipulated their strategic location as middlemen to monopolize power networks. Like other intermediaries and brokers of the medieval world, they shared the practice of restricting rivalry to the minimum. They understood that their favorable location in these coastal settlements could be sustained by forging and regularly renewing partnerships with the hinterland, other coastal communities, and foreign merchants. These partnerships involved formalizing affinal ties into long-lasting friendships that promoted peaceful coexistence, tolerance, and sharing of the region's diverse resources. Wealth accumulated from these interaction spheres created inequality. In time this would intensify the coastal region's social, class, and ethnic consciousness, which increasingly embraced a global Indian Ocean culture while strengthening its local networks. Ancient trade between the Swahili coast and Asia was a complicated global affair involving many communities and took several routes that traversed land and sea. The influences of this international trade are still visible today and are clearly outlined in the individual chapters of this volume.

Bibliography

Barendse, R. J. 2016. *The Arabian Seas and the Indian Ocean World of the Seventeenth Century.* New York: Armonk.

Beaujard, P. 2018. "The Birth of a Single Afro-Eurasian World System (Second Century BC–Sixth Century CE)." In *Trade and Civilisation: Economic Networks and Cultural Ties, from Prehistory to Early Modern Times,* edited by K. Kristiansen, T. Lindkvist, and J. Myrdal, 242–50. Cambridge, U.K.: Cambridge University Press.

———. 2019. *The Worlds of the Indian Ocean: A Global History,* 2 vols. Cambridge, U.K.: Cambridge University Press.

Bennison, A. K. 2009. *The Great Caliphs: The Golden Age of the 'Abbasid Empire.* New Haven: Yale University Press.

Bisson, M. S. 2000. "Precolonial Copper Metallurgy: Sociopolitical Context." In *Ancient African Metallurgy: The Sociocultural Context,* edited by M. S. Bisson, S. Terry Childs, P. deBarros, and A.F.C. Holl, 83–145. Walnut Creek, Calif.: Altamira Press.

Boivin, N., and D. Q. Fuller. 2009. "Shell Middens, Ships and Seeds: Exploring Coastal Subsistence, Maritime Trade and the Dispersal of Domesticates in and around the Ancient Arabian Peninsula." *Journal of World Prehistory* 22: 113–80.

Boivin, N., D. Q. Fuller, and A. Crowther. 2012. "Old World Globalization and the Columbian Exchange: Comparison and Contrast." *World Archaeology* 44(3): 452–69.

Boivin, N., A. Crowther, R. Helm, and D. Q. Fuller. 2013. "East Africa and Madagascar in the Indian Ocean World." *Journal of World Prehistory* 26: 213–81.

Boivin, N., A. Crowther, M. Prendergast, and D. Q. Fuller. "Indian Ocean Food Globalisation and Africa." *African Archaeological Review* 31: 547–81.

Brielle, E. S., J. Fleisher, S. Wynne-Jones, K. Sirak, N. Broomandkhoshbacht, K. Callan . . . and C. M. Kusimba. 2023. "Entwined African and Asian Genetic Roots of Medieval Peoples of the Swahili Coast." *Nature* 615: 866–73.

Donley-Reid, L. W. 1990. "A Structuring Structure: The Swahili House." In *Domestic Architecture and the Use of Space: An Interdisciplinary Cross-Cultural Study*, edited by Susan Kent, 114–26. New York: Cambridge University Press.

Dussubieux, L., C. M. Kusimba, V. Gogte, S. Kusimba, B. Gratuze, and R. Oka. 2008. "The Trading of Ancient Glass Beads: New Analytical Data from South Asian and East African Soda-Alumina Glass Beads." *Archaeometry* 50: 797–821.

Elverskog, J. 2011. *Buddhism and Islam on the Silk Road*. Philadelphia: University of Pennsylvania Press.

Evans-Pritchard, E. E. 1933. "Zande Blood Brotherhood." *Africa* 6(4): 369–401.

Fabian, J. 1991. *Language and Colonial Power: The Appropriation of Swahili in the Former Belgian Congo 1880-1938*. Berkeley: University of California Press.

Fagan, B. M. 1966. "The Iron Age of Zambia." *Current Anthropology* 7(4): 453-62.

———. 1969. "Early Trade and Raw Materials in South Central Africa." *Journal of African History* 10(1): 1–13.

Fuller, D. Q., N. Boivin, T. Hoogervorst, and R. Allaby. 2011. "Across the Indian Ocean: The Prehistoric Movement of Plants and Animals." *Antiquity* 85: 544–58.

Hammel, A., C. White, S. Pfeiffer, and D. Miller 2000. "Pre-Colonial Mining in Southern Africa." *Journal of the South Africa Institute of Mining and Metallurgy* 100: 49–56.

Harries, L. 1965. *Swahili Prose Texts: A Selection from the Material Collected by Carl Velten from 1893 to 1896*. London: Oxford University Press.

Herlehey, T. J. 1984. "Ties that Bind." *International Journal of African Historical Studies* 17(2): 285–308.

Kusimba, C. M. 2006. "Slavery and Warfare in African Chiefdoms." In *The Archaeology of Warfare: Prehistories of Raiding and Conquest*, edited by E. Arkush and M. Allen, 214–49. Gainesville: University Press of Florida.

———. 2017. "The Swahili and Globalization in the Indian Ocean." In *The Routledge Handbook of Archaeology and Globalization*, edited by T. Hodos, 104–22. London: Routledge Handbooks.

———. 2022. "Technological Innovation and the Emergence of the State in Eastern and Southern Africa." In *Studying Africa and Africans Today*, edited by Augustin F. C. Holl, 225–50. New Delhi: BP International.

Kusimba, C. M., and Sibel B. Kusimba. 2018. "Mosaics: Rethinking African Connections in Coastal and Hinterland Relationships." In *The Swahili World*, edited by Stephanie Wynne-Jones and Adria LaViolette, 403–18. London: Routledge.

Kusimba, C. M., Sibel B. Kusimba, and Laure Dussubieux. 2013. "Beyond the Coastalscapes: Preindustrial Social and Political Networks in East Africa." *African Archaeological Review* 30: 39–63.

Kusimba, C. M., and J. Walz. 2018. "When Did the Swahili Become Maritime? A Reply to Fleisher et al. (2015), and to the Resurgence of Maritime Myopia in the Archaeology of the Swahili Coast." *American Anthropologist* 120(3): 429–43.

LaViolette, A. 2008. "Swahili Cosmopolitanism in Africa and the Indian Ocean World, AD 600–1500." *Archaeologies* 4(1): 24–49.

Miller, D., N. Desai, and J. Lee-Thorp. 2000. "Indigenous Gold Mining in Southern Africa: A Review." *South African Archaeological Bulletin Goodwin Series* 8: 91–99.

Middleton, John. 2004. *African Merchants of the Indian Ocean: Swahili of the East African Coast.* Long Grove, Ill.: Waveland Press.

Miller, J. M., E. A. Sawchuk, A. L. Reedman, and P. R. Willoughby. 2018. "Land Snail Shell Beads in the Sub-Saharan Archaeological Record: When, Where, and Why?" *African Archaeological Review* 35: 347–78.

Mugane, J. M. 2015. *The Story of Swahili.* Athens: Ohio University Press.

Mutoro, H. W. 1979. *A Contribution to the Study of the Cultural and Economic Dynamics of the Historical Settlements of East African Coast with Particular Reference to Takwa Ruins North Kenya Coast.* M.A. thesis, University of Nairobi.

Mwacharo, J. M., K. Nomura, H. Hanada, H. Jianlin, O. Hanotte, and T. Amano. 2007. "Genetic Relationships Among Kenyan and Other East African Indigenous Chickens." *Animal Genetics* 38(5): 485–90.

Nabhany, Ahmed Sheikh. 2001. Personal Interview. Fort Jesus Museum, Mombasa.

Nicholson, S. E., D. J. Nash, B. M. Chase, S. W. Grab, T. M. Shanahan, D. Verschuren . . . and M. Umer. 2013. "Temperature Variability Over Africa During the Last 2000 Years." *The Holocene* 23(8): 1085–94.

Oteyo, G., and C. M. Kusimba. 2020. "The Consumption of Beads in Ancient Swahili East Africa." In *China and East Africa: Ancient Ties, Contemporary Flows*, edited by C. M. Kusimba, T. Zhu, and P. W. Kiura, 147–64. Lanham. Md.: Lexington Books.

Parker, Ian. 2017. "Bows, Arrows, Poison, and Elephants." *Kenya Past and Present* 44 (2017): 43–56.

Roberts, A. D. 1970. "Nyamwezi Trade." In *Pre-Colonial African Trade: Essays on Trade in Central and Eastern Africa before 1900*, edited by R. Gray and D. Birmingham, 649–701. London: Oxford University Press.

Robertshaw, P., M. D. Glascock, M. Wood, and R. S. Popelka. 2003. "Chemical Analysis of Ancient African Glass Beads: A Very Preliminary Report." *Journal of African Archaeology* 1: 139–46.

Robertshaw, P., B. Rasoarifetra, M. Wood, E. Melchiorre, R. S. Popelka-Filcoff, and M. D. Glascock. 2006. "Chemical Analysis of Glass Beads from Madagascar." *Journal of African Archaeology* 4(1): 91–109.

Robertshaw, P., M. Wood, E. Melchiorre, R. S. Popelka-Filcoff, and M. D. Glascock. 2010. "Southern African Glass Beads: Chemistry, Glass Sources and Patterns of Trade." *Journal of Archaeological Science* 37(8): 1898–1912.

Rowlands, M., and D. Q. Fuller. 2018. "Deconstructing Civilisation: A 'Neolithic' Alternative." In *Trade and Civilisation: Economic Networks and Cultural Ties, From Prehistory to Early Modern Times*, edited by Kristian Kristiansen, Thomas Lindkvist, and Janken Myrdal, 172–194. Cambridge, U.K.: Cambridge University Press.

Seland, E. H. 2014. "Archaeology of Trade in the Western Indian Ocean, 300 BC–AD 700." *Journal of Archaeological Research* 22: 367–402.

Sinclair, P.J.J., A. Ekblom, and M. Wood. 2012. "Trade and Society on the South-East African Coast in the Later First Millennium AD: The Case of Chibuene." *Antiquity* 86: 723–37.

Thomson, J. 1968. *To the Central African Lakes and Back: The Narrative of the Royal Geographical Society's East Central African Expedition 1878–1880*. London: Frank Cass and Company (orig. London 1881).

Ville, J-L. 1995. "The Waata of Tsavo Galana." *Kenya Past and Present* 27: 21–26.

White, L. 1994. "Blood Brotherhood Revisited: Kinship, Relationship, and the Body in East and Central Africa." *Africa* 64(3): 359–72.

Wood, M. 2012. *Interconnections: Glass Beads and Trade in Southern and Eastern Africa and the Indian Ocean, 7th to 16th centuries AD*. Uppsala, Sweden: Department of Archaeology and Ancient History.

Wynne-Jones, S., and A. LaViolette. 2018. *The Swahili World*. London: Routledge.

Zhao, B. 2012. "Global Trade and Swahili Cosmopolitan Material Culture: Chinese-Style Ceramic Shards from Sanje ya Kati and Songo Mnara (Kilwa, Tanzania)." *Journal of World History* 23(1): 41–85.

Zhao, B., and D. Qin. 2018. "Links with China." In *The Swahili World*, edited by S. Wynne-Jones and A. LaViolette, 430–44. London: Routledge.

11

Commentary

A Perspective from South Asia

Supriya Varma

I explore here several intersecting issues related to historical archaeology, a subfield of archaeology. It is well known that in the case of historical archaeology most studies have largely focused on the European colonial expansion in the last 500 years, and it is the Atlantic world that has dominated the narrative. This volume edited by Mark William Hauser and Julia Jong Haines seeks to be a much-needed corrective by shifting the gaze from the Atlantic Ocean to the Indian Ocean. There is an attempt to map the transnational world through a comparative method using multisited and multiscalar approaches. In their introductory chapter Hauser and Haines push us to "conceptualize a historical archaeology of the Indian Ocean as material practice: embedded within structures of history and power, including class relations and markets, *and* with a physical presence in the present."

In a way, doing a historical archaeology of the Indian Ocean also enables a far more expansive temporal frame that is not just limited to the modern world but goes back at least a millennium. This is indeed a significant contribution in redirecting historical archaeology to a period prior to the Europeans traversing the seas in the sixteenth century. As Hauser and Haines (this volume) also note: "Recasting the emergence of the modern world in a way that centers the Indian Ocean is not new to historians, anthropologists and literary scholars," but archaeologists have not paid much attention to the Indian Ocean in the post-1500 centuries (but see Seetah 2018), although that is not the case as far as archaeology of the Indian Ocean is concerned in the preceding millennia, be it the third millennium BCE or the first millennium CE. Hence the volume makes a valuable intervention in the field of historical archaeology as it seeks to initiate an archaeology of modern worlds in the Indian Ocean.

Just as a historical archaeology of the Indian Ocean is in a nascent stage, so is the case with this subfield in South Asia. A couple of years ago, when I was devising a graduate level course on historical archaeology, I realized that it was simply impossible to limit it to South Asia alone, primarily because so little work has been done in the subcontinent. The focus had to be on a transnational world and a course that emphasized a comparative method using multisited and multiscalar approaches, as we see in this volume too. Thus I came up with five themes that could form the core: gender, identity, power, inequality, and connectivity. A central concern in this course has been about the definition of historical archaeology. The Society for Historical Archaeology, even while defining this subfield in the broadest terms possible as "the study of material remains of past societies that also left behind documentary and oral histories," also slips in that it studies "the emergence, transformation, and nature of the modern world." In other words, does this subfield study the material remains of the modern world that are supplemented with documentary data and oral accounts, or is it also about method?

A much-needed and long overdue conversation on historical archaeology in South Asia has also been initiated with two panel discussions being organized in 2021.[1] As a discussant at one panel and a co-organizer of the second, I had flagged several issues that need further discussion. First is the problem of definition. How do we define historical archaeology, specifically in the context of South Asia? Here, my own sense is that rather than framing it from a temporal sense, we need to do so through a methodological lens. Second, if we accept the first premise, then what would be the method for a historical archaeology of South Asia? Third, how do we explain the near absence of archaeological studies of the modern and contemporary pasts in South Asia (but see Varma 2021)? Fourth, how would a historical archaeology of South Asia contribute to the subfield more broadly?

To an extent, this resonates with what some archaeologists are stressing about how the Indian Ocean World as a method contributes to an archaeology of the modern world. As Hauser and Haines have argued in their introduction, "no mercantile venture, colonial enclave, or settlement, including slaveholding plantations of the Atlantic, could have survived if its people had not relied on the circulations, commerce, and ways of doing things in the Indian Ocean." Thus transnational archaeologies also situate the many diasporas that circulated in the Indian Ocean and are a central narrative in several chapters of the book. Heritage studies too form an important component of historical archaeology, an aspect that has been discussed in some detail for the case of Velha Goa. Within the Indian Ocean World, historical archaeologists so far seem to be investigating primarily the two islands, Mauritius, and

Zanzibar, and two coastal zones of peninsular India, Coromandel, and Velha Goa on the Konkan, although in future more areas are likely to be explored as the potential is immense.

Seetah, Manfio, and Sarathi examine the interconnections between the islands of Mauritius and Zanzibar and the role of both Indigenous and diasporic communities in shaping trade, networks, and social development. By situating these two islands as critical nodes within much wider networks, they invert the conventional narrative of islands being isolated and connectivity ushering in superior technologies solely through colonization. Instead, they direct the gaze on the agency of human and non-human actors that formed the Indian Ocean World. Historical archaeology is taking the lead in several other areas too. For instance, Čaval and Cianciosi have initiated research on healthcare, especially from a gendered perspective, through surveys of quarantine stations as well as the excavation of a cemetery in Mauritius. Haines and Hauser have compared domestic spaces at the two ends of the South Asian diaspora, the Coromandel coast and Mauritius, to track facets of social identity, power relations, and everyday life.

Hauser and Selvakumar (2021) have also been documenting changes in the patterns and organization of settlements as well as material assemblages between the twelfth and nineteenth centuries CE at the Danish colonial enclave Tranquebar (Tharangambadi) and 23 associated villages and hamlets on the Coromandel coast. Their study involves a systematic pedestrian survey in conjunction with textual, epigraphic, and cartographic data. The aim of this project is to understand both changes and continuities between two specific settlement types, namely gardens and plantations, with the former emerging between the sixth and thirteenth centuries CE, and the latter in the seventeenth and eighteenth centuries CE. Apart from a larger concern of decentering the role of the Atlantic world in the establishment of commercial agriculture during the early modern period, it also demonstrates the importance of looking at the longer histories of a micro-region. With most histories of Tranquebar beginning in 1620 CE, this historical archaeology project has the advantage of uncovering the deeper pasts of commercial agriculture in this region, one that predates the early modern period.

In the case of Zanzibar, archaeologists had focused mainly on the centuries between 750 and 1500 CE and looked at the elements contributing to social change, which tended to be viewed in binary terms of internal (Swahili/African) versus external (Arab/Indian Ocean) factors. It is only in the last decade that we have witnessed an interest in the archaeology of Zanzibar in the post-1500 centuries. LaViolette and Norman have a project on the archaeology of Portuguese agricultural outposts in the seventeenth-century countryside that builds on a tradition of critical historical archaeology of East Africa. Such a tradition includes an archaeology of colonial processes but also looking at oral histories and ethnohistoric records. Once again, an archaeology of colonialism has been well studied, but not so much in the context of the Indian Ocean. LaViolette and Norman's research is significant as it examines failed colonial endeavors in the case of Zanzibar. There is also much to understand about how disruptive European settlements may have been in such colonized areas, especially from the perspective of the ordinary Swahili people and the ensuing power relations.

Wilson makes several important points related to heritage in his chapter on Velha Goa, which witnessed Portuguese rule for nearly 450 years. Most accounts of this Portuguese settlement have relied almost entirely on historical archives produced by elite Portuguese people and detailing large residences and ecclesiastical and administrative buildings. It was only when Wilson carried out an archaeological survey of the city that he could come up with an alternative narrative. In his survey Wilson identified a range of non-elite residences that revealed a large but integrated urban-agricultural system, which parallels the vernacular settlement pattern still seen outside the city even today. Such a pattern comprises dispersed homes built on high ground, amid low-lying agricultural fields and cashew plantations.

The discussion on the heritage management practices at Velha Goa, which was given UNESCO World Heritage status in 1986, has implications for several other sites in India, including Mandu, where I have my current project. A major problem with the UNESCO status is that this has been conferred just to the churches and convents and not to the entire site, as one would have expected. Even in the case of protected buildings, the practice followed in India of landscaping the areas with lawns around these protected monuments further creates an alienating space rather than something more organic. Further, the built landscape populated by the non-elites remains unprotected and vulnerable to destruction daily due to natural and human factors.

Ironically, what remains preserved is the ecclesiastical colonial heritage, but not the residences, elite and non-elite. Neither has there been any attempt to incorporate within heritage management practices in Goa other narratives that are equally valuable, such as the history of early agrarian capitalism and plantation agriculture or even the fortification. Often, heritage preservation (or destruction) draws on a range of conflicting tropes that include "nostalgia for the golden colonial era" alongside "anti-colonial and anti-Portuguese sentiments." As Wilson writes: "Velma Goa's archaeological and heritage futures may pose to us seemingly intractable questions of how we decolonize this history and its public engagements, and yet, the endeavor to do so and preserve this unique past remains one of the most important avenues of research to help us create an equitable and representative heritage management practice across India and the world."

There are important lessons to be drawn from the UNESCO status that has been selectively ascribed to the ecclesiastical buildings of Velha Goa. As a dossier is being prepared to make a bid for UNESCO World Heritage status for the fifteenth- to sixteenth-century CE capital city of Mandu in central India, can we learn from the case of Velha Goa? As part of our ongoing historical archaeology project, we are investigating society-environment interaction in relation to water management, climatic variability, and the making of the built environment in both urban and rural contexts (Casile 2021). The project has been designed to explore a range of questions; for instance, how did people live and transform the environment to adapt to monsoon rain variability in a semi-arid environment? What can the study of the long-term lives of water bodies (both natural and constructed) tell us about vulnerability, adaptation, and resilience in the face of climatic and monsoonal fluctuations? How did communities in the past respond to hydroclimatic variations, and how do they continue to do in the present? To investigate these questions, the project is relying on a variety of disciplines, data sets, and techniques by bringing together scholars from the humanities and the social and environmental sciences. The project is also tracing continuities and discontinuities in the historical landscape and waterscape, and failures and successes in water management, and analyzing them in ways that can give insights into the nature of change, vulnerability, and adaptation in the past as well as the present. The palaces, mosques, tombs, and caravanserais are only part of what constitutes the heritage of Mandu. What needs to be preserved is the entire landscape of Mandu, natural as well as built, but as at Velha Goa, only a few buildings (palaces, along with a few mosques and tombs) are being protected, while the rest are being destroyed, as we see happening right before us. Ultimately as archaeologists, when we envisage projects, perhaps we should also address issues of heritage, historic preservation, and rights of local communities.

Note

1 The two panel discussions were titled *Historical Archaeology in South Asia,* Society for Historical Archaeology, Germantown, Maryland, USA, Virtual International Conference, January 6–9, 2021; and *Towards a Critical Historical Archaeology in South Asia,* Theoretical Archaeological Group 2021, Stanford University, April 30–May 2, 2021.

Bibliography

Casile, Anne. 2021. "Climatic Variation and Society in Medieval South Asia: Unexplored Threads of History and Archaeology of Mandu." *Medieval History Journal* 24(1–2): 56–91.

Hauser, Mark W., and V. Selvakumar. 2021. "Gardens of the Coromandel Coast: Landscape Considerations of Commercial Agriculture in Tamil Nadu, South India." *International Journal of Historical Archaeology* 25(4): 1113–41.

Seetah, Krish. 2018. *Connecting Continents: Archaeology and History in the Indian Ocean World.* Athens: Ohio University Press.

Varma, Supriya. 2021. "Between History and Anthropology: Finding a New Home for Archaeology." *Social Scientist* 49(11–12): 59–76.

Contributors

Saša Čaval is research associate at the Research Center of the Slovenian Academy of Sciences and Arts in Ljubljana, Slovenia, and a lecturer at Stanford University, USA. Her research area includes medieval archaeology of plurality in the Western Balkans and historical archaeology in the Indian Ocean. She regularly publishes internationally.

Alessandra Cianciosi is a Marie Skłodowska-Curie Global Fellow at the University of Amsterdam, Amsterdam School of Historical Studies (ASH), in partnership with Stanford University. Her research focuses on landscape and funerary archaeology. She has been publishing in international journals and is an author or editor of seven monographs.

Mick de Ruyter is associate lecturer in archaeology at the College of Humanities, Arts and Social Sciences at Flinders University. His research investigates traditional watercraft across the Indian Ocean, Asia, and Australasia, specifically how they were used and adapted as the means for seapower.

Julia Jong Haines is a Mellon Postdoctoral Fellow at the Society for Humanities and Anthropology Department at Cornell University. She has published articles on her historical archeological research in the *International Journal of Historical Archaeology, Azania: Archaeological Research in Africa,* and *Journal of African Diaspora Archaeology and Heritage.*

Mark William Hauser is professor of anthropology at Northwestern University. Mark is a historical archaeologist who specializes in materiality, slavery, and inequality. These key themes intersect in the seventeenth, eighteenth, and nineteenth centuries and the Atlantic and Indian Oceans. His current research on the labor histories and social lives of two communities in the Caribbean and South India explores a "prehistory" of the global south by mapping the movement of people, objects, and ideas between two oceans.

250 · Contributors

Ellen Hsieh is assistant professor in the Institute of Anthropology, National Tsing Hua University. She has published articles in the *Journal of Archaeological Science, Ritual and Economy in East Asia: Archaeological Perspectives, Historical Archaeology of Early Modern Colonialism in Asia-Pacific: The Asia-Pacific Region,* and *The Routledge Handbook of Global Historical Archaeology.*

Chapurukha M. Kusimba is professor of anthropology at the University of South Florida. He has published a series of books and book chapters on a wide range of topics from slavery to trade to urbanism in East Africa to South Asia. He has published in a number of different venues including *Journal of Archaeological Science, African Archaeological Review,* and *American Anthropologist.*

Adria LaViolette is professor of anthropology at the University of Virginia. She recently published *The Swahili World* (coedited with S. Wynne-Jones), which received a Society of Africanist Archaeologists' Book Award for 2018–21.

Stefania Manfio is a PhD candidate in the Department of Anthropology, Stanford University. She is a maritime archaeologist who specializes in the slave trade, illegality, and shipwrecks. For her PhD Stefania is working on materials and shipwrecks from Mauritius, serving as an ideal case for Indian Ocean labor movements.

Neil Norman is associate professor of anthropology at the College of William and Mary. His publications include the volume *The Archaeology of Anxiety: The Materiality of Anxiousness, Worry, and Fear* (coedited with J. Fleisher).

Takashi Sakai is adjunct professor in the Graduate Institute of Art History, National Taiwan University. He has published volumes such as *Banten: A Port City State and Its Ceramic Trade,* and *Hizen Wares Excavated from Royal Capital Sites in Indonesia: Trowulan and Other Sites,* and articles in the *Archaeology of Ceramics from Middle Age and Early Modern Period* series, *Oriental Ceramics,* and the *Journal of Southeast Asian Archaeology.*

Akshay Sarathi is lecturer in the Department of Anthropology at Texas A&M University. His research focuses on Indian Ocean connectivity, globalization, and subsistence practices.

Krish Seetah is associate professor in the Departments of Environmental Behavioral Sciences & Oceans, Stanford Doerr School of Sustainability, and Department of Anthropology, School of Humanities and Sciences at Stanford University. He has authored and edited several books, including *Connecting Continents: Archaeology and History in the Indian Ocean World.*

V. Selvakumar is associate professor of maritime history and archaeology at Tamil University, Thanjavur. He has published widely, including in the *International Journal for Nautical Archaeology*, *World Archaeology*, and *Antiquity*.

Supriya Varma is associate professor of archaeology at Azim Premji University. She is a social archaeologist with expertise in the historical archaeology of South Asia over the *longue durée*. She has published widely, including the edited volumes *Traditions in Motion: Religion and Society in History* and *The Archaeology of the Medieval in South Asia: Contesting Narratives from the Eastern Ganga–Brahmaputra Basin*.

Brian C. Wilson, PhD, is associate director at the Mansueto Institute for Urban Innovation, University of Chicago. Some recent publications include "Culture, Ethnicity and Trade at Early Historic Arikamedu, South India," in *Cross-Cultural Networking in the Indian Ocean Realm, c. 100–1800*; "Towards an Historical Archaeology of South Asia," *Historical Archaeology* (50)4: 7–21 (with Mark Hauser, 2016); and "The City as Façade in Velha Goa: Recognizing Enduring Forms of Urbanism in the Early Modern Konkan," *Medieval History Journal* (24)1: 320–52 (2021).

Index

Page numbers in *italics* refer to illustrations.

Aapravasi Ghat (Mauritius): Immigration Depot, 84; UNESCO World Heritage Site, 113
Aapravasi Ghat Trust Fund, 196
Abolition Act (1807), 79
Abortion, 102
Aceh stone, 55, 57
Adas, Michael, 87
Agius, Dionisius, 29
Agriculture, 182; clove production and distribution, 79, 81–82; sugar plantations, 79–80, 84–86, 102; and Swahili culture, 144. *See also* Plantation economies
Agusan del Sur, Mindanao Island, 48
Ahmad, Anisah Bahyah, 63
Ahmad Qomi (Sheikh), 59
Ahmad Shah, 54
Akamba people, 234; trading societies, 231–232
Alauddin Khalji, 54
Albuquerque, Alfonso de, 208, 210, 211–212
Alders, Wolfgang, 143
Ali ibn Muhammad, 88
Allen, Richard B., 165
Ambar, Malik, 90
Anping jars, 59–61, *61*, 66
Antoninus Pius (Roman emperor), 48, 50
Arab manuscript painting. *See Maqāmāt* ship illustration
Arab Seafaring (Hourani 1951), 25, 42
Archaeological Survey of India (ASI), 223, 225
Archaeology: Atlantic World focus, 12; global vs. local movements, 4; historical, 243–244; Indian Ocean World (IOW) regional/local approaches, 6–14, 16; methodology, 1–2;

multisited approaches, 6; periodication, 72; perspectives/thinking, 4; transnationalism as framework, 5–6, 14–17
Architecture: Danish contrasted with Portuguese, 189; of domestic spaces, 187, 189, 194, 201–202; Islamic, 82; limestone, 77; plantation, 84; Portuguese, 133, 214, 219; temple, 53
Art Nouveau tiles, 62–64, *63*

Bagan Kingdom stupas (Myanmar), 52–54
Baldacchino, Godfrey, 74
Al Baleed (Oman), 28
Balfour, Andrew, 116
Baptiste, J., 89
Bates, Crispin, 186
Bauer, Andrew M., 7
Baužytė, Ema, 139
Bawbawgyi Paya Stupa, 52
Beaujard, Philippe, 228
Belitung (Tang) shipwreck, 9, 28, 39
Belle Mare Sugar Estate, 84, *85*
Bernard, Eugène, 102
Bhabha, Homi K., 86
Bhan, Surendra, 7
Blood brotherhoods among merchants, 233–236
Bois Marchand burial ground, 78, *107,* 108–109
Borobudur, stupa, 50–52, *51*
Botswana, 237
Boxer, C. R., 211–212
Bras d'Eau Sugar Estate, 78, 84–86, 88, 183, 195–199
Braudel, Ferdinand, 15
Broodbank, Cyprian, 75
Buddhism, 50–52, 53

254 · Index

Burial grounds. *See* Cemeteries
Burningham, N., 40
Burton, Sir Richard Francis, 207

Campbell, Gwyn, 72
Cantonment model, 84
Capitalism: and colonialism, 11–12, 154; late-stage, 7; legacies of, 4, 5; and plantation system, 82, 85, 224, 246; trade networks, 165, 172
Carey, Dwight, 195
Carita, Helder, 214–216
Carter, Marina, 186
Caste groups, India, 12, 160, 162, 168, 180, 186–187
Catholic Church, 210, 211, 213–214, 223
Catino map, 78
Čaval, Saša, 245
Cemeteries, 105–109; Bois Marchand cemetery, *107,* 108–109; Le Morne Old Cemetery, 105–106, *107*
Cenotaphs, 54–56, *55*
Ceramics: Anping jars, 59–61, *61;* Art Nouveau tiles, 62–64, *63;* double-happiness bowls, 64–66, *65;* Persian wares, 58–59, *59;* Vietnamese wall tiles, 56–57
Chakrabarty, Dipesh, 14
Chami, Felix, 77
Chedi Chula Prathon (Thailand), 52
Chen, Kuo-tung, 60
Chiang Mai (Thailand), 53
Child mortality rates, 106, 108
Chittick, H. Neville, 134, 140
Cholera, 103, 104, 108, 113
Christianity: Catholic Church, 210, 211, 213–214, 223; conversion to, 168; and slave trade, 79
Cianciosi, Alessandra, 245
Cindu (poetic tradition), 154, 169–172
Climate change, 7, 71
Clove production and distribution, 79, 81–82; clove-drying floors, 83
Code Noir, 79
Cohn, Bernard, 5
Colonialism: British colonial models, 62, 65–66, 78–81, 84, 103, 109–110, 133, 168, 186; Chola Empire, 160, 162, 164; colonial narratives, 208 (*see also* Goa [India]); colonial

thought, rejection of, 87–88; Dutch colonial models, 60, 78–79, 156–157, 166, 167, 216, 217; European, 2, 16, 128, 133, 228; French colonial models, 78, 80, 101, 109–110, 167, 183; legacy of, 2, 5, 12–13; Omani colonial models, 77, 79, 80, 81–82, 131, 133–134, 145; Portuguese colonial models, 16, 128–134, 140–141, 188–189, 207, 208–209; and reductionism, 86–87; and slave trade, Coromandel Coast (India), 166–173; Vijayanagara Empire, 162, 209. *See also* Goa (India)
Commerce. *See* Trade and exchange
Concubines, role on plantations, 83
Connectivity: archaeology of islands, 74–76, 86–90; background and overview, 71–74, 90; and de-emphasis of technology, 87–88; nature and human transformation of landscape, 86–90; node function of islands, 73, 76; Zanzibar contrasted with Mauritius, 76–86
Consanguineal kinship, 233–234
Contagious disease, 108. *See also* Quarantine stations
Corby, Thomas, 114, 117
Coromandel Coast (India): background and overview, 16, 152–156, 173; *cindu* (poetic tradition), 154, 169–172; colonial period, 165–173; debt bondage and wage labor, 164–165; migration from, 184–186, *185, 186;* precolonial period, 158–163; Sathagudi, 182, 188–194, *189;* slave trade, 166–173; South Asian diaspora, documentation of, *154,* 156–158, *157*
The Corrupting Sea (Horden and Purcell), 73
Coureur shipwreck, 80–81
Cowrie shells, 230, 231, 232
Croucher, Sarah K., 82–83

da Gama, Vasco, 130, 132–133, 210
Damborg, Jens, 188
Darwin, Charles, 74
Databases, comparative, 4–5
Debt bondage, Coromandel Coast, 164–165
DeCorse, Christopher, 145
DeRuyter, Mick, 9
Dhamekh Stupa, 52
Diaspora, South Asian, in Indian Ocean region: archaeology at Bras d'Eau, 195–199; archaeology at Sathangudi, 188–194; cenotaphs

and wall tiles, 54–57; ceramics, 16th to 18th centuries, 58–61; ceramics, Age of Imperialism, 62–66; and comparative archaeology, 199–201; and indentureship, *179,* 180–188; map, *49;* overview, 48–50, 66, 178–180, 201–202; stupas, 50–54, *51*
Dickey, Sara, 193
Digital Archaeological Archive of Comparative Slavery (DAACS), 4
Domestic spaces, 187–188; at Bras d'Eau, 195–202; Tamil houses, 189, *192,* 192–193
Dos Santos, Fr. João, 132
Double-happiness bowls, 64–66, *65*
Dutch East India Company, 58, 166
Dysentery, 108

Elephant people (Waata), 234
Enclosure and barriers, 17–18, 116, 135, 141, 143, 180, 198
Enslavement, 4, 79, 88–90, 164–167, 181; concubines' roles on plantations, 83; and conversion to Islam, 82; Coromandel Coast, 166–173; healthcare conditions in Mascarene Islands, 101–103; and landscape transformation, 85; and paternalism, 83; in Portuguese colonial situations, 140–141; runaways, 89; sexual exploitation, 102; slave trade/markets, 74, 78, 79–81, 103; status of enslaved persons in the IOW, 88; transition to indentured servitude, 83–84, 119; women as plantation owners, 83
Epidemic disease, 75, 108, 109, 110, 113, 119, 238. *See also* Quarantine stations
Ethiopia Oriental (Dos Santos), 132
Evans-Pritchard, E. E., 233
Evolution of species, 74–75

Fagan, Brian, 231
Fiji, 16, 179
Fitton, Tom, 135
Fleisher, Jeffrey, 131
Flewellen, Ayana O., 15
Fonseca, José Nicolau da, 217, 219
Fort Jesus (Mombasa, Kenya), 16, 133, 134, 144, 145
French Antilles, 16
Fukuchani (Portuguese colonial site), 77, 132, 135–143, *136, 138. See also* Zanzibar

Gendered segregation: gender binaries, 120–121; labor migration, 100–101; in latrines on ships, 105; plantation systems, 119; quarantine stations, 110–118; workspaces, 140
George, A. F., 35–36
Giriama trading society, 231–232
Glassman, Jonathon, 82
Globalization: and connectivity in Indian Ocean World (IOW), 73–74; in premodern Swahili world, 228–239
Goa (India), 207–210, *213, 215, 220, 221;* archival function of artifacts, 217–221, *222;* background and overview, 246–247; Catholic Church and Portuguese colonialism, 210, 211, 213–214, 223; cultural heritage, 223–225; decline, 216–217; design and layout, *213,* 213–216; Indo-Portuguese architecture, 214–216; Lisbon as model, 211–212; Portuguese colonial period, 211–216; tourism, 225
Goundar, Nettappakkam Narayanasamy, 171
Grabar, O., 27, 35, 40
"The Great Experiment" (importation of Indian workers), 80, 83–84
Guilds, in India, 158–159
Gujarat-style cenotaphs, 54–56
Gunpowder as commodity, 80, 81; mill explosion, 86

Haines, Julia Jong, 12, 85, 168, 231, 243, 244, 245
Hall, Martin, 11–12
Hariphunchai Kingdom stupas, 53
al-Hariri al-Basri, Abou Mohammad, 26, 36, 43–44. *See also Maqāmāt* ship illustration
al-Hariri Boat reconstruction, 39
Hauser, Mark William, 12, 15, 16, 90, 168, 182, 231, 243, 244, 245
Health: healthcare in Mascarene Islands during indenture period, 103–105; healthcare in Mascarene Islands during slavery, 101–103; modern health policymaking, 101
Heritage studies, 17, 244
Herlehey, T. J., 235
Historical archaeology. *See* Archaeology
Ho, Enseng, 5
Horden, Peregrine, 73

256 · Index

Hourani, G. F., 42
Hsieh, Ellen, 10
Human trafficking. *See under* Enslavement

Ibn Batuta, 164
Identity: caste identity, Indian peoples, 180; social identity and domestic space, 187; Swahili identity, 83; tension between "Arab" and "African," 82
Indenture, 83–84, 103–105, 119, 180–188
India: and labor migration in indenture period, 103–105, *105;* and slave trade, 79–80. *See also* Coromandel Coast (India); Goa (India)
Indian Immigration Archives, 184
Indian Ocean World (IOW); individual locations: contemporary situation, 3–6; in diaspora, 5; historical archaeology, regional/local approaches to, 6–14, 16; map, *2;* region addressed in book, 2–3; trade and commerce, early evidence, 9. *See also* Diaspora, South Asian, in Indian Ocean region
Infectious disease, 108. *See also* Quarantine stations
Interconnectivity. *See* Connectivity
Islam: among Swahili, 131; and cenotaphs, 54–56, *55;* conversion of enslaved peoples, 82; glazed wall tiles on mosques, 56–57; and laws concerning slavery, 88; mosque construction, Zanzibar, 77
Islamic manuscripts. *See Maqāmāt* ship illustration
Islands, as cultural/model systems, 74–76
Itinerario (Linschoten), 214

James, D., 31
al-Jassasiya (Qatar), 28, 41
Java, 50–52
Jensen, Niels, 188
Jewel of Muscat reconstruction, 38–39
João III (Portuguese king), 215
John III (Portuguese king), 211
Johnson, Matthew, 188

Kala pani, 180, 186
"Kappalerrum Kankaniccindu" (folk song), 169
al-Kazaruni, Umar bin Ahmad, 54
Kenya, 132–134; Tsavo region and commerce, 234–235

Khao Khlang Nok, 52
Kirkman, James, 72, 133, 145
Kizimkazi Dimbani, 77
Kuumbi Cave site, 77

Labor migration. *See* Migration
Lal, Brij, 186
Lamu archipelago, 229
Landscape transformation: and colonization, 17, 73, 120, 140, 208; and connectivities, 7, 86–90; and quarantine stations, 110; under slavery, 76, 84, 85, 88, 200; water capture and storage, 179–180, 194–195
Later Zanzibar Archaeology Project (LZAP): analysis, 143–145; background and overview, 128–132, 145–146; Fukuchani, 135–143, *138;* Kenya, 132–134; Mvuleni, 135–143, *138, 142;* Tanzania, 132–134
Latrines: in quarantine stations, 116, *118;* on ships, 105
LaViolette, Adria, 16, 245–246
Lazaret de La Grande Chaloupe, 111, *112,* 120
Lazaret of La Ravine à Jacques, 110–111
Le Morne Old Cemetery, 78, 105–106
Linschoten, Jan Huygen van, 214, *215*

Machada, José de Morais Antas, 219, *220*
Mahabodhi Temple, 53
Mahatma Gandhi Institute, 184
Majapahit Kingdom, 56
Malaria, 108, 113
Malekandathil, Pius, 212
Malik Ibrahim, 57
Malik Kafur, 209
Malikussaleh, 55
Malindi people, Kenya, 132–133
Mandu (India), 246, 247
Manfio, Stefania, 13, 245
Manuel (Portuguese king), 211, 214
Maqāmāt ship illustration: in archaeological contexts, 28–30; background and overview, 9, 24–25, 42–44; Baghdad-style manuscripts, 26–27, 28, 29, 33; British Library manuscript, 27–28; cultural context, 36–38; imagery and symbolism, 36–38; Istanbul manuscript, 26, 27, 28, 31; narrative and short story, 30–33; nautical research, 39–42; Paris Schefer manuscript, 24–27, *26,*

31–33, 39–42; reconstruction of ships, 38–39; shadow puppets/shadow play, 24, 35–36, *36;* ships in thirteenth-century manuscripts, 25–28; source material, 33–36, *34;* St. Petersburg manuscript, 26, *27,* 28, 31, 32–33, 39–42; versions of, 26–28

Marcus Aurelius (Roman emperor), 50

Marine shells, 230

Marronage, 88–89

Mascarene Islands, 78, 83

Mauritian Archaeology and Cultural Heritage (MACH) group, 113

Mauritius (Île de France), 100, 183; archaeo-historic background, 6, 78; Bras d'Eau Sugar Estate, 78, 84–86, 88, 183, 195–199; cemeteries, 105–106; commerce and trade, 78–81; contrasted with Zanzibar, 76–86; Flat Island, 113–116, *114, 115, 117, 118,* 120; healthcare during indenture period, 106, 108; healthcare during slavery, 101–103; migration from, 184–186, *185, 186;* plantation economies, 74, 76, 79–80, 83–86; quarantine stations, 113–118

Mauritius Archaeology and Cultural Heritage, 196

Meier, Prita, 144

Menzaleh puppets, 35–36

Middleton, John, 232

Migration: labor migration, gendered aspects, 100–101; labor migration in indenture period, 103–104; migration infrastructure, 100

Mijikenda people, 234, 235

Mindanao Island, 48

Mkama Ndume (Swahili settlement), 133–134

Mombasa, Kenya, 132–133

Monetization and currency use, 157, 158, 160, 162, 166

Monsoon cycles, 3, 73–74, 76, 87, 88, 247

Moquette, J. P., 54

Moran, Mary, 187

Moravian missions, 182, 190

Mosse, David, 194

Moulin à Poudre complex, 81, 86

Mozambique, 237

Mrozowski, Stephen, 7

Muhammad-bin-Taghlaq, 209

Mujani, Wan Kamal, 63

Mutoro, Henry, 229

Mvuleni (Portuguese colonial site), 132, 135–143, *136–137, 138*

Myanmar, 52–54

Nabhany, Ahmed Sheikh, 234

Nadar, Vellaiya, 190

Nagarakretagama, 56

Nangur excavation site, India, *161,* 161–162

Nautical research and *Maqāmāt* ship illustration, 39–42

Nayakkar, Ayirandu Sinnaiya, 169

Norman, Neil, 16, 245–246

Nyamwezi trading society, 231–232

Oman: forts and raids in Tanzania, 134; Omani landowners in Zanzibar, 82, 131

Orser, Chuck, 11

Ostrich eggshell beads, 230

Palm leaves, as sales records, 169

Pandemic disease, 103. *See also* Epidemic disease; Quarantine stations

Pedersen, Karl, 188

Pemba Island, 77, 133–134. *See also* Zanzibar

Periodization in historical archaeology, 72

Periplus of the Erythraean Sea, 209

Persian wares, 58–59, *59*

Petit marronage, 88–89

Phanom Surin shipwreck, 9, 28

Pigs, feral, 143

Pikirayi, Innocent, 143, 145

Plantation economies, 74, 76, 80, 81–86; connectivity and landscapes, 89–90; hospitals and healthcare, 102

Poison making, 234

Porcelain, 58, 62, 64

Portuguese colonial models, 16, 128–134, 140–141, 188–189, 207, 208–209. *See also* Goa (India)

Power, Timothy, 134

Pregnancy. *See* Reproductive health

Prestholdt, Jeremy, 134

Purcell, Nicholas, 73

Quarantine stations, 109–110, 118–121; Mauritius (Île de France), 113–118; Réunion (Île de Bourbon), 110–113

Qusier al-Qadim, 28

258 · Index

Rainbird, Paul, 75
Reductionism, 86–87
Religion: Buddhism, 50–52, 53; Catholic Church, 210, 211, 213–215, 223; conversion to Christianity, 168; Moravian missions, 182, 190; and slave trade, 79; Sufism, 37–38, 57; and Swahili identity, 83. *See also* Islam
Reproductive health, 108
Réunion (Île de Bourbon), 100; healthcare during slavery, 101–103; Lazaret de La Grande Chaloupe, 111, *112;* Lazaret of La Ravine à Jacques, 110–111; quarantine stations, 110–113
Revire, Nicolas, 52
Reza Abbasi Museum, 58 *59*
Rice trade, 165–166
Roxburgh, D. J., 38
Russell, Lord John, 181

Safavid ware, 58
Saghala people, 235
Said, Edward W., 86
Sakai, Takashi, 10, 60
San Diego shipwreck, 60
Santo Antonio de Tanna shipwreck, 133
Sarathi, Akshay, 13, 245
Sassoon, Hamo, 133
Sathangudi, 182, 188–194, *189*
Satmahal Prasada, 53
Scham, Sandra Arnold, 73
Schefer *Maqāmāt* ship illustration. *See Maqāmāt* ship illustration
Sebastian (Portuguese king), 211
Seetah, Krish, 13, 245
Selvakumar, V., 16, 182, 245
Settler-colonial activity. *See* Colonialism
Severin, Tim, 38
Shadow puppets/shadow play, 24, 35–36, *36,* 43
Ships in thirteenth-century manuscripts, 25–28. *See also Maqāmāt* ship illustration
Shipton, Ceri, 77
Shipwrecks: Belitung (Tang), 9, 28, 39; *Coureur,* 80–81; Phanom Surin, 8, 28; *San Diego,* 60; *Santo Antonio de Tanna,* 133
Shovel-test pit (STP) methodology, 129, 139, 140
Siddis of Janjira, 89–90
Sinbad Voyage, 38

Singapore River, 65
Slavery. *See* Enslavement
Smallpox, 103, 113
Snail shells, 230
Society for Historical Archaeology, 244
Sohar (Sinbad Voyage), 38
Somalia, 237
Sompur Mahavihara, 52
South Africa, 229
Spyer, Patricia, 9
Sri Lanka, 52, 53
Stephen, S. Jeyaseela, 165
Stoler, Ann, 208
Stone houses, 237–238
Stone Town settlement, 132, 134, 139, 144
Strandes, Justus, 137
Stupas, 50–54, *51*
Sufism, 57; Sufi mystics, 37–38
Sugar plantations, 79–80, 84–86, 102
Sunku Rama, 166
Suwanna Chedi, 53
"Swahili coast," 128
Swahili culture: agriculture, 144; commerce and trade, evidence for, 230–231; identity in Zanzibar, 82, 83, 128; premodern era globalization, 228–230; urbanism, 230–232, 239. *See also* Later Zanzibar Archaeology Project (LZAP)

Taita people, 234
Takwa (Lamu archipelago), 229
Tamil Nadu, 194–195
Tang (Belitung) shipwreck, 9, 28, 39
Tanzania, 132–134. *See also* Later Zanzibar Archaeology Project (LZAP)
Tara statuette, Mindanao Island, 48
Tatsimo people, Madagascar, 234
"Tea Garden" (Velupillai), 169
Technology, de-emphasis of, and connectivity, 87–88
Thomas, Nick, 9
Tobacco, 137
Tombs (cenotaphs), 54–56
Trade and exchange, 60, 65–66; merchant relationships, 233–236; modes of exchange, 232–233, *233;* Swahili, 230–238; Zanzibar, 78–81
Tranquebar (Tamil Nadu, India), 156, 178, 188, 245

Transnationalism as framework, 5–6, 14–17, 244–245
Trianon Sugar Estate, 78, 84, 195–196
Tumbatu, 77. *See also* Zanzibar
Typhoid, 104

UNESCO World Heritage sites, 17, 218, 223–224, 246, 247
Unguja Island, 77, 128, *129. See also* Later Zanzibar Archaeology Project (LZAP); Zanzibar
Urbanization: towns as ports of trade, 232–233, 236–238; urban spaces, archival function of, 217–222
Uungwana ("civilization" in Swahili), 82

Velupillai, C. V., 169
Venereal disease, 104, 110
Venkatapathi Devaraya II, 166
Vietnam, glazed tiles in mosques, 56–57
Vitousek, Peter M., 75
Vosmer, Tom, 39
Voss, Barbara L., 12

Waata people (Kenya), 234
Wage labor, Coromandel Coast, 164–165
Walls and boundaries, 143
al-Wāsitī, Yaḥyā ibn Maḥmūd, 29, 31, 32–33, 34, 37, 39, 40, 43
Wat Chama Thevi, 53
Wat Chet Yot, 53

Water: economic and symbolic roles, 179–180; management and use, Bras d'Eau, 197–199, *198;* management and use, Tamil Nadu, *189, 191,* 193–195
Wat Phra That Hariphunchai, 53
Weaving industry, India, 159–161, *160*
White, Louise, 233
Wilson, Brian C., 17, 144, 246–247
Wilson, Thomas, 229
Woman's Emigration Pass, 103–104
The World of the Indian Ocean (Beaujard), 228

Xavier, Angela Barreto, 137

Yasawi, Khoja Ahmed, 57

Zambezia, 229
Zambia, 231
Zanj Revolt (869–883 CE), 88
Zanzibar, 245–246; archaeo-historic background, 77; commerce and trade, 78–81; contrasted with Mauritius, 76–86; plantation economies, 81–83; slave markets, 74; Sultanate, 82, 86. *See also* Later Zanzibar Archaeology Project (LZAP)
Zanzibar Department of Antiquities and Museums, 135
Zanzibar Stonetown, 16
Zimbabwe, 229, 237
Županov, Ines G., 137